Illuminate
Publishing

D1353013

AQA Media Studies

for A Level Year 1 & AS

Stephanie Hendry • Elspeth Stevenson

Published in 2018 by Illuminate Publishing Ltd,
PO Box 1160, Cheltenham, Gloucestershire GL50 9RW

Orders: Please visit www.illuminatepublishing.com
or email sales@illuminatepublishing.com

British Library Cataloguing-in-Publication Data

A catalogue record for this book is available from the
British Library

ISBN 978-1-911208-03-7

Printed in the UK by Cambrian Printers, Aberystwyth

01.18

The publisher's policy is to use papers that are
natural, renewable and recyclable products made
from wood grown in sustainable fWorests. The
logging and manufacturing processes are expected
to conform to the environmental regulations of the
country of origin.

This material has been endorsed by AQA and
offers high-quality support for the delivery of AQA
qualifications. While this material has been through
an AQA quality assurance process, all responsibility
for the content remains with the publisher.

AQA examination questions are reproduced by
permission from AQA.

Editor: Dawn Booth

Design and layout: Jon Fletcher

Cover design: Nigel Harriss

Cover image: © Shutterstock / Dinga

Contents

How to use this book

Since 2015, English A levels have moved from a modular to a linear structure. From September 2017, A level Media Studies will be a two-year course. Assessments for this qualification are undertaken at the end of the second year and consist of two written examinations and one practical based non-examined assessment (NEA).

In addition to the full A level qualification, you will be able to take the AS level in this subject. This is a one-year course. If you are completing the AS you will need to sit one examination and one NEA at the end of the academic year. AS Media Studies is a standalone qualification and marks awarded for the AS do not contribute to the final grade at A level.

Your school or college may make different decisions as to how to structure their teaching. There are likely to be three common approaches to the course:

1 Two years of teaching for the A level with no external examination at the end of year one.

2 Two years of teaching for the A level with the AS exam being used as a 'mock exam' at the end of year one. The AS NEA may also be used at the end of year one to assess practical production skills.

3 One year of teaching, with the AS exam taken at the end of year one. You may complete your studies at this point or you may continue and sit the A level exams at the end of year two.

This book has been constructed to support the first year of study regardless of the assessment structure being followed. Chapter 9 looks at the AS examination requirements in some detail and Chapter 10 focuses on the AS NEA. These chapters offer support to those involved in external assessments at the end of year one, but Chapter 10 also offers useful advice as you develop your research and planning skills in the first year of the A level in preparation for assessment in the second year. The rest of the book covers the subject content required for AS Media Studies and can be used to prepare for the exam. This content also prepares you for the more advanced ideas you will have to cover in the second year, as subject content for AS is also a requirement for A level students. Chapter 11 offers advice and guidance on preparing for the NEA that is relevant for both AS and A level production work.

The AS exam does not contribute to the A level mark, but the subject content for AS Media Studies will also be assessed in the A level examinations. The NEA options for the AS production work will be repeated within the NEA options for the following year's A level.

At the heart of media studies is the theoretical framework. This framework provides ideas and methodologies that allow us to consider the way media products are constructed, the way media products make meaning, how audiences may respond to media products and the relationships between audiences and producers. The framework forms the structure of Media Studies and there is a range of key ideas that need to be engaged with as detailed in the AQA specification.

Chapters 1–6 offer a range of explanations, definitions and examples that cover the main ideas within each part of the framework. Each chapter, therefore, provides the background knowledge that is required for each element of the theoretical framework and examples of how to apply that knowledge. The theories and ideas only become meaningful when used to help explain how media products are constructed, when related to audience behaviours or industry practices. Some features you will find in each section include:

- **APPLY IT** The **Apply It** sections in each chapter aim to allow you to consider the ideas in light of your own media knowledge and experience.

- In the book you will find lists of key terms. These lists will help you construct a glossary of specialist terminology that you should try to use when discussing media products and processes. Using the correct language is a good way to demonstrate your understanding of concepts and ideas.

- Some theorists have been identified as **key thinkers** in each part of the theoretical framework and must be considered when preparing for the exam. These theorists have been identified and information provided on some of their ideas. Of course, you can use other theorists and other ideas in addition to these key thinkers.

- The elements of the theoretical framework can be looked at separately but it will soon become clear that each area impacts on and influences the others. Each chapter therefore offers a **link** feature that cross-references connected ideas from other parts of the book.

How the chapters relate to the AS and A level specifications

Media language (Chapters 1–3)

The practical choices made by media producers when creating media products. You need to be able to identify and analyse the way media producers communicate meaning in the way they use media language choices. You will need to understand how codes and conventions of form and genre are used and how narratives are constructed.	Required for the AS exam	Introductory knowledge for A level students

Representation (Chapter 4)

The way the media portrays events, issues, individuals and groups. You will need to consider how representations are constructed and how meanings are created by them. You should be able to critically evaluate how ideologies can be communicated through representations.	Required for the AS exam	Introductory knowledge for A level students

Audience (Chapter 5)

How the media targets and attempts to reach audiences and how audiences respond and interpret media products. You will also need to consider the way audiences can become producers of media products themselves.	Required for the AS exam	Introductory knowledge for A level students

Industries (Chapter 6)

The way media industries produce, distribute and circulate media products. You should consider the relationships between audience and producers, the economic issues that motivate media industries and the way industries are responding to changes in the media landscape.	Required for the AS exam	Introductory knowledge for A level students

Skills development (Chapter 7)

Chapter 7 offers practical tips on building the skills that are required in Media Studies. The chapter looks at the skill of analysis as well as using media theory and terminology in formal written work. These will help you develop the skills that will be assessed in examinations and so will need to be practised over the course of one (AS) or two (A level) years.	Provides examples of the underpinning skills required in Media Studies for both AS and A level students

Close study products (Chapter 8)

A number of media products have been selected and are identified as 'close study products' (CSPs). These are the products you must study before taking the AS examination at the end of the first year and/or the A level examination at the end of year two.	Provides examples of the application of the theoretical framework to media products for both AS and A level students
Chapter 8 offers some examples of detailed analysis using the theoretical framework and some of the CSPs. It is possible that CSPs may change in the future, so you must check with the most up-to-date information provided by the exam board to make sure you are using the correct products for the examination you are sitting. The analytic methods found in Chapter 8 can be used as a model for a detailed and considered analysis using aspects of the theoretical framework for other or, if applicable, newer CSPs.	
Chapter 8 offers examples of media products that cover all three platforms (broadcast, e-media and print) and three of the nine media forms (magazines, television and media) identified in the specification.	
The analysis of these products also uses many of the ideas and much of the language identified in the key terms features of earlier chapters as well as the ideas from the key thinkers. The examples here can help you prepare your CSPs for the AS examination or could be used to develop your analysis skills and your ability to apply theoretical ideas prior to engaging with some of the more advanced A level theories and ideas.	

So, whether you are working towards an examination at the end of the first year or only being assessed after two years, this book offers the subject content and a focus on the application of ideas that can be used as a textbook for a standalone AS course or for the first year of the A level.

Chapter 1 Reading print media

1.1 Decoding print media texts using basic semiotics

One of the key approaches you will be using throughout the course is **semiotic analysis**. Semiotics is the study of signs in our culture. These might be any aspect of print, audio-visual or digital media, including images, sounds and language. Semiotics is a complex field, and at A level you will not be expected to have an exhaustive knowledge of the subject, but you will need to have a working knowledge of some of the basics. You will find that some of the principles of semiotics you use over and over again; others you use less frequently.

When you use semiotic analysis to help you **decode** a text, you should use it alongside other elements of the theoretical framework and terminology associated with each field. Some of the introduction you'll find here is applicable across all the media forms you will be studying; other aspects are specific to print media. In Chapters 2 and 3 we will consider how the approach you use in this first chapter is modified to suit different mass media forms. As you begin each of those chapters, it is suggested you re-read this section to help you internalise the approach.

The origins of semiotic theory

Semiotic theory is the study of signs in our culture and how they communicate meaning. Semiotics is related to linguistics, and is part of two wider fields in critical theory known as structuralism and post-structuralism, which you will encounter later in in the full A level course. Many theorists have contributed their own models and ideas to the field. Three important contributors, together with a brief summary of their ideas, are referred to in this textbook. It is not absolutely necessary to associate each term that you use with one theorist in your writing, as all their approaches have produced terms useful to your analysis. If you would like to deliberately mention a particular theorist (e.g. Saussure) and explicitly say that you are using their approach, make sure that the terms you use are only those associated with their ideas.

Ferdinand de Saussure

Ferdinand de Saussure was a Swiss linguist, and is considered by most people to be one of the founders of semiotics, although the ideas that informed his work have much earlier roots. Saussure viewed semiotics as a scientific discipline, although it is not usually regarded in this way by modern theorists. Because of this, Saussurean thinking applied to reading signs is sometimes referred to as **semiology**, although it is fine to use the term semiotics when using his ideas.

Saussure believed that **linguistics** provided a good model for application to wider cultural phenomena. Written or spoken language is the primary form of communication between humans, but it is not the only form. The mass media are forms of communication that deploy traditional language structures, but also are full of other codes. Semiotics allows us to access these other codes and to understand the sense that audiences make of them.

At its simplest, Saussure's model of the sign and signification process can be illustrated as follows: **sign = signifier + signified**

It is usually drawn as shown on the right.

It would work as follows, where the word 'tree' conjures in the reader's mind the tree as a real-world object:

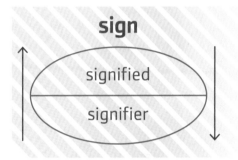

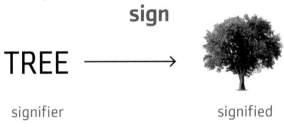

signifier   signified

A signifier cannot exist without a signified – the two parts of the sign work in tandem. The mental concept (the signified) is almost simultaneously triggered the moment a signifier (the symbol or real-world object) is perceived. This element of Saussure's work remains at the heart of how we use semiotics in Media Studies. The sign itself can be thought of as the overall effect of the two things combined. Signs can be simple or complex. Most media texts you analyse can be regarded as complex signs, comprised of many signifiers plus signifieds, which combine into a larger overall signification of the sign, although some print advertising will use simpler signs – which can be very effective.

EXAMPLE: The open or closed shop

In his book *Semiotics: The Basics*, Daniel Chandler gives the example of an 'OPEN' sign encountered by someone at a shop door. Because the word 'open' (the *signifier*) has a context – being on the shop door – the *signified* is that the shop is open for business. Similarly, a 'closed' sign would signify the opposite.

In order for the signification process to work in a culture, users have to agree on the signified. The relationship between the signifier and signified is sometimes referred to as an **arbitrary relationship**. The best example of this is European languages that use the Roman alphabet, which only makes sense to its users because they all agree what the letters and words mean – there is no literal relationship between the shape of the letters that form the words and the meaning of the word. Some other languages use lettering systems that do bear some resemblance to their meaning in the real world. In European culture, we inherit the meanings when we learn language from our parents and those around us.

APPLY IT

Depending on how confident you feel with this idea, either:

- Come up with five examples of simple sign construction using Chandler's example of an open sign on a shop door,

or

- Use the internet to help you find some simple examples of the signification process and how it makes simple signs.

APPLY IT
Source a text from a culture you are not familiar with. The further away it is from your own background the better. What aspects of the text can you understand within your own cultural frame of reference? Which aspects are more difficult to understand?

At the same time, we inherit the agreed meaning of a sign. Signs in popular culture are more complex than the meanings of words and, because of this, not all users may agree completely on their meaning. Their intended meaning, though, is usually understood by most, with only subtle variations in the decoding process.

EXAMPLE: Genre and the signification process

Watching a genre text from outside your own culture can be a strange experience, especially if you have no subtitles and are reliant on visual and aural codes to make sense of it. Some Bollywood films include a range of deliberate appeals for different sections of the audience in order to function as whole family entertainment – for a UK viewer, who is only used to Western generic codes, this can seem strange.

Charles Peirce

Charles Peirce (1839–1914)

Like Saussure, US-born scientist and philosopher Charles Peirce is credited with making some of the most significant contributions to the field of early semiotics. Although their models slightly differ, both are regarded as important figures.

Peirce's triadic model of the sign, meaning it has three parts, is less commonly used than Saussure's as it is a little more difficult to understand. He did, however, leave another important legacy. Saussure himself was not concerned with categorising signs into types, but Peirce did attempt to do so.

The categories he defined were:

- **Arbitrary signs**, or **symbolic signs**, where there is no physical relationship between the signifier and its concept (using Saussurian definitions). Language, which we discussed earlier while looking at Saussure, falls into this category.
- **Iconic signs** look like their signified, making the relationship between the two very straightforward and obvious.
- **Indexical signs**, where there is a causal relationship between the signifier and signified.

EXAMPLE: Chandler

In his book *Semiotics: The Basics*, Daniel Chandler gives some excellent examples of all three of these signs. Three such examples are given below for each sign category.

Symbolic signs – numbers, Morse code, traffic lights

Iconic signs – portraits, a scale model, sound effects

Indexical signs – footprints, a skin rash, a weathervane

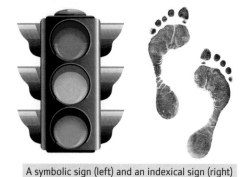

A symbolic sign (left) and an indexical sign (right)

APPLY IT
Depending on how confident you feel with these definitions, either:
- Come up with five examples for each type of sign, or
- Use the internet to help you find some simple examples of each type of sign.

Roland Barthes

 For more on Barthes see section '1.3 Narrative organisation in print media texts'.

Barthes was one of the most important French philosophers of the last century. His legacy in the reading of popular culture is huge. Barthes was also highly influential in the field of narrative.

One of Barthes' contributions to the field of semiotics was to study more closely the relationship between **denotation** and **connotation** in the signification process. We mentioned earlier that media texts are complex signs. Barthes believed there was a process taking place, which he referred to as the **order of signification**. This begins with denotation, which is often thought of as the literal meaning of the sign, although many semioticians argue that this is more complex. The signification process is view by Barthes as layered.

Connotation is the meaning arising from the sign. According to Barthes, a simple unit of signifier + signified can result in just identification – the recognition of an agreed meaning of a sign. We saw this earlier, with the example of the word tree and the concept it signifies. This is the first order of signification. The second order of signification is layered so that a signified becomes a new signifier – an intricate process, but one that actually describes very well the processes we all undertake when reading a sign as complex as a media text. In a media text, there may be several layers of signification operating at once, which give rise to much more complex meanings than simply understanding the meaning of a word.

Roland Barthes (1915–1980)

Another of Barthes' contributions to the field was the concept of **myth**, which remains very important in any study of culture. A myth is a group of shared cultural connotations that reflect a dominant ideology. Cultural myths are one way in which we share ideas about ourselves and make sense of our society. They are part of a higher level of signification. Myths help to naturalise the way in which things are in societies, so can be viewed as an important contributor to ideology. Barthes understood clearly that myths could be and often were created in society to political ends. He believed that ideology could be thought of as the third order of signification. Likewise, many myths about consumerism serve to generate economic revenue for big businesses. It is important to understand that Barthes uses the term myth not to mean something that is false – a myth can be true or false – rather that it is a way of rationalising daily life around us, and of connecting with our culture at almost every level.

For more on media representations see section '4.5 The ideological nature of common media representations and how we respond to them'.

EXAMPLE: *Omo* soap powder

In his book, *Mythologies*, Barthes looks at the advertising of a soap powder brand, *Omo*, and how it draws on wider myths about detergents and their cleansing power circulating in his culture at the time. He considers how the separation of dirt from cleanliness draws on ideas about perfection, and the ideas of depth (efficacy) and foaminess (luxury). These combine powerfully to create a persuasive message for the audience, interacting with myths about cleanliness and creating a false desire for the product.

APPLY IT

Choose three print advertisements for contrasting products. Can you identify any myths in our culture that they appear to draw on to promote the products? Write approximately 100 words about each one, using the ideas of either Saussure's or Peirce's model to support your ideas. Consider how denotation and connotation draw on myths, and how each advert perpetuates these.

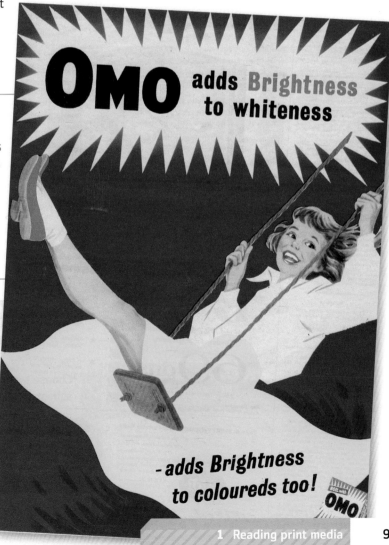

OMO adds Brightness to whiteness

- adds Brightness to coloureds too! OMO

Key terms in semiotic theory and their applications in print media analysis

As we discussed earlier, semiotics is a complex academic field and a sub-discipline in its own right within cultural analysis. There are many terms associated with its use, but the ones listed below are the ones you are likely to find yourself using most frequently.

anchorage	does exactly what the name suggests – it fixes meaning. In print media texts, anchorage consists of lexical codes that firmly establish the connection between an image and the reason it has been used. They may appear as slogans, copy, headlines or captions accompanying an image. This can add value to the use of the image and maximise its impact
arbitrary or symbolic sign	a sign that does not have an obvious connection with what it represents, but the meaning of which is agreed on by users of a particular code. Saussure referred to these types of sign as **symbolic**. Many road signs can be regarded as symbolic if you have to have read the *Highway Code* to understand what they mean
code	a system used to create meaning. Most forms of meaning production have specific codes: frameworks that are used to encode meaning. It is vital that codes are shared and their meanings agreed upon across a culture or they cannot be decoded. Where these are limited to a specific mode of expression in media productions or forms, they are referred to collectively as **technical codes**. The various kinds of code used in print media analysis are described in more detail in the technical codes and features used in print media texts
connotation	the meaning evoked by a sign – what it makes us think. It can be thought of as the end result of reading a sign, the mental image we have of its meaning

decoding	when audiences interpret a text in order to make meaning
denotation	may be understood as the literal meaning of a component of a code. You can also use the term as a verb, saying that an element of an image denotes – but be careful. The term is easily confused with **connotes**, which you would more commonly be using in meaningful semiotic analysis rather than description
encoding	the process of creating particular intended meanings within a text
iconic sign	looks like what it is representing. A portrait photograph is a good example of an iconic sign. Symbols such as the 'danger of death' sign you see on the side of an electrical substation are also iconic – they show someone being struck by a bolt of electricity, looking very much like the physical manifestation of electricity as lightning
indexical sign	has a relationship between the signifier and signified that could be described as causal or otherwise linked. The relationship between the two things is so widely recognised by users of the signification system that the indexical sign easily stands in for, or signifies, the concept it represents. Commonly used examples are smoke, which is an indexical sign of fire, a tear, which suggests sorrow, and footprints, which suggest someone was in a place

myth	this term is closely associated with Roland Barthes. A myth in critical theory is the way in which certain signs contribute to ideologies in our society. Myth is particularly helpful to print advertisers in promoting values that are consumerist and materialist in nature
sign	the sum of the signifier plus signified. Most print media texts can be referred to as complex signs, since they often comprise many individual elements and codes that need to be decoded in order to understand fully what they represent
signified	when we say that a particular message is signified, we are using it as a verb – it can also be used as a noun – the signified, the meaning that is intended
signifier	works in tandem with the **signified**, and together these combine into a sign. We consider signifier and signified to work together, because the association happens so fast when reading a text

To see the terminology of semiotic analysis in action turn to Chapter 8, which models how to approach close analysis of products.

APPLY IT **Choose two print media texts of your choice. Write a paragraph of semiotic analysis based on each text. Try to consciously integrate at least five terms from the list into each paragraph, looking back at the example to check you have used each word in context correctly. Highlight the terms you used to help reinforce their use in your memory.**

arbitrary relationship	a relationship between signifier and signified that is not obvious (e.g. the word 'cat' in the Roman alphabet and our mental image of the animal)	second order of signification	a layered and more subtle interpretation of a complex sign
critical theory	an approach to the study of culture that considers how various forces are at work in its production	semiology	Saussure's term for the study of signs, which he regarded as a science
first order of signification	the recognition of the agreed meaning of a sign	structuralism	a way of analysing culture that prioritises its form/structure over function according to codified systems
linguistics	the study of structural aspects of language, with many sub-specialisms	third order of signification	the relationship between the first and second orders of signification and myths and ideology
post-structuralism	later work on structuralism that both extends its ideas and critiques its approach	triadic model	common term used for Peirce's description of how we read signs

Charles Peirce	(1839–1914) American multi-disciplinary academic who contributed to the field of semiotic theory from his broad background as a mathematician, philosopher and communication theorist
Ferdinand de Saussure	(1857–1913) Swiss structural linguist often credited along with Peirce with the founding of semiotic theory as we know it today

1.2 The technical codes and features used in print media texts

In the previous section, we talked about codes as a group of conventions that are used to organise and create meaning. In addition to using semiotic terms when analysing print media texts, there are some other codes and features that are likely to be frequently used. Other terms, some of which have their origins in the industry, are specific to one or two forms.

In this section, we will explore the relevant codes and more general features first. You will find in Chapter 2 that some of these codes appear again, but in a slightly different context as their usage varies depending on the media form. In the final section, we will look at the features peculiar to each main print form in turn – newspapers, magazines and print advertisements.

Dress code

Dress code forms an essential part of the signification process in any print media text. The clothing worn by anyone can be used to signify particular meanings about their social status, lifestyle, age and many other factors. It isn't enough to simply identify a dress code as 'casual' or 'formal' – look at the details of how the clothing is being worn, any accessories or details, the colours, whether they coordinate, connoting more simple ideas, or clash and suggest contradictory meanings and conflict, and to what extent they help meet generic expectations.

Colour codes

Colour codes may be inherent in the environment in which a photograph is taken, particularly if it is photo-journalism. Colours may still be subject to manipulation such as colour correction or saturation of the whole or part of an image in post-production. The extent to which this is acceptable is a grey area of **ethics** in photo-journalism and documentary photography. In the case of photo-journalism, colour codes are part of the factors considered in the editorial process, along with framing and cropping. For magazine shoots or print advertising, colour codes are often derived from a limited palette that strongly signifies a mood, theme or atmosphere.

Framing or cropping

Where everything about the subject is within the control of the producers, such as on a magazine or studio/location shoot for a print advert, framing is used in order to carefully construct meaning. Everything that appears in the frame is styled to contribute to the meaning of the sign. In the case of photo-journalism, photographs are not only selected for the best match of meaning to accompany the article, but also frequently cropped as a further way of anchoring meaning. Cropping a photograph has the power to significantly change the way in which it is read and, like processing of colour, can be controversial.

Non-verbal codes

The visual expression, eye-line and posture in this photo are all non-verbal codes that this girl is probably upset.

Gestural codes, facial expression, eye-line and posture are all significant non-verbal codes in print media images. In combination these can have a subtle or powerful effect. Make sure you look at the whole-body language, rather than just focusing on one aspect of meaning. Consider any apparent communication implied between multiple subjects in the frame as well as the direct/indirect address of the audience.

Typographical codes

The font style chosen for various elements of the design are typographical codes, which can signify house style in a magazine or newspaper – in fact, many magazines and newspapers use proprietary fonts that contribute to brand recognition.

Lexical codes

Lexical codes work in combination with other codes, contributing to the anchoring of meaning in captions and headlines in magazines and newspapers, and consistently being selected from a vast paradigm to ensure a preferred reading. It isn't within the scope of the course to conduct a linguistic analysis of a whole article, and neither do you have time – but there are clear cases where selecting for comment some of the wording used, and identifying how it contributes to meaning, is going to form an essential part of a balanced analysis.

Props, décor and location

Similar issues arise with analysing props, décor and location as when you are studying framing and cropping. Remember to consider every tiny detail of image content, and treat it as though it has significance initially, even if you then select from these ideas later, in the case of photo-journalism, discarding any elements that seem incidental to the dominant reading or don't contribute much overall to your analysis.

Camera positioning and proxemics/para-proxemics

The positioning of the subject within the frame is vital in communicating meaning, as is the hierarchy of positioning of multiple people within the frame. Studying these relative positions and their meanings is known as proxemics.

There is another consideration that affects the mode of address – sometimes known as camera proxemics or para-proxemics. This is the technique whereby the shot selected affects the perceived distance between the subject and the person, created by their proximity to the camera and how much of their body is shown. This creates an artificial, imagined relationship between the subject and the audience.

Graphical elements

Graphical elements is a broad term that encompasses many different features and techniques. Whenever you notice a design feature, computer-generated, that does not fit comfortably into any other category, you are considering a graphical element. These may be used in a minimal way, or they may dominate a print media text. They may be used on their own as a main feature, or to add to photographs – they can be used alongside typography and add to its effect (logos are a great example of this in action) or constitute a whole, computer-generated scene or image. Many of the other aspects of technical code listed above are applied to graphical elements to signify the appropriate meaning.

Exploring the technical codes and features used within a specific media form

Newspapers

Despite their differing readerships and proportional variations, the same technical codes are deployed across different newspapers. The terminology you will use when discussing layout remains the same. What does vary according to the type of newspaper – whether it is regional or national, tabloid or broadsheet – is the proportion of text to image, size of headlines and so on. The easiest way to understand these differing uses of the same technical codes to establish genre is to collect the front pages from a range of newspapers and look at them all together.

All newspaper front pages have a flag or masthead, which is the term for the newspaper name, positioned at the top. Above this there is often a skyline, which describes other content or promotions inside. Headlines and photographs with captions are usually the most obvious other elements of a front page, but these are of course also used throughout the newspaper. A byline often accompanies an article, giving the name of the journalist. Body text is organised into columns, with width and number varying according to the house style of the newspaper. Between the headline and body text, leading into the copy, there is a standfirst. This introduces the story with further attention-grabbing details, which supplement the headline.

Inside the newspaper, further technical codes are used to lead the reader's eye and break up the page in a visually appealing way. A folio title may be used, which you could think of as a header, to describe the section of the newspaper, such as 'National' or a supplement such as 'Education'. A sidebar, containing graphics or pictures, may be included as a panel on a page, which adds information to a story. This, or a photograph, may be used as a centre of visual interest (CVI): something to catch the eye as the reader peruses the paper. Sometimes, a standalone may be used on the front of a paper or in the centre. A standalone image is one that works with a caption and very little supplementary information. Other features might include a crosshead, where enlarged text breaks up a column visually and draws the eye on through the story, or a pull quote interview extract, which is used for the same reasons.

 To see the terminology of print media analysis in action turn to Chapter 8, which models how to approach close analysis of products.

APPLY IT

Collect one example from each of the three main print media forms you study on the course: a magazine feature, a newspaper article (with image) and a print advertisement. Make notes on the contribution of all the features described on these pages to guide you.

Write a 500-word case study of each example, exploring how it uses the technical codes and features of print media language.

Collect examples that show how variations in technical code appear across the presentation of a news story featured in both a tabloid and a traditional broadsheet newspaper. Write about the differences.

The three examples below show clearly the kind of differences in uses of technical codes you can expect to see across a range of newspaper types, purely on the basis of the front page.

Magazines

Generic variation, particularly evident in house style, is considerable across magazines. As with newspapers, you will find that there are certain consistent elements that recur. A strong analysis can take place when you understand what these features are before you begin to account for their specific meanings.

Front covers of magazines will include a masthead. This is the name of the magazine, and may also be associated with a strapline. Straplines sometimes make claims about the merits of the magazine or simply give more information about its contents. Usually, at least some of the most appealing content that month/week will be picked out in the form of coverlines, which entice the audience by letting them see the scope of articles included – particularly the lead article. Coverlines frequently use a personal mode of address and help to signify the genre codes. The area in the middle and to the left of the cover, where the eye tends to rest, is sometimes used to engage the audience by positioning either a prominent coverline such as a feature article, an important element of an image, or a puff – a feature that may be a promotion or other item that adds perceived value to the purchase. This part is known as the sweet spot, but commonly the whole of the left side third is considered prime space when attracting the consumer's attention.

Menu strips are another common feature. They are usually found at the bottom of the page, although variations in house style and edition may see them moved to the top (sometimes referred to as the skyline) or, less commonly, positioned as a side bar. Menu strips may have different functions, but their most common use is to promote familiarity by displaying regular content. A large proportion of your time is also likely to be spent considering the image or images used on the cover. This may consist of one large primary image. It is equally possible that you may have a number of images with a sense of hierarchy in size and positioning, or one primary image with a number of secondary images.

Despite wide variance in subject matter and target audience, all four of these covers deploy the same technical codes adapted to suit their house style – each is still instantly recognisable as a magazine.

Inside the magazine, there are other aspects of technical codes that you will see repeated. Headlines draw our attention to the feature and allow us to see at a glance whether or not the magazine is likely to interest us. These are often accompanied by a **slug**. Slugs appear in a larger typeface than the main body text and provide more information for the reader. They can also act as a **hook** or create a **narrative enigma**. Columns are included, and their width and number for a particular type forms a crucial part of the house style. Pull quotes may also be used if the article is an interview, or any other subtitling techniques. These function to visually break up the text, providing relief for the eye and contributing to the ease with which the material is absorbed. **Drop caps**, an example of typographical code where the first letter at the beginning of an article is enlarged for stylistic effect, can also appear at the start of an article; again, these function partly as an aesthetic device, and partly to signal clearly to the reader where to begin.

Magazines are necessarily visually rich and appealing. Depending on the genre, some prioritise visual content over written. Feature articles are sometimes referred to as **entry points** in the magazine – these are the articles that, as you flip through the magazine, are most likely to draw your eye. Unlike the capturing of real events that we expect to see in newspapers, these are often highly stylised **studio shoots**. Digital manipulation of these images is common, with a great deal of retouching and other post-production work being undertaken to get exactly the right look for the magazine brand and article. In interviews, it's common to see the subject gazing into the lens, creating a direct **mode of address**.

APPLY IT

Collect three different examples of double-page spreads from three different magazine genres. What do you notice about the ways in which they deploy the technical codes of print media? What similarities do they have and what differences? How have text and image been combined to appeal to the target audience? Write a 1,500-word exploration of your three chosen texts.

Print advertising

Genius has no race. Strength has no gender.
Courage has no limit.

TARAJI P.
HENSON   OCTAVIA
SPENCER   JANELLE
MONÁE   KEVIN
COSTNER   KIRSTEN
DUNST   JIM
PARSONS

HIDDEN FIGURES

BASED ON THE UNTOLD TRUE STORY

IN CINEMAS FEBRUARY

The poster for the film *Hidden Figures* is a good example of the use of composite images.

Much advertising depends on a process known as **AIDA**, which stands for Awareness, Interest, Desire and Action. This simple model defines very well the aims of print advertisers, who may only have a single page or double-page spread or one space such as a billboard or other outdoor display context to sell their product or service. Print advertising is necessarily high impact, with every production decision being taken with extreme care to maximise response. At the stage of awareness, the consumer's eye needs to stop and be cast over the brand or product name. The advertisers then hope to encourage a more intense lingering over the page or place, which is interest – that interest turning into a desire means the signification processes at work in the advert are successfully selling the product. Action could be viewing other promotional material such as digital or social media presence, looking up reviews of the product, visiting the company's website, purchasing the product as it appears at eye level in a supermarket and so on. AIDA is relevant and applicable to all adverts, but is vital where purchase space is at a premium.

Composite images, rarely seen in magazines or newspapers, do appear in adverts. These are particularly common in film posters, where they are a common convention and, in fact, one of the most obvious signifiers of film promotion as a form. There is huge variation in the ways that print adverts are used. **Advertorials**, which appear in the body of a magazine (or newspaper), will tend to replicate to some degree the house style of the destination publication. By law, advertorials must be labelled as such.

Most adverts make some use of lexical coding. In some cases this may be fairly minimal. Usually, we would expect to see the product name, perhaps a slogan, or information about where we might buy the product, or social media and web links as a minimum. Some adverts may include supplemental information about the qualities of the products, or to make clear their **brand values**. Advertising copywriting is a specialist field, and huge importance is placed on every element of lexical coding included – you will need to reflect this by giving it due attention in any analysis you make.

The majority of print advertising sells its products on some kind of image. The image will usually feature the product, although there are exceptions to this. Some of the styles of print advertisement you might see are:

- **Conceptual** – the product is depicted through an idea or feeling conveyed visually, sometimes in a hyperbolic way. On occasion, the product itself may appear to be almost incidental.
- **Informative/demonstration** – the product may be shown in action.
- **Pseudo-scientific or technical** – often combining graphics to construct the product as one that makes the most of advanced technologies.
- **Narrative** – the advert takes the reader on a journey of some kind.

Many advertisements will use a combination of these techniques in a single-page space.

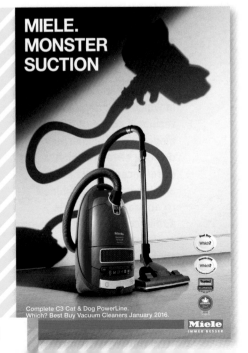

MIELE.
MONSTER
SUCTION

Complete C3 Cat & Dog PowerLine.
Which? Best Buy Vacuum Cleaners January 2016.

Miele
IMMER BESSER

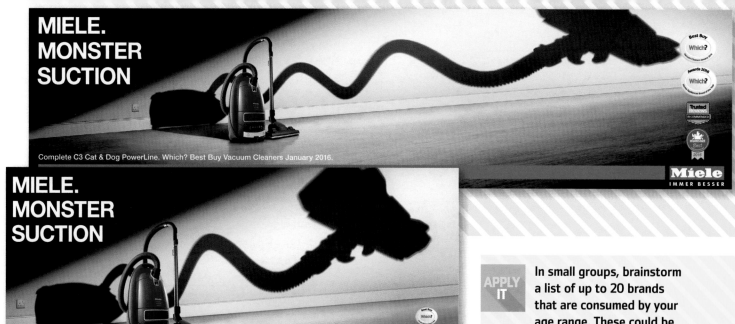

Semiotic approaches to image analysis are therefore really important when decoding visual images, but need to be consistently used alongside narrative codes and generic expectations of the product or advertising style. Logos also contribute strongly to brand recognition, and will usually be placed prominently to reinforce consumer associations between the product and the brand. Don't forget to analyse logos, which are often neglected by students new to print advertising analysis.

KEY TERMS

advertorial	an extended print advertisement that may resemble editorial in its use of codes, but will be clearly labelled 'advertisement' under UK media law
AIDA	Awareness, Interest, Desire, Action
body text	the majority of article text, usually at the smallest size, appearing in a magazine or newspaper
brand recognition	when an audience becomes familiar with a brand
brand value	the image a company intends to convey of its product or service
byline	journalist's credit, usually at the start of an article
camera proxemics	sometimes known para-proxemics – the distance/relationship between subject and audience

caption	written anchorage accompanying an image and fixing its meaning
centre of visual interest (CVI)	in newspapers in particular, the headline, photograph or graphic that intentionally dominates a page
composite image	presentation of images using a montage effect
copy	the term used for body text in a newspaper, print advertisement or magazine
coverline	feature and secondary articles promoted on the front of a magazine
cropping	the removal of sections of an image to emphasise its subject or remove clutter or unwanted signs
crosshead	small amount of text enlarged as a hook for visual contrast with body text
décor	selection of the appearance of interior locations

direct/indirect address	the way in which a text addresses its audience; for example, where a subject is gazing into the lens of the camera, this could be said to be a direct mode of address
drop cap	an enlarged first letter – an attention-grabbing aesthetic device
entry point	a visually appealing and prominent spread in a magazine
flag/masthead	the name of a newspaper or magazine
folio	titling at the top of a section of a newspaper identifying the content in that section
framing	careful selection of what will appear in a final shot
graphical elements	any graphics generated that do not consist of pure typography or photography
headline	large type promoting article content, especially on the front of a newspaper

hook	any technique used to draw the audience into a narrative	non-verbal codes	in human subjects, this is facial expression, posture, body language	sidebar	photographs or graphical elements in a newspaper to accompany an article and provide visual interest
house style	the way in which codes combine in print media to produce a familiar and recognisable brand	para-proxemics	sometimes known as camera proxemics – the distance/relationship between subject and audience	skyline	strip often used to promote other content running along the top of a newspaper or magazine, sometimes referred to as a menu strip
lead article	in print media, this is usually clear from the front page or cover, where one article will be selected for promotion over others	primary image	the image that predominates visually where more than one has been used	slug	a line in larger print introducing a feature that acts as a hook
left side third	area of a magazine cover where key content is usually positioned	proprietary fonts	fonts that are developed exclusively for a particular publication	standalone	prominent image without accompanying copy used to attract attention on the front page of a newspaper
lexical codes	words selected to generate specific effect	props	items that are consciously added to a shoot because they contribute to meaning	standfirst	an introduction/introductory summary
linguistic analysis	detailed analysis of the ways in which language is used over a whole section of copy in the English language	proxemics	power relationships signified by relative positioning within the frame	strapline	sometimes accompanies the masthead on a magazine – a promotional slogan
location	choice of place for an exterior shoot	puff	a call-out feature, often circular in shape, that draws attention to a price or promotion on a front cover	studio shoot	a highly contrived photographic set-up, usually in an interior location
logo	a design, sometimes consisting of typography and a symbol, that identifies a brand	pull quote	excerpt from interview enlarged as a hook device and for visual contrast with body text	sweet spot	position to the centre left of a single page of print media, where the eye naturally falls
mode of address	how the text 'speaks' to the audience – can be formal or informal – created by use of codes	secondary image	an image that appears to be hierarchically less important when more than one is used	typographical codes	selection of font and graphical choices
narrative enigma	puzzles or questions set up by the text to maintain audience engagement (see Barthes' five codes, Chapter 2)				

1.3 Narrative organisation in print media texts

Approaches to reading narratives in print media

One of the dominant features of narratives in any form or genre is that they centre on humans as primary causal agents. This is true even if you are considering a text that has anthropomorphised characters, who are symbolic humans interpreted through character traits we all recognise. We have a strong desire, rooted as far back as civilisation goes, to experience the world through the eyes of others and learn from their experiences in a vicarious way. This is why children for thousands of years were told folk tales, why medieval troubadours sang ballads, and why we watch soaps. The need to render the world comprehensible through storytelling is probably as old as the human race.

In Media Studies, we often use narrative theories to explore how texts organise information in a way that tells a meaningful story that the audience can correlate with their own experience. Some of these are more suited to print media texts than others; in Chapters 2 and 3 we will be looking at how some of the narrative terms and techniques first encountered in this chapter can be explicitly applied to other forms.

It's really important, though, that you don't try to apply narrative theories in a slavish way at the expense of your own observations about the form, structure and progression of the text. There are a few terms that can be used outside of narrative theories that will help you to make insightful points about narratives alongside your application of the some of the best-known narrative theories.

For example, when talking about the shape of a narrative, you should always consider what kind of ending and format it has. Is it an enclosed narrative, where all the loose ends are tied up? This kind of narrative often is said to have narrative closure, or narrative resolution. You might also consider whether a narrative is serial or self-contained – the majority of print media texts, with the exception of comics, are mainly self-contained. Remember that narrative study should be applied to both fiction and fact-based media. Some fact-based narratives are simultaneously open-ended, such as news stories, and also have serial qualities that leave the story open for further reporting.

Hook is a term widely used in narratology to describe any technique used to gain the interest of the audience. Cultural tropes are simple, over-used devices that, when connected with universal themes, help us to constantly re-evaluate our affiliation with a culture as well as what it means to be human.

Tzvetan Todorov

Tzvetan Todorov was a Russian structural theorist, whose work on narratives in culture has been used in the fields of literary, film and media theory. He described narratives as having a chronological quality outside of plot; a process shared in common.

A state of equilibrium is present at the start of a narrative. This isn't necessarily a good state of affairs, but it can be considered a stable starting point for the rest of the narrative to flow from. At times, the equilibrium can only be discerned from the disruption to it.

Some kind of disruption occurs to the equilibrium. This is the jolt that drives the narrative, which gives us a story and sense of movement.

Tzvetan Todorov (1939–2017)

A recognition of disruption occurs next (sometimes this is almost simultaneous with the disruption itself). Someone realises that something has gone awry, or discovers a need. This then sets the scene for the next stage.

The attempt to repair in a narrative can be extensive. It may be broken down into a series of narrative segments. This stage will persist until the final one is reached.

A new equilibrium is reached at the end of a narrative. This is not a simple reinstatement of the original equilibrium – even a cyclical narrative will be typically a metaphorical journey for those featured within it. Lessons will have been learned, and losses and gains incurred.

EQUILIBRIUM
↓
DISRUPTION
↓
RECOGNITION
↓
ATTEMPT TO REPAIR
↓
NEW EQUILIBRIUM

Summary of Todorov's theorem

APPLY IT

Apply Todorov's narrative theory to a crime report from a newspaper, a double-page feature from a celebrity or 'true life' magazine, a children's comic and an interview with a prominent person in any lifestyle, sports or entertainment magazine.

How easy was the theory to apply? Were there any texts that didn't seem to fit comfortably with the five stages and, if so, were elements of it still useful – or would you choose another theory to support what you wanted to say about the narrative organisation?

Claude Lévi-Strauss (1908–2009)

Claude Lévi-Strauss

Lévi-Strauss was a structural anthropologist. One of the much-valued ideas in his work was binary oppositions. These could be, at their most basic, light versus darkness, good versus evil, or death versus life. Lévi-Strauss was heavily influenced by Saussure. He is considered a key figure in modern anthropology, mainly because of his belief that the 'savage' and 'civilised' minds were no different and both held the same essential humanity. According to Lévi-Strauss, we all understand the world in terms of opposites. He theorised that this way of viewing the world was common to people across all cultures, and that the stories we tell in all societies are heavily driven by opposite qualities and characters of all kinds. As someone who studied the similarities between myths (in the fantastical story sense of the word) across cultures, he found that many of them had very similar qualities and, particularly, presentations of recurrent conflicts.

Binary oppositions are especially useful when reading those print media texts that may not have sufficient length or complexity to apply Todorov's theory. Binary oppositions can be very usefully applied to whole genres as well as to the individual text, making them a very interesting way of approaching meanings of whole clusters of signs. It is the tension between oppositions – or the imbalance caused by the presence of one thing and the absence of a countering opposition – that drives all our stories, with the pairings acting like counterweights, pushing and pulling the narrative ebb and flow. These tensions are more important than the chronology of a narrative – the order in which things happen.

EXAMPLE: Brexit coverage in news stories

Consider the conflicts suggested in the presentation of a news story about the UK's departure from the European Union – leave versus remain, togetherness versus isolation, harmony versus disruption, known versus unknown, nationalism versus Eurocentrism, are just a few of the binary oppositions that repeatedly dominate these stories.

APPLY IT

Find four print advertisements that span the categories of conceptual, informative, narrative or technical. For each advert, try to identify three pairs of binary oppositions that establish a limited narrative for the consumer about what the product can offer.

Some Media Studies students initially find the theory difficult, as the identification of the oppositions is up to them rather than being prescribed. Sometimes a pairing of oppositions can only be identified by the absence of the other, but in reality this is the beauty of this theoretical approach to narrative, making it truly versatile once you have the confidence to use it. It is also worth remembering that rather than simply identifying the pairings you believe are present in the text, their real value lies in your explanation of the pairs and their subtle interplay with and manipulation of our perceptions of the 'story'. Binary oppositions can also be used to articulate Barthes' concept of myth.

Roland Barthes

We first encountered Roland Barthes in the first section of this chapter, where we looked at semiotics. Barthes is also renowned for his work on narrative, and particularly his organisation of aspects of narrative into five different narrative codes. Barthes described these codes as functioning like a 'braid'. No single code is prioritised in the functioning of a narrative – they all take on their own comparative significance and then recede at different points in the text. These codes and their key features are outlined below.

Hermeneutic code – these are sometimes known as enigma codes. They are used to describe any element of a narrative to which the audience requires answers. The function of the hermeneutic code is connected with narrative chronology, since it functions in print media to keep the audience interested until the end of an article, to make them look closer, or to encourage them to buy the next issue.

Proairetic code – proairetic codes are sometimes called action codes. They describe small, quickly resolved units of action that drive the narrative forwards and maintain the interest of the audience. Any proairetic code suggests that another will follow. Proairetic codes are also connected with chronology, since they are often about cause and effect. All 'plots' are composed of numerous units of completed actions.

Semantic code – Barthes uses the term semantic code to define anything that is strongly connoted by a particular element of a text; meanings that go beyond the denotations that are present in any text.

Symbolic code – symbolic codes are also present in text outside of structure. Symbolic codes tend to be the deeper meanings we can draw from a narrative, sometimes as a result of repetition of particular semantic codes, more often as the result of binary oppositions in the text.

Cultural/referential code – these codes relate to our shared understanding of how the world works and the established understanding of its properties. These could be behaviours or events that have psychological realism, historical resonance, literary precedents or medical verisimilitude. Cultural codes can be a reference to almost anything in the body of human knowledge we can see being applied in the construction of a text. Genres can even be considered to be cultural codes.

APPLY IT

Choose three posters for films currently on general release. How does each make use of hermeneutic and proairetic codes to engage the audience's interest?

Choose a more complex text, such as a magazine feature. Can you find any examples of the semantic, symbolic or cultural codes being used? Be aware that you won't necessarily find all in a single text.

KEY TERMS

attempt to repair	in Todorov's theory of narrative, attempts made by the protagonist or other characters to bring about a new equilibrium
binary oppositions	narrative theory proposed by Lévi-Strauss that describes narratives as driven by pairs of opposing qualities that are in tension
chronology	the time order of narrative events
cultural/ referential code	one of Barthes' five narrative codes; the frame of reference that is human knowledge
cultural tropes	plot elements, themes or figures of speech that are used repeatedly in literature or popular culture
disruption	in Todorov's theory of narrative, an event that disturbs the equilibrium
enclosed narrative	a narrative that is complete
equilibrium	in Todorov's theory of narrative, the stable situation or balance at the beginning of a narrative, and the new state achieved by the end
hermeneutic code	one of Barthes' five narrative codes; enigmas or puzzles in a narrative
hook	any technique used to draw the audience into a narrative

narrative closure	a narrative with a satisfactory ending
narrative resolution	the way in which a narrative concludes
narratology	the structuralist study of narrative
primary causal agents	the driving factors in a narrative, usually people
proairetic code	one of Barthes' five narrative codes; units of resolved action through cause and effect
recognition	in Todorov's theory of narrative, the realisation that a disruption to the equilibrium has occurred
self-contained narrative	a narrative that stands on its own
semantic code	one of Barthes' five narrative codes; connotations in a narrative
serial narrative	a narrative that may be extended over a number of episodes or editions
symbolic code	one of Barthes' five narrative codes; deeper meanings and binary oppositions
universal themes	themes to which many people across cultures can relate

KEY THINKER

Tzvetan Todorov	(1939–2017) Bulgarian-French theorist who contributed to a range of academic disciplines in his time, including literary theory, anthropology, history and philosophy

1.4 Genre and print media texts

Genre development

Some of these technological changes are explored more fully in Chapters 5 and 6.

Print media products and genres have experienced technological changes in keeping with every other aspect of production and consumption.

One effect of market competition and globalisation can be to homogenise content and reduce variety. Simultaneously, the comparative cheapness of production technologies allows more access to digital production and distribution.

Print media is the only mass media form that has experienced a permanent and irreversibly negative impact on its sales as a result of the technological revolution. Despite dire predictions of its imminent demise in the early 2000s, print media still persists.

Some newspapers still retain a settled level of circulation despite losses to digital news sources – and magazines still offer the pleasure of having something tangible for your money. They seem a luxury in a world where most of our films are now held in clouds, and, rather than buying a boxed set of DVDs, we simply wait for a series to appear on whichever service we subscribe to. Genre texts in print – particularly magazines – offer something that is not yet being absolutely replaced by digital.

EXAMPLE: Genre development – a brief history of the film magazine

Film magazines have a long history in the UK. The first recorded example was only 16 pages long. Published in 1911, *The Pictures* proved very quickly that there was an appetite among fans of cinema – which was still very new at the time – for written material about their favourite stars and films.

These magazines really were the first celebrity magazines, often filled with gossip, Hollywood fashion and forthcoming releases. The industry was quick to capitalise on this for promotional purposes, and so a long-standing co-promotional relationship was born.

One of the most famous historical titles was *Picturegoer*, which was published first monthly and then weekly from 1921 for almost 40 years.

Although film magazines were initially popular with both men and women, television impacted on sales of film magazines, with film entertainment no longer at the heart of women's lives in particular.

In the intervening years, a number of magazines, such as *Film Review* for mainstream audiences and *Sight and Sound* for people with a specialist interest in film, continued to survive, with a number of titles appearing and disappearing as the market adjusted to who their target audience now were.

The brand leaders today, *Empire* and *Total Film*, launched in 1989 and 1997 respectively with very much a male target audience in mind. Both maintain good circulation figures despite online competition for film news, with glossy exclusives on upcoming releases, big director and star interviews, and privileged access to sets.

APPLY IT

Research the history of a print media genre of your choice. Write a 500-word case study of its origins, any significant setbacks or sub-genres and modern incarnations.

Exploring codes and conventions in print media texts

Print media genres are relatively straightforward to study. Newspapers are often categorised by the area they serve – local, regional or national press – their political leanings – right or left wing – or their approach to news – whether they have the values of a traditional tabloid or broadsheet. Magazines are often categorised by audiences and media producers alike according to their content – there are sport magazines, gaming magazines, lifestyle and so on. Some of these have clear sub-genres, although, unlike audio-visual or digital media, they constitute a smaller corpus with fewer examples making up each since the magazine business is less prolific in terms of individual titles than other media forms. They can also be grouped by target age range of audience or sometimes by gender of the majority of readership. Print advertising is often studied generically by looking at similarities between adverts for similar products – car advertising, for example, might be considered to be a genre, with family or luxury car advertising a sub-genre.

One interesting aspect of genre study is that print media genres do not exist in a vacuum – they will also borrow from other genres and be related to them. This is particularly the case with print media products that are advertising another media form, or functioning as a sub-promoter of that form, as do TV themed magazines and film magazines. When studying a print media genre, it is quite possible to collect all the examples on the market in the UK at any one time for analysis – something that would be almost impossible to do with digital or audio-visual media.

Much genre theory has evolved from film study, and has been appropriated by Media Studies students for its interest and relevance in looking at a whole range of texts. One of these theories was proposed by Dudley Andrew in his book *Concepts in Film Theory* (1984). These definitions of how we understand the term genre, and the different ways in which the term is meaningful to both print media industries and audiences are summed up here:

Genre as **structure**

- Typical articles, content, technical codes and representations.
- Typical locations such as sports photographs or studio shoots.
- Iconography – typical images we associate with a genre.

Genre as **blueprint**

- Useful to industry – the observation of previous successes and cultural trends.
- Dictates hybridisation.
- Influences how many of a particular type of text appear on the market; successful texts spawn imitators.

Genre as **label**

- The way in which audience and industry connect and understand print media titles.
- Widely used by audiences to describe their print media consumption.
- Industry labels might differ from those used by audiences, e.g. young men's lifestyle, lad mag.

Genre as **contract**

- Audience expectations about the content of their print media products.
- Crucially, the front page of a newspaper or the front cover of a magazine arouses expectations – if these are not met, audiences consider the contract broken.
- Audiences exchange money for a media text in most cases. If they don't get what they expect, they won't repeat the purchase.

APPLY IT

Choose a genre of product advertising and collect at least five examples from it. identify any relevant sub-genres, common codes, and conventions and techniques used.

The front covers of these magazines arouse expectations about the contents.

🔗 Some of the theoretical approaches to genre are explored in more detail in section '2.4 Genre and audio-visual/audio media texts'.

Crime magazines are a niche genre of the form. It is difficult to define the readership, but the majority will obviously have an interest in crime, and particularly a fascination with violent crimes and murders, the police and investigation procedures. This is not so strange when you consider that television crime drama series are a very popular genre in that media form. There is possibly a level of coincidence between fans of the genre and the readership of this genre of magazine.

This might seem macabre, but these magazines in many ways fulfil the same audience pleasures as might be experienced by a horror film viewer – they are reminded by their experience of the text how comparatively safe and happy their own life is. It's highly unlikely that someone whose real world in any way came into collision with any of the kind of experiences recorded in these stories would want to read them. Most of the crimes selected in the coverlines appear to be extreme examples of their kind, not the more common crime events such as the regular murders that happen every week in the UK as a result of domestic violence. They offer a safe way of closing down fears about violence in society – they are all about how perpetrators of crimes, no matter how cunning, were ultimately caught, exposed and punished.

There are five main titles on the market in the UK – *True Crime, Real Crime, True Detective, Master Detective* and *Murder Most Foul*. Some also produce special editions. From looking at the series of images, it is clear that each individual title shares some features in common with others. Historical crime cases from around the world form most of the coverline content. All of the editions feature a crime focus, which in four of the five cases is positioned on the left-hand side around the sweet spot. Other secondary images are used in conjunction with coverlines to emphasise the human nature of the subject matter and to hook the readership in. The lexical coding uses frightening words with strongly negative connotations – *monster, lethal, hell, slaughter, rape, slayer*. These emphasise that the magazine covers the extremes of human experience of crime in a sensationalised way.

The majority of the magazines use similar iconography – many black and white images indicating the starkness of the subject matter and the historical nature of some of the crimes. Red and black, which can have a connotation of danger, and yellow – which combined with these can seem to be a sickly or disturbing colour – form the majority of the palette. The background selected in each case is dark and cold, blue or black. The house style is not dissimilar in its cluttered look to many women's weekly titles that feature a mixture of true stories, puzzles, some celebrity news and lifestyle elements, or even soap weeklies. This suggests a plausible consonance in mode of address with an audience age range of predominantly middle-aged and older women in lower socio-economic categories.

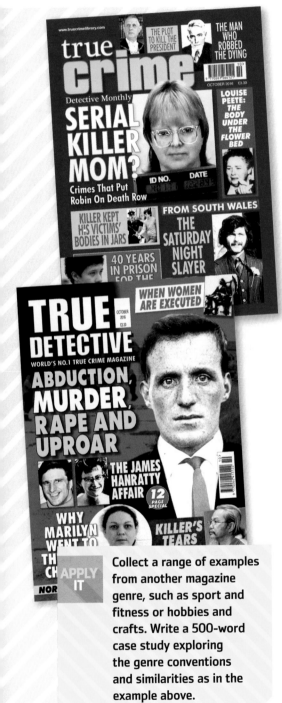

APPLY IT

Collect a range of examples from another magazine genre, such as sport and fitness or hobbies and crafts. Write a 500-word case study exploring the genre conventions and similarities as in the example above.

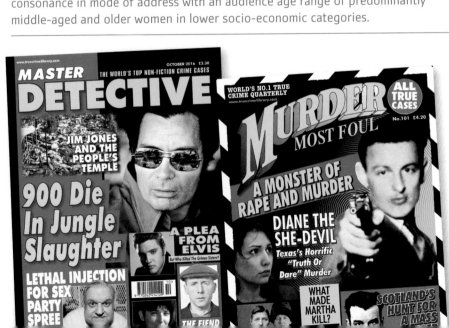

Intertextuality and print media

Intertextuality as a term first began to appear in writing about the mass media from the late 1960s onwards. It is often used in conjunction with **post-modern theory**, which you will learn more about in the second year of your A level course. It is a difficult term to define with precision, partly because the nature of what it describes is often quite intangible. An intertextual product is one media text that is making a reference to another consciously and deliberately, in order to create a new meaning. This retains some of the reference text but imbues it with new qualities and meanings specific to the new text. Since all texts are part of a continuous cycle of the production of meaning, and continued cultural re-referencing, some critics suggest that the term is actually redundant in today's media climate.

In print media, fortunately, we sometimes see some very concrete examples of intertextuality. A magazine cover or advertisement might reference another famous media image, such as a propaganda poster. A feature interview with a celebrity might use a dress code associated with a film genre to depict them in a particular way. Although a lot of intertextuality can be seen in iconography, it can also be present in lexical coding, with conscious and deliberate referencing of any popular catchphrase from a sitcom or game show. Advertising slogans, long-gone television drama series and historical newspaper headlines continue to imbue the new text with an element of the original meaning, although this will often be conducted in a playful or ironic way.

Season 6 Episode 1 of animated series 'Family Guy' saw the story of Star Wars retold featuring the regular cast of characters.

EXAMPLE: *Wired* magazine and intertextuality

This front cover from *Wired* technology and culture magazine April 2016 clearly references Maoist propaganda posters from the cultural revolution in China to promote its feature on China and technology and its interview with Chinese technology entrepreneur Lei Jun.

APPLY IT

Look through a supply of magazines and newspapers for an example of intertextuality. Can you find online the original text to which your example refers? What meanings were present in the original text? How are these meanings being incorporated into the new?

KEY TERMS

intertextuality	the process by which one media text consciously references another text or genre, therefore deriving further layers of meaning for a reader who has experienced both texts

post-modern theory	a school of thinking that questions the idea of 'reality' as anything other than a collection of constructs apparent in any culture – the mass media is seen as playing an important role since it helps shape and reflect our understanding of our culture. The movement resists solid definitions and answers in many disciplines within the arts, humanities and even sciences

sub-genres	the formulation of a new subgroup within a genre which shares some of the qualities of the parent group but also has defining qualities of its own

CHAPTER SUMMARY

- Semiotics, which is the study of signs, is an essential way of understanding how media products communicate with their audiences.
- Semiotics is an early structuralist theory derived from linguistics as a field of study. It is continually revisited and expanded by theorists.
- Two of the most significant early theorists are Ferdinand de Saussure and Charles Peirce. Saussure is mainly remembered for his discussion of the sign as the product of signifier plus the signified, which he regarded as being indivisible.
- Peirce developed a method of categorising signs into symbolic or arbitrary signs, iconic signs and indexical signs, which all function in slightly different ways.
- Another important contributor to the field was Roland Barthes, who further added his ideas about different orders of signification that increase in complexity – the first order being denotative, the second connotative, and the potential third order operating on the level of ideology and myth.
- There are some key terms associated with semiotics that you need to be confident in using when analysing print media forms and language.
- Print media has its own technical codes and discrete terminology used in discussion of technical codes.
- The main forms – newspapers, advertisements and magazines – all have their own combinations of technical codes that allow them to be easily recognised by the audience. Each form may also have its own form-specific terminology.
- Narratives are present to some extent in all media texts, even those with the simplest form such as a single-page advertisement.
- Narratives are ways in which we organise media texts to make sense of their content. There is a range of narrative terms that can be used outside of specific narrative theories, and using these to support your own insights into narrative organisation can be useful.
- Todorov's theory of narrative suggests that many narratives may be broken down into five stages that describe the movement between two equilibriums. This is useful for newspaper stories and magazine features, but less so for print advertising.
- Lévi-Strauss' theory of binary oppositions is one of the most versatile narrative theories available to Media Studies students, and oppositions can be identified in any text, from the very simple to very complex.
- Barthes' five narrative codes work together to produce a holistic view of how narratives operate on a number of different levels. If you're not sure about using all five codes in analysis, start by just using hermeneutic and proairetic codes.
- Print media genres are often simple to demarcate, consistent in their conventions and very centred on content or product.
- All genres can be thought of in different ways and approached with slightly differing emphasis depending on the point being made – as structure, blueprint, label or contract.
- Intertextuality is widely used in print media texts, and this is particularly evident in borrowed iconography.

FURTHER READING

Bronwen Thomas (2015) *Narrative: The Basics.*
Daniel Chandler (2007) *Semiotics: The Basics.*
Paul Cobley and Litza Jansz (2010) *Introducing Semiotics: A Graphic Guide.*
Roland Barthes (2014) *Mythologies.*
Stephen Neale (1980) *Genre.*

Chapter 2 Reading audio-visual media

2.1 The technical codes and features used in moving image texts

In Chapter 1, we explored the main theories and terminology associated with a structuralist approach to reading signs. It would be a good idea to revisit this section before undertaking any analysis of moving image texts.

In the previous chapter, we considered some of the separate terminology associated with the three main print media forms. In this chapter, we will be looking at technical codes in a slightly different way to help us understand the codes common to all the audio-visual forms you study, which are music video, television and audio-visual advertising. Video games and apps are also audio-visual in their nature, and some of what you learn in this chapter is also relevant to their study. Although some industry-specific terminology is associated with production of certain genres and forms, such as documentary, television advertising and news, these are beyond the scope of this chapter – although you may find it very useful to explore them if you are undertaking study of a particular genre.

To help you understand how to approach audio-visual texts, examples are supplied of how certain codes are deployed within a range of textual examples from different forms, to show how they operate in a way that works when located in a particular chosen text. You can use these approaches as a springboard to adapt the techniques to help you analyse any text of your own choosing with confidence.

Mise-en-scène

Mise-en-scène is the term used to refer to the placement of everything within a frame. It is one of the most significant decisions taken by directors and production designers of almost any moving image product. One of the easiest ways to begin to analyse mise-en-scène is to take screenshots from a text to study; picking out the elements of mise-en-scène takes a lot of practice while a moving-image text is playing. These elements are:

- setting/location, both interior and exterior
- dress code
- props
- lighting and colour
- non-verbal communication such as facial expressions and gestural codes.

What you will learn in this chapter

- How audio-visual media language can communicate in different ways and be used to influence meaning
- What makes audio texts distinctive as a medium
- The contribution of narrative to our reading of audio-visual media texts
- How genre theory can inform our understanding of audio-visual texts

Revisit the main theories and terminology associated with a structuralist approach in Chapter 1.

For more on video games see Chapter 3.

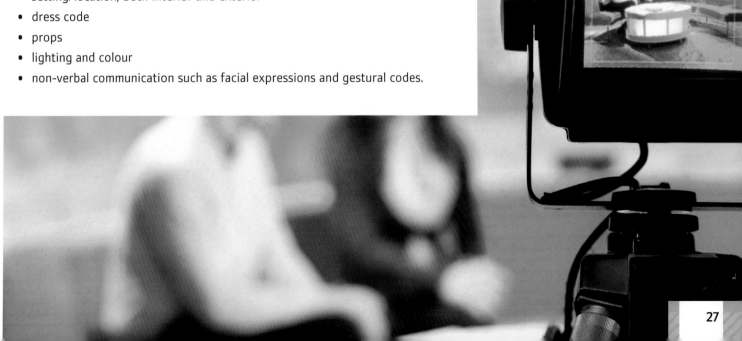

In reality, well-developed mise-en-scène analysis rarely focuses on all the signs within a single frame – it is used alongside the discussion of other technical codes, and selected significant elements are picked out for discussion across a whole sequence. Mise-en-scène analysis can also be useful in genre identification, and contributes strongly to our understanding of the iconography of a genre, conventional symbols or images associated with it.

Mise-en-scène is controlled by framing. The positioning of props and people within the frame is just as important, if fleeting, as it is in the photographic images used in print media texts. The same codes used in photographic images take on significance – dress codes, colour codes, décor, location and non-verbal codes. Non-verbal gestural codes and gait also become more significant when a person can be seen moving. Proxemics and para-proxemics are still significant, sometimes with more complex hierarchies as movement is introduced. Lighting is also significant, and can be used to create a range of moods and effects through contrasts in lighting temperature between scenes, along with the control of highlight and shadow, and apparent time of day.

Spike Jonze, director of the 'Kenzo: World' perfume advert.

EXAMPLE: The mise-en-scène of the 'Kenzo: World' perfume advert, 2016

The 'Kenzo: World' perfume advert follows the recent trend of commissioning well-known directors (in this case, Spike Jonze) to produce extended and highly cinematic adverts featuring established stars. This often means a sumptuous and grand-scale mise-en-scène.

The narrative features a young woman who escapes from a dull formal event in a large hotel or conference venue, only to playfully unleash herself on the corridors. She dances a riot around the venue to a specially commissioned and unconventional track before finally leaping through a huge model eye positioned outside. The main contributor to meaning within the mise-en-scène is the unusual use of non-verbal communication and gestural codes.

Iconography of perfume advertising: This is apparent in the advert's focus on a glamorously dressed and physically attractive female star. In this case, this is Margaret Qualley, an American television actor and formally trained ballet dancer. Throughout the advertisement, she dominates the frame, reiterating her status as the star.

Dress code: Qualley has her hair neatly arranged up to suit the unnamed formal occasion she is attending at the start of the advertisement. Her make-up is low key but immaculate. She wears a long, formal ball gown, also matched to the occasion, which becomes more revealing throughout the sequence. The gown is deep green, a colour relating to superstition. It's also a strong signifier of nature in this context; Qualley fights back against convention in the text and her own 'nature' is unleashed.

Non-verbal communication: Qualley's performance style as an actor and dancer is highly energetic. At the beginning she is polite, sober in manner and subdued. The others around her appear to be absorbed by the formal event, which Qualley's character clearly does not feel any enthusiasm for; this is evident from her facial expression, which connotes disengagement. Once free to dance the corridors, stairs and stage of the venue her face contorts, puppet-like, into a series of outrageous expressions. Throughout, the character repeatedly directly addresses the audience by looking straight into the lens, reducing the distance between the audience and text, and making us feel complicit in her playful adventure around the venue. Energetic sequences in which elements of gestural codes are borrowed from action films – kickboxing and a range of dance styles and puppet-like movements – are used to transport her from one part to another. These gestural codes combine elements of the masculine and feminine. They culminate in her final graceful leap and landing to where she rises and beats her chest.

Location, décor, props: The location uses a vast and luxurious (connoted by the plentiful floristry and chandeliers) but bland hotel or conference centre. A significant prop used in the advert is the mirror, which has a long tradition of being used symbolically for reflection on the self and identity. The rose-covered wall-hanging against which she performs lends a stuffy, stale and claustrophobic backdrop. The pink flowers on the table at the start, and in the display stands inside and outside the venue, seem to symbolise a stifling femininity. Other aspects of the décor include a quietly feminine palette of peach, pink, pale gold and beige tones, against which Qualley's performance can really stand out. The other notable props are a bust of Winston Churchill, which is licked – symbolising a lack of deference to authority – and the eye that she leaps though at the end. This is open to interpretation, possibly symbolising all eyes being on her, expecting her to act her part. The generally muted lighting is broken by the use of strobe as she attacks the man engaged in a serious mobile phone conversation.

Camerawork

Shot types are one of the most important codes in audio-visual texts. The basic shot types of **close-up** (CU), **medium shot** (MS) and **long-shot** (LS) can all be modified to describe incremental changes in shot using terms such as extreme (e.g. extreme close-up) and medium (e.g. medium close-up).

Other shot types are named more for their function. A **two-shot** is the common term for a shot that has two people in it; an **establishing shot** is used to establish a change of scene. A **point-of-view shot** (POV) makes us feel as though we are seeing events unfold through someone else's eyes, and an **over-the-shoulder shot** gives us a sense of participation in a conversation. Other shot names – such as a **cutaway shot**, **reaction shot** or **nodding shot** only make sense in the context of other shots, so really form part of the codes relating to editing.

Some shots are named after specialist lenses that may be required to shoot them effectively – a **wide-angle shot** allows us to see more of an expanse of an exterior or interior location in one shot, with a **fish-eye shot** giving us a distorted perspective that introduces even more extreme wide angles and can feel very claustrophobic.

Extreme close-up

Medium shot

Long-shot

Fish-eye shot

Just as important as the type of shot used is the angle of the camera. A camera placed roughly at eye level with its subject creates a sense of equality with it on the part of the audience. A slightly higher angle can easily make its subject appear inferior, and a low angle elevate it. A canted angle ('Dutch' angle) can feel edgy and disorientating in some texts, but in music video canted angles are very common. A worm's-eye shot is sometimes a point-of-view shot, either pointing directly upwards as though on the ground, or an extreme low angle that makes its subject loom. A bird's-eye shot offers the reverse perspective.

As with shot types, some camera angles are named after the techniques used to capture them – an aerial shot is used to show vast areas of location, and usually requires air transport to shoot. Aerial shots span the categories of both shot type and movement. Crane shots also do this – a crane is used to provide some exceptionally fluid and unusual movements, often following action from perspectives that would be impossible from the ground. Jib shots, where the camera is positioned on a metal arm and operated remotely, are often used in studio shoots, such as those you might see in a studio-based television show.

Hand-held shot is a generic term for any use of camera operated by hand rather than situated on a tripod or dolly. These have many applications across genres. They are highly practical in documentary or news filming situations, where advance planning is not always possible, and spontaneity and portability are of the essence on the shoot. This code can sometimes be re-appropriated in fictional media texts, where the effect is to create a feeling of instability to the subject matter or a documentary style that implies verisimilitude.

Other terms are used to describe very specific movements. A tracking shot – sometimes also called a following shot, is used to follow a moving subject by travelling alongside it. It can be filmed either by a vehicle with an on-board mount, or by a long track set up parallel with the line of movement, which then has a dolly move along it. A short tracking shot (often also slower) is called a crab. A following pan can also follow an object, but in this case the camera stays in one position and moves on its axis to follow the subject of the shot. Used at speed, this becomes a whip pan. A surveying pan can follow the same movement, but is more languorous and has no subject. When a pan occurs on the y-axis it is referred to as a tilt, and is often divided into tilt up or tilt down, since it is unusual to see both movements in one take without an edit.

Working with the camera on a dolly.

Although not strictly shot types, focus techniques and lens movements are often considered alongside these as they form part of the same paradigm. Zooms, both in and out, are strictly lens movements in which the subject is brought closer or made more distant. Zooms can be fast or slow, and the effect of speed on interpretation can be significant. Faster speeds are associated with action, and slower speeds with manipulating para-proxemics and sometimes contributing to the emotional response we experience to a subject on-screen. Selective focus is used to bring attention to a particular part of the frame to show its importance. A pull focus may be used to change this, and form a kind of in-shot edit, where the audience's attention is drawn first to one thing then another by changing the focus. Using this technique, a subject in the foreground may be defocused in preference to the background. The effect of this is usually quite contemplative, although very fast focus pulls can also be seen deployed in action sequences and point-of-view shots.

EXAMPLE: Music video: *Angels*, Chance the Rapper featuring Saba (2015)

Music videos are interesting examples to use when beginning to study camerawork. They often use very dynamic shot ranges because of their innately bold visual style, and feature a range of shots that can be explored out of the sequence.

- *Tracking shot* – used in the opening to bring us on the boy's journey and allow us to sense his place in the city.
- *Establishing shot of the city* – shot as aerial footage, which feels like a POV perspective of Chance flying over the city.
- *Extreme low angles* – give an impression of the size and scale of the city, contrasting with the sky through which Chance flies.
- *On-board vehicle shots* – used on the top of the train, showing Chance's performance and lending a highly mobile and journey-like feel to the narrative.
- *Close-up* of shoes – signifying the introduction of dance moves to the sequence.
- *Tracking shots* in the train – both back and forth – allow for focus on different characters and their performances.
- *Hand-held camera work* on train – reflects the movements of the vehicle.
- *Camera work* – reflects two spheres of action, the train/below and the train/above.
- Numerous *two shots* – used on the street to film two performers dancing.
- *Crane shots*, *dolly shots* and *hand-held work* including *low-angle shots* – elevate the importance of the performers, and are all used in the dance sequence.
- *Bird's-eye shot* – at the end on the boy, as though the 'angel' is looking down on him.
- Video ends with a *tilt up* – as the song finishes with the boy who drew us into the narrative at the start, we share his perspective on the city.

APPLY IT

Choose a music video from any genre you enjoy. Watch the video several times, pausing where you need to make notes. List some of the camera shots used, describing the effect of each.

Use your notes to write a paragraphed analysis of how camera work contributes to the construction of meaning, in around 500 words.

Editing

Many techniques are used in editing, and it is only possible to cover here a few that are seen most frequently. The majority of texts you study will use **continuity editing** style, the predominant type of editing in mainstream media. Continuity editing constructs time and space in straightforward ways that make sense to us because we have been reading its codes since childhood. Most of the time it provides a seamless experience of viewing that does not draw attention to the **apparatus** – the physical nature of its construction.

The other common editing style you will see used is **montage editing**, which has many uses from film trailers to music videos. In montage editing we see a number of shots, which we understand are not occurring consecutively in the chronology, played in close sequence. This creates a strong impression of a character's journey or an event, or to create atmosphere. It is usually used quite sparingly.

Space is constructed according to technical laws and norms such as the **180-degree rule**, where the camera must not 'cross the line' in a straight cut from a film sequence in order to preserve the illusion of a particular perspective on a scene. If the perspective needs to switch to another side of the room, a connecting shot with a movement, such as a dolly or jib shot, will usually be included, or the narrative will cutaway to another scene before returning to a new camera position.

Similarly, to preserve visual logic, we have the **30-degree rule**, which states that the camera must move more than 30 degrees when showing a new shot of the same subject. Failure to do so results in a **jump cut**, which is disorientating for the audience – and actually looks like a mistake. At times this can be deployed for effect (usually with several jump cuts being edited together). Although it is important to understand how editing constructs space, you will rarely need to actually comment on this in an analysis. Understanding it will make you more aware of editing and more likely to spot other more relevant techniques.

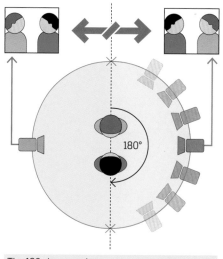

The 180-degree rule

The way in which we experience the passage of time is also controlled by editing. The depiction of 'real' time is compressed – in fictional narratives, this is carefully controlled to manipulate our experience of the narrative. More screen time will be given to certain characters at particular points, and events that unfold over a number of days – or would if they were real in the case of fictional narratives – will be compressed into an hour or 30 minutes. Parallel development may be used, where we understand that two events are supposed to be happening in simultaneous time, even though the edit requires that we cut between the two events alternately. The only real alternative to this is the use of split screen, which is acceptable for more experimental TV dramas, but would appear odd in a soap opera.

Some other techniques that involve using editing to play with our perception of time include the multi-take, where the effect of an action is shown by repeating it several times, sometimes shot from different angles or distances. Decelerated motion is frequently used to contribute to the emotional power of a sequence, and is a convention so familiar we barely notice it. Accelerated motion adds to our perception of speed, but usually has to be deployed with a much lighter touch, since, unlike decelerated motion, it jars when used deliberately, and is only suited to deliberate use in a small handful of contexts, such as comic effect.

Transitions are used to get from one shot or scene to another. The overwhelming majority of transitions you will see in audio-visual texts are straight cuts. Other common techniques are fade in, fade out and fade through black. These are subtle and slower-paced transitions. Also in this category is the cross-dissolve, where one image is slowly superseded by another, creating a whimsical effect.

Relationships can be created by editing. The juxtapositioning of a high-angle with a low-angle shot can easily imply a relative power positioning between two characters. An eye-line match is created when we see someone looking, then see what they are looking at. Matched cut is another term used for pairs of shots that make sense together. Over-the-shoulder shots are used to film conversations, and reaction shots commonly allow us to see the impact of almost anything else that has happened in the previous shot.

Titling can be used in all kinds of versatile ways. Cutaway shots are used in factual media, sometimes to contribute additional meaning or add weight to a person's dialogue, at other times for illustrative purposes. Cutting rhythm and cutting rate are used to refer to the way in which footage is cut to create a particular pace. You should also remember that sound, covered earlier, is also a significant part of the editing process. This is discussed further in the next section, but is also relevant to audio-visual texts. Other post-production techniques rendered so much easier in the digital age include special effects, graphical elements and subtle post-production practices such as colourisation.

Over-the-shoulder shot

For more on tilting see section '3.4 Genre and digital media texts'.

For more on sound see section '2.2 The technical codes and features used in audio texts'.

EXAMPLE: Editing in an episode of *Take Me Out*, a television dating game show (ITV, 2016)

Editing style in television game shows varies across the genre and sub-genres, but will always match the style of the show. A frenetic physical or youth-targeted game show will have a faster editing pace and more use of score. A quiz show will be more sedate. Editing usually deploys straight cuts between a standard paradigm (range/group) of familiar shots, and the sequence in which these are cut together may vary very little. This helps to underline the format of the show and encourages familiarity. It is useful to identify these recurring groups of shots.

Take Me Out uses hyper-kinetic 'MTV style' editing, which matches the feel of the show and the target audience. It has a fast cutting rate, and makes some use of cutting rhythm, with shots edited on the beat of popular tracks used in the soundtrack. The pace of editing slows significantly in the date segment. There is frequent repetition of certain sequences of shot, for example *high-angle crane shot of whole set, LS host, MCU of each female participant, MCU or CU reaction shots intercut of male contestant.*

The date scene has significantly compressed screen time – location filming of the date is sampled to give a snapshot that supports the views given in interviews. If an annoying quality of the date is described by the other participant, several instances of that behaviour or quality are edited together in montage to exaggerate it. Each participant's reflections on the date are carefully controlled through editing, with some cutaway footage used of their interviews. Reaction shots are also made use of in much the same way they are controlled in reality television, to articulate and construct relationships.

The host of *Take Me Out*, Paddy McGuinness, with contestants

Sound

Sound makes a huge contribution to audio-visual texts, but is sometimes neglected by students during analysis in favour of the seemingly more dominant visual codes. This is a shame because aural codes can contribute a great deal to our reading of a text if we listen carefully. The sound mix is an important part of post-production, and can be considered alongside editing.

The term diegetic sound, meaning from the diegesis (the 'story-world', the construct) is often used to label the apparent source of sound and to understand how we should read it. A common mistake made by new Media Studies students is to assume that any sound that is added post-production rather than recorded on a location is non-diegetic. In fact, regardless of how it was technically integrated into the soundtrack, any sound that supposedly originates in an audio-visual text is diegetic. An easy way to remember this with texts is if the participants or characters in a recording can hear the sound, it would be classed as diegetic. Parallel sound is a term used to describe sound that fulfils our expectations. Sometimes, sound that doesn't match the scene can be deployed – this is known as contrapuntal sound, and has a disconcerting or even sinister effect.

From this example, you can see that very few sounds are commonly categorised as non-diegetic. The most significant of these are voice-overs, which can be provided by an extra-diegetic narrator (who is unseen) or an intra-diegetic narrator, who also appears in the text's diegesis. This second kind of narrator can bring an additional layer of uncertainty into a fictional text, as we might question the reliability of their interpretation of events. A score is also considered non-diegetic, although music can also appear diegetically, heard by characters and part of the scene.

Background sound, known also as atmosphere or soundscape, can be very interesting to analyse, as we rarely notice it, but it often makes a very significant contribution to our level of immersion in a text. At the other end of the scale, we can sometimes detect the use of selective sound, when one sound is deliberately amplified in the mix to draw attention to it.

APPLY IT

Choose a reality television show and watch an episode. Note down the key editing techniques you observe that are used at different points in the show. Consider in particular whether editing is used to represent participants in a particular way.

Write your findings as a 500-word case study.

APPLY IT

Choose a film trailer in a popular genre. Watch it first with sound, then without. Identify a number of sounds you hear used. Try to find examples of as many of the techniques mentioned on this page as you can.

Group your examples of sounds heard under diegetic and non-diegetic column headings. Are there any other ways in which you can group certain sounds? Try to decode the qualities of the sound.

a What can you decode from the soundscapes used in the trailer?

b What qualities are there in the range of vocal performances in dialogue?

c Which sounds are prominent in the sound mix?

d Does the trailer make use of a score? If so, what does the music contribute to meaning?

e Does the trailer use a voice-over?

KEY TERMS

30-degree rule	one of the rules that constructs space in visual language – the camera must move more than 30 degrees in order to avoid an ugly cut
180-degree rule	one of the rules that constructs space in visual language – the camera must stay one side of an imaginary line when filming a scene, unless a cutaway or visible movement leads the audience to another perspective
accelerated motion	the speeding up of footage during editing
aerial shot	from in the air, often shot from an aircraft
apparatus	term used for the equipment and methods used in media production
atmosphere/ soundscape	background sound, especially in fiction media texts, which is constructed to contribute to verisimilitude
aural code	term used to describe all the techniques relating to sound
bird's-eye shot	extreme high angle or directly from the sky downwards
canted angle	sometimes known as a 'Dutch' angle – a shot that leans over to the side
close-up	often just face and shoulders
colourisation	the way in which the saturation or other elements of how we perceive colour may be altered post-production, either to harmonise footage from different shoots or locations, or to achieve a particular aesthetic
compression of screen time	the way in which media texts, through editing, reduce the 'real time' in which events would unfold
continuity editing	dominant mode of editing that does not draw attention to itself, allowing the audience to focus on the subject-matter
contrapuntal sound	sound that does not seem to match the action, often deliberately used to unnerve the audience or even create a blackly comic effect
crab	short tracking shot
crane shot	any footage taken using a crane – highly mobile and versatile in terms of movement

cross-dissolve	the gradual fading of one shot into another
cutaway shot	footage that shows another subject before returning to the original
cutting rate	the way in which pace is controlled in editing – many shots of short duration lend a fast cutting rate; longer duration results in a slower rate
cutting rhythm	the length of shots, particularly when edited to a soundtrack or score, when these appear to have rhythmic qualities
decelerated motion	the slowing down of footage during editing
diegesis	the world of the media text, the 'story world' especially in fiction-based media
diegetic sound	refers to sound supposedly generated within the diegesis
dolly	fixing for camera that allows it to be moved smoothly over a set floor or on a track
elements of mise-en-scène	the individual components of mise-en-scène such as props or lighting
establishing shot	often exterior locations, but can be interiors – used to set a scene
extra-diegetic narration	voice-over provided by an unseen person from outside the diegesis
eye-line match	usually means the pairing of a shot of a person with the object of their attention in the next frame
fade in/out	the gradual dissolution of a shot
fade through black	technique that allows the audience a moment to reflect, by placing a short breathing space over black between scenes
fish-eye shot	a shot, usually using a specific lens for the purpose, which brings in a range of angles of view
following pan	movement where the camera remains in one position but is turned on its axis to follow an action
gestural codes	the way in which we read expression through movement
hand-held shot	footage taken using a camera operated by a person
high angle	a shot positioned slightly higher than the subject that diminishes it

iconography	repetition of certain visual images or symbols, usually associated in media with particular genres
intra-diegetic narration	voice-over provided by a person or character from within the diegesis
jib shot	any footage taken using a camera, remotely controlled, on a metal arm
jump cut	where the camera moves less than 30 degrees, creating an ugly and dissonant effect – sometimes used deliberately, but is not part of continuity editing style
lighting temperature	the feel lent to a scene according to how it is lit – warm or cool, for example
long-shot	full body at any distance
low angle	a shot positioned slightly lower than the subject, which elevates it
matched cut	pairs of shots that have a logical connection
medium-shot	mid-body shot
montage editing	editing style where we are given a 'snapshot' of different clips
multi-take	non-continuity technique, where a dramatic event may be filmed from several angles and the moment duplicated for effect
nodding shot	in documentary, used to show an interviewer is listening to the subject, but is often cut in later
non-diegetic narration	voice-over created by an unseen person from outside the diegesis
over-the-shoulder shot	shot in which the back of someone's head and shoulder will be partially in view – often used to shoot dialogue – and makes the audience feel they are sharing in the exchange
parallel development	the apparently simultaneous presentation of another narrative strand in a text, which is actually achieved by alternating between the two spheres of action
parallel sound	a sound mix that meets the audience's expectations of a particular scene
point-of-view shot	shot that allows us to share someone's perspective
pull focus	shifting the focus in the frame in the same shot

reaction shot	demonstrates a response to an event or person	split screen	simultaneous depiction of two events on screen by physical splitting of the frame	transition	the way in which movement from shot to shot is managed in editing, most often a straight cut
score	music composed specifically to accompany a media text – existing music redeployed in a text is usually referred to as soundtrack	surveying pan	slow pan on the camera's axis, often to establish either exterior or interior environment	two-shot	two people in the same shot, often implying a relationship between them
screen time	the amount of 'real' time a character is present on screen for, e.g. two minutes	tilt down	movement where the camera is angled down on its axis	whip pan	rapid following pan, widely used in action sequences
selective focus	use of the lens where a particular section of the frame is in focus	tilt up	movement where the camera is raised up on its axis	wide-angle shot	a shot, usually using a specific lens for the purpose, which shows a wide field of view
sound mix	the combination of sound into a soundtrack, and the differing emphasis placed on certain sounds for effect	titling	the use of lexical coding over black or over image – has become very common in digital media texts	worm's-eye shot	extreme low angle or directly from the ground upwards
		tracking shot/ following shot	follows action by travelling alongside or behind it	zoom	movement of the camera lens to bring a subject closer or to distance it

2.2 The technical codes and features used in audio texts

The nature of radio as a medium

Radio and podcasts are what is usually referred to as a 'blind' medium. The type of discussions we have already had about sound in audio-visual texts are still relevant to reading purely audio texts, but, in the case of these, the weight that the auditory codes carry is of so much more significance.

Radio is an old medium, but it has endured. It is a cheap technology, and has an immediacy that is hard to match, except perhaps in certain new digital media forms such as social media platforms, whose distribution methods may be more haphazard, although can have a global reach in a very short space of time.

For more on the historical development and modern contexts of radio, see section '6.1 The diverse nature of media organisations'.

Podcasting is a newcomer on the scene, appearing only as the internet made it possible to digitally share and broadcast files. Many of the codes applicable to radio are also present in podcasts – some podcasts are in fact radio shows made available for listening outside the scheduled time. This first section, where we explore what is distinctive about radio as a medium, will allow you to think, possibly for the first time, about what is truly distinctive about it. In academic terms it receives far less research attention than television or film, but it is consumed daily by large audiences.

The characteristics of radio are defined very interestingly by Andrew Crisell in his book, *Understanding Radio* (1986). The following points are summarised from the first chapter:

- In agreement with most commentators on the role of radio in culture, Crisell refers to radio as a blind medium in that it functions purely on auditory codes at a semiotic level.
- Radio uses speech codes, but without features such as phatic remarks, paralinguistic features and metalingual checks that we would experience if we were face-to-face in the interaction.
- Radio is a form of mass communication and therefore lacks feedback from all of its listeners. Recent advances in digital technologies have meant

APPLY
IT

Listen to three contrasting programmes from three different radio stations.

Write a short report on each programme.

Did you find any evidence of signposting, framing or boundary rituals?

a Did you notice any examples of conscious avoidance of ambiguity?

b Did you hear any examples of processes being explained to help the audience visualise something?

c Were you conscious of any strong mental images you formed in response to any of your listening?

that some almost live feedback on the show such as tweets, texts and emails are integrated into live topical content to give the illusion of a more conversational or two-way relationship between the sender and receiver.

- Talk on radio is necessarily free from ambiguity because there are no other technical codes to support its interpretation.

- Processes we would 'see' in other media forms have to be described verbally to clarify them to the audience.

- Signposting is used to allow the audience to sense the structure of a programme or schedule.

- Beginnings and ends of programmes are used to frame their content, with this framing sometimes being referred to as boundary rituals that distinguish one programme type from another, for example a fictional play from a news bulletin.

- Radio is not the only medium to appeal to the imagination, which is experienced through all the senses, but it is perhaps the medium that requires us to exercise it the most. It is this quality that makes it what Crisell calls an 'intimate medium', which seems to address us in a more personal way since our brains are so necessarily active in generating the mental images and sense that necessarily accompany our reading of auditory codes.

- Radio is flexible, because the audience is able to undertake other tasks when they are listening, such as household chores or driving – but this can sometimes mean that the audience is sometimes distracted from its content and messages (they may 'dip in and out').

- Radio's auditory codes exist in time the same as audio-visual codes do, so they feel more immediate than reading a magazine or newspaper.

- The modes of listening to radio have been categorised in the past as either predominant, where it is the focus as a provider of entertainment, or secondary, where listeners are not fully engaging. Crisell suggests that there is a whole range of listening practices between these two points.

Technical codes in radio

All radio and podcasts depend on sound to communicate their messages. Collectively, the speech codes, music and sound effects that drive radio are known as noise – but there is another very important technique used in radio that is more regularly used and has far more significance in radio than in any other medium, and that is silence. Radio genres and programmes that work particularly well in using these codes are sometimes described as radiogenic.

Speech codes in radio take on far more nuance than in other media – in looking at the characteristics of radio, we saw how language has to be used in a way that is unambiguous, and how explanations are often used to help the listener imagine a particular scene in both fiction-based texts and factual programming such as documentaries. Since radio is an intimate medium, it elicits something that has been identified as co-presence in its reception, which means that listeners feel as though they are almost sharing a room with the presenter and to some degree other listeners.

Because the impact of the spoken word in radio is so much stronger, swearing is very powerful – a radio station that broadcasts instances of swearing is very aware of this and has made a conscious stylistic decision to include it, well aware of the impact that it will have on the listener. This is different from audio-visual use of bad language, where its effect is lessened. 'Shock jock' is a term used to describe a brand of deliberately provocative and offensive radio presenter/DJ,

particularly in the US. These earn their popularity among a small, often right-wing audience, for deliberately challenging the polite conventions of the majority of radio. The increased weight of the spoken word in radio has long been employed to propagandic effect by different nations in history and is also used, disturbingly, in hate radio today.

A sound mixing desk

The sound mix in the radio world is usually created to build a simulation of the way in which the brain works when interpreting sound in the real world. We innately treat certain sounds as background, tuning in to those that are important. This is mimicked by the way in which soundscape at the beginning of a change of environment in a radio programme will be heightened to orient the listener, then fades to give priority to speech codes. Sound effects to which a strong signification is attached punctuate the action. The complete withdrawal of sound, either abrupt or using fades as a framing device, is sometimes used to change scene. As with the continuity system of editing in audio-visual texts, these conventions are understood by the audience. Sound effects have a context to them, and do not have to be 'realistic' in order to be read correctly in the way intended.

Music is sometimes used to evoke a time or place in documentary and fact-based media, working in exactly the same way as it would in an audio-visual text. It can also be used as a theme or jingle to frame programmes, and even as a score, underlining particular moments of drama in a fictional radio text. However, it is true that the majority of music used on radio – and it forms a high proportion of the output of many stations – is used precisely because it lacks any one meaning for the audience.

KEY TERMS

Andrew Crisell	author of *Understanding Radio* (1986), an important text and one of the few available that really explores radio from a Media Studies perspective
auditory codes	sometimes also known as aural codes – sound and particularly its uses in radio and podcasting
blind medium	radio or podcasting – one that is wholly reliant on auditory codes
boundary rituals	another term for framing devices in radio and podcasting
co-presence	the audience's audio-texts experience of almost being in the same room as the presenter and other listeners

framing (in radio)	contextualisation of sections or delineation between programmes in audio texts
hate radio	radio broadcast used to incite racial/ethnic hatred or persecution of minority groups
mass communication	a medium that has the power to communicate very quickly with large numbers of people
metalingual checks	in linguistics, elements of speech used to clarify understanding
noise (in radio)	the sum total of speech, sound effects and music in audio tracks

paralinguistic features	additional information we gain during a face-to-face conversation, which lends meaning to the words used – in audio-visual texts called non-verbal codes
phatic remarks	talk that has a social function
radiogenic	a text that lends itself very easily to radio production
signposting	in radio or podcasting, clearly signifying a change of some kind or designating structure and organisation of an audio text
silence	the deliberate absence of sound in a radio programme or podcast

2.3 Narrative organisation in audio-visual and audio texts

Approaches to reading narratives in audio-visual media texts

Most approaches to reading narratives distinguish between 'story' and 'plot'. Story refers to the overall narrative. Plot is the order in which information is presented organisationally in the text. In discussing plot, you may need to use the terms **analepsis** and **prolepsis**, meaning flashback and flashforward, referring to disturbances in the chronology of events.

Another consideration is the style of narration. Narration styles are sometimes described as either **restricted** or **omniscient**. Restricted narration means that some information is withheld from the audience to preserve suspense, or enhance cognitive enjoyment in some way. With omniscient narration, the audience occupies a privileged position where they are able to gain perspective on all the relevant events, although characters will not.

Narrative perspective is also important – the idea that we share a character's particular view of events as they unfold. Connected with this is **focalisation**, where we can relate to different characters as we move through texts. This might be in terms of the perceptual – what the character can see, hear and so on – the psychological (how they understand it) or ideological (the external frame of reference) interpretations of the narrative events. This suggests that when we read narratives, we are subconsciously encouraged to shift our awareness of the storytelling to explore different dimensions to the narrative in many different ways through the realms of each character. It allows for the identification and understanding of different characters at different points in the narrative. If you would like to read more about focalisation, which comes from the work of French theorist Gérard Genette, a very useful introduction to how it works is provided in Bronwen Thomas' *Narrative: The Basics* (2015).

Gérard Genette (1930–)

When reading complex fictional narratives, or even fact-based media such as documentaries, reality television and hybrids such as scripted reality shows, you need to have the terminology to talk about several things that may be going on at once. One of these is **narrative arc**, which can be used to describe an individual character's journey through the narrative. You can use the term **narrative strands** to discuss separate contributory elements to the overall narrative. Also important when thinking about how a narrative moves forwards is the sense of narrative progress and delay. Another important idea when reading fictional narratives in audio-visual texts is the diegesis. The easiest way to imagine the diegesis, or story world, is as a bubble that contains the world of the text. We enter that bubble through the suspension of disbelief.

Applying narrative theories to audio-visual texts' sphere of action

For an overview of each of these theories and their origins see section '1.3 Narrative organisation in print media texts'.

Todorov's theory of narrative can be a useful tool for exploring longer narratives in either audio-visual or audio texts. Modern media texts are complex, and it can be difficult to apply the theory in its simplest form to complex narratives that may contain many sub-plots. This does not mean the theory is redundant – just that it can be applied in different ways to fragments of narrative and sub-plots that could be mapped across a longer text such as one of the high-engagement, high-budget television series that tend to be binge-watched on video-on-demand services.

When approaching a text like this, you might even find that virtually all stages can be applied to an individual episode of a television series, to its respective sub-plots, or even to the overall narrative formed by all the episodes together. This is one of the most interesting ways of using theory, to see how it can be used to discover coherent units of narrative that build together like blocks to create a whole.

Be aware that, as with any narrative theory, it is best to give it a light touch when responding under time pressure to an exam question. It's rarely useful to apply a whole theory in its entirety – although you will need to do this initially when you encounter it to be sure how it works. It is far better to drop in occasional references to parts of the theory in an integrated way, using them to support what you want to say about the text.

Stranger Things, Netflix, 2016

EXAMPLE: Todorov's theory of narrative applied to the first episode of *Stranger Things* (Netflix, 2016)

Stranger Things is a Netflix Originals series that was broadcast in 2016. The science-fiction/horror series follows a mother's efforts to get back her missing son. This example clearly shows how Todorov's theory of narrative can be applied to a complex text, even though it is a serialised narrative.

EPISODE 1: Main narrative, 'The Missing Boy'

Equilibrium: Four boys, firm friends, are playing Dungeons and Dragons in the basement of one of their family homes on a school night.

Disruption to equilibrium: On his way home, one of them – 'Will' – is accosted by an unseen creature, chased to his home and vanishes.

Recognition of disruption: Will's mother realises he isn't at home the following morning; his friends miss him at school.

Attempt to repair: Will's mother visits local law enforcement and a search party is called. The boys decide to form their own search without the knowledge of their parents, who have forbidden it.

New equilibrium: It could be said that there is no true equilibrium to a first part of a serial narrative, as it relies on a continued state of disequilibrium to retain audience engagement until the next episode. Even so, often a situation will be left that has some kind of balance. Although the search party find Will's bike in the woods and fear the worst, Will's mother is convinced her son is still alive when she receives a strange telephone call in which she believes she hears his voice – and vows not to give up on him.

Elements of further disequilibrium are suggested by clips from the next week, which hook the viewer in.

EPISODE 1: Secondary narrative/sub-plot, 'Eleven'

Equilibrium: A girl appears in the woods near a secretive research facility, with a shaven head, a tattoo on her forearm that reads '11' and wearing only a nightgown.

Disruption to the equilibrium: Eleven, who seems almost non-verbal, is caught stealing fast food at a remote restaurant by its kindly owner, Benny.

Recognition of disruption: Benny senses the girl is in trouble and is distressed but cannot get any information from her.

Attempt to repair: Benny tries to help; he calls social services to collect her.

Disruption to equilibrium: Fake social services workers arrive to collect Eleven, and shoot Benny dead.

Attempt to repair: Realising she is in grave danger, Eleven defends herself using supernatural powers, and escapes.

New equilibrium: Eleven is found by Will's friends, who decide to hide her in the basement, dovetailing the sub-plot with the main narrative arc and substituting the missing friend with a new, very intriguing one.

APPLY IT

Choose a serial television drama series you know well. Either re-watch the first episode or find a detailed episode synopsis online to help you.

Sketch out a map of the episode, showing a timeline of key events in the plot, and adding in any sub-plots. Try mapping the stages of Todorov's theory against these key plot events. Can you slot the slices of theory together like building blocks to provide a picture of the whole?

Lévi-Strauss was referred to in Chapter 1 as a theorist whose work can be used to understand any narrative no matter how apparently simple the text. Binary oppositions can be used to explore themes and expose dominant ideologies in a text. It is a highly adaptable theory to use with any moving image text.

Two of the young subjects in *The Secret Life of 4 Year Olds*, Channel 4, 2016

EXAMPLE: *The Secret Life of 4 Year Olds*, Episode 1 (Channel 4, 2016)

This series places a group of young children together in a school and play environment and measures how they react to one another socially, leading to often conflict-fuelled encounters. It offers an excellent opportunity to observe how texts can reflect our basic human understanding of rules and norms. As you would expect for a largely **fly-on-the-wall documentary** that has such young subjects, the tone is light-hearted and non-judgemental.

Social acceptance versus social rejection

Two children in particular are depicted as finding it hard to fit into the group: one is quiet and shy, the other attention-seeking and indifferent to authority. Both are initially socially rejected by other members of the group, and by the end of the first episode have formed a bond with each other as a result of exclusion by the others.

Behavioural compliance versus anti-social behaviour

One child is repeatedly shown to not comply with adult demands during the activities and tasks set for the children, such as resisting temptation to gain an additional reward. He is shown to be judged and blamed by the rest of the group, who miss out because of his behaviour.

Shyness versus confidence

Some children's behaviours are selected to show them not joining in, or being cautious in the new social situation; others are shown to be socially at ease and integrating successfully.

Leadership versus followers

One child is shown to play a particularly dominant role in the group, easily commanding the respect and attention of the other children. This quality is voiced over by the two child psychologists and designated as 'exceptional for his age', suggesting this is a desirable quality.

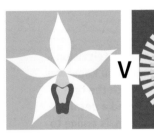 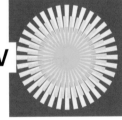

'Orchids' versus 'dandelions'

The child psychologists who mediate children's behaviours for us through their covert observations use the term orchid to describe a child who requires a particular set of social conditions to flourish, who is seen as less 'easy-going'. These are compared with 'dandelions', which are children who will 'flower anywhere'.

Social sensitivity versus thoughtlessness

Some behaviours are shown that suggest those children are thoughtful and considerate – but one boy in particular, in an extended sequence, is shown to disregard the feelings of his partner in an activity, when he gives away a reward without consulting with her in order to reinforce his status with others in the group.

Roland Barthes' five codes in narrative are useful in decoding audio-visual texts, and you should remember that it is not necessary to identify every example of each type of code. You may also find that it isn't always possible to list all the ones you can identify, preferably focusing on accuracy and care in identifying fewer examples and explaining fully how they contribute to the meaning of the text for the audience. The only two codes that refer to the chronology of the text are the hermeneutic (HER) and proairetic (ACT). You will often find it easiest to think of semic codes (SEM) as the connotations of individual technical codes you are already used to identifying.

Symbolic codes (SYM) are often best expressed in terms of binary oppositions. Cultural codes (REF) are very broad, and you will usually be able to find specific examples that relate to our cultural knowledge and practices without too much difficulty.

EXAMPLE: John Lewis Christmas advertisement 2015, *Man on the Moon*

Released part-way through November, the extended television advertisement for UK department store John Lewis (right) has become an annual event that is greatly anticipated by the audience. The advertisements often seek to evoke a nostalgic or sentimental feel, appealing primarily to a female target audience who usually do the majority of gift buying in a household.

The narrative of the two-minute advertisement features a young girl with a telescope who believes she can see a man on the moon, and wishes to contact him. As the advert progresses, we see her thinking through the problem, and attempting to send messages to him in different ways unsuccessfully. By the end, we see the girl send him a gift from under her Christmas tree using helium balloons. The man in the moon receives his gift, a telescope, and is able to see the girl waving back at him.

All of the five codes have been applied, although if you watch the advertisement for yourself, you will see more.

Hermeneutic codes: (HER) Close to the beginning of the advertisement, we ask ourselves, will the girl ever be able to communicate with the man in the moon?

Proairetic codes: (ACT) The girl adjusts her telescope and sees the man on the moon. The girl climbs a ladder to hold her letter up but isn't close enough. The girl shoots an arrow with the letter on it towards the moon, but it misfires. The letter is thrown from her window as a paper plane, but falls to the ground.

Semantic codes: (SEM) The man on the moon is shown from a high angle in long-shot, connoting isolation. His gaze is repeatedly shown as fixed on Earth, connoting his desire for contact. His facial expression connotes sadness in a close-up and an extreme close-up. The girl writes a letter, connoting that she wants to communicate with the man. The extreme close-up of the tear in the eye of the old man and the smile in the eye of the girl connote gratitude and a human connection/relationship.

Symbolic codes: (SYM) The Christmas spirit is contrasted with loneliness and isolation, the importance of cross-generational ties is emphasised through depiction of the relationship between someone at the start of their life and someone who is close to the end.

Cultural codes: (REF) The children's story of the man in the moon, Christmas as a time for the ritual of gift giving, selflessness and charity.

APPLY IT

Using YouTube, find examples of previous or subsequent years' John Lewis advertisements. Try to apply Barthes' five narrative codes to two of these. Are all the codes relevant? Some texts do not offer you an example of every one.

KEY TERMS

analepsis	commonly known as a flashback
fly-on-the-wall documentary	style of documentary where the camera work is as unobtrusive as possible in order to capture events in a candid way. This technique can be created easily today by the miniaturisation of digital cameras that can be placed unobtrusively to capture many angles, as well as the habituation of subjects to the presence of cameras

focalisation	term used to describe our tendency to follow particular characters at individual points in a narrative, dependent on a range of encoded strategies and our own conceptual maps
Gérard Genette	French narrative theorist who proposed focalisation as an alternative to structuralist readings
narrative arc	the journey of an individual character

narrative strands	different 'storylines' or sub-plots that usually contribute something to the main narrative subject
omniscient narration	style of narration where the audience is privy to most contextual narrative information even where this is withheld from characters in the diegesis
prolepsis	commonly known as a flashforward
restricted narration	style of narration where information is withheld from the audience

2.4 Genre and audio-visual/audio media texts

Genre development

Genre study becomes more complex when exploring audio-visual texts. In Chapter 1, we explored Dudley Andrew's idea that the term genre can have different nuances depending on the context in which it is used. In this chapter, we will be adding to your understanding of genre approaches to studying texts, and equipping you with some new terms to use in writing about genre from enabling theorist Stephen Neale, as well as considering some of the problems with approaching study of a text through its genre. Some genres are enduring; others are more short-lived. This is part of what makes them so interesting to study.

Hancock's Half Hour

Steptoe and Son

EXAMPLE: Situation comedy across radio and television through time

The situation comedy is an enduring genre spanning both audio-visual and audio media forms. It is a series of episodes where each has an enclosed narrative, making it distinct from the comedy drama and sketch show. It usually features a group of main characters who are thrown together in some way. Families and workplaces are very common settings, and there needs to be a sense that the characters cannot avoid each other in order to bring out the best comedic situations.

A traditional sitcom should have humour and entertainment as its primary purpose. There are occasional serial elements to the narrative, but it usually resets at the beginning of each episode, with no reference being made to previous events. US sitcoms tend to run for much longer series, so are more likely to have serial elements and gradual changes to narrative or situation over time. The narrative shape sometimes varies across cultures, too – for example, in UK sitcoms we frequently see a character who is down on their luck gain an opportunity to escape their circumstances, but be ultimately unsuccessful. US sitcoms vary this formula much more. Usually, stereotypes are heavily used to increase comic effect. Sitcoms are usually quite cheap to produce (with the exception of some of the star-studded US casts, who have commanded some of the highest salaries paid in US TV), and locations are limited with much filming taking place on a regular set.

Sitcoms were popular programming on the radio before becoming a mainstream part of television schedules. Some of the early popular radio sitcoms in the UK, such as *Hancock's Half Hour* (1954–1961) later transferred to television. *Steptoe and Son* was made concurrently for both television and radio in the 1960s and 1970s, proving popular with listeners and viewers. *The Mighty Boosh* is a more recent unconventional BBC2 sitcom, which changed between series from its setting of a zoo to being a flat-share and later a shop. It began on Radio 4 in a late-night comedy slot before having its early episodes rewritten to suit the more visual medium.

In recent years, the sitcom has seen many changes, such as the reduction of the laughter track, and increased hybridisation with the comedy-drama and even the spoof documentary. However, although audience tastes may be hungry for new incarnations of the genre, traditional sitcoms continue to be made.

 APPLY IT Choose an example of a television genre you enjoy to research. Write a 1,000-word case study in which you trace its origins, identify its codes and conventions and how these have changed over the years, the influences on its development, and cite some key examples.

The Mighty Boosh

Stephen Neale

Stephen Neale is a prominent UK-based film theorist who has made an enormous contribution to the field of genre studies. In exploring Neale, there are three main sources you can use, which are all detailed in the 'Further reading' at the end of this chapter. Like Dudley Andrew, Neale's work was conducted initially in the field of film theory, but has relevance for Media Studies students because genres in other media forms behave in very similar ways.

Neale views genre as a process, rather than a collection of static groups that consistently draw on an identical repertoire of elements. Audio-visual genres evolve over time, meaning sometimes it is difficult to pinpoint exactly where a genre begins, disappears or evolves into a genre so different it is no longer considered part of the same genre category. Genres do evolve continually as new texts are added to the body of similar texts, which Neale calls the corpus. This may involve hybridisation between genres or the formulation of sub-genres.

Some genres have historic specificity (meaning they are associated with certain time periods) and tend to have been popular at a particular moment in time due to other cultural, economic or historical factors. The reasons for the popularity of a particular genre at a particular point in time are often complex. Sometimes, genres that have been popular in the past – or at least sufficient in number to qualify as a genre – experience revivals, or suddenly become far more popular than before.

Genres are subject to change because of tensions of all kinds that push and pull texts. There is a dynamic relationship between audience, industry and text, which is constantly being renegotiated, with the locus for that process evident in the genre texts we have available to view or listen to. The main tensions are between repetition and sameness versus variation and change. This means that genre text producers walk a fine line between repeating successful formulas with only minor variations – which may eventually bore the audience – and varying it sufficiently to still allow familiarity but also make the audience feel the product they are consuming seems fresh.

Like Andrew, Neale believes that genre labels are familiar to the audience and are important to them. They carry a narrative image that is communicated and perpetuated by word of mouth (other audience members) and marketing materials. This is closely connected with their various expectations and hypotheses based on their previous experience of the genre. Audiences find the action of prediction based on generic expectations a crucial pleasure of some genre texts and are easily disappointed if these are not fulfilled, which can be a disaster for media producers. This is true of factual media such as documentaries as well as television serials.

In order to immerse themselves fully in a fictional diegesis, the spectator must suspend disbelief (i.e. 'buy into' the film or TV narrative, characters, etc.). In fictional media texts it is vital that we care about the characters, and allow ourselves to share their world for the time allotted to the narrative to play out, whether that is a 45-minute radio play or a 26-episode television serial. We have all experienced an occasion when this has failed to happen, and distraction and disinterest wrest us from the narrative. At this point, when consuming a television text or radio narrative, we tend to switch off, transfer our attention to something else or switch to another channel.

The suspension of disbelief is associated with the two regimes of verisimilitude. The generic regime of verisimilitude refers to what is probable or likely in a genre text; the ways in which texts match up to both our experience of other texts and of the real world. We are happy for events to take place in a science-fiction TV series using technologies that don't exist, because this is part of the norms and laws of

The viewer must suspend disbelief if they are to enjoy watching the Ood on *Doctor Who*.

the genre. The **cultural regime of verisimilitude** is connected with the spectator's experience of the 'real' world, and can be subtle in its influence. Texts that are set in a real historical time period or offer a fictionalised interpretation of real events may suffer credibility issues if the fictionalisation departs significantly from the known facts. This operates similar to Roland Barthes' cultural code, which we encountered in Chapter 1.

Rick Altman

Rick Altman (1945–)

In Chapter 2 of his book *Film/Genre* (1999), Rick Altman explores the idea that film genre criticism has evolved from literary genre criticism. In turn, as Media Studies students, we then appropriate elements of film theory approaches to our own study of more varied texts. Altman sums up ten claims that have been made about genre, which are really useful to media students because, rather than leading us to believe that there is a single 'right' way to study genre, he demonstrates that there are a number of different approaches to understanding its significance that we can select from. He does this through a series of statements that define different approaches that have been taken to genre study. Seven of these are explored below:

'Genre is a useful term because it bridges multiple concerns'

- Genre is not a term that should be seen to have a single meaning, but rather one that can mean different things in different contexts – Altman refers us back to Andrew's four definitions of genre as structure, blueprint, label and contract.
- To 'prove' this flexibility of the term, critics tend to choose straightforward examples where this is the case to 'prove' their point.

'Genres have clear, stable identities and borders'

- This assumption underlies much genre theory and historical study.
- It is problematic, since it disregards non-genre texts or those that don't quite match entirely, focusing instead on a core of examples that fit the conventions.

'Individual [media texts] belong wholly and permanently to a single genre'

- Once a genre label is affixed, there is an assumption that a text's qualities can no longer be reviewed and reconsidered.
- This fails to account for the fact that genre labels are largely a product of the culture that uses them to designate media products, so are subject to changing perceptions over time.

'Genres are transhistorical'

- This suggests that genres exist, frozen, outside of media histories.
- It seeks to historicise genre development and to trace the lineage of a genre, a process that is appealing and neatly accounts for the phenomenon but doesn't always reflect the messy and divergent nature of real media texts.

'Genres undergo predictable development'

- The metaphor of human life is often used to describe genres – they are born, they peak, they decline, they 'die'. This can be useful to identify broad trends.
- This approach, as with the transhistorical, is easy to apply when studying genre, but again provides an all too convenient narrative that negates the complexity of genres and their constant tension between repetition and variation/change.

'Genre [media texts] share certain predictable characteristics'

- Emphasises the characteristics of media texts that are repeated frequently – themes, situations, narratives, iconography.

Swiss Army Man (2016); although it could be loosely labelled a 'buddy movie', this unusual film resists the usual genre classification.

- This approach, like many others, tends to look only for similarities between media texts and not to consider what they might be doing that is a little different.

'Genres have a ritual or ideological function'

- This suggests that all genres grow out of a society's stories it tells about itself, and can have a role in social cohesion and problem-solving. Some genre critics see genre texts as reinforcing dominant ideologies, as they are usually generated by powerful media institutions that have an investment in keeping consumers consuming.

- These privilege a certain reading of genre texts without any real justification why other explanations go unexplored.

Codes and conventions in audio-visual genre texts

It is tempting to think initially of fiction texts when approaching the study of the media genres, probably because so much genre criticism has grown out of film theory. What we do know is that fact-based media texts have just as many interesting genres, and their features can be identified as clusters of codes and conventions just as with any other text. When undertaking study of a genre in an audio-visual text, one of the first things you're likely to do is to research and/ or try to define for yourself what the codes and conventions are based on your experience of a group of texts from the corpus.

This kind of approach produces a 'checklist' of generic codes and conventions that is a useful starting point. In keeping with the arguments you have already encountered, you should be aware that this method is only the beginning for generic discussion, albeit a useful one. It is worth including in your 'checklist' other factors such as audiences you associate with the products, and some of the economic factors affecting their production and scheduling. This will allow you to begin to access some of the other arguments about the genre you are studying that might be relevant in helping you to connect up the theoretical framework.

APPLY IT

In small groups, choose three statements from the list of Altman's claims and discuss what each suggests to you about television genres. Make notes and present your findings to the wider group.

a Do you agree or disagree with the statement? Why?

b Can you put the statement into your own words, or explain it more fully?

c Can you explore the statement using three of your favourite genres as examples?

d Is the approach useful? Altman seeks to look at these approaches in an objective way, but knowing there are faults with a theoretical approach doesn't mean you can't use it, just that you need to be aware of its potential limitations.

EXAMPLE: Television news

Television news has expanded hugely as a genre because of the opportunities offered by 24-hour programming. However, its programme content remains quite stable – it is the visual iconography of news that has shown the most changes, with improvements in graphics technologies being particularly evident in the last couple of decades. At their core, though, the genre conventions of TV news actually remain quite stable:

1 News is prioritised according to an agenda from hard to soft. Events that are very dramatic or have a strong visual impact are the primary focus.

2 NVC of presenters reflects seriousness of hard news – they may appear more relaxed and friendly towards the end (especially true of regional news).

3 Hi-tech studio settings are commonplace.

4 Use of graphics to create visual interest.

5 Formal dress codes.

6 Recognisable news presenters.

7 Recognisable branding – logos, colour schemes, etc.

8   Most stories last less than a minute.

9   Forms an essential part of public service broadcasting.

10   Ownership of TV news is connected with other big media organisations.

11   Reassuring formats for each segment – introduction, cutaway to interview or journalist in the field, wrapped up by a return to presenter.

12   Repertoire of familiar camera angles, shots and editing conventions.

13   Signature theme and graphical sequence.

14   Stories selected for their simplicity, visual interest and ease of narrative presentation.

15   Format varies little, often ending with sport and weather.

16   References made to links with social media and other communications such as texts.

17   Newsreaders appear unflustered and authoritative.

18   Use of powerful language to increase dramatic impact.

19   Internal advertising ('Coming up …') maintains viewing.

20   Polite and professional mode of address maintained by participants at all times.

APPLY IT Choose a genre that is not fiction-based from audio-visual media. See whether you can produce a 'checklist' like the one in the Television news example, which not only considers the technical codes of the genre but also any other relevant contextual information.

Intertextuality, which we first encountered in Chapter 1, is rife in audio-visual texts. It is so rich in these media forms it has almost become a redundant concept, since so many mass media forms constantly make references to others. This does not mean you should ignore it – sometimes it is used to greater effect than others.

⊂⊃ For more on intertextuality see Chapter 1.

EXAMPLE: Intertextuality and *The Simpsons*

The long-running US animated sitcom series, *The Simpsons*, is popular all over the world. It is also very well-known for its conscious and deliberate referencing of a whole range of texts ranging from pop culture, political and social to the literary canon. Intertextuality in *The Simpsons* resides in many parts of the text – it can shape an overall narrative structure, be found in particular lines of dialogue, be evident in the construction of mise-en-scène or dictate the reaction of a character to a situation. Sometimes it is subtle; at other times blatant.

Here are a few examples:

- *Them, Robot*: The narrative of this episode (and its title) makes conscious and deliberate reference to the film *I, Robot*. Mr Burns replaces the workers of his nuclear plant with more efficient robots that must abide by the three laws of robotics.

- *Bart to the Future*: Playing on Donald Trump's media image as a power-hungry businessman, this 2000 episode features Lisa Simpson elected to the US Presidency as the successor to Donald Trump. When viewed retrospectively in 2017, this episode takes on even more nuances.

- *The Springfield Files*: The character of Chewbacca from *Star Wars* appears in a line-up of suspects when the FBI begins investigating strange happenings in Springfield.

- *The Tell-Tale Head*: The title is a reference to Gothic American writer Edgar Allen Poe's story *The Telltale Heart*. Widely read in the US, Poe's stories and poems feature regularly. Lisa creates a diorama of a scene from the story in another episode, and in a Halloween episode a whole segment is devoted to the reading of the poem *The Raven*.

APPLY IT Choose an episode of *The Simpsons* to watch, looking for examples of intertextuality. Compile your answers as a class to see the breadth of intertextual sources used.

Genres are sometimes clustered in radio around the schedules that a particular radio station specialises in. Most local commercial radio stations, for example, will have a mixed daily schedule that consists of local news and music. Other radio stations may define themselves not by the geographical boundaries of their listeners, but by the predominant content, e.g. music or talk radio. It is true that many radio shows are made in genres that cross media – quiz and comedy panel shows, soaps, documentaries, magazine shows with short snippets of topical content and so on.

Neil Caddy and Lucy Start, presenters at Pirate FM

EXAMPLE: Pirate FM (Cornish local commercial radio station) schedule, Monday 7 November 2016

Neil & Lucy: 5:00am
Neil Caddy & Lucy Start wake you up great music and Cornwall's essential travel news! Including: 7.15 Cornwall's Secret Sound 8.10 The Thousand Pound Minute

Non-Stop at Nine: 9:00am
Top tunes to kick-start your workday, including 30 minutes non-stop at 9!

Scott Temple: 10:00am
Sarah sits in with More Music to get you through the day.

Johnny & Holly: 3:00pm
Cornwall's biggest Hometime show, with Johnny Cowling and Holly Day! Including: 3.15 Place on Your Face 5.30 Beat Johnny's Organ

Ben Moseby: 7:00pm
Great music in the evening with Ben Moseby on Cornwall's Pirate FM.

The Nightshift: 10:00pm
Great Music through the night on Cornwall's Pirate FM.

APPLY IT

Listen to a radio show that exists as a genre across television and radio. Compare it with a programme in the same genre on television. What similarities can you identify in the codes and conventions and the way in which these are expressed? How might the audience differ and relate to the genre when broadcast on radio rather than television?

KEY TERMS

corpus	group of texts identified as belonging to the same genre
cultural regime of verisimilitude	our connecting of a genre text with our wider cultural knowledge
expectations and hypotheses	requirements to be fulfilled, and narrative and other predictions made by an audience based on their prior experience of a genre
generic regime of verisimilitude	the norms and laws of a genre; what is probable or likely in a genre text
historic specificity	belonging to a particular time period (e.g. a genre)
hybridisation	the mixing of one genre with another

narrative image	the expectations of a genre text based on its label, often passed by word of mouth
repertoire of elements	identifiable aspects of texts belonging to the corpus in genre theory
repetition and sameness	the tendency of genre texts to repeat aspects of successful formulas – always in tension with variation and change
suspension of disbelief	allowing yourself to be immersed in a fictional world
variation and change	the tendency of genre texts to reformulate with new qualities to prevent audiences from becoming tired of a formula

KEY THINKER

Stephen Neale	(1950–) Neale has written numerous books about film and genre, and is widely reputed as an expert in the field

CHAPTER SUMMARY

- The principles of semiotic analysis, explained at greater length in section 1.1, are readily applied to audio-visual and audio texts.

- The technical codes of audio-visual texts are combined in different ways in different audio-visual forms, but all these use the same codes.

- Mise-en-scène is used in both fact-based and fiction media to carefully construct meaning using dress codes, framing, props, décor, lighting, locations and non-verbal codes.

- Camera work is used to create relationships between subject matter and form in a text and the audience. Many aspects have to be carefully considered – shot type, camera angle, camera movement and lens.

- Editing is fundamental to your understanding of time and space in audio-visual texts. The two dominant modes you will encounter are continuity editing and montage editing.

- Sound is often neglected in favour of the visual aspects of the text and its contribution should never be ignored in analysis.

- The characteristics of radio as a medium are distinct from any other.

- Radio is a 'blind' medium, and the auditory codes it deploys are tailored to avoid ambiguity.

- Radio differs from other media forms in that many of its consumers may be engaging in other activities while listening rather than giving it their full attention.

- Audio-visual and audio narratives are time based, so narrative theories are used in a way that considers this.

- All three of the theorists we encountered in Chapter 1 – Todorov, Lévi-Strauss and Barthes – are useful in decoding the narratives in audio-visual texts, and in this chapter you looked for the first time at some examples of how these theories might be applied to three varied popular texts.

- Much of the genre theory you use in Media Studies comes from film and literary theory, but has relevance for you too – it may need to be adapted intelligently to suit the texts and contexts you encounter across media forms.

- Stephen Neale is an important theorist in genre, and from his work terms and associated ideas have been gained that allow you to discuss the relationship between audience, industry and text in a precise way.

- Rick Altman's ideas are also useful, since they not only sum up the dominant traditions in genre analysis, but they also suggest some of the weaknesses in certain approaches.

- Using a 'checklist' of codes and conventions is a good way into genre study for Media Studies students, but can be quite limited if not used alongside other contextual information about production and reception contexts.

- Intertextuality is rife in audio-visual texts, but you still need to be able to recognise the contribution made by it to meaning, and the examples that seem most conscious or deliberate can still form an interesting part of your discussion.

FURTHER READING

Andrew Crisell (1986) *Understanding Radio.*
Bronwen Thomas (2015) *Narrative: The Basics.*
Hugh Chignell (2009) *Key Concepts in Radio Studies.*
Rick Altman (1999) *Film/Genre.*
Stephen Neale (1980) *Genre.*
Stephen Neale (1991) *Questions of Genre.*
Stephen Neale (2000) *Genre and Hollywood.*

Chapter 3 Reading digital media

3.1 The technical codes and features used in online texts

In Chapters 1 and 2, we looked at some of the ways in which we can access the meanings of print and audio-visual media texts. When approaching any kind of digital media text, you will be drawing on many of the same skills and much of the same terminology you used earlier. It's essential that you revisit these chapters and consider what can be applied to the new texts you are looking at. Many digital media products, for example, draw on a combination of print media codes with audio-visual content and increased interactivity. Many of the significant differences lie in the ability of the user to also be a contributor to such media. In addition to this, they demonstrate the user's ability to construct the text, within certain parameters, to suit their own aims and preferences.

What you will learn in this chapter

- How to extend your knowledge and understanding of reading print and audio-visual media texts to digital media and computer games
- The codes and conventions of digital media forms and products
- How to understand some of the unconventional ways in which narratives can operate in digital media texts
- How to approach the study of digital media genres

Websites

Websites deploy many of the features to attract attention that we have already seen being used in newspapers, magazines and print advertisements. The majority offer us a familiar combination of a banner, usually positioned at the top, navigation features and clickable links (interactivity). These are sometimes also placed as a skyscraper. On conventional sites, this will often be on the left, but on blogs the convention is for a skyscraper of archived posts, adverts and links to be on the right. Single skyscraper adverts are also common. They use a combination of lexical codes, photographs, graphical images and large typography to sub-section content and draw the eye. The hero image has also become a feature of many contemporary websites, positioned centrally, sometimes filling the whole screen as a single image, video or rotating gallery. A slideshow such as this may also have clickable content, and is a common design feature that allows the site's designers to order its most topical content in an attractive and appealing way. Similarly, many web designers now use cards to display dynamic content and encourage clicks, attributing the popularity of card-based design to the influence of Pinterest.

Logos, house style and branding are all as important to websites as they are to magazines, advertising campaigns or newspapers. Background images are increasingly used, adding a dimensionality and depth to the look of the site that would appear cluttered in print media. Skins came from software apps and websites that were originally designed to be customisable, but many websites have adopted the look of skins without the functional personalisation, often using a hero image as a background.

The rise of video-on-demand and TV player services means that many TV channels have standardised the look of their websites, with pages for individual programmes acting as a gateway to accessing viewing rather than being a more complex promotional tool. Most pages for programmes contain a single hero image that signifies the genre or promotes the show on star value, and a brief synopsis. They also usually provide links to clips, extras or available episodes. The tendency is for video content to predominate over written, taking advantage of the immediacy and popularity of short video form on the web. This is what we see on immediate entry to the science fiction series *Humans* webpage on the Channel 4 site (Channel 4, 2015–present). The webpage can be found at www.channel4.com/programmes/humans.

Scrolling down, we see an additional banner not present on most series websites. This suggests that Channel 4 is putting a high value on the marketing of this programme. It also maintains the narrative image of other cross-media promotional strategies for Series 1 of *Humans*, which consisted of convincing teaser trailers that followed the form and conventions of advertisements for the 'product' itself; the synthetic humans around which the premise of the series is based.

The Channel 4 house style now appears to be blended with what at first looks like an advertisement. Clicking on the advert takes us to another site, www.personasynthetics.com/productrecall/, which immerses the audience into the fictional diegesis of the series. The Channel 4 branding and look is absent here. The site positions Channel 4 as customers of the company selling the synthetic humans that appear in the programme. It adds cultural verisimilitude to the show, is immersive and has a game-like quality. However, the video makes it plain that this is not a genuine technological company – the video is a conventional trailer for the second series. This positions the audience by using two separate modes of address: the audience is simultaneously drawn into the diegesis and maintain their presence outside it.

The colour codes used on the site are clean: a cool combination of aqua blue (connoting cleanliness and symbolising the purpose of the synths to serve) and plenty of white space, signifying order. A predominantly white mise-en-scène is commonly used in dystopian science fiction to connote a world that appears initially free from problems, and later is revealed as anything but. The symmetrically placed images of the male and female synth suggest balance and harmony; all very reassuring to the user when coupled with the clean, discreet logo and branding of the imaginary company. Despite the alarm that could be caused by the lexical coding of the 'safety recall', they appear expressionless and are young and physically attractive. Their eye-line matches the audience's, which perhaps suggests equality with humans – striving for which is part of the series' narrative. The artificial look is signified by colourisation of the eyes to an unnatural green – connoting mistrust and envy – and the faces are heavily airbrushed to given them an artificial look.

As we scroll down, the illusion that we are visiting the site for a real technological product is maintained. The two models are positioned stiffly here and appear more like mannequins – in fact, far less 'human'. As on many real technological product sites, detailed information in the lexical coding lists familiar features such as model, processing power and so on that we would expect to see when purchasing a product. Clicking on the returns toggle provides a PDF of a realistic looking returns label, and a live chat-bot also pops up on the left hand side. Further down the site, viewers are treated to a cheerful marketing message asking for 'malfunctioning' synths to be returned to the manufacturer.

The site clearly shows that it is still possible – and desirable – for programme-makers to use some supplemental creative marketing to create a buzz around a new series.

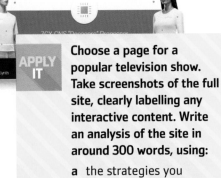

APPLY IT

Choose a page for a popular television show. Take screenshots of the full site, clearly labelling any interactive content. Write an analysis of the site in around 300 words, using:

a the strategies you already have from your study of print media, and

b your understanding of how websites use similar codes in addition to some of their own.

Other multi-media content, such as video content, and animated features, such as gifs and galleries, may be used to produce a limited but eye-catching effect. Embedded content such as video players can often also be found. Most sites feature numerous links, giving rise to a concept related to intertextuality known as **hypertextuality**, where the site's producers are able to physically link not only to other content within the site but also to external content. Banner adverts and pop-up ads are also a common part of the web-user's experience – often these are external adverts, and can be analysed as texts in their own right using standard print and audio-visual methodologies.

The way in which a website is designed and structured is sometimes referred to as its **architecture**. Other menus and **hyperlinks** are always provided as the online equivalent of a contents page. Most professionally produced websites try to avoid too much scrolling, so will limit the content of the first page. This makes the rest of the site's content easily navigable from prominently placed and well-organised menus. Website design varies enormously, depending on the function of the site, its content and the design aims, but you will tend to see the same basic elements present: interactivity, **dynamic content** (content that changes regularly), navigability and copy. **Plugins** are also used such as social media buttons, which increase web flow and ease of content sharing.

Websites tend to deploy a grid layout, which organises content in a visually appealing and harmonious way. Templates, used by the majority of amateurs such as bloggers, offer these ready designed. This means that in some cases there is a limit to customisation – consider, too, that when looking at a site designed using a template (such as a Wordpress Blog) the only means of individualised communication is through the populating of images in placeholders, the lexical codes of the copy and headers, and categorisation of links.

Although any website can theoretically be analysed using semiotic methods, some genres are more interesting and productive to study than others. This is because of their clear contextual link with other areas of the subject.

Common genres of websites of interest to Media Studies students

Film marketing websites	Promotional websites for films vary from embedded trailers, simple information about plot, cast, crew, release date and press/awards, to complex sites that play with some aspect of the film's diegesis or contain extras such as games, behind-the-scenes interviews and footage.
Television websites	Television websites range from simple episode lists and outlines on bigger channel pages, to immensely rich and complex sites for the most popular shows.
Fansites for other media content	Fansites are interesting because they select from the wider meanings of a particular film or television show and offer a real insight into what drives the popularity of a media text with its core audience. Sometimes lacking on the aesthetic front, some are very professionally produced, with the best often being fed exclusive content by the producers.
Dedicated websites of existing print media products	Most magazines offer a digital version. Some have quite rich websites in their own right, but some exist simply to drive custom towards digital or paper subscriptions.

PR sites such as sports team or event sites	PR sites for events that occur on a diarised basis are often now maintained between these events to sustain interest. They tend to contain a great deal of detailed information for people with a specialised interest, whether they are following a sports team or anticipating a music festival.
Game promotion websites	Game sites give information about release dates, have trailers and serve mainly to promote the game. With a big game franchise, sites often host associated message boards for the gameplaying community.
News sites	The majority of news websites are related to other media, creating a cross-platform presence.
Sites promoting musical acts or artists	These serve to promote the musician/band, and announce forthcoming tours and album releases.

APPLY IT

Choose a website that promotes an event. Take screenshots of the full scroll on the home page. Annotate them to show which features of analysis can be used from print media, and which aspects clearly follow the design conventions of a website. You should also pay attention to hyperlinks, elements of the site that move such as galleries/slideshows, social media buttons and feeds, and other opportunities for the user to interact with the text.

In addition, choose a short piece of video from the site. Analyse the contribution it makes to the audience's experience of the text.

EXAMPLE: Event websites

The Team GB and Glastonbury Festival websites function to raise awareness of a sporting team and an event respectively. Both are excellent examples of how a website is designed to appeal to its specific target audience. The Glastonbury Festival site draws on psychedelic colour codes but combines these with contemporary black and white graphics, reflecting both its origins in 1960s counter-culture and its modern popularity with youth audiences. The homepage is relatively static to the eye but features clearly delineated clickable toggles for navigation and news items relating to the line-up.

The clean design of the Team GB website uses the primary colour codes of red, white and blue to connote Britishness and reflect the branding of the team. Rather than a banner header, the website Team GB and Olympic logos appear to the left, with a gallery featuring headlines relating to sporting success and a promotional video that plays a montage of British Olympic successes from the Rio games in central position as a large banner. A Twitter plugin is positioned in the bar at the right-hand side, which emphasises that British sportspeople are continuing their presence in other competitions in the four years between Olympic events. This helps to maintain interest in and support for the team during the years in between, and to promote British sport in a more general way.

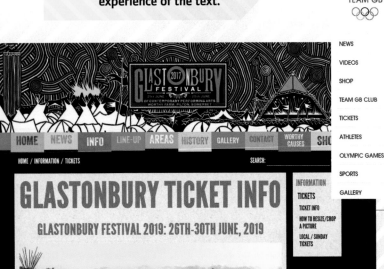

Video content on the web

When we think of video on the web, we most commonly think of YouTube. The length of internet video content is often very short – initially, this was due to connection speeds and bandwidth, but it also quickly became clear that abbreviated forms of audio-visual text were highly suited to the internet environment. Short videos are now an established part of our internet experience, whether we are consciously seeking them out through a dedicated video-sharing platform such as YouTube, or whether we are using social media or visiting a news site. Video is such a popular and powerful feature of the new media age that web video has become a defining feature of an increasingly post-broadcast era. Media consumers seem increasingly less satisfied with the imposition of traditional schedules on their viewing, and video content is an important way of enriching any other digital presence.

The ability of audio-visual digital video to deliver high-impact content in a short space of time makes it very suited to web browsing habits. The impact of the viral video (simply meaning one that has been shared and viewed many times) on popular culture is a dramatic one. When you are analysing any kind of video content online, you can start by asking the following questions:

1 What are the *stylistic conventions* of this kind of video? This could be locations, mode of address, camerawork, mise-en-scène editing.

2 What is the *purpose* of the video? Does it belong to an identifiable genre? If so, what are its conventions?

3 What kind of *duration* is typical for it, and how would you describe its *narrative progression*?

4 Where is the content typically *posted* initially, and does it *move* from platform to platform?

Use the four numbered points above combined with screenshots to create a five to seven-slide presentation of an online video of your choice.

Present it to the rest of the group, including a screening of your video at the beginning.

Create a mind map showing as many uses as you can of the presence of digital video online.

Video content online is a mixture of professional and amateur texts, ranging from user-generated prank or cat videos on YouTube to highly polished promotional content, with every shade in between. Short video can even be used in war zones or protests as citizen journalism, countering an authorised version of events or documenting abuses of human rights.

Video logs, usually referred to as vlogs, are for a youth audience one of the most popular genres on YouTube. According to a recent Ofcom report, between 33% and 44% of 8- to 15-year-olds watch vloggers and other YouTube stars such as gamers on a regular basis.

As with podcasts, users can subscribe to vlogs in various ways to ensure they are notified of the latest instalment from a favourite vlogger. Vlogs feature personalities, often with big followings. Similar to blogs, which reach a much older target audience, their content can be about almost anything. Popular genres include game walkthroughs and release reviews, beauty and lifestyle – where the personality of the vlogger and their opinions are usually of great significance. Some topics are less pop-culturally focused, such as popular science vlogs, where scientific principles are often tested out in entertaining ways. One of the key presentational devices in vlogs is that they are dominated by the personality of the presenter – it is the combination of the presenter and their particular take on their subject matter that earns them subscribers.

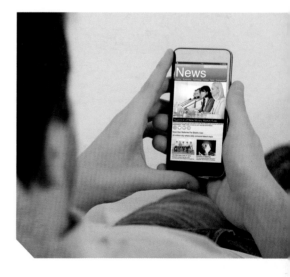

Zoella is a UK-based fashion and beauty blogger who has an international YouTube following. Known to millions of YouTube users, she is almost unknown outside a youth audience and only receives limited attention within mainstream media.

Web series, both produced professionally and user-generated, continue to appear. These are increasingly providing alternative new forms of fiction-based entertainment and many are available on YouTube and Vimeo. They are broadcast in **webisodes**, which are typically less than 15 minutes in duration. These provide yet more competition for traditional broadcasters. The majority of web series can be analysed in a straightforward manner by Media Studies students, as most use conventional codes of audio-visual media. It is in their subject matter and distribution method that the most significant differences can be seen. Since web series can be made on quite small production budgets, there is much less risk attached than to a conventional serial drama broadcast on television. This means that all kinds of subjects can be explored and find an audience. Some do fulfil the definition of modern alternative media, and some are examples of transmedia or distributed narratives, which are discussed further in 3.3.

EXAMPLE: *LARPs* (YouTube, 2015)

LARPs is a comedy web series featuring a group of people who play Live Action Role Playing games. It is produced by a collaboration of media industry professionals and YouTube enthusiasts. In the first episode of *LARPs*, we see each of the characters in their day jobs, and then all of them meeting in role. In the first episode, a new gameplaying character is introduced as a device to familiarise us with the existing players.

Another online video style on the rise is 'explainer' videos, which have their origins in business and promotions but have since been used in many playful, ironic, awareness or political ways. They are short videos that can be distributed on any media platform. They can use animation, photographs, graphics and video edited in montage, usually to a single music track. The 'explaining' is done using titles, sometimes called **captioning**, either as **intertitles** or superimposed on the footage.

APPLY IT

Choose an example of a vlogger you either regularly follow or one who your research shows has many subscribers. Watch two or three of their vlogs. Note the use of mise-en-scène, the editing style and the mode of address they use to communicate with their audience. Write a 300-word case study, including three screenshots, which focuses on the use of audio-visual information combined with subject matter that makes the vlog appealing to its target audience.

🔗 For a discussion on transmedia see section '3.3 Narrative organisation in digital media texts'.

APPLY IT

Research a popular web series. Analyse the first episode using the codes of audio-visual media.

The *Guardian* newspaper regularly produces explainer videos on a range of lifestyle and news topics for distribution on their own website and apps, and for sharing across social media. In the example on the right, a short soft news story about the discovery of a skeleton on an ancient shipwreck receives 'explainer' treatment.

With the discovery of these bones

For more about soft news see Chapter 5.

In another variant of the explainer, often used to tell personal stories, lexical coding can appear as handwritten placards accompanied by only facial expressions. These usually feature very little editing, and consist of one long take with the static camera position level with the subject. This means there is very little technical skill required to produce one. This kind of short film is extremely cheap to produce, although many users report that they find them irritating. This may be due to the simplicity of the style and its didactic nature.

There are some advantages to both styles, strengthening the preferred reading of the text. The heavy reliance on relatively unambiguous language also means firm anchorage for the message. The language chosen is often simple, and frequently emotive, as it is selected in an economical and clear narrative for its suitability to appear as titling on screen. These videos have proven popular with users of many sites who may not wish to use audio – either because they are in a public space or they simply prefer not to.

APPLY IT

Choose an example of an amateur and a professionally produced explainer video. Analyse how the lexical coding and soundtrack interplay with other technical codes to produce the preferred reading.

EXAMPLE: Campaigning video from YouTube

Corey Maison, a transgender teen from the US, made a video to raise awareness of bullying and issues relating to transgender. The video uses placards and the location of the bathroom combined with expressive non-verbal communication to tell her story. Search for it online and watch it on YouTube.

Social and participatory media

Social and participatory media involves the use of platforms that allow users to make themselves heard. These are based on the idea of virtual communities, and operate through profiles, a digital projection of a person's individual identity in that community. There are image-sharing sites, video-sharing sites, social networking sites, micro-blogging sites, communication-based apps, discussion and news aggregation sites, idea cataloguing sites and so on. They are a medium that is generated by the masses and consumed by the masses. They are highly accessible and differ significantly from traditional media in their ease of access, self-regulation and immediacy. To some extent they are less permanent than traditional media. New social media platforms, which draw on aspects of the perceived benefits of social media, appear fairly regularly – some endure, others are more transient and appear, flourish, and then disappear as their popularity wanes.

EXAMPLE: *Vine*

Vine was a video-sharing app that allowed users to record a tiny clip of footage (or capture it from elsewhere) and loop it continuously into a six-second clip. Its abbreviated form and potential to reinforce a single telling moment made the videos very popular, shared on a range of other social platforms, with some becoming memes. *Vine* itself closed to new uploads in October 2016, but existing vines and their influence on other videos can still be seen travelling around digital space.

Self-regulation of websites and social media is discussed more in Chapter 6.

Most social media platforms are used for similar reasons, even though the focus of membership might vary. Their users have usually come together to share content, either found elsewhere on the site or that they have created, to discuss things with other people and network with like-minded individuals. All these things can be true of social features of websites such as message boards and forums. Most digital culture experts now believe that any content-sharing platforms can now be regarded as social media, including video- and picture-sharing sites.

A meme is the term for any element of culture that is passed on through imitation rather than due to genes, and comes from the work of evolutionary biologist Richard Dawkins. Just as 'viral' has come to describe the way in which internet memes spread, the term has changed from its original meaning. An internet meme is any short video, image or graphic/typographic content that is shared, imitated, subverted or co-opted, so its original meaning is hijacked for a different purpose. Memes can be used for entertainment, advertising or political purposes. Users regularly manipulate photographic images in both simple and complex ways for entertainment purposes. Meme-generating sites are hugely popular with social media users, and memes can be passed around globally in a matter of minutes. A meme only becomes a meme once it is shared and is travelling around social networks with an impetus of its own due to sharing.

Social media usage can be a platform for presenting a person's own identity and gives people a sense of a presence in the online world, and of belonging to a community outside the daily grind of the real world. In this community, they may have a reputation that exists, at least in the first instance, exclusively online. Social media is all about the power of communication, and a sense of belonging to a culture outside the everyday.

Web comics are also often shared on image-sharing sites, as well as being linked to dedicated cataloguing sites. These can range from complex serials read using universal platform e-reader software, to simple one-page or strip examples shared on social media. Although many printed comics seem to be in decline, there is a thriving community online who both read and produce these. As a highly visual medium, they have adapted well to online consumption, and can be read – as can any image shared digitally – using the standard semiotic processes and technical codes you might use for a traditional comic.

EXAMPLE: A web comic with a serious purpose

This short web comic was produced by 'Maeril', a French Middle Eastern woman, and posted on Tumblr. It offers a quick visual guide to an effective psychological technique for intervening in a hostile social situation, and has been widely shared on social media internationally in solidarity with Muslim women.

APPLY IT

Find an example of a web comic on an image-sharing platform or dedicated web comic indexing site such as comic-rocket.com. You can either choose a short comic or a section from a longer one.

Write an analysis of it in around 1,000 words, using your knowledge of semiotics, narrative theories and transferable print media codes.

This is Bill.
Bill sends an important message on Facebook to a friend.
The friend sees the message but he doesn't answer.
Bill doesn't have that friend anymore.
Bill is smart.
Be like Bill.

KEY TERMS

architecture	the structure and navigation of a website
banner	commonly used term for any block of information at the top of a website; can also refer to the site's 'masthead', its identity
captioning	the adding of subtitles to a video, sometimes used as another term for titling
card-based design	trend in web design that prioritises visual rectangular clickable links – 'cards' that often have a picture and captioning
citizen journalism	the passing of footage or photographs taken by witnesses as events to either mainstream or alternative news distributors
dynamic content	content that is regularly updated
hero image	use of a large, dominating image that fills the majority of the viewable homepage before scrolling occurs

hyperlinks	links within a web page to other parts of the site or external content
hypertextuality	web 'intertextuality' – the linking from site to site of other content
intertitles	title cards used in silent cinema – a style of titling in modern video where the titles are placed in between other footage
meme	an image, concept or behaviour that is rapidly disseminated online, mainly through social media
participatory media	digital media that the audience interact with, help construct and distribute
plugins	additional features such as social media buttons or embedded YouTube players that encourage sharing and connectivity

post-broadcast era	term sometimes used to define the shift away from scheduled media consumption
skin	personalised look to software or apps – a style in web design where a background image such as a photograph is layered behind other content
skyscraper	object positioned to run up the side of a website – sometimes a narrow advertisement
virtual communities	groups of people who come together in cyberspace through a shared interest without geographical barriers
web comics	comics that are published and designed to be read solely online
web series	a short form collection, usually fiction, of videos released online
webisode	individual 'episode' of a web series

3.2 Computer games

In this book it isn't possible to explore all the rich diversity of computer games available to players, and game studies is a discipline in its own right. In this section, we look at some of the factors that need to be taken into consideration when analysing games. This should allow you to identify for yourself which of these are the most significant, depending on the game you are looking at.

Computer games differ from other media. The way in which they are experienced is significantly more immersive than other mass media forms, and requires many modifications of the traditional ways in which media texts are read to make sense of the space they have opened in popular culture. During the first year of A level, the best way into the study of computer games as media texts is to look at ways in which the technical codes of media language you have already encountered in reading other texts may be adapted to allow you to begin to explore the nature of these rich, diverse and interesting media forms.

One way to study a computer game is either to use one of the many examples of gameplay footage available on YouTube, or to play segments of the game yourself. Pause regularly to take notes on what you experience in terms of mise-en-scène, graphical information, framing and perspective, sound, narrative and so on. This should in turn lead to consideration of representations. Signification in computer games is layered, as suggested by Barthes' model. It is dependent on the interests of the player and their enthusiasm in engaging with the world of the game, its social and cultural contexts playing a very important role in this process.

Mise-en-scène analysis has to be amended for computer game analysis, because very often the framing is being done by the players themselves in an environment. Props, location design, character design (including dress code) and non-verbal communication are all still relevant. Artificial environments can be procedurally generated in computer games – others are quite rigid and vary little as game progression occurs, with the key differences revolving around engagement with other characters and selected views of the environment.

Graphical information plays an important role, and in many games appears permanently on screen to give the player information and statistics about their progress, score and environment. Also highly significant in considering the mise-en-scène of computer games is the notion of 'simulation' – the blending of the real and virtual in visual style. Games that are based on augmented reality take this to a new and more literal level.

EXAMPLE: Mise-en-scène in GTA V

The environment of GTA V is huge, encompassing spatially connected desert and urban and mountainous environments. The style is hyperreal – it has very detailed dress codes and numerous small details in the environment, offering one of the key pleasures of the game. The appearance of the environment depends on how the player interacts with it – crashing into a lamppost will damage it – as well as whether the action is taking place during the day or at night, with sophisticated light quality generating realism. Weather is also simulated, adding to the sense of immersion.

 APPLY IT

Source some screenshots for a game. Consider how mise-en-scène analysis can be applied in a conventional way to understand how it contributes to the gamer's experience of the game.

APPLY IT

Find a game score online to listen to, preferably one you don't usually play. Research what you can about the game's genre, gameplay and narrative.

Listen to the score without visuals – can you describe any of the techniques being used to evoke a particular atmosphere? Does the score signify genre? Are any sound effects integrated into the score? Since game scores are usually primarily electronic, are there any acoustic sounds mixed into the track?

'Camerawork' and 'editing' are interesting aspects of games. In the absence of continuity editing (although some cut scenes observe its laws) the player essentially constructs the proxemics, para-proxemics and framing/view. 'Editing' takes place through a combination of player selection from a paradigm and responses in the game's programming to player interaction. Other optional views available for the player to choose from, such as maps, are a significant part of the gamer's rich visual world. First-person shooters almost always have weaponry in view, and the character in such games might only be seen at the start.

Since the gameplayer controls their own movement through the environment, we have to consider the limited usefulness of using the terminology of traditional camera shots. Graphic interfaces take on a much higher significance in many computer games; often the gamer is the character, so everything they see is a point-of-view shot.

Sound in a computer-generated environment may encompass effects, ambient music and character voice dependent on the scenario. Aural codes are vital in gaming, since they often provide essential feedback on gameplay as well as having the usual functions of creating atmosphere and verisimilitude through soundscape. Some soundscapes in games differ from conventional media texts in that they are often more experimental, and may seem to blur the boundary between extra-diegetic and diegetic – ambient sound in an alien landscape may combine soundscape with score in interesting and evocative ways that contribute enormously to the gamer's experience of the game.

US-based game score composer Ben Prunty, who has gained recognition for his work on indie games Gravity Ghost and FTL: Faster Than Light, sells his work for digital download on his website. You can preview the named atmospheric tracks generated for different points in the game at https://benprunty.bandcamp.com/album/gravity-ghost-soundtrack.

3.3 Narrative organisation in digital media texts

Some digital media narratives function in a way that is quite different from traditional media. This is due to the hugely participatory nature of most digital narratives. While a viral or user-generated video can be analysed similarly to any other short audio-visual text, some digital narratives are more challenging to decode when applying traditional theories. Roland Barthes, whose ideas about myth and the five narrative codes we encountered earlier, also raised another issue about the ownership of meaning in media texts in his famous 1967 essay, 'The Death of the Author'. Barthes suggested that the Western habit of privileging the author's intentions in writing a text over the reader's experience of the text in interpreting it was losing its relevance in contemporary culture.

This signified a move away from the earlier structuralist theories of narrative, which tended to see the meaning as being inherent in the text. It began to move us towards an era in participatory and gaming culture where narratives can be used in all kinds of non-linear and non-traditional ways. This might include the reappropriation of game footage in machinima, for example. This is an interesting approach to apply to digital media texts, which are often highly intertextual and derivative. Narratives that exist in many digital forms may be fragmentary, have many contributors and be open-ended, with many opportunities for variation in between.

Conventional narrative theories can be applied in a modified way to digital media texts, but you might find yourself doing this in a much more fragmented way. Before considering how narratives work, it is worth revisiting the sections on Barthes and Todorov, especially, in the first two chapters.

Distributed narratives – Jill Walker Rettberg

Digital culture theorist Jill Walker Rettberg has been influential in defining the non-traditional ways in which narratives can work over digital networks.

Distributed narratives are an important new concept in reading narratives that occur across time and digital space. They are difficult to define because of the ways in which we usually think about a narrative, as a complete 'product'.

Examples that currently are considered to be examples of distributed fiction vary from the quite conventional and familiar, to some highly experimental projects:

- Blogs, which are either fictional projects or have genuine identities behind them and narrate an aspect of the writer's life, are narratives distributed in time.
- Some narratives are also distributed in space, as was the case with a science-fiction story that began to appear as conspiracy-style comments in voices of different characters on various Reddit posts.

Jill Walker Rettberg (1971–)

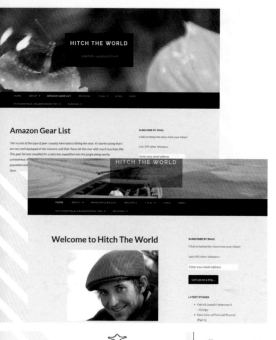

EXAMPLE: *Hitch the World* and *The Modern Nomad*

Patrick Joseph Falterman was the author of a blog called *Hitch the World*, in which he periodically updated readers about his travels across the world, eventually fulfilling his dream of canoeing on the Amazon. His blog posts were written as travel writing, described as 'chapters' written in the present tense, complete with reported dialogue exchanges. Falterman's blog was necessarily only updated on an infrequent basis. The random nature of events due to travel and the dangers he sometimes faced meant his readers were never sure what would happen next. This makes it an example of a simple distributed narrative.

In 2016 Falterman was killed in an air crash aged 26, and his blog has been memorialised. Now it becomes a more traditional narrative of a short period of adventure in someone's life. His adventures are also now summarised in another more conventional digital narrative, a web comic by an artist friend called *The Modern Nomad*.

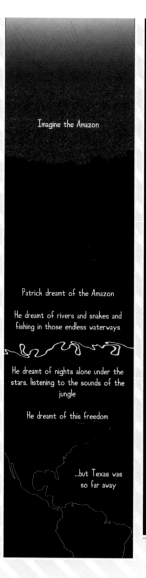

An early Web 2.0 example of a much more complex distributed narrative was *Online Caroline* (2000). Attracting the attention of both the internet and academics, *Online Caroline* was an interactive story that functioned by sending links to webcam footage, a personal website and personally addressed emails. The content was tailored to the information provided by the user, and the interactive story unfolded over a minimum of 24 days depending on how often it was used. For more about *Online Caroline*, see Jill Walker Rettberg's online essay 'How I was Played by Online Caroline' at http://jilltxt.net/txt/onlinecaroline.html.

Transmedia storytelling

The theoretical definition of transmedia narratives, and even the term itself, is still under formulation as an area of new media theory. Transmedia narratives are often highly experimental, and should not be confused with, for example, the simple cross-platform presence of a marketing campaign for a film. In his 2008 book, *Convergence Culture: Where Old and New Media Collide*, Henry Jenkins uses the example of the Wachowski Brothers' wider digital project surrounding the *Matrix* film series. Rather than being a pure cross-promotional film campaign, the print and web comics, webisodes and other digital connections with the film series contributed to and expanded its world for fans of the franchise. Some elements of the film trilogy's narrative and meanings could only be fully understood through supplementation by digital media.

Henry Jenkins (1958–)

Fan texts that extend the world of a conventional media text can sometimes fulfil the definition of transmedia narratives. Many transmedia projects deliberately challenge our idea of authorship; others do so in a more organic way. To be truly transmedia, a text should exist in more than one media form. This can mean using different storytelling techniques across different digital platforms, such as a blog, webisodes on YouTube and posts on a social media account.

Transmedia is defined by Carolyn Handler Miller (2008) as follows:

- *The project exists over more than a single medium* – the media may all be accessed digitally, but should use distinct digital media forms and narrative techniques.

- *It is at least partially interactive* – users must be able to engage with the narrative in some way – it should not be straightforwardly 'read'.

- *The different components are used to expand the core material* – the narrative should be enhanced by the different contributions to it – the narrative should be a sum of parts with different dimensions not encountered in a linear way.

- *The components are closely integrated* – 'trans' can mean across, beyond or through – there must be a crossing or connecting of digital divide between elements of the narrative; a way of moving referentially from one to the other.

- *The story contains at least one public entry point* (the 'rabbit hole') – this is the place from which any user can find a way into the story – where they go from there will vary depending on the strutural organisation of the transmedia narrative.

- The story contains spaces that are designed to invite members of the audience to contribute content ('cheese holes').This is very important, since it draws on the idea that many transmedia stories will be in some way participatory.

In her blog, *The Writer's Platform*, US-based academic Donna Hancox provides a series of links to some examples of transmedia storytelling, some of which are also distributed narratives.

Choose one of the texts referred to in the blog, and spend some time exploring and experiencing it. Write a review of your experiments with this different style of narration to explain the experience to someone who has never encountered a transmedia narrative. Her blog can be found online.

Four of the examples she mentions are:

- *Welcome to Pinepoint*
- *Highrise*
- *The Hollows*
- *Lowlifes.*

- Transmedia stories, while not necessarily games, often contain some gaming elements and a playful sensibility.

It's important to understand the resistance of transmedia narratives to fitting our expectations of the ways in which traditional media engages its audience, and to apply some of the decoding relationship between text and consumer.

EXAMPLE: *Highrise*

Highrise is an interactive digital documentary project that exists solely online, capturing the histories and experiences of people living in high-rise flats. The latest version of the project in 2015 looks at the digital lives and participation of people living in high-rise accommodation in digital culture. It is accessed in a highly exploratory way, with the user creating their own route though the content.

Narratives in computer games

Gameplay produces a different kind of experience compared with traditional media texts. Most of us recognise that computer games are more cognitively immersive than most mass media, but they are also very 'kinetically' immersive because of their sensory properties. These types of immersion will vary according to the game being played.

Another key difference is the experience of many computer games through a first-person narrative. This is especially relevant in role-playing games (RPGs), where the experience of creating an alternate 'self' can be especially powerful and personal. It may even be an expression of some or many aspects of a person's identity that only find a release in that environment. Even when the game allows control of an environment that features a third-person narrative, the audio-visual aspects of the interface often make the player feel as though they 'know' them. They feel a sense of ownership of the character(s) not usually experienced by mainstream viewers of other media forms. The exception to this is fandoms, explored more in the second year of A level, where a niche section of a mainstream audience may indeed feel 'ownership' of characters.

The narrative of many computer games lies not so much in the sequential order or route through play, although for many games it is possible to identify a structure through the game's architecture. Some games also use **backstories** conveyed through **cut scenes**: non-interactive sequences of action that often provide contextual information about the next section of gameplay. Cut scenes can be more easily analysed using traditional narrative theories, although the actual cut scenes experienced by the player may be dependent on the route though gameplay. Because of the limited capability of the game experience to generate complex characters, narratives often depend heavily on the predictably in behaviour of character archetypes. These in turn signify a broader cultural understanding and consensus in reading the text in order to engage fully with the narratives presented.

Some elements of traditional narrative theory still retain a certain level of usefulness when beginning to explore games. Todorov's theory, for example, could be applied to a game that has a strong 'plot' that drives the gameplay and a defined resolution or outcome. Lévi-Strauss' theory is non-linear, so works well when analysing any computer game narrative. Of Barthes' five codes, proairetic codes (PRO) are obviously of most significance, but symbolic (SYM), semic (SEM) and even cultural codes (REF) can also be applied.

Use conventional narrative theories to analyse games in order to answer the following questions:

a Find a synopsis of a video game plot from a source such as a games wiki. Print it out. Highlight the synopsis and annotate it to see whether and where Todorov's five stages of narrative can be applied.

b Research one of the top ten current best-selling games in the UK. Choose one, then read reviews and a synopsis of it. Which binary oppositions can you identify in it?

c Choose one game that has a setting that relates to the 'real' world such as a combat-based game or a sim game. View a couple of game walkthroughs and cut scenes. Can you observe any use of hermeneutic codes (HER) in the cut scene? Which proairetic (PRO), symbolic (SYM) and cultural codes (REF) are used?

There have been some sophisticated attempts to describe the radically different understanding we need to have of how narratives work in computer games, such as the cybertext. This is a text that is presented electronically, the meaning of which is generated by the process the reader uses to access it. This can be applied to games where the experience is more important than the ending.

Another framework is the ergodic narrative, defined by Espen Aarseth. In an ergodic narrative, the rules are in-built. It is up to the 'reader' of the text whether they succeed or fail in getting the message of the text, which does not exist without the player to play it. These approaches form part of a discipline called ludology, which opposes the idea that games can be studied using the more traditional approaches of narratology. Ludology emphasises the nature of the algorithms in the game that control outcomes depending on the actions and behaviours of the player. The fact that players can sometimes add their own modifications to games and are even encouraged to do so by game developers also emphasises their ergodic nature.

Research ludology and Game Studies and make some notes on what you find out.

a What principles and interests seem to drive the discipline?

b How do you think a Media Studies approach differs from a Game Studies approach?

c What do the two disciplines share in common?

d Discuss your findings in a group.

KEY TERMS

backstories (in computer games)	contextual narrative information, often fed in through cut scenes
cut scenes	non-interactive animated sections of games that contexualise an element of play
cybertext	a digital text that is constructed through effort by the reader in a non-linear and highly individual experience through the act of consumption
distributed narrative	fragmented or fractured narrative distributed in different places and at different times

ergodic narrative	in ludology, a narrative that has different outcomes according to the interaction between the 'user' of the text and the 'rules' of the game
ludology	the study of games, especially video games
transmedia narrative	product that exists over more than one media form, with different forms contributing different dimensions to the narrative

3.4 Genre and digital media texts

For more on digital media genre see sections '1.4 Genre and print media texts' and '2.4 Genre and audio-visual/audio media texts'.

APPLY IT

For each of the website genres listed in the grid in section '3.1 The technical codes and features used in online texts' (pages 51–52), create an entry in a case study document listing around five conventions you believe these sites to have in common.

Digital media texts populate a space created by technologies that are constantly on the move. Because of this, new genres are often emerging and old ones disappearing. You can use the genre theories you encountered in 1.4 and 2.4 in just the same way to explore digital media genres. At the beginning of the chapter, we explored the typical features of some websites and other digital media forms such as social networks and content sharing sites. Using this information, you should be able to work out the conventions of most websites and other digital texts with relative ease.

Genre and computer games

There are some broad genre labels used in computer games, which can be understood even by people with a limited knowledge of the medium. Some game genre labels also evoke genres in other media in describing a setting, such as science fiction, war or sport. These have only a limited usefulness, since innovation in genre constantly leads to genre mixing and very little generic stability. These might include, but are not limited to:

APPLY IT

1 Look at the table on the right. Find three examples for each of the categories. What do they have in common?

2 Can you think of three further examples that are generic hybrids of these categories? What does this suggest to you about genre labels and mode of play?

Combat games	Games where beating opposing forces is the primary goal.
Sport, fitness and dance	Games that require very active physical participation.
Role-playing games	Games where the player has a strong role in creating the appearance and persona of the character they play.
Simulation-based games	These games focus on the simulation of an environment or situation – may also be a mode of play within other games.
Strategy	Games that need a combination of cognitive skills and knowledge of the games' challenges.
Platform/ environment	Games that often cluster around levels and are driven by certain repeated skills and how to overcome new challenges, which are offered progressively.
Puzzles	Games that require problem-solving to complete.
Racing	Games where speed and competition are the primary pleasures.

Game genres are sometimes clustered around what is known as the 'pillars' of game design, and the modes of play engaged in by the players. Players and designers alike understand the broad language of design pillars and play modes, and definitions of what these are vary from source to source. Pillars include world design, game mechanics and game writing. Other generic labelling language used by players might refer more closely to the modes of play – the actions that preoccupy the gameplayer in using it.

EXAMPLE: Genre and play modes in No Man's Sky

No Man's Sky was a much-anticipated indie game released in 2016. Players were excited by the alleged complexity of the world design and its highly appealing aesthetic. It is a science-fiction exploration game in which players explore and conquer different worlds in a procedurally generated 'universe'. Although it was one of the most downloaded games for Playstation and Windows that summer, its popularity soon went into rapid decline. Players rated the game poorly due to technical issues surrounding the multi-player function and mechanics of gameplay, with some gamers reporting the game to be repetitive.

The four modes of gameplay in No Man's Sky are combat, exploration, trading and survival. Players can specialise in any of these four areas to progress through the game, or focus on different skills at different points in their gameplay.

Intertextuality and digital media texts

As discussed previously, intertextuality in digital texts is so widely used that many cultural commentators have coined a different term – hypertextuality – to describe the endless interlinking practices of digital media forms. However, you will still be able to identify instances of intertextuality in a more conventional sense – the conscious re-referencing of existing texts in other media forms or other digital forms. Many memes are examples of intertextuality, where the original meaning of an image is reappropriated time and time again until it is almost entirely self-referential. Computer games offer rich opportunities to see connections and influences across popular culture more generally, and within digital and gaming culture.

EXAMPLE: Intertextuality in Life is Strange

Life is Strange (2015) is an episodic third-person adventure game/sim, which is strongly focused on characterisation and narrative arc. Its protagonist, Maxine Caulfield, is named after Holden Caulfield in the classic American novel, *The Catcher in the Rye*. This signifies to the audience the off-beat, youth appeal of the game.

Forerunners to Life is Strange can be seen in other media. A key part of the gameplay is the pop-cultural interpretation of the butterfly effect, which has provided inspiration for many television serials and films featuring time-travel, alternative universes and the notion that small events can change whole histories.

Another essential aspect of the gameplay is Maxine's special skill – that she can rewind time – and the high-school setting. These are both explored in the Japanese anime, *The Girl Who Leapt Through Time* (dir. Mamoru Hosoda, Japan, 2006), which in turn was based on a serialised narrative that appeared in a teen-oriented Japanese magazine in 1965. A live-action version of the film was also made in Japan in 1983.

APPLY IT

Find three examples of games that make conscious and deliberate references to a textual world outside the game.

a Where is the intertextuality located in the game? Is it in narrative and themes? Iconography? Characterisation?

b Create an infographic to map your findings, using screenshots and other visual reminders of intertextual links.

CHAPTER SUMMARY

- Many digital products, including video content and websites, can be analysed using strategies you are already familiar with from your study of print and audio-visual media. Much of our work on the process of signification, narrative theory and approaches to genre can be adapted to help you understand digital media texts.

- Digital texts have their own codes and conventions, and it is important to be able to understand these. You need also to recognise the unique way in which digital media are designed to promote their nature as interactive media, consumed in new ways.

- Social and participatory media are a crucial part of the way in which you encounter much digital media content.

- Some traditional media forms have made the transition to a digital existence: serialised audio-visual narratives previously encountered only on television now appear as made for web series; short documentaries and self-contained international news stories fly around social media sites; and web-only comics continue to develop huge followings.

- Computer games are experienced in a completely different way from other media, and some conventional techniques of media analysis have limited usefulness to access them.

- You can borrow approaches from disciplines such as ludology to help you understand the immersive nature of computer games and the meanings made by the user/game interaction.

- New types of narrative are emerging in digital culture, such as transmedia storytelling and distributed narratives, which sometimes challenge traditional narrative studies, or require us to modify our use of narrative theories.

- Genre study offers similar challenges when studying digital media texts, but genre analysis is possible of digital media forms such as websites, YouTube videos and computer games.

FURTHER READING

Bronwen Thomas (2015) *Narrative: The Basics.*

Carolyn Handler Miller (2008) *Digital Storytelling: A Creator's Guide to Interactive Entertainment.*

Espen Aarseth (2008) *Cybertext: Perspectives on Ergodic Literature.*

Franz Mayra (2008) *An Introduction to Game Studies: Games and Culture.*

Henry Jenkins (2008) *Convergence Culture: Where Old and New Media Collide.*

Jill Walker (2004) Distributed Narrative: Telling Stories Across Networks, http://jilltxt.net/txt/Walker-AoIR-3500words.pdf.

Chapter 4 Media representations

4.1 Representation as process – who or what, how and why?

The process of representation is the essence of Media Studies. Media texts mediate the world around us. Meanings in these texts are not fixed in a particular way, and do not necessarily have one single interpretation in our culture. They are constructed through what we call signifying practices. These signifying practices, including the study of semiotics, attempt to anchor meanings. Other signifying practices include genres and narratives, and their connections with cultural myths and ideologies. Study of the values of the sector of the industry that produces and distributes the text also contributes to meaning. Producers will guide the audience towards the preferred reading of a particular text – the one intended by them and accepted by the majority.

Media texts are polysemic signs, meaning they have potentially more than one meaning depending on who interprets them. Elements of the sign and the signification process will show variations in interpretation between consumers. Not everyone will accept the preferred reading, or even read a sign in exactly the same way. The social and cultural factors that come into play when reading a media text are important for us in understanding the broader significance of the media texts we consume.

We often think of the mass media as relying heavily on stereotypes in creating representations, but it is important to remember that stereotypes are not necessarily negative. In his 2013 book, *Representation: Cultural Representations and Signifying Practices*, Stuart Hall refers to stereotyping as a form of cultural shorthand. It allows the audience to quickly assimilate ideas, but is not the only factor in how an audience reads a media text. If stereotypes of a social group are used in a persistently negative way, this could of course be harmful. In reality, media producers can play in a sophisticated way with our understanding of stereotypes, or even consciously challenge them.

What you will learn in this chapter

- How to approach the study of representations

- The way events, issues, individuals, groups, places, events and abstract concepts are represented through processes of selection and combination

- The way the media through representation construct versions of reality

- How and why stereotypes can be used positively and negatively, and why counter-types exist

- How media representations convey values, attitudes and beliefs about the world and can inform our sense of our own identity

⟳ Read about Stuart Hall's reception theory in Chapter 5.

⟳ Stereotypes are explored in more depth in section '4.4 Stereotyping and counter-representations'.

APPLY IT

Think of the difference between a tabloid newspaper's coverage of 'migrants' compared with a documentary telling the story of a 'refugee' family from Syria such as *Exodus* (see right). Both texts nominally represent the same social group in completely different ways.

Choose a social group or issue, and source two texts that represent them/it in contrasting ways. Write a 1,000-word case study exploring the reasons for the contrasting representations. Make sure you use your knowledge of the relevant technical codes and analysis techniques for your medium as evidence (see sections '1.1 Decoding print media texts using basic semiotics', '2.1 The technical codes and features used in moving image texts' and '3.1 The technical codes and features used in online texts').

In his book, *The Matter of Images* (2002), Richard Dyer explores some different ways of understanding what we mean by the term representation. If we think of it in terms of representation, reality is mediated to the audience in various ways, and is constructed using media language. The world both within and beyond the audience's experience is represented to them, often in ways that seem familiar or match their existing ideologies.

Dyer also considers the process as a presentation of what is 'typical' of a given people, place, time, etc. This can be understood in terms of stereotypes, and is perhaps most obvious when the complexity of representations is secondary to narrative or generic factors.

Sometimes, a great deal of care is taken over the process of representation as a way of speaking for or on behalf of a group of people or person. Deliberately signifying certain values often creates what is termed a counter-representation. This idea is explored in more detail later in this chapter. We can also recognise **audience reactions** to different representations and consider them in terms of these and how they might vary from person to person.

For more on using semiotic analysis see Chapter 1.

Representations are constructed using media language. It's essential that you are familiar with the technical codes of the media form you are trying to analyse. You will also need to be able to use semiotic analysis and genre and narrative theory to evidence your ideas.

The relationship we perceive between representations and reality will always be a complex one. Producers of media texts make deliberate choices about how they reconstruct the world in limited time and space in print, in audio or on screen. These choices are encoded to guide the reader to the preferred reading. Assumptions are made about how the audience will read a text all the time, and producers rely on us having attitudes and values that they can either reinforce or counter, depending on the intended meaning.

Almost all study of representation has to begin with some simple exploratory questions. The following sections will look at each of these questions in detail to understand why they are so significant.

Who is being represented?

People are the main focus in the majority of media texts. We are drawn to people above all else in many of them. This is why who appears in the text and how they are portrayed is so significant. People can be represented quantitatively. This involves considering how many representatives of a social group or treatment of a theme we see. Many research studies have used this idea as a tool to explore visibility, meaning the profile given to these groups and the frequency with which they appear, or measuring as a sub-category the prominence their appearance has. Are they on the front cover? How long are they on screen for? Quantitative representational analysis does not usually explore in detail the nature of the representation. Results of quantitative studies are sometimes impressive, but they are still open to a range of interpretations and reasons for them.

We are normally drawn to people first when looking at a media text.

EXAMPLE: Researching crime, ethnicity and television news representations

In 2010, a study was conducted into the reporting of ethnicity and crime in the US. The study is not particularly well-known, but it is useful because it is very typical of a quantitative study. *Race and Ethnic Representations of Lawbreakers and Victims in Crime News: A National Study of Television Coverage* conducts a review of findings already given by other researchers, and then uses content analysis to corroborate those findings. An extract is given from the study below:

... although official national crime statistics indicate that violent perpetrators are predominantly White ... Whites are not significantly more likely than Blacks to be portrayed as perpetrators in television news stories ... Such a relative over-reporting of Black offenders accords with the predictions of power structure, racial threat and racial privileging explanations, but the media representation of Hispanics and Others is more consistent with market share and normal crime expectations. (page 3)

This study draws its conclusions from a random sampling of television news stories, both local and national, from all over the US and shows clearly the usefulness of quantitative methods.

Qualitative representational analysis is the set of tools, including semiotic theory and related ideas, that we use to understand the quality – the nature – of the representation. This kind of analysis is often more useful, since it allows careful evaluation of the possible messages encoded within a particular representation. It is important to understand that different people will read representations in different ways. You will do this yourself if you are taking the full A level – think of the difference between a feminist analysis of a text and a neo-Marxist analysis. One would consider the representations in terms of gender; the other social class and power structures. There are also numerous smaller variations in the way in which a media audience receive texts.

 The ways in which audiences do this is discussed in more detail in section '5.3 How audiences read the media'.

The significance of different technical codes of media language will vary depending on the media form. For example, radio representations are constructed primarily through vocal performance, soundscape and audio cues. Computer graphics in a game will almost always have a hyperreal feeling to them, and colour codes are deployed in evocative ways that are far richer than we would see in other media forms. When you are exploring representations of a person or people, try to consider the following questions:

- What gender are they?
- How old are they?
- What is their ethnicity?
- Can you identify any signifiers of social class in the representation?
- What does their dress code, including their hair, jewellery, accessories or make-up, suggest about them?
- Is there anything distinctive about the way in which they speak or the language they use?
- What do elements of their non-verbal communication, such as facial expression, posture or gait, communicate?
- What sense do we make of the behaviours and actions?
- How are technical codes such as framing contributing to the production of meaning?

APPLY IT

Find a selection of vox pops on a television programme from a current schedule. Vox pops are sometimes used in light investigative documentaries (e.g. food programming) and local news broadcasts. Consider the mix of people used by age, gender, ethnicity and so on. Summarise briefly the range of views they express. What kind of representation of the subject of questioning is created by their responses?

EXAMPLE: Vox populi

Vox populi (known as vox pops) are used to give viewers of news, documentary or magazine programmes on television a sense of other people's opinions. They involve the cutting together of a broad sample of people's responses, usually to the same question or approach by an interviewer. The interviewer may or may not be present in the final edit. Excerpts are then edited together to suggest a range of opinions and, where possible, social mix. Vox pops are not as equitable as you might think – quite often they are edited to a particular bias required to match the preferred reading.

What else is being represented?

It is not just people who are represented in media texts. Almost every aspect of our lives and the world around us has to go through similar processes of mediation.

Think about how the places you see are represented. The settings chosen for any one media text are highly significant. They might be historical, present day or futuristic. They might be small or large. They might be interiors or exteriors. If you're listening to a radio show recorded in a studio, even that studio is signified through the reactions of the audience (if there is one) or the relationships between presenters. There may be excerpts recorded elsewhere, and the way in which that sound has been mixed will further contribute to our impression of the place.

It is also really important to consider the way abstract concepts are represented. Marriage or romantic love might be represented quite differently in a crime drama featuring a storyline about domestic violence, a situation comedy featuring a married couple, a banking advertisement or a trailer for a romantic comedy. You should be able to identify relatively quickly what the dominant themes and ideas are in factual media texts. In the case of fiction texts, these sometimes take longer to emerge. We can sometimes think of abstract concepts in terms of themes, and there are close connections between themes and narratives.

Events are also represented in particular ways. Consider a sporting event, where the winning team will be heralded as heroes in their own region, the losers being either denigrated or represented in a melancholy or contrite way. The way in which historical events are interpreted and reinterpreted can also be very interesting, with the same stories retold in different time periods in different ways. News providers have to constantly consider how they are presenting events to their audience. What is highlighted by one news source may differ from the angle of another.

⊂⊃ For more on the selection and presentation of news, see section '5.1 How the media industry targets audiences'.

The women's cycling team were widely lauded for their gold medal-winning performances in the Rio Olympics.

What is the nature of the representation?

Selection, **focusing** and **combining** play a vital role in constructing a representation. Numerous techniques are used to influence how we read a text. Selection of material is essential to the process of representation. Without selection and focusing, texts would be difficult to make sense of. In audio-visual media, camerawork and sound as well as editing combine to create meanings. Non-verbal communication in actor or participant performance can be essential in encoding meaning. In factual media, such as news and documentary, shot selection is vital.

The following list suggests some of the ways in which the main media forms you study on the course control the selection and focusing aspects of representations, mainly through technical, narrative and genre codes but also institutional factors. The list is not intended to be exhaustive but serves to highlight some of the most important processes.

APPLY IT

Look at the list of forms in the table on the following page and choose five to work with. Find a textual example for each and evaluate the nature of the representations it contains. Create a grid modelled on the one on the following page. Sum up the nature of the representation and explore ONE important representation in each text using some of the techniques used to create it.

Form	Techniques
Television	• Editing – screen time can be manipulated and relationships implied through editing • Shot types and angles – close-ups make us more likely to empathise with someone, high angles can make someone look either inferior or vulnerable • Mise-en-scène and para-proxemics – the context in which people appear or events take place, and relative positioning within a frame or perceived distance from the audience (proxemics); how people and places are lit • Inclusion – who appears and the social group they represent – shot selection • Sound – who speaks the most, selection of score, social class or region conveyed through accent, voice-over
Film marketing: trailers/web/print	• Narrative image and compression of screen time • Genre conventions embody the focusing process; selection of numerous elements from a particular paradigm because of audience expectations and hypothesis • Voice-over and titling; lexical codes • Typography • Use of composite images to establish key character hierarchies and relationships as well as locations • Menus that select material such as press reviews and awards for positive content and elevate the profile of particular characters or stars
Music video	• Mise-en-scène and dress code • Lyrical content • Camera angles, screen time, editing, repetition of visual motifs • Locations • Signification of artiste or band • Form – the majority of music videos fit into the style of performance-driven or concept-driven

Form	Techniques
Radio	• Vocal performance • Music • Atmosphere/soundscape, signposting • Lexical coding – audiences are far more attuned to language use and its nuances in radio than any other medium • Scheduling and running order
Online and participatory media	• Profiles and shared content • Marketing algorithms and tracking; moderated content; censorship via filtering • Selection based on personal engagement and preferences; most-read – 'echo chamber' effect • Alternative voices can be heard; new communities emerge with their own powers of selection
Video games	• Embedded behaviours in characters • The player/character/agency and power • Binary categorisation, e.g. of genders, can lead to simplified representations • Hyper-masculinity • Which characters have a voice • Self-representation in MMPORGs
Newspapers	• News values • Headlines • Selection of images and captioning (anchorage) • Choice of quotations • Experts • Bias
Magazines	• Coverlines • Features and column space • Inclusion – who or what appears in the magazine • Lexical codes in sluglines, captioning and pull quotes • Illustrative photography and artwork accompanying an article • Non-verbal codes
Advertising and marketing	• All of the above may be used depending on the form in which the promotions appear

MMPORG = massive multiplayer online role-playing game

Cancer Research UK advert, Channel 4, September 2016	Advert features a middle-aged woman talking about her hopes and dreams	Advert represents an organisation making a difference to cancer sufferers, but still needing support	• Personal mode of address. Positive non-verbal communication – smiling • Selection of 'ordinary' person • No mention of cancer itself, which can have negative and frightening connotations as a disease • Head shot, one continuous edit – like being in conversation. High level of focus on subject matter
One-page article about Katie Price, *Heat* magazine, 2016	Article describes the celebrity's behaviour in response to marital breakdowns	Represents Katie Price as being taken over by her 'party girl persona', 'Jordan'	• Two close-up paparazzi shots (below left) taken in club locations 17 years apart, in which the celebrity appears to be inebriated • Copy uses quotes from a 'friend' close to the star and the subject herself in a previous article to create a present-moment narrative of self-destruction • Archive photographs of Price partying after each marriage has broken down support the representation of her as her alter-ego, 'Jordan'

For more on representations see section '4.5 The ideological nature of common media representations and how we respond to them'.

Important questions to ask yourself when considering the nature of a representation

- Is the representation positive?
- Is it negative?
- Is the representation neutral?
- Is it simple or complex?
- Does it fit with mainstream ideologies about the social group, individual or subject matter?
- How open is the representation to alternative readings?
- Does the text conform to established stereotypes, or offer any counter-representation(s)?

Why are these representations the way they are?

Once you have done the work of identifying what the representations are and how they are being constructed using media language, the next stage is perhaps the most important.

You need to explore what the maker of the media text is trying to convey about their subject matter – what is the preferred reading? You don't have to agree with the preferred reading, but you need to be able to identify it.

What factors might have influenced their decision to represent their subject matter in a particular way? Do these relate to the institutional values of the media organisation that produced the text? Are they trying to promote something? Is there an informative aspect to the text, or does it exist purely for entertainment value?

As a genre, reality television is one of the most criticised for its selective use of editing and construction of particular narratives, often from many hours' worth of footage. The problem is a perceptual one, in that the genre has its origins in documentary form, which audiences expect to be offered as a factual perspective.

In fact, all documentary makers also have to create narratives and decide which stories they want to tell from the footage they have. The problem is that the genre exists primarily for entertainment value rather than to inform. In the early days of reality TV, participants frequently complained of misrepresentation.

The contestants on *The Apprentice* (2017)

APPLY IT

Choose a reality television show episode. Draw up a single-page profile for each participant. Include a screenshot of them all. Explore their representation using both the individual episode and any wider knowledge you may have of the show. Bullet point five clear examples of how media language is used to construct the representation.

KEY TERMS

combining	using elements of more than one aspect of media language and form to achieve a desired representation
counter-representation	a representation that offers an alternative to stereotypes
cultural shorthand	a way of understanding how stereotypes communicate ideas quickly to the audience
focusing	building of a representation through techniques such as repetition or elimination of comparisons
polysemic signs	possible multiple meanings of a sign

qualitative representation	using techniques such as semiotic analysis to draw conclusions about the nature of media representations
quantitative representation	using techniques such as content analysis to draw conclusions about representations in media texts
representation	the way in which people, places, abstract concepts and events are mediated in a particular way in media texts
selection	choosing to represent one thing over another

signifying practices	techniques used to construct representations
stereotypes	reduction of a social group to a limited set of characteristics
visibility	how high profile a particular issue, group or event is in media analysis
vox populi	soundbites and/or visual clips of different respondents discussing a topic or answering a question intended to reflect a range of opinions

The Little Mermaid statue by Edvard Eriksen, in Copenhagen, Denmark

4.2 Constructing 'reality' through representation – Stuart Hall

Stuart Hall outlined two systems of representation. The first correlates with our conceptual map and is the way in which we group representations in our minds, using features such as similarities or differences. This can be applied not only to social groups within our direct experience, but also to ideas outside of it. In his book, *Representation: Cultural Representation and Signifying Practices* **(2013), Hall uses the example of angels or mermaids, which we all have a clear representation of in our minds even though we could never have seen either of these mythical beings.**

The second system of representation is the language we use – the signs that stand for the concepts. This process was covered more fully in Chapter 1, where we looked in detail at the process of the production of meaning.

Stuart Hall outlines three approaches, as shown in the grid below, which have been taken to understanding the relationship between reality and representations. These approaches take differing stances on the way in which we understand how the process of representation works.

APPLY IT

Discuss what features you would associate with any collection of mythical beings – ogres, giants, mermaids, angels, the devil and so on. Consider where you might have gained these ideas from. Most of our knowledge of mythical beings comes from ancient narratives retold in different ways within cultures.

Identify a cluster of signs you would associate with each being. Search the internet and collect three visual representations of the beings. Do their features correlate with your conceptual map? Do they contribute to it? Annotate the images with your reactions to them.

Reflective approach	• This approach to representations suggests that meaning is inherent in the aspects of the real world that are being represented. Media language therefore simply 'mirrors' the real world as we experience it
	• This approach has limitations, because it doesn't account for a whole range, from slight to significant, of variations in readings of a text. It ignores the fundamental process of mediation
Intentional approach	• This approach has the producer of the text constructing the world as they see it, and the audience accepting those values encoded in the text at face value. Since signs are polysemic, any sign system is open to variations in interpretation. There would be no room here for a negotiated or oppositional reading
Constructionist approach	• The constructionist – or sometimes 'constructivist' – approach is the one most useful to us, and the process Hall believed best described the relationship between representations and reality
	• Concepts and signs do have some shared meanings, but they are not all inherent, and the audience for a text play a large role in their active interpretation and use of conceptual interpretation of signifying systems
	• Hall says, 'We must not confuse the material world, 'reality', where people and things exist, and the symbolic processes and practices through which representation, meaning and language operate' (page 25, *Representation: Cultural Representations and Signifying Practices*)

APPLY IT

Choose a media text from any of the forms you are studying on the course. Try writing a paragraph that uses the reflective approach to discuss representations. Then do the same with the intentional approach and, finally, the constructionist approach. How does each change the significance of the encoding process? Discuss your findings with the rest of the group.

What is very clear from Hall's work is that sign systems can never reliably depict 'reality'. All sign systems are open to differing interpretations across and within different cultural groups. All signs in the media are representations – a version of reality that subtly steers audiences towards a particular reading, but can never guarantee that they will respond quite as intended.

constructionist approach	readers of a text or its producers can wholly fix meaning	reflective approach	approach that suggests meaning is inherent in what is being represented
intentional approach	approach that suggests meaning is imposed by the producer of the text	systems of representation	identified by Hall – our conceptual map, and the language we use to navigate it

Stuart Hall	(1932–2014) prominent cultural theorist. Born in Jamaica, Hall worked most of his life in the UK, and became a highly influential thinker respected for writing about cultural practices in many disciplines, including Sociology and Media Studies

4.3 Representations and the wider world – people, events, issues and social groups

Why does it matter how individual people are represented?

Media Studies assumes as a starting point that representations in the mass media are important. Some of the discussions you will be having will consider the relative importance of these. No two media theorists agree completely on the extent to which media representations are thought to affect the treatment of social groups in the real world, since this is impossible to measure.

Some texts seek to actively shape or change public perceptions of an individual public figure through the way in which they are represented. In the case of prominent public figures, journalists and documentarians, who seek to portray the individual in any way that challenges their mainstream media portrayal, typically encounter obstacles. These might range from legal challenges to difficulty in gaining access to subjects.

EXAMPLE: *When Louis Met Jimmy* (2000) and *Louis Theroux: Savile* (2016)

Off-beat documentarian Louis Theroux made his name in the late 1990s with a series of documentaries on BBC2 known as *Louis Theroux's Weird Weekends*. He spent time with a range of people who would be considered examples of pariah groups or out-groups. Theroux quickly built on his reputation as someone who would go where other people wouldn't and ask the questions no-one else would with a series entitled *When Louis Met ...*

When Louis Met Jimmy (right) features his encounter with Jimmy Savile, who was subsequently revealed to be one of the most dangerous and prolific sex offenders in UK history. The relationship between Theroux and Savile has since been re-evaluated in a different light, with many people retrospectively considering the documentary a gross misrepresentation of Savile as a mostly harmless eccentric.

Apparently seeking to explore his own gullibility further, in 2016 BBC2 screened a one-off follow-up documentary, *Louis Theroux: Savile*, in which Theroux re-examined the experience of making that documentary. As part of it, he spoke to some of the victims of Savile in an attempt to re-frame the context of the original documentary.

Gender and sexuality

The field of gender studies and the mass media is huge, and is an area you will become much more familiar with in the second year of the A level course. On the whole, stereotypes associated with gender are remarkably slow to make progress in keeping with societal attitudes.

Deborah Meaden, who appears in *Dragons' Den*, conforms to the stereotype of the ruthless business-woman.

🔗 For more about cultivation theory see Chapter 5.

For further reading about gender and media stereotypes see David Gauntlett's (2008) *Media, Gender and Identity: An Introduction.*

Traditionally, women in the media have been the focus of a great deal of representational study. This is because of the unique position they occupy in our society. Women constitute 50% of the population, yet are still treated very differently from men in the mass media. Most of the feminist explanations for this relate to **patriarchy** as a social system. Traditional femininity is very much based around the role of women as child-bearers and at the heart of domestic activity. The other strand to this is the sexualised image of women as beings to be looked at and appreciated by men, and valued according to their perceived attractiveness. These examples demonstrate to us just how contradictory stereotypes can be – that they can simultaneously embody many different qualities. This is related to the concept of myth – since several myths can co-exist about a social group, and are perpetuated by repeated exposure.

Representations of women in more powerful roles in the contemporary media frequently depict women as having to make sacrifices for their role. They can degenerate into unflattering stereotypes. An example of this might be the ruthless business-woman who is cold and unfeeling, inflicting misery on her employees.

Much of the focus in gender studies over the last few decades has been on women, because they have gone some way to challenging some of the pervasive historical stereotyping of women that is a product of patriarchy. Increasingly, more critical studies have been undertaken in the field of masculine representation.

Traditional masculinity has men as breadwinners, and authoritarian and paternalistic figures in the family. Outside the family they are macho heroes who are independent, capable and fearless. Showing emotion is generally frowned upon.

Newer stereotypes relating to masculinities are emerging, but again the media struggles to keep up with the changes men have experienced in real life in their roles. Many newer modes of masculinity are still often depicted as though they are **emasculating**. Reading masculinities in media texts is therefore complex. Plural masculinities that are a blend of old and new are apparent in some contemporary media texts, and those that draw exclusively on traditional masculinity are becoming fewer. Nonetheless, as with female representation, it seems that it is simply easier to represent both men and women in a binary way.

EXAMPLE: The marketing for *Jason Bourne* (2016)

The online trailer for the action/spy film *Jason Bourne* (2016, left) uses codes associated with traditional masculinity to signify the action genre. The film hit the headlines when it was released, partly because the lead actor, Matt Damon, only says a total of 288 words in the film.

Despite the appearance of a seemingly powerful female ally in the trailer, traditional masculinity is very much in evidence. Bourne continues to signify for us the macho hero, able to cope with anything while showing no emotion and with immense physical strength, combined with combative skill. Bourne represents the qualities theorists studying masculinity in the Hollywood hero have identified over and over again – coolness, toughness, hardness – and silence.

Another field that is explored much more closely later on in your course is representations of the lesbian, gay, bisexual and transsexual (LGBT) community. This is a very interesting area of study. Just as it is sometimes difficult to find progressive representations of new masculinities and femininities in the media, so it is equally difficult to find examples of people from these communities being

APPLY IT

Collect a range of images from across the media that signify more traditional modes of femininity and masculinity. Create a collage as a class, using large sheets of paper taped together to display your findings. Talk about what you notice.

represented in a positive and rounded way. Common historical representations in the media have tended to portray people in this social category as deviant, dangerous, victims or a source of comic relief. Sadly, many of these stereotypes still persist despite some changes in social attitudes.

Race, ethnicity and religious representations

Race representation continues to be a source of productive discussion about the nature of media representations and their relationships with real groups in society. The race and ethnicity representations that predominate in a culture tend to vary according to the make-up of that culture and its histories.

In the US, representation of African-Americans is considered a contentious area. This is partly because of the significant proportion of the population they represent, but also due to social issues relating to power and poverty. One of these might be the disproportionately high level of incarceration of young black men, and ongoing social problems such as the deaths of young black men shot by police. Historical sensitivities still exist in both white and black communities around the legacy of slavery.

In the context of the current climate of global terrorism and conflict in the Middle East, in the UK many negative representations of Muslims as a people and Islam as a religion have emerged. If unchecked, these can contribute to Islamophobia. Concerns have also arisen over the representation of Eastern European migrants and workers, with some blaming negative tabloid representations of this group for inciting persecution.

Age

We are all familiar with some of the most common stereotypes relating to age, although we rarely consider the real-world implications of these. Stereotypes relating to age tend to affect mainly those at the higher or lower end of the spectrum – the elderly and teenagers.

Teenagers are often particularly negatively portrayed, using stereotypes relating to youth crime. History shows us that youth, as a time of exploration of new-found independence and risk-taking, has always been viewed with suspicion by older generations. This is strange when you consider that all these people were once teenagers themselves. Over-representation of youth crime and other negative factors associated with youth are often at the root of moral panic, where news media give a greater proportion of reporting time to stories that have currency such as abuse of legal highs and games addiction.

Older people also suffer from entrenched stereotypes – that they are bored, lonely, senile or physically infirm. This could lead to a lack of respect for the elderly and reluctance to allow them to participate fully in society – including continuing to work should they wish to do so.

Social class

Despite social mobility in the last century being experienced by British people on a scale never seen before, the class system still exists in the UK. There are still large sections of society who are born into privilege, just as there are still as many who find their chances hopelessly limited by their family circumstances and real barriers to social mobility such as the cost of childcare, housing or higher education.

As a society, we are hugely class conscious, and many areas of media representation from comedy to news still reflect this. We are very sensitive to signifiers of social status and class, such as outward displays of wealth, cultural practices, dress code,

Using age, race/ethnicity or social class as the basis to choose a text from the range of forms you are studying on the course. Write a 500-word case study exploring how the text uses either stereotypes associated with that social group or counter-types.

education and profession, manner of speech and region. The UK is still a country that has wide variations in standard of living with both very wealthy and extremely poverty stricken citizens, even if some of the signifiers of these situations do not match traditional structures and delineations of social class.

EXAMPLE: *Believe in Me* (2016)

In 2016, the children's charity Barnardo's departed from its history of shocking and disturbing advertising campaigns to promote a more positive marketing strategy based on children's potential. In the 2016 *Believe in Me* advert, we see a range of children, each depicted against a stark mise-en-scène and shot in muted colours, demonstrate talents – in sport, music and dance. This is a departure from previous advertising campaigns, when the focus tended to be on the stark consequences of neglect and abuse.

Disability

People with disabilities have for a long time been categorised as an out-group, despite the fact that the majority of people with disabilities live fully integrated with the rest of society. They are an incredibly diverse group, but like others tend to suffer from recurrent reductive stereotypes in the mainstream media.

Representations of people with disabilities should not be confused with representations of mental illness or temporary physical impairment due to illness, which also have separate stereotypes associated with them. Think also of how different the treatment is of people with mental illnesses in fictional narratives compared with physical illnesses.

In 1991, Colin Barnes followed up some of the work by well-known disabled rights activist Paul Hunt. Barnes explored the perpetuation of a number of common stereotypes of people with disabilities in the mass media of the time. Traditionally, the field of disability studies distinguishes between the medical model of disability, where the disability is perceived as a flaw that focuses on what people with disabilities are not able to do rather than what they can do. This is the model that often persists in culture. The second model is the social model, where the disadvantage is perceived as a fault on the part of society for failing to recognise people's strengths, and focusing on the impairment rather than the person.

Barnes also outlined some very common stereotypes that persist about people with disabilities in the mass media:

1 Pitiable and pathetic; sweet and innocent; a miracle cure
2 Victim or object of violence
3 Sinister or evil
4 Atmosphere-curios or exotica in 'freak shows', and in comics, horror movies and science fiction
5 'Super-crip'/triumph over tragedy
6 Laughable or butt of jokes
7 Having a chip on shoulder or aggressive avenger
8 A burden/outcast
9 Non-sexual or incapable of having a sexual relationship
10 Incapable of participating in everyday life

EXAMPLE: *Meet the Superhumans*, Channel 4, 2012/*The Undateables*, Channel 4, 2016

Trailers advertising the Paralympics are always interesting in their representations of people with disabilities.

In the award-winning trailer for Channel 4's coverage of the games, athletes are shown in footage that shows them at the top of their game, as well as flashbacks showing disability to sometimes result from injury, and at other times being present from birth.

Of course, there is a danger that this advert could be considered to be falling within the 'super-crip' or triumph over tragedy stereotype, but we should question here whether that is relevant given that the marketing of able-bodied sports heroes also coincides with this approach in mainstream media.

The Undateables (2012–2017), also broadcast on Channel 4, is a reality dating show that follows people with physical disabilities or learning difficulties. The show initially met with controversy for its suggestion that people who belong to these groups are unwanted or cannot participate in day-to-day life: a claim that was denied by the show's producers, who intended the title to reflect mainstream attitudes rather than reality. However, critics praised the warmth and positivity in the portrayal of its subjects.

 APPLY IT

Source and view other trailers for the Paralympics and an episode of *The Undateables*. Do they conform to the medical or the social model? Do they reinforce certain stereotypes or attempt to counter them?

Place

Place in our culture is often defined in terms of binary oppositions. The countryside is quiet and dull while the city is loud and vibrant; or the countryside is a place of beauty and connections with nature while the city is an ugly sprawl and an unnatural environment. We often read representations of place as points of contrast with our own experience, a locus of certain events or values, or as a projection of our desires and imagination.

Place as geographical location also can be influenced by political and economic factors such as the relative power positioning of the industry doing the representing and the audience watching it, or the legacy of colonialism, past conflicts and foreign policy. An area can also be represented in quite different ways depending on who is actually doing the representing, and who is the intended audience. Institutional values come into play that can result in very highly contrasting representations of the same place.

For more about place see section '1.3 Narrative organisation in print media texts'.

EXAMPLE: *Poldark* and *Grand Theft Cornwall*

Cornwall is frequently represented in both fiction and documentary in a highly romanticised way. As a popular UK holiday destination, the county enjoys a largely positive reputation of laid-back and friendly locals, clean beaches, great surf, pretty harbours and rugged landscapes. In reality, many Cornish people struggle to make ends meet and economic poverty is rife. This side of Cornwall is rarely shown as it fails to match the entertainment values of the programmes using it as a location.

Poldark is a successful BBC costume drama, made in both the 1970s and again recently from 2015. Part of the reason for the show's success is its use of location filming and the depiction of a wild and romantic setting as a backdrop for an intense family saga. Although avidly watched by many Cornish people, the series as a whole is intended to appeal to a cross-section of the BBC 1 audience.

Grand Theft Cornwall is a YouTube machinima production made by user 'Colin Leggo'. It utilises in-game footage from GTA V cut to create a narrative of a local man complaining about parking due to holidaymakers and trying to buy a pasty in a gun shop. He argues about where to get building supplies with a workmate with a south-eastern accent, and finally ends up in an altercation with a lifeguard on a beach. Voiceover in strong Cornish accents using in-jokes and local dialect, it is subtitled '*If GTA was set in our beloved home*' and is a comically affectionate portrayal of Cornishness, made by Cornish people for a predominantly Cornish audience.

APPLY IT

Choose an audio-visual media text that represents a particular historical time period or place. Think about how it represents that place or period through mise-en-scène.

KEY TERMS

emasculate	to remove masculinity
medical model	approach to representing disability that perceives it as a flaw

patriarchy	a system where men predominate in power structures
social model	approach to representing disability where society is to blame for failing to recognise what disabled people can do

4.4 Stereotyping and counter-representations

Stereotyping as a term refers to the practice of reducing a group or an individual to a limited set of preconceived ideas that already circulate about this group in society. Stereotypes are a means of quickly constructing representations in an accessible way for the audience. They are constructed in many of the ways already discussed, and may have more significance in some genres than others.

Richard Dyer provides an interesting discussion of this in *The Matter of Images*. Like Hall, Dyer believes that stereotypes function in part as a short-cut for the audience. He describes them as an ordering process, a way of rendering social groups and people both within and outside social reality as understandable. Dyer also accepts the dual nature and central problem of stereotypes – the debate as to whether stereotypes exist to serve dominant ideologies in society in the interest of powerful groups, or whether they simply reflect the shared cultural ideas of the majority. Most theorists agree that stereotypes are based on a limited set of ideas and assumptions that stand in for a whole, rich and varied representation.

In-groups and out-groups

APPLY IT

Using an example of a moving image, and an audio, web and print advertisement, identify four stereotypes that are common in the popular media. The stereotypes should not be limited to gender or age – try to cover as much ground as you can across the texts. Considering working or familial roles is a good way to ensure variety.

When looking at social groups, an important concept is **in-groups** (the dominant culture) and **out-groups**, who are usually in the minority. This is not always about numbers of people in a society, but about who holds the power. For example, women have historically been considered an out-group within patriarchal systems of representation. In-groups often hold stereotypes about the out-groups as a way of understanding their presence in the context of their own group; stereotypes are often based on difference – a set of binary qualities that the out-group may use to compare the group characteristics with their own. Sometimes this process consciously defines the out-group as inferior. There is then a danger that this treatment in the mass media either reflects or reinforces real treatment of members of that out-group in society. Out-groups can be instrumental in the formulation of alternative representations and counter-types. These can begin to make their presence felt in mainstream media; more often they will be confined to alternative media.

EXAMPLE: Three advertisements from *Attitude* magazine

The three advertisements below all appeared in *Attitude* magazine, an established lifestyle, fashion and culture magazine, in September 2016 for an audience of gay men. In the magazine, a range of advertisements appear targeting this audience. Some are for mainstream companies who are seeking the custom of a gay audience; others are companies that exclusively cater for the audience's needs. All of them demonstrate how an out-group in British culture redefines itself outside of the imposition of stereotypes held by the in-group of heterosexuals. This is also known as counter-representation.

For more on counter-representations see page 84.

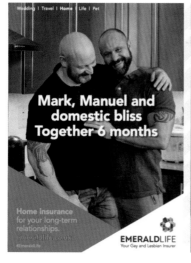

- *Emerald Life Insurance advert:* Reinforces the idea of the committed, loving, long-term gay relationship, countering the out-group's belief that gay relationships are transient. This belief possibly originated in the necessity of secrecy faced by gay men in previous decades whose relationships were outlawed by the state.

- *Holding the Man film release*: This advert promotes the release of a romantic drama that centres on two gay characters and their desire to be together. This counters the idea that romantic love is entirely the province of the heterosexual norm, and that gay relationships are based on primarily physical aspects. That particular stereotype owes more to binary categorisations of masculinity and femininity rather than real gay experiences of falling in love.

- *iCandy pushchair advert*: Promotes the pushchair rather like a car, as a fashion and status symbol; exactly the strategy used for the product in mainstream publications. The presence of this advert shows that gay men are parents too, and have the same interests in related products and the status their purchase might confer. Most mainstream representations of gay men do not represent them routinely as parents.

APPLY IT

As a class, source a copy of *Attitude* magazine or another magazine that caters for an out-group. Choose three advertisements and explore how these may challenge stereotypes held about that group by the in-group.

Another really important idea is the notion of **otherness**. This is a well-established concept in **post-colonial theory**, which explores representations of different ethnicities in Western culture. In the case of **the other**, people belonging to the out-group are defined exclusively by their differences from the dominant culture. This can be used in political justification for repression of groups or limitations of their rights within a host culture. It is also used in other demeaning ways, such as sexualising black women by portraying them as 'exotic'.

Choose four examples in different media forms that appear to correlate with Alvarado's stereotypes. Look beyond these – can you find any counter-representations? Are there any examples of representations where the subject's skin colour is irrelevant and they are depicted as fully integrated into the dominant culture? Present your examples to the group for discussion.

EXAMPLE:

Manuel Alvarado identified four common stereotypes of black people as 'other' in Western media (*Learning the Media*, 1987). He found that four common stereotypes were reinforced time and time again:

- *exotic* – to be looked at, sexualised, glamorously different
- *pitiable* – starving, victims of violence and oppression
- *humorous* – clown-like, entertainers, non-threatening
- *dangerous* – savage, barbarian, uncivilised, violent, threatening to whites.

Problems of misrepresentation in a global culture

In Chapter 6, we will be discussing more about the global nature of media industries and how this affects media consumption. It is certainly true that today's media audiences are exposed to more varied representations of people from other cultures. Although the Westernised values embedded in these predominate, on this course you will be considering media that is produced by other cultures, and also media that is produced by out-groups. These often challenge the dominant representations encountered in other texts. A number of the issues presented by the global nature of some representations are outlined below:

1. A reduction in diversity of representations due to their repetition in dominant media forms, e.g. English language content, particularly from the US
2. The transmission of negative stereotypes from one culture to another – bad news travels faster than good
3. Media censorship – the state censoring of some content may lead to skewed representations that are difficult to make sense of
4. Reduction in perceived value of indigenously produced media content – the inability of indigenous groups to find a platform for self-representation in a competitive media industry
5. Value judgements – alternative representations and modes of self-representation perceived as less important than the dominant representations we are exposed to on a regular basis

Are stereotypes fixed?

Some stereotypes are certainly more persistent than others in both society and media histories. Since society and culture are constantly changing, the mass media is in a state of perpetual flux itself. New stereotypes and sub-categories emerge all the time while others remain surprisingly constant.

'Geeks' in the digital age are often the subject of negative stereotyping.

EXAMPLE: 'Geek or Chic? Emerging Stereotypes of Online Gamers'

In their 2012 article, 'Geek or Chic? Emerging Stereotypes of Online Gamers', Rachel Kowert and Julian Oldmeadow explore a new stereotype relating to digital media – that of the online gamer. In the article, the authors argue that the social stereotype of *'isolated and lonely couch potatoes'* is less interesting than what it can tell us about what they term the cognitive stereotype – society's attitudes towards gaming as an activity. In the study, they propose that online gamers are:

> *stereotypically unpopular, unattractive, idle, and socially incompetent, a characterisation that seems to match common stereotypical portrayals in the media, television and internet fora.*

The study, which tested a range of supposed traits associated with gamers among both gamers and non-gamers, found a marked distinction between gamers, who tended to refute the stereotype, and non-gamers, who appeared to have internalised it.

Tessa Perkins wrote an important article called 'Rethinking Stereotypes' in 1979, which is very useful reading to help understand the significance of stereotypes in the media. It still represents some of the most powerful and focused consideration of the nature of stereotypes and the problems with them that can be found anywhere. In common with most theorists, Perkins accepts that stereotypes do not come from nowhere. She also sees the contradiction that stereotypes can be both true and false at the same time. She does suggest that some stereotypes are simple, whereas others are more complex and that they are attached to complex social meanings, for those who both replicate and decode them. Stereotypes, Perkins argues, are always held by a particular social group about another social group.

One of the most interesting aspects of Perkins' work is her identification of who we hold stereotypes about:

1 *Major structural groups* – these are the largest categories we can think of: gender, age, class and race all fall into this category.
2 *Structurally significant/salient groups* – smaller categories with a defining quality, such as working as a teacher.
3 *Isolated groups* – transgender people might fall into this category.
4 *Pariah groups* – groups about whom there is a sense of disapproval attached to their status in society – alcoholics, for example, or gay people. Pariah groups can also fall into any of the first three groups.
5 *Opponent groups* – feminists, the Alt-right in the US.
6 *Socially/ideologically insignificant groups* – Apple users, Harry Potter fans.

Another well-known aspect of Perkins' work was her identification of some of the problems with the way we understand stereotypes. She identifies, for example, our assumption that stereotypes are always 'erroneous in content', which, as already discussed, cannot be true. She also questions whether stereotypes are always pejorative (negative) – many are, but not all. Positive or laudatory stereotypes can also play an instrumental role in elevating the visibility of an oppressed group, as well as validating a group who are already powerful or respected in society.

Stereotypes are often used in the media because they support another aspect of the product's form. Stereotypes recur commonly in genre-based narratives. They are an essential part of the ordering process, and an important part of how audiences relate to characters in a genre text. Characters drive narratives, and part of the pleasure of narrative is the characters. Stereotypes are a quick way for audiences to understand a story. This can be seen in many computer games that pit the player against some kind of threat, often embodied by 'bad guys'.

Industry values can also be highly significant in dictating the observance of stereotypes. These are central to the success of the tabloid press in the UK. Often accused of vilifying social groups and individuals, they nonetheless persist in using them because the formula works.

 APPLY IT
Explore a stereotype relating to new digital media. Examples might be the 'Pinterest mum'/blogger, beauty blogger, stereotypes relating to teenagers and social media use, comic and fan-flic geek, or the coder/hacker. Try to collect at least two textual sources that help you to assess the nature of the stereotype. Set up three photographs: one a portrait of someone who represents the stereotype, and two others showing behaviours you might associate with them. Present as a 'wanted' poster. How do they all look displayed together?

 APPLY IT
Think of three different laudatory stereotypes we hold about people in society. For each type, identify an example of this being reinforced in a mainstream media text. This is more difficult than you might think, so choose your examples carefully. A good place to start is with Perkins' 'salient groups', since there is often a pre-existing neutrality about these compared with, for example, pariah or opponent groups, which tend to bear more ideologically significant aspects to their associated stereotypes.

Counter-representations

Counter-representations are sometimes present in mainstream media texts. They can work to increase suspense, promote awareness of an issue or simply to serve a niche audience. Counter-representations are often far more consciously constructed than stereotypes, and structurally reinforce a stereotype by opposing it. Counter-representations are therefore interesting to study alongside a structuralist theory of narrative such as Claude Lévi-Strauss'.

For more on Claude Lévi-Strauss see section '1.3 Narrative organisation in print media texts'.

Counter-types can have an educational role in the media, challenging prejudices and increasing awareness of issues relating to stereotypes. Like stereotypes, they may also appear more commonly in some genre texts than others. Counter-types are particularly likely to emerge in social media, shared as viral messages that provide an alternative to dominant representations. These may attempt to raise awareness or galvanise social change. Although better than no representation at all, it should be remembered that often this kind of video will not reach the kinds of people it is intended to, tending to be shared by those who are already receptive to alternate viewpoints. Documentary is a common genre to find the counter-type in, as it usually aims to inform people about a topic. It may also aim to expose something, to leave the audience thinking about a subject from a new perspective or re-evaluating attitudes.

EXAMPLE: *Exodus: Our Journey to Europe*

This three-part documentary was shown on BBC1 in 2016, shot by refugees on their own phones as they made the treacherous escape from Syria. The documentary challenged many people's views of 'migrants' by showing the desperate reasons they are fleeing war zones, allowing them to connect with the stories of individuals rather than just a number. This allowed self-representation from a group who, because of their obvious lack of power and status in society, do not usually have a voice. It is also a powerful reminder of the potential of digital media and devices to tell stories that otherwise might not be heard.

We should take stereotyping seriously. It would be too easy to dismiss it as a cultural signification practice, which most of the time is harmless. Some of the time, perhaps it is. Given that we know the relationship between stereotypes and real-world attitudes and values among media consumers informed by them is a complex one, media producers have an ethical responsibility to try and represent people in a fair way. Derogatory stereotypes can inform attitudes and have been used as a part of negative propaganda campaigns throughout the relatively short history of the mass media. It is essential that across the media people have access to different perspectives and counter-types in order to avoid what began as a cultural short-cut becoming entrenched beliefs, particularly worrying when it concerns one part of a population's view of another.

APPLY IT

Create a 60-second video using a music track, titles and graphics as well as original footage, that constructs a deliberate counter-type of teenagers. The video should be suitable for distribution on social media.

KEY TERMS

in-groups	members of a dominant culture	pejorative stereotypes	stereotypes who demean their subject
laudatory stereotypes	stereotypes that contribute positively to views of social groups	post-colonial theory	field that explores the legacy of colonialism by Western powers and how it contributes to race representation
otherness	the state of being defined as 'different'– views of an out-group held by an in-group	the other	the state of being defined as 'different' due to cultural differences
out-groups	minorities living within a dominant culture		

4.5 The ideological nature of common media representations and how we respond to them

Throughout this chapter we have referred to the way in which media producers encode messages into their texts to create a preferred reading. We also know that not all audiences accept the preferred reading. Stuart Hall's reception theory is introduced in more detail in the next chapter. In this final section of Chapter 4, we will be looking more closely at why audiences frequently do accept the preferred reading, and the sometimes complex reasons for differing responses to the same representations that might lead some audience members to question dominant representations.

Ideologies – what they are and why they matter

The study of ideology is a complex field. For the purpose of the first year of A level Media Studies, we will use the term ideology to mean the shared value and belief systems of a culture. Dominant ideologies tend to be perpetuated and reinforced by preferred readings. Mainstream media texts will tend to support the dominant ideology in a culture. They have a role in both maintaining the status quo and reflecting the values held by a large part of a population. The problem with this is that not everyone within a particular culture will share the same values and ideologies. Popular ideologies are often slightly conservative and pro the role of the individual and traditional family structures in society. They tend to be predominantly hetero-normative, pro-work, and supportive of the government and democracy. These kinds of values pervade our media texts.

Some political theories of the mass media go even further. Marxist theorists suggest that the mass media is a tool of the state, serving the wealthy and powerful, and protecting the interests of the ruling class as a passive ideological state apparatus by naturalising values that preserve their power. This was first proposed by Louis Althusser. Antonio Gramsci, another Marxist theorist, referred to the process of coercing the population into conforming with mainstream ideologies as cultural hegemony. Texts that have a hegemonic function may simply convey mainstream ideologies in a simplistic way, or they might test out alternatives and then resolve them in favour of the ruling elite.

EXAMPLE: *Hello!* magazine

This publication is well-known for its positive portrayal of society's role models, such as celebrities and particularly the monarchy. It publishes exclusive interviews and photoshoots with the wealthy, which are positive in tone and uncontroversial. Because of this, they are often the only invited presence at celebrity weddings, and have a higher than normal level of access to the younger generation of the monarchy. *Hello!* could be considered to play a role in upholding the status of the wealthy and powerful in society, reinforcing their significance in the lives of ordinary readers, promoting values such as patriotism and validating distinctions in social class.

This idea was also explored by Noam Chomsky when he wrote in 1988 that the mass media helps to manufacture consent in a society by playing out and resolving in favour of the ruling class any contentious issues. Chomsky believes that a galvanising force is necessary as a background to his propaganda model of communication, which unites the majority of a population in the face of a threat that is real and can be maintained over a long period of time. An example of this today, both in the UK and the US, is the War on Terror.

Not all political theorists share this left-wing perspective. The dominant mode of considering the relationship between audiences and the media they consume in most

APPLY IT

Identify some popular ideologies around the following in our society: work ethic, the family, the monarchy, body image, consumer culture, celebrity.

Now find evidence for each of these in a range of print media products. Include magazines, newspapers and print adverts.

Collate your findings as a slide presentation to share with your group.

Fans of *Star Wars* attending a *Star Wars* convention are expressing an aspect of their identity.

For more on identities see section '5.1 How the media industry targets audiences'.

Western capitalist countries is liberal pluralism. Liberal pluralists do not think that the media controls people's beliefs about society; more that they offer choices and can even reflect diverse identities and ideologies. This approach suggests that media consumers, when faced with a multitude of ideologies, select those that match their own and reject others that don't. This is also suggested by what David Gauntlett called the pick and mix theory. Consumers will tend to ignore texts that challenge their way of thinking, seeking out instead those that reinforce their view of the world. This appears to support the idea of preferred readings – a consumer who encounters a text that disturbs their view of the world may simply disengage from it.

This is really important in considering the relationship between how we respond to dominant ideologies in the mass media and how they might contribute to our sense of our own identity.

How does the media we consume impact on our sense of our own identity?

There has been a great deal of critical thinking in recent years, particularly in light of developments in participatory and digital media, about the role of the mass media in shaping and reflecting multiple identities in society. This is inextricably linked with representations, since not only do audiences draw on their media consumption in informing their own identity, with new media they may also use the media interactively to help display it.

Identity is often separated into cultural identity and personal identity. Aspects of cultural identity are common across large groups of people – personal identity is much more nuanced. The way in which these combine uniquely in every person is one of the reasons media texts are so open to different readings of the same content by various people, especially when the text seems to force a conflict between the two. It is certainly true that conforming with mainstream identities means a sense of acceptance by society, and is very reassuring for significant numbers of people – the mainstreamers of society.

Most research into identity over the past few decades makes the assumption that identity is a fluid concept. Some believe identity is fractured or fragmented. Many individuals do have a complex identity, made up of several components. Our identities can also change as we go through life, and position ourselves differently in relation to wider society and how we understand or represent ourselves when measured against it. If we accept that the mass media offers us role models and ways of being that we can select from if we choose, then this renegotiation process has a far wider frame of reference at this point in history than ever before.

Some people may choose not to conform with mainstream identities, and reframe their own identity in alternative ways – Web 2.0 has changed the ways in which people are able to connect with like-minded individuals significantly. The internet offers numerous spaces where people can build and share alternate ways of being or select from more eclectic media influences. People can also take pleasure from having a collective identity – feeling that they are sharing values or even just acts of consumption with others. This can be seen in the case of fan sites and forums.

A more pessimistic view of identity formation would suggest that this happens only infrequently, and that the majority of people frame their understanding of their own identity from a narrow range of media representations and societal roles.

APPLY IT

Choose one of the examples on the right and find out more about the issue of representations and identity. To get a really rounded exploration, choose a range of texts – or extracts from them – as examples.

1 **Make notes on how groups are being represented and how these representations have been constructed.**

2 **Consider how they might be read by their intended audience, possibly contributing to the sense of their own identity.**

Share the texts you chose and your focus with your group, using your notes to talk about them.

Young women and material consumption

This study could take in conventional advertising of clothes and beauty products that targets young women, as well as magazines that promote cheaper as well as high-end brands and products also targeting young women. A great addition to this would be to look at the sub-cultural phenomenon of 'Haul Girls' on YouTube (girls who upload videos of themselves, showing off what they've bought on a shopping spree).

Skaters/surfers and masculinity

This study could choose as its texts online culture such as official websites of particular well-known skaters or surfers, and cover brand endorsements and advertising. It could also include surf and skate magazines. The focus should be on how new and old masculinities and heterosexuality as the norm are represented and responded to by the audience. An interesting site for alternatives might include www.gaysurfers.net.

Music genres and youth identity

This could focus on any of the musical genres that have a strong dress code associated with them, and reference music videos, other cultural products consumed (e.g. Grime and the marketing for films such as *Kidulthood*, the association between Goths and horror series, etc.). Alternatively, a short-lived phenomenon such as Seapunk and its transition from meme into the cultural mainstream could be studied.

David Gauntlett – enabling Ideas

In his 2008 book, *Media, Gender and Identity* 2nd edition, David Gauntlett considers the relationship between representations in the mass media and how people construct their own identities. Although his main interest is in gender, much of what he says about gender is more widely applicable. Gauntlett's book makes interesting reading, partly because he evaluates the thinking of other key thinkers as he works through ideas relating to media representations and our sense of identity.

At the beginning of the book, Gauntlett considers why media influences are important in thinking through how representations affect people's sense of self and relationships with others in society. He wonders:

David Gauntlett (1971–)

> *Do domestic and romantic dramas influence how we know what to do in a romantic relationship, since we don't typically see other people's from the inside? Do media texts show us what is meant by friendship?*
>
> *How can we possibly avoid the influence, if we read them, of women and men's lifestyle magazines, with their continual suggestions as to how we should improve our looks, our physique, our well-being, our relationships?*
>
> *Film heroes are remarkably similar to one another, and we are repeatedly exposed to these very similar representations which reinforce certain qualities.*
>
> *Why wouldn't we begin to assume some of these traits in the way we present ourselves to others?*
>
> *The overall attractiveness level of people in the mass media must surely affect how we evaluate the appearance of ourselves and others around us.*
> (Gauntlett, 2008, page 3)

These are questions that Gauntlett suggests as examples of some of the most pervasive media influences – he does not suggest that we can prove these influences on identity; more that we should be aware of the power and prevalence of them and consider them as possibilities.

Towards the end of the book Gauntlett tries to make sense of some of his exploration both through his own experimenting and the ideas of other prominent theorists. Some of his conclusions are as follows:

- People tend to view their identities as a single thing, rather than perceiving them as fragmented. They may see what some theorists term fragmented or multiple identities as co-existing within a whole.
- Most people actively dislike the idea that they are the same as everyone else, and will try to differentiate themselves from the masses in some way while at the same time wanting to feel a part of society. This is known as the individuality paradox.
- The media does not exist in a vacuum – it is a part of most people's everyday social reality and not a separate field that they enter and then leave. In order to study the media's contribution to our sense of identity through representations, we need to understand how it fits into people's worlds.
- Media Studies tends to treat audiences as a faceless mass – and even though it is often acknowledged that audiences are made up of individuals with their own tastes and ideas, this only touches the surface. The real issues of complexity of the individual and how that affects the ways they make sense of their media consumption are almost infinite.
- Most people don't actually rate influence from the media all that highly when questioned about influences on their identity, unless the media is specifically mentioned.
- Despite all these issues, the media does influence how we feel about our identities, because it offers us frames of reference and ways of understanding how people fit into society – the stories we tell about ourselves use some of the points of narrative and symbolic reference we gain from the media, even if we find that a hard thing to acknowledge.

KEY TERMS

collective identity	aspects of our identity we share with others
cultural hegemony	described by Gramsci – the process of indoctrination through cultural products of the dominant ideologies in a society
cultural identity	aspects of our identity that are derived from cultural influences such as region, religion or family
hetero-normative	using the perspective of heterosexuals (and therefore omitting alternative perspectives)
ideology	in the context of A level study, dominant ways of thinking in a society shared by many people within it
individuality paradox	a known philosophical quandary in studying identity, that most people wish to simultaneously be seen as an individual while experiencing commonality and social belonging
liberal pluralism	the belief that the mass media offers a range of ideologies that we can choose to accept or reject
manufacture consent	the process, identified by Chomsky, that media institutions persuade audiences of the validity of national policies, particularly military
passive ideological state apparatus	according to Althusser, the function of the mass media in maintaining the status quo
personal identity	identity made up of individual preferences and views
pick and mix theory	David Gauntlett's assertion, comparable with most liberal pluralist views, that audiences simply don't consume aspects of a media product or whole products that don't appeal to them or are not consistent with their sense of self
propaganda model of communication	the sustaining in media profile of a genuinely threatening event for political purposes

KEY THINKER

David Gauntlett	(1971–) formulated ten influential criticisms of media effects theory

CHAPTER SUMMARY

- The study of representation means studying the process of mediation.
- Representations are constructed using other codes, particularly the technical codes of media language and generic and narrative codes.
- The process of reading representations is particular to the individual.
- In reading any representation, we must ask ourselves who or what is being represented, how they are being represented, and why?
- Stuart Hall is a key thinker on the subject, and defined two systems of representation and three approaches commonly taken to it.
- Gender, sexuality, age, race, ethnicity, religion, disability and social class are all interesting areas to explore when considering representations of social groups.
- Abstract ideas, places and time periods can also be represented through media texts.
- Stereotypes are an important aspect of how representations work, but are not simple and need to be examined carefully.
- Stereotypes are not necessarily negative.
- The analysis of representations may be quantitative, where content is analysed for the presence of someone or something, or qualitatively, where the nature of the representation is evaluated more closely.
- Stuart Hall defined three ways in which representations might be understood to work – the reflective, the intentional and the constructionist.
- The codes that play the greatest role in the selection, focusing and combining of representations vary according to the medium in which they appear.
- Social groups and places are commonly represented in the media, but so are abstract ideas and events.
- Counter-types exist in the mass media that can serve to challenge predominant stereotypes.
- Representations are considered by some theorists to have an important ideological function that relates to power relationships in society.
- A large part of many people's identities may be contributed to by the representations that are common in the mass media.
- David Gauntlett explored at length how identities and gender could be linked with the mass media, to find that the role of the mass media in shaping how people explained their identities to others was smaller than might have been expected, and that we need to understand media consumption as an influence on other people's identities in light of the role the media plays in their lives – as a contextual influence.

FURTHER READING

David Gauntlett (2008) *Media, Gender and Identity.*

E.E. Bjornstrom, R.L. Kaufman, R.D. Peterson and M.D. Slater (2010) 'Race and Ethnic Representations of Lawbreakers and Victims in Crime News: A National Study of Television Coverage', *Sociology Problems* 57(2).

Noam Chomsky (1988) *Manufacturing Consent: The Political Economy of the Mass Media.*

Rachel Kowert and Julian Oldmeadow (2012) 'Geek or Chic? Emerging Stereotypes of Online Gamers', *Bulletin of Science Technology & Society* 32(6), https://www.researchgate.net/publication/258127460_Geek_or_Chic_Emerging_Stereotypes_of_Online_Gamers.

Richard Dyer (2002) *The Matter of Images.*

Stuart Hall (2013) *Representation: Cultural Representation and Signifying Practices.*

Tessa Perkins (1979) *Rethinking Stereotypes.*

Chapter 5 Media audiences

5.1 How the media industry targets audiences

Constructing audiences

The media industry is sometimes said to 'construct' audiences. This is an interesting idea, since as audiences we tend to think of ourselves as having free choice over what we consume without really considering that we can only choose from content that is available to us. Often we are subtly steered towards particular content by a whole range of profiling techniques.

Genre is one of the most powerful tools available to media producers in 'constructing' an audience. Genre was originally discussed in the first three chapters from a media language perspective, but is integral to the dynamics that are at play in the relationship between audience, industry and text. Current television schedules seem to be saturated, for example, by reality television and its sub-genres, and it constitutes one of the most popular genres in television viewing today. Television producers have built on the successes of early examples and deliberately refined earlier formats to appeal to a whole range of audiences.

Audiences are not always predictable in their tastes, and ensuring a product is a hit can be challenging. Traditional marketing such as billboards, print advertising, radio and TV spots, and trailers are still important, as is word-of-mouth (including social media), as it increases the audience's sense of having a foreknowledge of the product. This enables the audience to feel as though they identify with the content. Audiences do not, crucially, want to feel targeted. They want to feel as though someone is catering for their needs and desires, not selling them something. Manufacturing this illusion drives the entire marketing machine that shifts a media product from concept to product.

Market research techniques as well as mass media proliferation have both been revolutionised by the advent of digital media and media convergence. Information gathering has become increasingly sophisticated, meaning media producers have better access than ever before to complex data about who is consuming their products. Once a media producer knows who they think their audience is and what similar content they might be consuming, they have to consider carefully how the audience will engage with that product and market it accordingly.

The mass media industries are finding increasingly sophisticated ways to reach the right audience for a particular product. Often, there is a good financial incentive to do so where media industries are driven by a dependence on advertising revenue for their profit. Other subscription-based media products or public service producers, which are not answerable to advertisers, still need to ensure that their products get to the right audience sector in order for people to continue to subscribe, or to justify their reach to trustees or stakeholders.

Publishers of print media in particular have often used demographic information about their audiences to increasingly target them more closely.

There are some common factors used to identify and target audiences that help media producers and advertisers to reach the right people. Some categories initially seem too unwieldy and broad to be useful, but when combined with others can segment the audience powerfully. Producers of mainstream media rather than niche products are most likely to use these, although they are important to anyone who wants to find the 'right' audience.

Age and gender

Age is a significant factor in targeting audiences. A simple way into understanding age-centred targeting is to look at media products that target children. Some large media producers may produce products that cater for quite distinct banded age ranges.

APPLY IT — Produce a report on all the different ways in which mass media products and services are marketed. Do this by considering each media form in turn: radio, television, websites, games, magazines and newspapers.

More detail about how media industries measure their audiences is available in Section '6.2 Distribution and circulation: what they are and why they vary across media'.

EXAMPLE: How the BBC caters for its younger audience

The BBC has two channels that target three different age ranges – CBeebies, which is for three- to six-year-olds, and CBBC, which states its age range to be 7–12. A version of the video on demand (VoD) service iPlayer, containing only the content for these two channels, is available for children to use independently. The age of the child is input into a profile at point of set-up, and this is then used to offer age-appropriate content.

Somewhere around the time of transition to secondary school, tweens and then younger teenagers begin to join their parents in family viewing. Tea-time and early evening pre-watershed viewing on various channels now begins to dominate. Family viewing of big reality contests such as *Strictly Come Dancing*, *Masterchef* and *The Great British Bake-off* is common. Soaps and long-running serial dramas, such as *Eastenders* and *Casualty*, sport and pre-watershed drama series such as the phenomenally successful *Doctor Who* are also popular with this age range. Scheduling is therefore really important when targeting a family audience.

Once teens begin to discover their own identity and interests, it's likely that a lot more of their viewing separates out from that of their parents. Many older teens will also be viewing on their own devices, or in their rooms. At this point, targeted programming for 18- to 34-year-olds is available in the form of BBC3's online-only service, which was controversially withdrawn from standard scheduled broadcasting on 16 February 2016.

The Oldie, a light-hearted magazine for older people

The British Film Institute (BFI) commissioned a survey to explore the effect of age and gender on television genre preferences, which appeared to show that men preferred sports, factual entertainment and culture programmes. Women were found to enjoy more reality television programmes, soaps and chat shows. In some areas though, such as sitcoms, news and wildlife or nature programming, as well as music concerts, no significant gender gaps in viewing were found. For all of these genres, variations were significant in terms of age. This means that gender and genre may both be useful considerations to schedulers looking to cater for a wider range of audience members on their channels.

Children's magazines, particularly those that are film or TV spin-offs, dominate the younger end of the market. As these children move towards teen years, there are a few lifestyle magazines for girls that bridge the gap between adult titles. This readership may also move towards celebrity interest. Many boys by this point will read sports, gaming, music or film titles, depending on their interests. Beyond the fashion, lifestyle and technology titles that appeal to those in their 20s and 30s, there are the hobby and interest magazines that cater for the changes in lifestyle many people experience as they start their own families. Finally, there are the puzzle, craft and hobby, and lifestyle magazines that appeal to those entering a more sedate or leisure-dominated phase of their lives. Some estimates suggest that by 2030 half the adult population will be over the age of 50. Catering for this ageing population in terms of media content will become a more and more lucrative sector. From early childhood to retirement, there is a title for most of us out there.

A clear gender divide can be seen in purchasing patterns in the magazine market and, in terms of primary readership, there is quite clear delineation between the male and female market. The exception to this is the sports rather than fitness sector, where some popular titles that sell worldwide aim to appeal to both genders.

Social class, income, location and political leanings

Social class is a complex area and, just as with age and gender, it is difficult to make broad generalisations. Clear delineations no longer exist in the way that they did a few decades ago. Increased access to education beyond 16 and higher education beyond that for working-class youth initially lead to an expansion of the middle class, but more recently to an increase in educated adults doing jobs that no longer fit comfortably into old definitions of working-class or middle-class jobs, some of which are lower income – for example call centre work and IT services.

Daytime television is viewed not only by pensioners and non-working mothers, but also a significant number of unemployed men and women. Another group it reaches is people who are unable to work due to illness or disability. People who work part-time or from home may also participate in daytime viewing. The advertising carried by some channels during the daytime, consisting of many for domestic products and services of interest to retired people, does suggest the first of these two groups forms a large part of the audience, but their needs are actually very varied. This shows how careful we must be before making any generalisations about who consumes a particular form of media.

Some sectors of the mass media face criticism for being focused on the interests of people living in the south-east of the UK, and ignoring the issues and interests of people living in other parts, where there may be subtle but important cultural differences. Income is also a factor in targeting audiences. The cover price of a magazine may be a significant factor in an audience's purchasing decisions. It does not necessarily follow that the more expensive a product or service is, the wealthier the uptake of the target audience who consume it. Some families on a lower income may choose to spend a significant proportion of their money on, for example, a comprehensive satellite subscription package, because it represents good value for money for something the whole family can enjoy.

One of the places in the media industry where the divide in social class is still quite apparent is in national newspaper readership. Traditionally divided into tabloids and broadsheets, there is a clear link between readership of traditional tabloids such as the *Daily Mirror* and the *Sun* and the 'quality' tabloids such as the *Daily Mail* and the *Daily Express*. These have a majority working-class and retired working-class readership. Content is matched accordingly with the perceived interests of the social class, with a heavier focus on entertainment, domestic and soft news stories. Traditional broadsheets such as the *Guardian*, *The Times* and the *Daily Telegraph* tend to be read by a more middle-class audience, who may have a stronger interest in current affairs, international news and the hard news stories. Soft news tends to be relegated to supplements and in most cases appears mainly in weekend editions: the weekend being a traditional time for leisure in the middle-class lifestyle.

EXAMPLE: Crossing class boundaries with the *i*

An interesting development in the traditional notion of social class being signified and even in part constructed by newspaper owners, was the introduction of the *i*. Defying the odds in a culture where traditional newspapers are all experiencing a decline in circulation of their print editions, the *i* has been very successful. Originally produced by the politically middle-ground newspaper the *Independent* and now owned by Johnston Press, the *i* has appealed to both working-class and middle-class audiences, with its blend of contemporary layout, mixed selection of news, lack of strong political bias and moderately in-depth reporting. Crucially, it also has a cheap cover price.

Star appeal

Celebrities have become increasingly valued by audiences, and their correct placement on the cover of a magazine or as host of a new game show can make or break that edition or series. A whole self-sustaining sector of the mass media has sprung up around the manufacture of celebrities and the provision of 'news' about traditional celebrities such as film and television stars, sports personalities and artists from the music industry. Buying in the services of the right celebrity with the right image for a media product has now become a must for whole sectors of the media.

Celebrity endorsement is a highly valued aspect of marketing for many big brands. Television channel proliferation and the continuing popularity of the reality television genre have created an unending appetite for new reality stars, although many find their fame is ephemeral. Celebrities have become far more visible in politics and charitable causes, their views echoed by fans sharing them many thousands of times.

Ethnicity

Ethnicity is a consideration for targeting audiences in the UK, with contemporary producers in some sectors becoming more aware of cultural distinctiveness and consumption preferences among sections of their audience. Some traditional research into ethnicity and the mass media is problematic, because it often comes from a white ethnocentric approach, which can draw conclusions that have more to do with preconceptions about a culture than the reality of the varied cultural diversity and readings within it.

Targeting an ethnic group does not necessarily mean providing ethnic minorities with access to imported satellite or cable shows from their own culture, or the publication of newspapers such as *Eastern Eye* and lifestyle magazines such as

Black Beauty and Hair. It also involves considering which kinds of mainstream programming are appealing to different cultural groups as part of the wider audience, and increasing that share of the market by making subtle changes to content and representations to make them more socially inclusive and appealing to a broader audience.

The cast of *Neighbours* in the 1990s.

One ethnographic study (Mary Gillespie, 1995) found that in Southall, London, in the early 1990s, the Australian soap opera *Neighbours* was popularly viewed by young people of both genders from the Punjabi community. Although highly specific and narrow in its range, Gillespie's study seemed to suggest that despite having a distinct set of cultural influences, which differed from those of the white, culturally British teenagers around them, there were still plenty of pleasures in the text for this group. These included accessing the 'other', offering reference groups of families, and seeing a small distinct community of people confronted with challenges and resolving difficulties.

The 'reader'

To help them to promote their publication to advertisers, most magazines include in their **press packs** information about their market share – its size, nature, interests of readers and so on. By regularly commissioning polls of their subscribers, the magazine industry is able to discern its readership, and draw logical conclusions about the content that will keep them buying and continue to generate advertising revenue.

EXAMPLE: *GQ* magazine's press pack

GQ refers to itself in its press pack as:

> *the only brand in Britain dedicated to bringing together the very best in men's fashion, style, investigative journalism, comment, lifestyle and entertainment. GQ is the go-to brand for discerning, affluent men, delivering award-winning content across multiple platforms: in print, digital, online and social.*

LUXURY INFLUENCERS

INFLUENCERS

85% of readers are passionate about **sharing** their knowledge and **47%** regularly write blogs/reviews online

97% of readers and 83% of GQ.co.uk users have influenced others to **purchase their recommendations**

89% of readers have **researched** products and 88% have **bought** or plan to buy products they've seen in GQ

STYLE INVESTORS

92% of readers own **designer fashion** and 87% of GQ.co.uk users agree 'Fashion & grooming are an **integral** part of my lifestyle'

Collectively, the GQ audience have spent **£800 million** on fashion in the last 12 months.

VANGUARD

GQ's online audience are **40%** more likely to be **'High Net Worth City Workers'** who are **64%** more likely to be **early adopters** of technology.

Source: The GQ Portfolio Survey 2015 (based on regular GQ readers). Hitwise (based on 4 rolling week data ending 16th September 2017). The GQ Style Survey 2015.

GQ

Psychographics and lifestyle profiling

A highly influential method for targeting people by their lifestyle attributes and ways of thinking about purchases was developed by US-based advertising agency Young and Rubicam. The model was based on Maslow's hierarchy of needs, a well-known system already exploited by advertisers to better understand people's priorities when purchasing consumer goods or services. According to the hierarchy of needs, humans value basic physiological requirements for survival first – as these are met, they are free to strive for more motivational needs to do with their personal growth and sense of fulfilment.

Young and Rubicam's model developed this further, creating seven categories that fully describe the consumer market. It became known as cross-cultural consumer categorisation, or the 4Cs.

The system grouped consumers by psychological approach to lifestyle. Understanding people by segmenting them into these groups makes targeting advertising much easier. Rather than trying to appeal to everyone, advertisers can instead have a stronger focus on the people with the qualities who are most likely to buy their product. Young and Rubicam's model has been highly influential and adopted by many advertising agencies worldwide, but it is used alongside other market research. The qualities of consumers are summarised in the following grid:

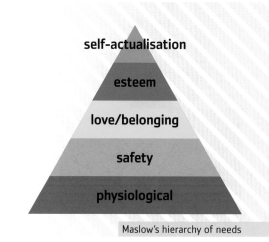

Maslow's hierarchy of needs

Consumer category		Summary of qualities
	Explorer	• Needs discovery, challenge and new frontiers • Often the first to try out new ideas and experiences • Respond to brands that offer new sensations, indulgence and instant effects • Their core need in life is for discovery
	Aspirer	• Materialistic, acquisitive people, who are driven by others' perceptions of them • Respond to what others perceive as being superficial: image, appearance, persona, charisma and fashion • Packaging is important to them • Their core need in life is for status
	Succeeder	• Possess self-confidence, have a strong goal orientation and tend to be very organised • Tend to occupy positions of responsibility • Often seek out the best • Their core need in life is for control
	Reformer	• Value their own independent judgement • The most anti-materialistic of the seven groups, often perceived as intellectual • They are socially aware, and pride themselves on tolerance • Their core need in life is for enlightenment
	Mainstreamer	• People who live in the world of the domestic and the everyday • Largest group of people within 4Cs across the world • Respond to big established brands, to 'family' brands and to offers of value for money • Their core need in life is for security

	Struggler	• Live for today, and make few plans for tomorrow • Heavy consumers of alcohol and junk food • Visual impact and physical sensation are an important element of their brand choices • Their core need is for escape
	Resigned	• Predominantly older people with constant, unchanging values built up over time • Respect institutions and enjoy acting in traditional roles. Their brand choices are driven by a need for safety and economy • Their core need is to survive

Source: Young and Rubicam's booklet, available online at www.pdf-archive.com/2016/10/20/4cs/4cs.pdf.

You can probably work out which group or groups you and your family and friends fit into by reading the descriptions, but it's worth noting that most of us are a blend of different categories – or we may even fit into different categories for different products. The categories work by thinking through consumers' needs, from the most basic connected with safety to the things that are desirable, the things we can attain if all our other needs are satisfied. This means we could fit anywhere between from 'survival' and 'security' to 'control' and 'enlightenment'. These qualities are mapped to the categories according to what people's greatest needs are – someone who would count as having reached a point where they feel 'enlightened' would be characterised as a reformer, whereas someone who is a struggler would be needing to 'escape'.

News values

All news sources have their own **news agendas**. These dictate the stories that receive top priority in the broadcast, edition or site/app. Work conducted by Galtung and Ruge in the 1960s still informs much of our understanding of why particular stories are considered newsworthy across media forms today.

Some of these news values can even be adapted to specific sectors such as entertainment magazines, celebrity magazines, fashion and trend-based websites, and so on, whose agendas may be quite different from a mainstream news provider's. News providers of all kinds select the news that they believe to be most relevant to their audiences in order to maintain them. This is sometimes offset against the demands of ownership and control as well as advertisers.

For more on ownership and control see section '6.3 Issues of ownership and control'.

A news room

An introduction to news values	
1 Negativity	'Hard' news – bad news will almost always be prioritised. The worse the news, the higher up the news agenda it will be placed.
2 Proximity	Things that happen close to home (domestic news) or that involve people from close to home in global events are seen as important.
3 Recency	'This just in' – the scramble by news channels to report events as they happen.
4 Currency	The 'value' of a story. If a story is seen as valuable for other reasons, it will continue to be reported on even though not much new might be happening.
5 Continuity	Stories that are likely to continue for a long period of time.
6 Simplicity	The easier a story is to understand the better – or an angle will be found on a story to make it easier to understand.

7 Personality	Often 'soft' news surrounds personalities in whom the public have an interest, such as the Royal Family, celebrities, e.g. actors and singers, and sportspeople.
8 Uniqueness	If a story is unusual or surprising.
9 Expectedness	Includes diary events – things that particularly happen at a certain time of year – as well as stories that match public expectations because of previous similar events.
10 Elite nations/ people	Western societies such as European countries and the USA will tend to dominate the news above developing countries and places perceived as having a very different culture from our own. Politicians and other prominent people in our society such as the owners of large businesses or managers of important organisations also receive a lot of coverage.
11 Exclusivity	When a news channel or programme has footage or interviews that are not yet in possession of others. Citizen journalism can contribute to this.
12 Threshold	How many people are impacted on a by an event – its size.

APPLY IT

Look at an edition of a gaming magazine such as *Playstation* magazine, and a celebrity news magazine such as *Heat*. Can the traditional model of news values help you understand the way in which they select content for their readership?

What other factors have to be considered when selecting editorial that might impact less upon traditional news media outlets?

KEY TERMS

British Film Institute	(BFI) organisation that promotes the work of British cinema and studies cinema as a pastime among British people
celebrity endorsement	the process by which a celebrity is paid to become the face of a brand. This might include appearing in advertisements, using the brand in high-profile places, being a spokesperson for the brand
cross-cultural consumer categorisation	system developed by Young and Rubicam to categorise consumers outside of the usual factors. Also referred to as psychographics
demographics	studying how populations may consume the media in different ways according to where they live
ethnocentrism	seeing an issue from the perspective of your own cultural heritage – usually refers to a white European perspective
hard news	news that focuses exclusively on serious issues relating to domestic or world events
Maslow's hierarchy of needs	pyramid-based model offering a hierarchical visualisation of human needs

media convergence	the coming together of many aspects of media businesses, including commercial, technological and cultural
news agenda	the priority given to particular news items by a news organisation
press pack	information released by a company to promote its work, often to prospective investors or advertisers
profiling techniques	ways by which media producers discern their target audience
scheduling	in traditional television viewing, choosing the optimal time of broadcast to reach the highest potential target audience
soft news	news that can be seen as focusing mainly on entertainment or celebrity-focused stories
supplements	extra inserts to newspapers that tend to have a specific focus; issued particularly at weekends or on a certain day of the week. May be themed by finance, business, arts or other categories

Young and Rubicam	one of the biggest advertising agencies in the world, established in New York in 1927

5.2 The impact of new technologies on patterns of media consumption

For a fuller discussion of mass media convergence, see section '6.3 Issues of ownership and control'.

Media audiences are changing. The way people use the media, the content of the media they are consuming, the access they have to the media and the devices they consume it through have all undergone rapid change with the technological and digital revolution and convergence in media technologies, where the social and cultural uses of technologies, the businesses who run them, as well as the ways we access them, increasingly combine in new and interesting ways.

Celebrity status has become within reach of ordinary audience members more than ever before. YouTube in particular acts as a showcase for talent or notoriety, which sometimes translates into a mainstream media career, albeit often short-lived. Celebrities are expected to engage with audiences on social media, and barely a day goes past without the reposting in the gossip columns of some misdemeanour on social media, the escape of some inappropriate material, or a row breaking out on Twitter.

The *Ofcom Communications Market Report* in 2011 used the term 'solus media use' to define media consumption where the consumer was wholly focused on one form. For example, it used to be commonplace for someone to watch a television programme giving it their full attention. It is much more likely now they are dipping in and out of the action, while connected to social media or even playing a computer game. Computer gaming technology has been one of the fields to really harness and integrate the social aspects of digital media, including massive multi-online roleplaying games (MMORPGs).

It is understood by most people today that the historical barrier that existed between media industries and their audiences no longer has the same clear boundaries. It would be pleasing to think that new technologies have increased the right to reply for the audience, but this does come at a cost. The reality is that it is still the companies themselves who benefit the most from the digital age, garnering huge swathes of marketing information from people's online behaviours, and making the most of their presence there to expose them to greater quantities of advertising than ever before. Audiences can literally make their own media, but generally on the terms of those who host and control the platforms that they use – and those terms generally involve advertising.

Technological determinism is a complex field of thinking that is explored more in the *AQA A Level Media Studies Year 2* book, but it is a very useful consideration when thinking about changes in our leisure time. The theory suggests that technological progress – particularly the development of the internet and faster connections – develops independently of most other cultural influences. The thinking follows that we then experience a kind of forced uptake of a particular technology, which can then change the direction of human development, whether for better or for worse. Certainly, our access to such technologies has changed the way in which we consume the media forever. Critics would argue, however, that users of technologies assimilate them culturally, and that the ways in which inventions are actually used are determining our behaviours and actions.

Globalisation

Globalisation began more than 100 years ago with the invention of the telegraph and improvements in the worldwide infrastructure of transportation. Although the origins of the idea are old, the term today often refers to the increasing technological, economic and communications-based interconnectedness of the global community that has mainly resulted from the **digital revolution**. Another term widely used to refer to this is the **global village**, first coined by media and

APPLY IT

Produce a single-page infographic showing how technological advances have impacted on media consumption.

What advantages and disadvantages do you believe changes in media consumption have brought about in society? Produce a bullet pointed pros and cons list. Make sure you consider both local and global audiences. Do certain technologies disadvantage some and benefit others? Do people within populations have different views on technology? How many issues do technology and the mass media touch on that relate to other areas of people's lives?

communication theorist **Marshall McLuhan** in the 1960s. Globalisation has had a clear effect on media consumers. Not only has technological connectivity given us more choice in how we spend our leisure time, it has also provided us with rapid access to mass media production from other countries – most notably a sharp increase in the uptake of US-produced content.

For more on the impact of globalisation on the media industry, see section '6.2 Distribution and circulation: what they are and why they vary across media'.

Print media

The magazine sector has had to adjust to numerous changes. A standard publishing profile for a major magazine will now include digital editions, some of which are subscriber only, some of which are free, on a website, tablet or mobile, and produce videos as well as maintaining a strong social media presence. This is in addition to the print edition. Newspapers have struggled to maintain income from their circulation, and some have moved to either online web subscriptions and paid apps, or open content that generates revenue from clicks on advertising.

EXAMPLE: How newspaper publishers are adapting to the digital climate

The *Daily Telegraph* and the *Guardian* are both traditional broadsheet newspapers, but have responded quite differently to the challenges of freely available digital news.

The *Daily Telegraph* was the first UK news provider to launch an online version in 1994. *My Telegraph* is a feature of the site, where users can sign up to have a blog hosted and connect with other readers. The online version is not free to view in its entirety, and requires a subscription to access all content. There are various packages available, but one that includes web access, e-reader and tablet access, rewards and giveaways plus the print edition currently costs around £470 annually.

The *Guardian* makes all of their online content, including archived news stories, free and have a policy of equal and open access to their website. In the UK, the popularity of the *Guardian* online is challenged only by the *Mail Online*. Like its tabloid competitor, the *Guardian* has a strong culture of allowing moderated comments and discussion by audience on some of its content. A similar digital and print subscription to the package offered by the *Telegraph* costs around £390 per year. A much cheaper app-only subscription can be purchased, which simply eliminates advertising.

Television

The ease with which video files can now be uploaded online has led to an explosion in piracy, which affects television producers as well as film copyright owners. The major change most consumers have experienced in recent years is a move away from traditional scheduled viewing, and increased use of **VoD**. The growth in the DVD box set and use of physical media to record in the home has slowed with the availability of **digital locker** systems and VoD services. Binge viewing has increased as an audience practice, leading producers to concentrate on high-budget and extremely immersive and lengthy series that are increasingly cinematic in style. Back catalogues of all kinds of classic programming are increasingly available to audiences thus broadening the popular cultural and generational experience of the mass media. Audience expectations of high-budget, computer-generated imaging (CGI) effects in television shows continue to grow. The vast range of competing VoD services gives audiences more choice and increased convenience.

Radio

The main changes to radio are connected with digital broadcasting and the increase in both public service and commercial stations away from standard broadcasting. Audiences not only have more listening choice, but are in some cases also able to choose programmes to listen to again at their leisure. Podcasting is another significant growth area that continues to maintain a small but often devoted audience. This was caused in part by the development of MP3 players, meaning offline broadcasting was available for people to listen to anytime, anywhere. Streamed radio is also now much more common, and interactivity has become a key feature of modern radio, which has embraced the dynamics it offers.

Video on the web

Video upload sites are an entirely new feature of the digital age. They have allowed audiences to make and upload their own content and run their own channels. This has revolutionised not only the way in which younger media users spend their time, but also the whole relationship between the producers of media and their audiences. Many of the styles associated with short video production borrowed from amateur producers of videos continue to influence mainstream media organisations operating in digital spaces.

Gaming

Gaming is one of the areas that, because it is entirely driven by technological and communications advancements and has no legacy form, sees the most technological changes. The gaming industry has a high degree of crossover in effects technology development with the film industry. One of the major developments in gaming has been the increase in communal gaming and the interconnectivity of players over broadband connections. Gaming has become much more of a social pastime, with gamers on major platforms using headsets to communicate with each other. The gaming industry is also at the forefront of virtual reality (VR) development and sets. These are revolutionising the game experience, and are likely to continue to be a huge growth sector in the near future. Another significant area is augmented reality games, which blend elemnts of the real world with graphical information that is artificially generated.

EXAMPLE: The 2016 craze for Pokémon Go

In July 2016, an augmented reality app called Pokémon Go became the latest version of a game that has had various incarnations on different consoles since 1996. The game encouraged users to 'catch' various Pokémon characters, which were positioned in various real-world locations using GPS. The app was free on both IOS and Android platforms, and was widely downloaded. It caused a temporary spike in negative media reportage of related issues such as muggings at 'Pokestops' to instances of careless driving by people using them while in control of a vehicle.

The personalisation of news and other digital media content

News delivery is rapidly changing. News apps for phone and tablet allow people to effectively have more control over the news they consume – partially setting their own news agenda. The set-up in news apps allows users to tailor the content they want to see.

Many other websites, viewing services, producers using social media platforms to distribute content and so on also use information stored about their users to profile their use and offer similar content that might be of interest to the audience. Personalisation of content is therefore one of the most successful developments in connecting a wealth of content to the audience it appeals to the most. Clicking on suggested content refines this process and allows more precise targeting of the audience. This is one clear way in which the digital media audience is clearly constructed. Cookies and web tracking are used to follow audiences around the internet, with advertising spaces on subsequent sites filled personally with content from previously visited sites.

EXAMPLE: The BBC news app

The BBC news app for tablets and phones allows selection from numerous categories, providing a great deal of opportunity for personalisation. Here are some recently listed examples:

TOP STORIES | UK | ENGLAND | NORTHERN IRELAND (and other regions) | MEDIA | EDUCATION AND FAMILY | PARENTING | CHILDREN | SCIENCE | SPACE EXPLORATION | HEALTH | MENTAL HEALTH | NUTRITION | FILM | PHYSICS | ENTREPRENEURSHIP | FILM | MOST POPULAR | BUSINESS | TECHNOLOGY | MOST WATCHED | SCIENCE AND ENVIRONMENT | ENTERTAINMENT AND ARTS | SPORTS

APPLY IT

Choose three digital services and/or websites that you visit or use regularly. Write a 300-word report on how their content is personalised for you as a consumer.

KEY TERMS

digital locker	system whereby a television show or film is purchased (sometimes as a physical copy) but also exists for that buyer to watch on other devices	globalisation	the increased interconnectivity of businesses and cultures worldwide
digital revolution	sweeping changes brought about by the internet and advances in digital technology	technological determinism	the idea that technological advances dictate the path societies take
global village	term coined by Marshall McLuhan in the 1960s to describe the impact of media technologies on global culture	VoD	video on demand – any service where users can choose what they want to view and when

Marshall McLuhan (1911–1980) photographed in 1945

5.3 How audiences read the media

The ways in which we understand how media audiences make sense of the media products they consume have changed over time, and this is an issue that is widely discussed among academics. The following section will give you an overview of thinking in this area of Media Studies, and allow you to explore some of what each approach offers when applied to contemporary and historical media consumption. Key thinkers in the field and their approaches are simply explained here. This will make it easy to select an appropriate theory to study the relationship between media audiences and their consumption.

Effects theory

Approaches that explore the effect media have on audiences are known collectively as the **effects theory**. In the early days of the mass media, much study of the supposed effects centred on anxieties regarding the changes in society and leisure time brought about by widespread access to media consumption. The earliest of these is the **hypodermic needle model**, which considered the relationship between audiences and media content to be a simple case of the direct inception of ideas from media texts into the ideologies of the audience. This approach views audiences almost like sponges, absorbing ideologies passively from the media they consumed and engaging with them very little. These theories are associated with neo-Marxism, which we encountered in Chapter 4.

The **two-step flow** model of communication followed in the 1950s, which suggested that, rather than taking the mass media at face value, people have their interpretation of it formed by opinion leaders – people who reinterpret the mass media's messages who are trusted by the audience. Although treated with caution by subsequent theorists, the two-step flow of communication is quite useful in a limited way in explaining the campaigning by some celebrities or other prominent people in society about a certain political issue on social media.

Effects theories are **passive audience theories** – in other words, they tend to assume a connection between media consumption and behaviour in the real world. Many examples exist of this assumption being made, and apparent links between violent acts in the real world and specific media texts thought to have been consumed by those who are responsible are a mainstay of tabloid news stories. Effects theory often assumes that popular/mass culture is inferior to high culture and art, and as such could have a pernicious effect on its individual consumers and society as a whole.

The problem has always been that this is difficult to prove. It is very hard to separate the mass media from other influences. One of the other issues is that effects theory-based interpretations of social violence can contribute to **moral panics**. Some of the original research was politically conservative; researchers often already suspected the media to have a negative influence on society, and were therefore looking for evidence that supported this assumption.

Audiences have also become much more sophisticated in the time that has elapsed since the original studies, and could be assumed to be better educated and more media-literate than their counterparts two or three generations ago.

Orson Welles broadcasting his adaptation of H.G. Wells' *The War of the Worlds*.

For more on these theories see section '4.5 The ideological nature of common media representations and how we respond to them'.

EXAMPLE: *The War of the Worlds* radio dramatisation

One of the most famous examples of media effects was the 1938 broadcast of Orson Welles' radio adaptation of *The War of the Worlds*. The programme was clearly announced as a drama, but some people were still panicked by its presentation as a series of seemingly live news bulletins reporting on an alien invasion.

This was not the first time such a technique had been used, with both the UK and Australia having used similar formats for dramas as early as the 1920s, which were credited by Welles as an influence, but the resulting fear caused a public outcry.

Assurance in the validity of media effects theory is behind much of the censorship of the mass media worldwide. The fear that a culture will be negatively impacted on by outside influences, or that the mass media might cause unrest in a population that has become in some way dissatisfied with their conditions of living, is a valid one. Even censors in some Westernised countries are mindful of exposure of audiences to taboo acts or violence. Interestingly, what is acceptable to censors will still see slight cultural differences from place to place.

Despite some of the problems, it would be wrong to suggest that the mass media has no effect at all on people who consume it. Positive effects of the mass media are studied far less, yet they certainly exist. Think of the central BBC remit and its educational component. How could the media educate and inform if it had no effect on its audience? How could telethons raise money for charitable causes? And what about other 'neutral' media effects, such as the transmission of cultural ideas such as fashions?

For more on media consumption see section '6.5 How our media consumption is regulated in the UK'.

EXAMPLE: The Belstaff Millford coat

The Belstaff Millford coat worn by Benedict Cumberbatch in *Sherlock* sold out rapidly following the first broadcast of the series. *GQ* magazine ran a series of online articles about the sourcing of the mainly British clothing brands worn by the two actors in the show. How do we explain the spike in sales of a coat worn by a particular actor in a drama series following its broadcast if the media had no effect at all on the audience?

Another exploration of media effects that seeks to interpret audience behaviours in the real world and their connections with the media is cultivation theory.

Social learning theory, Albert Bandura

Social learning theory was one of the earliest theories surrounding media consumption. It was derived in the early 1960s primarily from the experiments conducted by **Albert Bandura**. From his famous Bobo doll experiment (where children in a controlled lab setting appeared to re-enact violent acts they had just seen on-screen on a doll) Bandura concluded that children who viewed violent content on television or film might well go on to behave violently in the real world. This is called social learning, because it suggests that children 'learned' violent behaviour vicariously from the actions they saw on-screen. The study became well-known, and appeared to validate fears many social commentators already had about the effect of television. It still carries weight today, despite there being issues with the methodology.

Social learning theory is a little more complex than this element of the study might suggest. Bandura acknowledged that other processes also contribute to behaviours. In the real world, it is difficult to establish whether individuals with other social problems may seek out violent texts and have preference for these, rather than the viewing of violent texts causing a behaviour.

Social learning theory tends to be brought out to justify criminal or deviant acts and blame the mass media as a main influence in these, but the positive effects of social learning theory as applied to the media are rarely heard about. Social learning theory is observable in action in the **Sabido method**, which has been deployed in many developing countries to help change attitudes to gender and homosexuality,

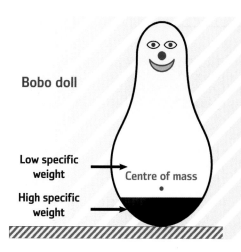

Bobo doll

Low specific weight → Centre of mass

High specific weight

A mini-project exploring social learning theory

Research examples of contemporary outcries about media texts and their supposed influence over events or people in the real world. Create a timeline of events, criminal acts or moral panics that have been linked causally to mass media consumption.

Research the Bobo doll experiment. What problems can you either identify yourself, or what criticisms can you find, of the conclusions gained from it?

Find out more about Miguel Sabido and his influence in the educational programming sector around the world. Create a slide presentation explaining his method and give five examples of the method in action.

For a more developed explanation of Barthes and his theory of myth see section '1.3 Narrative organisation in print media texts'.

George Gerbner (1919–2005)

give populations information about sexual health, reduce class prejudice (the caste system in India) and promote literacy. This is achieved by carefully populating casts and storylines with positive and negative role models who change very little and are repeatedly rewarded or punished in the narrative. Transitional characters are also included, who have experiences and test out ideas, in a sense representing the audience themselves.

EXAMPLE: The Sabido method in action

In Afghanistan during 1994, the Taliban tried to ban a popular BBC World Service drama called *New Home, New Life*. The soap promoted women's rights, and also taught safe conduct around areas that were heavily land-mined. Follow-up studies showed a decrease in the number of injuries and deaths caused by landmines in areas where people could access the broadcast. Banning the soap proved to be nearly impossible, since a number of Taliban senior figures were also said to be gripped by the popular series.

In another example, a group in the US, called the Hollywood, Health and Society, works in an advisory capacity with mainstream US dramas such as *House* and *Gray's Anatomy* to support accurate portrayal and raise awareness of issues in storylines.

For more information and examples, see the BBC article 'How Soap Operas Changed the World' (Hegarty, 2012).

Cultivation theory – George Gerbner

The work of **George Gerbner** in the 1970s was interesting because it explored violence and crime on television for slightly different more perceptual reasons. Gerbner's team of researchers considered television to be the foremost influence in modern people's lives, ahead of religion and the state. Their research appeared to show that the more hours of television people watched, the greater their belief that America was a violent and dangerous place. Television appeared to be literally 'cultivating' their ideologies and beliefs, acting as a form of socialisation and aligning them with the world they saw on television. It is also known as **enculturation**. This is a highly problematic finding, when you consider that news values dictate that higher priority should be given to the most shocking stories. Fictional storylines containing violence are clearly not representing reality in any kind of straightforward way and should be taken at face value. Barthes' concept of myth can be used to enhance your understanding of this issue.

The other finding of the study was that television appeared to be moulding people's understanding of issues and people around them, rather than real experience of life. This was termed by Gerbner as **mainstreaming** – a mainly political effect whereby people exposed to similar messages and viewpoints regularly on television find their own ideologies and those perpetuated in televisual texts beginning to synchronise, therefore affirming their views and shared symbolic language. Mainstreaming is also very useful to advertisers for economic reasons, since it means that brand and product awareness appear to take hold relatively easily in the minds of people who have frequent and lengthy exposure to television.

Another effect Gerbner identified was **resonance**. In the case of resonance, people find examples of aspects of their own lives that appear to correlate with what they see on television. This has an amplifying effect on perceptions of the world around them, where their own experiences, thoughts and feelings about society appear to be congruous with what they see on television. This can result in **mean world syndrome**, where people believe the world to be a more dangerous place than they actually experience in reality.

Gerbner's work has remained very influential. Although it was television that was the original subject of his research, his ideas have become extremely useful for studying digital media, which among younger members of society could be considered to have an even stronger influence than television. Social media and computer gaming are particularly interesting areas to explore using some of Gerbner's ideas.

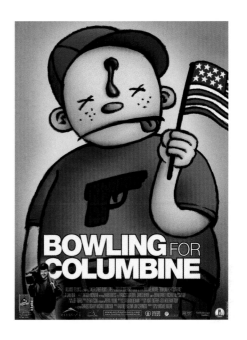

EXAMPLE: Bowling for Columbine

Michael Moore's 2000 documentary, *Bowling for Columbine*, is almost a visual essay exploring Gerbner's and Bandura's ideas. Moore is a left-wing documentarian, known for his outspoken critiques of US society. In the documentary, Moore explores how moral panics, attitudes to race, perceptions of personal safety and gun violence can all be influenced by the mass media.

Moore claims that simple myths and a culture of fear and exclusion perpetuated in the mass media seem to have a real impact on the quality of people's lives, and that the absence of views other than the mainstream can be harmful to people who feel disenfranchised from society. At the same time, he refutes an absolute cause and effect link between media consumption and violent acts, arguing that other influences such as government policies and deep cultural beliefs in the US such as the right to bear arms are neglected since the media is an easy target.

Desensitisation and compassion fatigue

Desensitisation occurs when a media audience is repeatedly exposed to shocking or violent content. **Compassion fatigue** is when a person repeatedly subjected to a situation or media content that would usually elicit an empathetic response ceases to be affected to the same degree. It can be caused by repeated exposure to either fiction or fact-based media. In a sense, compassion fatigue and other forms of desensitisation could be thought of as a defence mechanism. The human mind seeks to protect itself from things it finds disturbing or difficult to process in the face of continual exposure.

Both desensitisation and compassion fatigue are phenomena that appear to support cultivation theory, since they both involve a lessening of emotional or empathetic response to seeing traumatic events played out in mass media consumption. Whether either phenomenon would apply to real-world experience of these events is difficult to prove.

EXAMPLE: Desensitisation and compassion fatigue in routine television consumption

Suicide bombings used to be considered shocking in the West. The increased frequency of their occurrence as well as an increase in the level of 24-hour news reportage could cause the audience to care less for the victims, as well as dropping the story down news agendas.

Our fictional television consumption has also contributed towards our increasing acceptance of violence, with shows such as *The Walking Dead* and *American Horror Story* regularly borrowing from the body horror iconography of the horror film genre.

Criticisms of media effects – David Gauntlett

David Gauntlett is a contemporary academic who has studied a range of issues surrounding mass media consumption. Some of his early work centred on critiquing social learning effects theories in particular, which he believed assume a simplistic cause and effect relationship between the media consumed and behaviour in the real world.

APPLY IT

Write a 500-word case study on an aspect of digital media of your choice. Apply and evaluate the range of media effects theories you have just read, and discuss how useful or influential they might be in informing public opinions about digital media.

Three of his criticisms of effects theory can be summarised as follows:

1 Effects theory historically tended to focus on fictional media texts when looking at violence in particular. It is assumed that fictional texts have a greater influence over audience behaviour than non-fiction forms of visual media such as the news or documentaries. This is clearly not the case – think, for example, of how television news coverage might contribute to the radicalisation of a young European-born teen and their indoctrination into a far-right group or Islamic fundamentalism.

2 Effects theory has 'flawed methodologies' – Gauntlett suggests that many of the experiments such as the Bobo doll experiment simply do not scientifically prove the separation of the mass media from other influences and cannot measure this. Bandura himself was aware that subjects' learning from what they saw on-screen was only one part of acquired behaviours, but perhaps viewed it as more powerful.

3 When questioned, many people hold a widespread belief that violence in media texts affects other people in a potentially dangerous way, but not themselves. This suggests that the vast majority of people can consume computer games or films with 18-rated content without exhibiting any subsequent signs of social deviance – so something else is clearly contributing when a tragedy occurs.

When you are studying the relationship between the mass media and its supposed effects on audiences, remember that you can only ever really identify an effect as a possibility. Make sure you learn the cases for and against the various approaches to studying media effects, and apply these to your own discussion.

Active theories of audience

A decreasing suspicion of the potentially negative impact of an expanding mass media on society by the 1970s led to a change in the way in which the relationship between audiences and the media was understood. This made way for the development of more active theories of audience.

Uses and gratifications theory – Jay G. Blumler and Elihu Katz

The early work conducted by **Jay Blumler and Elihu Katz** on television viewing led to the development of one of the first widely recognised active theories of audience: the **uses and gratifications theory**. This theory considered that audiences might not be passively consuming television, but instead were using it in some way – gaining social uses and psychological gratifications from it. The theory regarded television in particular to contributing in a positive way to people's personal and social lives. It famously divided these into four main groups:

Elihu Katz (1926–)

- **Diversion** – this correlates with most people's understanding of the mass media as a form of escapism from the stresses and strains of daily life.

- **Personal identity** – the media was believed to supply people with role models, and ways of understanding their own place in society.

- **Social relationships** – many people seemed to gain an element of sociability through the media. People discussed television shows with each other, giving the act of viewing a socially cohesive function. People often showed an enthusiasm and liking for particular performers and presenters and enjoyed the sense of familiarity they felt with them.

- **Surveillance** – the mass media contributed to people being informed about the world around them through the viewing of news and current affairs, and the consumption of documentary programmes, as well as enjoying keeping up to date with entertainment trends.

EXAMPLE: The application of uses and gratifications theory to four popular British TV shows broadcast in 1979

Diversion – *The Paul Daniels Magic Show* wowed audiences with a glittering presentation of magic tricks, transporting them from the everyday grind. The magic, if not the ratings, was to last until 1994.

Personal identity – *Top of the Pops* celebrated the tribalism and vibrant presence of the UK's popular music scene, with the show peaking at its highest ever viewing figure of 19,000,000 in this year.

Social relationships – generations and workforces were brought together in their shared enjoyment of the second series of much-loved situation comedy *Fawlty Towers* (right), which enjoyed numerous re-runs despite a total of only 12 episodes ever being made.

Surveillance – *Brass Tacks*, a current affairs documentary series, investigated issues close to the heart of the British public. This year saw the broadcast of one of its most famous and influential episodes, 'Are the Kids Alright?'

The uses and gratifications theory still has currency today, and is often used by media students to understand media content it was not specifically designed for, since the approach is transferable to other aspects of the mass media. An interesting expansion of uses and gratifications can be found in Arthur Asa Berger's *Media Analysis Techniques* (2011). Berger develops the model to include further sub-categories of more specific pleasures that may be gained from mass media consumption.

These include to:

- satisfy curiosity and be informed
- be amused
- identify with the deity and divine
- reinforce belief in justice
- reinforce belief in romantic love
- participate vicariously in history
- see villains in action
- experience the ugly
- find models to imitate
- experience the beautiful.

Many other researchers have gone on to identify the uses and gratifications for contemporary media device usage such as mobile phones, social media sites and so on. This is a very interesting growth area for media students to explore.

Utopian solutions – Richard Dyer

In his 1992 book *Only Entertainment*, Richard Dyer suggests that, far from being trivial pastimes, most forms of popular entertainment have a great deal of value to the individuals consuming them, helping them to regulate for themselves some of the 'problems' inherent in modern life.

One of the frameworks developed by Dyer, which can be used to understand any form of contemporary media consumption, is his theory of utopian solutions. It develops our instinctive understanding that the mass media offers us escapism from our daily lives. As the name suggests, Dyer considers that entertainments can offer us compensation for some of the inadequacies of modern life, which he referred to as social tensions.

 APPLY IT

Can you apply the four-part model to examples from current TV scheduling?

Does the model work when applied to other mass media forms? Try applying the uses and gratifications theory to popular magazines, computer games and YouTube.

Think of examples for some of the more specific uses and gratifications suggested by Berger.

Social tension	Utopian solution
Exhaustion	Energy
Scarcity	Abundance
Dreariness	Intensity
Manipulation	Transparency
Fragmentation	Community

The opening ceremony of the Rio Olympics was an example of a televisual event that demonstrated energy, intensity and abundance in particular.

For more on Stuart Hall's ideas, see section '4.2 Constructing "reality" through representation'.

EXAMPLE: The opening ceremony of the Rio Olympics, 2016

EXAMPLE: The opening ceremony of the Rio Olympics, 2016

Energy – complex choreography and staging, lively performances

Abundance – lavish décor and costumes, thousands of participants, no expense spared on this major televisual event

Intensity – brightness of mise-en-scène and dress codes, climactic nature of ceremony

Transparency – simple values of sporting excellence and celebration

Community – sense of support for Team GB or other country; global sporting community

Reception theory – Stuart Hall

Stuart Hall extended his work on representations to form a simple model that allows us to consider that different audiences will not necessarily respond to media texts in the same way. Hall suggested that this is partly due to each person having a different conceptual map, meaning that they bring their own understanding of the world. This then affects the conditions of consumption of any given media text. Hall also proposed that texts are polysemic, meaning that they can carry more than just the meaning encoded by the producer. Hall's ideas therefore challenge the thinking behind the hypodermic needle model, where the audience is passively 'injected' with the meanings of a particular text and decode these meanings exactly as intended.

Reception theory suggests that when audience members consume a media text, they actively choose how they respond. Their own conceptual map, affected by variations in social class, gender, ethnic background, political leanings, life experience, education, cultural preferences and so on produces a decoding of the text, which correlates with this sum of experiences.

The three types of response are described:

- **Dominant reading** – the most common response to the text. It is the meaning encoded – or 'preferred' – by the producer of the text.
- **Negotiated reading** – some of the audience may partially accept and partially reject the text. Negotiated readings can happen for all sorts of reasons, and can vary a great deal from person to person.
- **Oppositional reading** – some of the audience will completely reject the text. This might occur because of conflict with their values or ideologies, or may be as simple as a matter of personal taste.

Hall's theory reminds us that we should not make simplistic or reductive assumptions about audience members based on generalisations such as age or gender, as they can and do have complex and differing responses to texts. Some texts are more likely to provoke a strong reaction than others.

EXAMPLE: Identifying differing potential readings of *Preacher*

Preacher is an original US drama series made for Amazon Prime. It was brought to the small screen in 2016 by producer Seth Rogen and is based on the 1990s comics by Steve Dillon and Garth Ennis. The series tells the story of Jesse Custer, a Texan preacher (left) who acquires an extraordinary superpower. The series was given a Video on Demand (VoD) certificate of 18 by the British Board of Film Classification (BBFC).

Dominant reading: the show is intended to be an entertaining, blackly comic look at life in a small Texan town, which features larger than life fantasy characters and satirises Christianity in a way that is impossible to take too seriously. It features high production values including exceptionally cinematic visuals and soundtrack, and strong, characterful performances by the whole cast including minor characters.

Negotiated reading: someone who experiences a negotiated reading might appreciate one or more of the series' qualities – that it is well-written with sparkling dialogue, or that the cinematography is very appealing. They might at the same time find the comic-book-style violence too extreme, or find the narrative pace too slow and the number of secondary storylines tiresome.

Oppositional reading: someone might reject the text on the grounds of their religious beliefs and find its treatment of the subject matter offensive. Others might simply find the level of casual violence gratuitous and in bad taste.

It is worth being aware that active theories of audience are considered by some people to decrease the relevance of the media in forming attitudes and ideologies, and that they do not sufficiently account for the power and pervasiveness of the mass media in our society. When you are writing about active theories of audiences, you need to be just as careful not to assume that they explain everything, but to see them as making a contribution to a rounded discussion of how people can understand, be affected by and use the mass media in different ways.

APPLY IT

Choose one print, two audio-visual and two digital media texts. Using reception theory, write a 600-word case study that explores the differing ways in which audiences might hypothetically receive the media texts you have chosen.

KEY TERMS

compassion fatigue	the process by which the media audience lose empathy for victims of crime, disaster or war zones due to repeated exposure (especially to news)
conceptual map	our inner reference points dictated by the sum of our social and cultural experiences
cultivation theory	branch of effects theory that looks at the effect of media saturation (particularly television) on the audience
desensitisation	the process by which media audiences can become used to seeing violent content and better able to tolerate it
effects theory	the collective term for media theories that explore the correlation between media consumption and audience behaviours or interpretations of the real world
enculturation	the adjustment of people's values to mesh with the culture and society they inhabit
hypodermic needle model	simple effects model that assumes the audience to be passive recipients of media content
mainstreaming	in cultivation theory, the process of ideological alignment between media audiences and content
mean world syndrome	in cultivation theory, the belief that the world is a more dangerous place than it actually is due to viewing of violent acts on television

moral panics	term coined by Stanley Cohen to describe the press reaction to a negative event in the real world
passive audience theory	another term for effects theories, since they do not sufficiently explain the uses audiences may make of media consumption or how this varies from person to person
reception theory	considers that different audience members may interpret a single text in varying ways
resonance	in cultivation theory, the reinforcement of ideologies or experiences by mass media content
Sabido method	named after its creator, Miguel Sabido, who has acted as a writer and advisor on television serials in many parts of the world, and created a method for embedding educational messages successfully into the series
social learning theory	branch of effects theory that considers vicarious learning to be a highly significant factor in how people respond to media content
social tensions	sources of displeasure in people's lives, compensated for by utopian solutions
two-step flow	communications-based model that highlights the significance of opinion-leaders in the transmission of messages in the mass media

uses and gratifications theory	theory that suggested audiences make use of the media they consume for personal fulfilment
utopian solutions	gratifications-based model that suggests audiences use the media to make up for a lack of something in their lives

KEY THINKERS

Albert Bandura	(1935–) credited with developing social learning theory
George Gerbner	credited with developing cultivation theory
Jay Blumler and Elihu Katz	(1924– and 1926–) credited as two of the key developers of uses and gratifications theory

5.4 Interactivity and media audiences

One of the most significant changes that has happened with the impact of new technologies is the shift in audience expectations regarding their right to respond to and interact with media texts in such a way that their voices are heard.

Media consumers now experience the highest level of autonomy and control over their consumption than at any previous point in history. Web forums, fan sites and social media, which can be considered as a channel for this feedback, are considered here in light of other forms that they are connected with, rather than in their own right.

Contemporary newspapers have found themselves needing to produce online editions in order to maintain competition with free news websites such as the BBC, and newer phenomena such as *BuzzFeed* and the *Huffington Post*. Audiences increasingly share news stories that interest them on social media. Some news websites and apps allow comment facilities, with varying levels of moderation. Such additions often add to the colour of the reportage, allowing audience members to respond to news stories and lend their views, thus contributing to the entertainment values of the content. At their worst, such sites can be used for political ends in the same way that reviews on commercial sites can be hijacked for promotional purposes. Magazines have adopted social media, and some titles have ventured into dynamic content in some of the digital or web editions, but this has overall been lower in terms of real audience response.

Television has clearly moved away from traditional scheduling as its only means of reading the audience, with viewers able to add favourite programmes to their profile. Many producers hoped that early interactive features such as the red button service and other functions allowing you to see different views of a sports game, for example, would be popular with audiences. This turned out not to be the case. It is online where we have seen the biggest growth and changes in the ways in which audiences interact with the shows they love – review sites, fan sites and forums covering broad televisual entertainment or dedicated to particular shows and Twitter hashtags are readily accessible to anyone interested in finding out more about a show. There is evidence that producers sometimes even listen to these legions of fans.

EXAMPLE: Fan power in the US

Chuck, a 2007 US comedy-drama, was saved by its fans using a number of strategies when ratings fell and rumours began of cancellation. Social media and fan forums were key in allowing fans to connect with one another to promote the tactics used to persuade producers to keep the show on air.

Traditional techniques such as letter writing and petitions were part of the campaign, but two of the methods were more unusual. One involved raising money for a US heart disease charity, which became newsworthy. The other directly targeted Subway, the global sandwich chain, as a sponsor for the show – fans caused a spike in sales and got their views heard by buying a huge sub on the day of the season finale and posting positive comments about the show on the store's comment cards.

The show eventually reached a natural conclusion with a series finale in 2012.

She's the Agent.　He's the Secret.

CHUCK

Saving the world at $11 an hour.

SEPT 24 MON 8/7c NBC

APPLY IT

Find three examples of different television shows that have been continued beyond their anticipated lifespan due to fan intervention. What techniques were used?

Radio has always been to some degree an interactive medium, from the day when listeners wrote in letters and took part in phone-ins to today, when emails and text messages are read out on air. BBC Radio 1 is an excellent example of a station that has fully embraced interactivity, changing both production values and the way in which it is consumed.

Games are clearly the most interactive of all media, since much of the progression and action in many games is directed by the players themselves. This is particularly true of 'sandbox' games, where the pleasure of the game is on the roaming, choosing of tasks and interaction with the gameplay world rather than a set progression. But all digital media forms have at their heart interactivity – it is this that distinguishes web destinations of every kind, from music and fan sites to user-generated video channels, from traditional media.

For more insight into the development of traditional media into new media, see section '6.1 The diverse nature of media organisations'.

CHAPTER SUMMARY

- Audiences are constructed by media producers. Audience interactivity has changed some of the dynamics of this relationship in recent decades, but fundamentally they are still reliant on the choices offered to them through media channels.

- Media producers factor in complex information, obtained though market research, about their audiences when creating products for them. Some of these are age, gender, social class and income, political leaning, level to which they are influenced by celebrity and ethnicity (although we should be cautious about making assumptions about this complex and diverse area).

- Media producers use systems such as monitoring detailed figures about readership, genre and schedule-based progamming, cookies and web tracking, news agendas and psychographic or demographic profiling to target their audiences as precisely as they can.

- The methods used to target the audience appropriately vary across media industries, and almost all industries now use digital technologies to their advantage in monitoring in some way who consumes their products.

- New technologies and globalisation have both changed the level of access we have to the mass media. This is more noticeable in some sectors than others, but no sector has not been impacted on by developments in technology.

- There are two broad schools of thought in media study regarding how audiences interpret the media. These are known as passive and active audience theories. Both comprise a number of different theories and approaches, each with its own distinct way of theorising audience/media relationship, but some sharing features in common with others.

- No theory of audience should be considered as definitive – media students should be able to select from their ideas as appropriate, and should be able to see potential flaws in the application of a particular theory and consider alternative viewpoints.

- Traditional media forms vary in the degree to which they offer the potential for interactivity. Some of the interaction displayed by audiences occurs outside of the text in contexts such as social media and web forums.

FURTHER READING

Arthur Asa Berger (2011) *Media Analysis Techniques.*

Jennings Bryand and Dolf Zillman (2002) *Media Effects: Advances in Theory and Research.*

Jib Fowles (1976) *Mass Advertising as Social Forecast.*

Mary Gillespie (1995) *Television, Ethnicity and Cultural Change.*

Nick Redfern (2015) 'Age, Gender and Television in the United Kingdom', *Journal of Popular Television*, www.researchgate.net/publication/274073135_Age_gender_and_television_in_the_United_Kingdom, https://nickredfern.wordpress.com/2013/04/11/age-gender-and-television-in-the-uk/.

Ofcom Communications Market Reports, annually published at www.ofcom.org.uk/research-and-data/cmr/communications-market-reports.

Philip M. Napoli (2012) *Audience: Evolution.*

Richard Dyer (2002) *Only Entertainment.*

Stephanie Hegarty (27 April 2012) 'How Soap Operas Changed the World', BBC World Service, www.bbc.co.uk/news/magazine-17820571.

Chapter 6 Media industries

What you will learn in this chapter

- An overview of significant changes in the media industry spanning a number of decades
- What is meant by processes of distribution and circulation in the mass media, and how these vary across industry sectors
- The importance of ownership and control
- The significance of economic factors such as commercial and not-for-profit public funding to media industries and their products
- How the media is regulated in the UK
- How digital technologies have changed the demands of media regulation, distribution and circulation, including the role of individual producers

APPLY IT

Write a 1,000-word article on the ways in which you experience the mass media compared with the media consumption practices of your parents and grandparents. Use a range of contrasting authoritative web-based sources, including at least one article or book found using Google Scholar. Gather interview material from a sample of subjects from different generations. Record the interviews using your phone, and be sure to supply a list of your internet-based sources at the end of the piece.

6.1 The diverse nature of media organisations

Traditional media

Just a couple of generations ago, the media landscape looked very different from the one we know today. Pre-television, most people's main sources of news were the radio and printed newspapers. Leisure time in terms of media consumption was dominated by the cinema, the ultimate in moving image entertainment. By the 1970s, UK television broadcasters were routinely broadcasting the majority of their schedules in colour. Black and white – and the more expensive colour – television sets were the centrepiece in most homes.

By the 1980s, some homes had satellite television in addition to the four terrestrial channels and some newspapers included colour pictures for special editions. The magazine industry had continued to expand exponentially in health and lifestyle titles, and many of the traditional town cinemas were closing due to competition from the out-of-town multiplexes, video recorders and video rental. Young people were spending more and more of their time in arcades gaming and – more and more – on games consoles in the home. Music was still being bought on vinyl, but there were plenty of fans of the cassette, which had introduced another real headache for the music industry – widespread piracy. By the end of the 1980s, the younger generation and plenty of older cash-rich early adopters were buying their favourite albums on compact discs (CDs).

Moving on another 15 or so years, digital technologies had begun to impact on people's lives and consumption habits in ways they could only have dreamed of a couple of decades previously. Social media, cheap digital cameras, digital television, huge leaps in computer gaming technologies, the internet, Freeview and cable television, and devices such as phones and tablet computers had now changed the media landscape forever.

To understand the constantly evolving nature of media industries, we have to understand the impact of technological change, which is covered in more detail later in this chapter. Each sector has its own unique history, patterns of ownership and consumption, and market leaders. A short overview follows of the key characteristics of the main forms of traditional media, and a brief introduction to some of the most significant advances that have impacted them. Advertising is not considered here as a separate topic, since it is integral to the economic viability of many producers of traditional media forms and can be considered in relation to them.

Newspapers

Newspapers in print are one of the oldest forms of mass media, and can be traced back at least 300 years. When mass literacy became the norm, in the decades following the 1880 Education Act, newspapers began to enjoy a much wider circulation. Broad generic expectations began to be established. Local newspapers reported primarily on local news. Some of the newspapers founded in bigger cities began to focus on national affairs. Eventually, three main types of newspaper emerged with quite different news values: local papers with a regional focus that reported only on national events that concerned local people; broadsheets with a hard news agenda debated politics and reported on global affairs; and tabloids which became increasingly entertainment and soft news oriented, tended to focus on domestic issues and headline-grabbers such as crime and the latest moral panic. In recent decades, this trend has been magnified.

Almost all major newspapers have suffered a decline in circulation due to two factors: the increase in use of the internet as a news source and the advent of 24-hour-news culture on television. Many have tried to migrate a proportion of their services to digital models, some with more success than others. Since newspapers are heavily reliant on income from advertising, they have been unable to command the same high-level payments from advertisers, who can often find other online hosts for their content at a much more competitive price.

Magazines

The history of the popular magazine title offers a fascinating insight into the study of culture, leisure and other areas such as gender politics. It is also inextricably linked with the history of print advertising, since most magazines make their commercial revenue not just from their circulation, but also, primarily, from the advertisers they can attract who have a message for that magazine's readership. The exception to this is comics, and some niche publications where publishers rely instead on high turnover and profit from a smaller number of units sold. Individual titles have appeared and disappeared over time, but many of the owner-publishers have remained the same. The magazine industry is extremely competitive, with successful titles quickly spawning imitators and titles whose circulations have slumped, vanishing abruptly. The editorial content of magazines is often highly consumerist in its nature: understandable when you consider that their readership is defined not only in terms of interest in subject matter, but also in marketing parameters. Publishers must maximise revenue and define their target audience through the brands they are likely to purchase.

Magazine publishers, in common with newspapers, have struggled with the growth of the internet and the information age. With much of their editorial subject matter now available elsewhere for readers to access for free, it has been a challenge to maintain readership and continue to sell what many view as an outmoded concept for which they are reluctant to exchange money.

For more on how the media industry has adapted to technological changes see section '6.4 How the commercial or not-for-profit nature of media organisations shapes the content they produce'.

APPLY IT

Create a visual timeline from the 1970s to present day following a specific media production or reception technology. Suitable examples could include television, the computer gaming console or newspaper production methods.

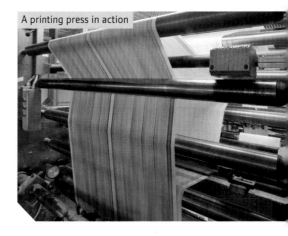
A printing press in action

The range of magazines available in most supermarkets today is huge.

Magazines, a visual medium where editorial has been consistently supplemented by artwork through most of the twentieth century, have had to become still glossier and more visually appealing, or cheaper and still more packed with advertising. An increase in cover price at the higher end has resulted in some titles costing as much as a paperback book. Price wars abound at the cheaper end of the market where readership may be only as loyal as the price puff or giveaway. There has also been an increase in hybrid magazine books, particularly in the hobby sector.

Some magazines have responded by moving part of their publishing to **digital subscription platforms** such as Zinio, where readers can access their archived back copies and re-read any issue when signed in to a tablet device. Forays into providing exclusive digital content for e-platform readership have had mixed results. This is partly because there is little understanding as yet of what consumers really want as additional benefits from a paid-for digital magazine subscription that they cannot already access readily elsewhere online.

Television

It was not until the 1950s that TV became a must-have fixture in homes. The BBC began broadcasting in 1936, with the introduction of the first commercial television station, which carried advertising, in 1955. The year 1982 saw the introduction of a new model of partial semi-public service broadcasting in Channel 4, followed by the launch of the purely commercial Channel 5 in 1997. The rapid expansion of digital technologies meant huge developments in cable and satellite television, which offered more global content in packages and an upsurge in niche broadcasting, for example genre-based providers such as the Horror Channel or Alibi, which specialise in crime series.

By 2012, internet television and the analogue switch-off meant that all television became digital. This was made possible by huge advances in broadband cabling and wi-fi. With this, the floodgates opened to **TV player** and VoD services, with content subscription packages challenging the market leaders in cable and satellite television, forcing them to make their own packages more competitive. In some cases, these services failed to predict the market switch by a new generation of **binge-viewers** who had sufficient disposable income for low-cost subscription packages. This was coupled with an increasing reluctance to pay for packages where content is frequently interrupted by conventional advertising.

Radio

Radio sets used to be the centre of the family home and, in many cases, were the sole provider of popular entertainment ('light' programming) and news. Many popular genres we know on television have a predecessor on radio. Well-known examples we still watch today on television include the crime drama, situation comedy, panel game show and soap opera. Radio, unsurprisingly, was hugely impacted by the arrival of television in people's homes. For years, ratings went into decline – yet public service broadcasting, community radio and commercial radio all persist today.

By contrast with the seeming positives reaped by many television companies, radio was not revolutionised by uptake of digital broadcasting. Initially, sets that could receive the signals were very expensive, and there was poor reception due to insufficient investment in transmitters even in urban areas. This meant that some early adopters of **DAB** (digital audio broadcasting) receivers, who tended to be hard-core radio fans, abandoned the technology and re-tuned to their favourite FM and MW services. At the time of writing, no date has been set for the switch-off of the analogue signal. However, the provision of digital radio in new cars and increased affordability of radio sets, coupled with coverage equal to analogue, has seen a determined move towards wider adoption and talk of a 'tipping point' being reached where analogue switch-off can be planned.

We shouldn't, however, ignore other surprising developments in audio broadcasting. Podcasting, which first appeared in 2004, has continued to retain a small audience of internet devotees. Some genres have translated particularly well to podcasting, such as comedy shows. There has also been some take-up of the availability of BBC radio content to subscribe to at no cost. The BBC also released a radio version of iPlayer called iPlayer Radio. Using the service, listeners could catch-up ('listen again') with programmes they might have missed without having to scroll through numerous podcast choices on third-party sites such as iTunes. Many small community radio stations have also circumvented large broadcasting licence costs by streaming content online, for which smaller webcasting licences are available.

The arrival of new media technologies

Computing technologies began to appear as early as the 1960s, but it wasn't until the late 1970s and early 1980s that a small number of enthusiasts began to use computers in the home. The first emphasis was on programming as a hobby and video gaming.

EXAMPLE: Early video gaming

The first video gamers used specialist consoles such as the Atari system and players enjoyed simple platform games on the ZX Spectrum. Word-based adventure games were also rapidly gaining popularity with the first PC users, and many of the genres of gaming we know today had their antecedents in these early ventures.

By the mid 1980s, computers were becoming commonplace in the workplace, and many processes that occurred in the media industry that had been quite laborious, such as the touching-up of silver photography by hand in art departments and the preparation of newspaper front pages, began to be digitised with the use of Photoshop and desk-top publishing software. By the early 1990s there was widespread adoption of home computing, connected to the internet (which began to be widely used by the public around a similar time). Connection was still through slow dial-up modems, meaning much content was text- rather than image-heavy. At the same time, the games console market and PC gaming were taking off radically.

Widespread improvements and access to broadband and wireless technologies meant the arrival of Web 2.0. Some of the characteristics of Web 2.0 include:

- The advent of social media as a form of leisure activity
- Advances in digital image-capture technologies combined with portability, accessibility and affordability, and the ability to embed them into the fabric of the web with ease
- Increased human communication and connectivity across the world through collaborative networks and information sharing. Wikis and crowdfunding are also an aspect of this
- User-generated content – decreased necessity for technical knowledge to have a web presence – and ease of content sharing
- The increase in a user's capacity to interact with web content, which might previously have been static sources of information, and user expectation of dynamic properties in the websites they visit

EXAMPLE: YouTube and Web 2.0

YouTube is often cited as a typical product of Web 2.0. People spend time on it as a leisure activity, and are able to contribute to it using cheap, digital video-capture technologies. It crosses continents and cultures, and, at its more serious, can promote the sharing of information. It requires little technical expertise to submit a video, and other users are free to comment on them.

One of the outstanding developments related to Web 2.0 was the rapid progress made in smartphone technology: the ultimate devices in technological convergence. Consider all the functions that can now be performed on a smartphone: emails, traditional work such as creation of documents, basic photo and video editing and graphics packages, gaming, telecommunications, information access, GPS navigational device, personal organisation and diary, health tracker, weather forecast, instant means of communicating with friends and family without the necessity of a phone call, etc.

Some now argue that Web 2.0's characteristics are now so fully expressed that we can understand the phase we are moving into as Web 3.0 or the semantic web. Commentators such as Tim Berners-Lee, inventor of the World Wide Web, think that Web 3.0 is not about connections between people but more between the individual and the information they require. This also dovetails with the development of the internet of things, where products such as fridges can order what's missing from the weekly shop, and a single search could choose you the holiday you can afford without having to go through multiple processes for bookings.

In terms of media consumption, we are already seeing within tools such as the Facebook algorithm the capacity to offer personalised media and advertising based on personal interests, harvested from keywords, a person's published information, their activity and 'likes' and posts. This has resulted in an experience that is far more relevant and tailored to a person's personal preferences.

For media producers, and advertisers in particular, this is a tool that allows still deeper penetration of a market to the consumers who really matter.

This personalisation of digital content can already be seen in other new media services and changes in the way we access digital media. Music and podcast purchases, online film rentals, use of TV players and so on are all likely to lead to us being recommended similarly categorised content, although often based at present on simple analysis of what else other viewers watched or downloaded rather than our own personal preferences.

KEY TERMS

24-hour-news culture	delivery of news around the clock on satellite and digital TV services since the 1990s, and its impact on the reporting and cultural perception of news	internet of things	connecting of appliances to online services using smart technologies	TV player	service sometimes known as 'catch-up' television, where channels make content previously broadcast traditionally available to viewers on demand for a period of time following broadcast
binge-viewers	people who watch between two and six episodes of a given television show in one sitting	news values	the categorisation of news into types, some of which may be favoured more highly over others depending on the news agenda of an organisation. Refer to the work of Galtung and Ruge		
circulation	amount of copies of a print media publication sold (paid circulation) or distributed (free publications funded entirely by advertising)	niche publications	print media publications serving a special interest or with a small circulation	Web 2.0	phase of internet development summed up by increased human connectivity
commercial revenue	profit generated by a media organisation	podcasting	distribution of audio files using RSS (really simple syndication)	Web 3.0/ semantic web	developments anticipated in internet use where user experience of the internet is much more highly personalised
DAB	digital audio broadcasting	technological convergence	the gradual combining of separate technological devices into fewer devices or one device with multiple functions	webcasting	the streaming of live audio content online – 'internet radio'
digital subscription platforms	offering of traditional forms of publishing such as magazines and newspapers on tablets or other digital devices				
editorial content	original content written for magazines distinct from advertising	traditional media	media forms that predominated before the digital age		

6.2 Distribution and circulation: what they are and why they vary across media

The term distribution refers to any way in which a mass media product reaches its target audience. These can be physical, technological or instigated by the media producer or their agents. They may also be audience-driven, as is the case with any carefully managed viral advertising campaign on social media. Distribution in the digital age can be via a mechanism as apparently simple as the uploading of a new game trailer to YouTube – even so, it is likely that a knowledgeable digital marketing specialist is maintaining the channel on which it appears, and observing closely how it performs.

There are formal methods of distribution common to traditional media such as films, where some studios own their own distribution arms.

These can co-exist alongside very small specialist distributors, which may focus, for example, on releasing DVD documentaries from non-English-speaking countries. Each stage of the distribution process can potentially be handled by a different distributor that has a limited role to play. Each distributor takes a percentage of the profits every time the product is moved on.

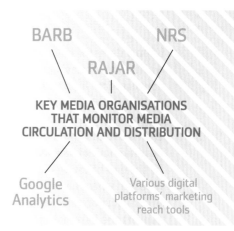

BARB NRS RAJAR

KEY MEDIA ORGANISATIONS THAT MONITOR MEDIA CIRCULATION AND DISTRIBUTION

Google Analytics

Various digital platforms' marketing reach tools

Find out more about the impact of technological change in section '6.3 Issues of ownership and control'.

In television and radio, distribution refers to the processes involved in broadcasting the programme on a particular channel or station. This might include the selling-on of spent content to other channels that will pay for it in order to refresh their own schedules. It also involves considering issues of placement in a traditional television schedule, and more recently the featuring and availability of content on TV player, VoD or podcast services.

BARB, the Broadcasters' Audience Research Board, measures ratings for television and TV players. Established in 1981, BARB is now recognising the challenges of providing accurate up-to-date measures of audience ratings that encompass all types of television viewing as well as the standard schedule. This information can be used by channels or programmers themselves to make decisions about the performance of individual content; crucially, it is also used by advertisers.

BARB measures representative consumption patterns by installing monitoring software in the homes of 5,100 people in the UK from a mixed demographic. Each week it produces a range of reports that show channel share, performance of individual programmes and so on. The most recent of these is the *TV Player Report*, based on device usage. The report uses a measure known as APS, average programme stream, which measures both live streaming and on-demand viewing, as well as downloads that are watched offline.

Produce a grid comparing the pros and cons of traditionally scheduled television and TV player use for both TV channels and audiences. What competing interests seem to emerge?

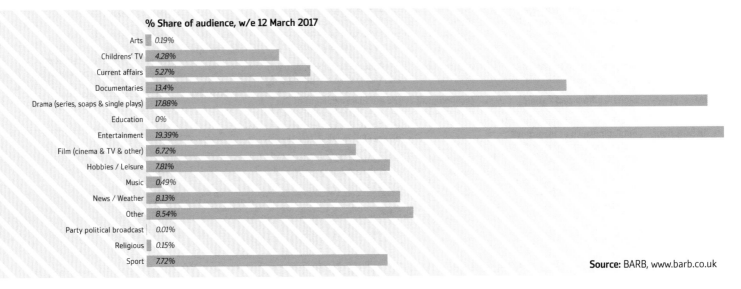

% Share of audience, w/e 12 March 2017

Arts	0.19%
Childrens' TV	4.28%
Current affairs	5.27%
Documentaries	13.4%
Drama (series, soaps & single plays)	17.88%
Education	0%
Entertainment	19.39%
Film (cinema & TV & other)	6.72%
Hobbies / Leisure	7.81%
Music	0.49%
News / Weather	8.13%
Other	8.54%
Party political broadcast	0.01%
Religious	0.15%
Sport	7.72%

Source: BARB, www.barb.co.uk

Keep a diary for one week of your television consumption. If possible, include the viewing of other family members. Count each episode viewed as a separate unit of viewing. At the end of the week, research where each programme originated, and convert the information into a percentage of your household's viewing of domestic and imported television content.

In the case of radio, ratings are measured by an organisation known as RAJAR (Radio Joint Audience Research). The methodology of RAJAR involves the use of listening diaries, in which a large number of listeners record their radio listening over a period of a week all year round. RAJAR tells us that radio listening is less varied than television consumption, with most listeners on average listening to a maximum of three radio stations. Interestingly, RAJAR research in 2016 shows that just over 1% of all radio listening hours are from on-demand services. Since 2013, a twice-yearly report into online listening such as on-demand, podcasting, on-demand music services and live streamed radio, known as MIDAS (measurement of internet-delivered audio services) has been published to ensure any significant trends are observed.

Circulation tends to refer more specifically to print media, and the amount of units sold – or, in the case of free publications, distributed – of a particular print product. Another key measure is readership.

The National Readership Survey (NRS) measures the readership of any magazine or newspaper using a currency known as AIR (average issue readership).

This information, although more an indication of statistical potential rather than a reflection of reality, is used by advertisers to inform their decisions about placement of advertisements within publications. It is an established organisation whose data are considered to be very reliable.

For many of the 250 print brands the NRS measures that also provide online content, digital subscriptions and so on, there is a new service measure – **NRS PADD** (NRS print and digital data), which partners with the US-based organisation Comshare, a leader in measuring digital performance.

In digital media, circulation can be counted in terms of views or **clicks** and **click-throughs**, and the majority of web hosting services, from blogs to social media business sites, offer detailed breakdowns of the performance of web content. A popular blog can gain over 100,000 clicks per month. Performance can also be measured in terms of:

- **reach** – how many people see something in their news feed, or turn it up as a search engine hit
- **views** – how many people click on the content to look at it
- **engagement** – how many people interact in some way with the content.

Google Analytics is also used by many digital advertisers to assess how their web content might be performing, and is used to improve targeting of content and rate of click-throughs.

Every year in August **Ofcom** publishes a very useful document called the *Communications Market Report*. This document provides a statistical examination of what media forms people of all ages are consuming. It offers breakdowns by factors such as age and gender, providing important evidence of evolving consumption patterns, which are invaluable both to industry and media researchers.

All of these measures of distribution and circulation are under constant review by marketing companies keen to ensure that their product remains competitive in the market. Given the hugely profitable nature of media production, it is unsurprising that there are many independent marketing companies regularly measuring performance and commissioning paid-for reports of mass media sectors.

Although the contemporary media landscape sometimes seems to be shifting in its dynamics day by day, many of these changes are subtle, with audiences being reluctant to replace traditional media overnight – rather to add to it.

Globalised patterns of circulation and distribution and their variations

Audiences may find accessing products easier in a globalised media market due to more streamlined services and provision of content. One of the most powerful arguments in favour of the communications revolution brought about by the internet is that it leads to increased **democratisation of the mass media**. In theory, bigger global audiences' opinions are heard more powerfully due to the prevalence of internet forums, fan sites and other unofficial channels of responses to texts. Conversely, they may find there is less diversity of products available to consume, as some products naturally fall by the wayside. However, some media companies may continue to offer riskier or less profitable lines on the basis that failure of one product for a huge parent company can be absorbed by the organisation as a whole with little impact.

Large, Western media company output is often readily available through communications infrastructures around the world. The result is often a side-lining of **indigenous media production**: products that are culturally and linguistically

The Readership Currency: AIR

NRS Print

APPLY IT

Explore the NRS website (www.nrs.co.uk). Prepare a 1,000-word report on the work of the organisation. This can be sequenced using the website's own subheadings if you wish. Include a section on the readership habits of your own family and/or friends.

Find out more about the impact of technological change in section '6.5 How our media consumption is regulated in the UK'.

APPLY IT

Research and write a 500-word case study on the journey from commissioning to broadcast of a popular TV programme you enjoy that has a global reach.

a Which aspects of the process do you believe to be common to other products in this media sector?

b What can you find out about the key players in the distribution chain?

c How does it add to your understanding of the way that media producers get products to the right audiences around the world?

produced by that region. **Domestic markets** without the equivalent economic buoyancy are often hard-hit by American television and film. These usually have high production values and budgets with which they cannot compete. A good example of this is some of the lengthy US-based television drama series that become popular via VoD services. Some countries may respond to this by restricting the availability of content through a **quota** method.

EXAMPLE: The case of Netflix and its global reach

Netflix is a VoD subscription service that has become increasingly popular, partly due to its affordability. It does, however, show a great deal of American content. Recent moves have been made within the European Union to impose a quota on Netflix, which would demand a minimum of 20% European-made content. It was also suggested that this content should be prominently positioned within menus to highlight its presence.

In 2013, Netflix began to commission production of its own original series. In some cases it has set the bar for high-quality, immersive series. Its reach is currently 190 countries worldwide and, despite a slight loss of subscribers when prices were increased, continues to be widely used.

Connected with this concern are debates relating to **cultural imperialism**, where members of the host culture begin to assume some of the values and ideologies of the media content they are consuming. Cultural imperialism offers us a different perspective from the more positive view of globalisation as a positive force that can unify cultures. Such unification is viewed instead as a dilution of national identity. We also might see the suppression of cultural heritage in favour of increasingly bland genre-based content. Where domestic media production survives, often its only option is to reproduce local variations of the big genres to which audience tastes have shifted.

KEY TERMS

AIR	average issue readership
APS	average programme stream
BARB	British Audience Research Board
click-throughs	viewing of deeper website content
clicks	viewing of the homepage of a website
cultural imperialism	transmission through the mass media of ideologies and/or cultural practices from a dominant media market to a smaller nation
democratisation of the mass media	increased ability of the audience to have their voices heard, and to interact with media producers and content
distribution	the way in a which a media product is transmitted from its originator to the audience

domestic markets	media content made by and for a particular country
engagement	click-throughs or other interaction with a page or other digital content
Google Analytics	market analysis of a website's performance
indigenous media production	media products made by and for a particular culture or nation
MIDAS	measurement of internet-delivered audio services
NRS	National Readership Survey
NRS PADD	National Readership Survey print and digital data
Ofcom	Office of Communications
on-demand viewing	viewing a channel or provider's content outside the traditional schedule

quota	imposing a restriction on certain kinds of foreign media imports
RAJAR	Radio Joint Audience Research
reach	the amount of people who see a link or site, for example in a newsfeed or search engine result
readership	the approximate number of consumers estimated to read a print media text
schedule	traditional way of organising broadcasts in a chronological way to transmit at specific times of day

6.3 Issues of ownership and control

Power Without Responsibility

In their 1997 book, *Power Without Responsibility*, James Curran and Jean Seaton explored the huge power yielded by owners of the large press groups such as Rupert Murdoch's News International (right). The book has been updated a number of times, and is considered very important in understanding the relationship between who owns the mass media and their output. They also discuss public service broadcasting, and who it is really answerable to. The latest edition looks at web ownership and controls, and considers who will control the future of new media.

Some of their key ideas are as follows:

- The mass media is driven and influenced by political agendas that are difficult to separate from other economic influences, but it often dovetails with them. These are perhaps the most obvious when we look at newspaper reportage, and the relationships between media conglomerates and politicians. However, it is also evident in television news and in competition for broadcasting licences as well as infiltrating many other areas, including the influence of politics on themes and subject matter of documentaries and fictional media texts.
- Technological change in the newspaper industry in production methods, where processes are increasingly digitised, has reduced the power of journalists, with stories that displease editors or owners easily pulled and replaced at short notice.
- The era of technological optimism heralded by New Labour in 1997 was still afflicted by the same attitudes to deregulation of the media, and the process was accelerated. The removal of controls over ownership is an issue because it can lead to concentration of ownership and domination of the market by a few big media organisations.
- The new media market has tended to feature many of the same big brands that dominated old media, which still account for some of the most visited websites. Globalisation has simply allowed big companies to become bigger and more powerful. Web 2.0 is complicated by the takeover of some initially independently owned companies, with audiences and consumers often unaware that sites and services they use and perhaps believe to be 'independent' are in fact owned by the same few companies.
- The rise of new media is thought to be associated with a decline in quality across the mass media, which affects every sector, including public service broadcasting.
- Curran and Seaton view the web as a place where dissenting voices can still be heard, but also a place where big businesses can operate in a less visible way, since most politicians are more focused on national political and business affairs.
- The seventh edition of *Power Without Responsibility* considers the web to still be a contested space. Big business could yet be counter-balanced by the strength of web users united in particular activities and with more socially responsible attitudes to the potential of the web.

EXAMPLE: The Leveson Inquiry

During the phone hacking scandal, high-profile employees of tabloid newspaper brand News International were summoned to appear at the Leveson Inquiry in 2011–2012. The outcome of the inquiry was that huge criticisms were made of the way in which some newspapers disregarded journalistic ethics and it led to the withdrawal of the Press Complaints Commission and its replacement by the Independent Press Standards Organisation (IPSO) in an attempt to more powerfully regulate the industry's activities.

Lord Leveson

21st Century Fox is one of the many companies owned by News International.

APPLY IT

Okido, a small independent magazine for children, was started in 2009 with just £5,000 of the owners' personal money. It has built a cult following in the UK, including a digitally animated spin-off kids' television programme on CBeebies, *Messy Goes to Okido*.

Research the magazine. What does it offer compared with more mainstream competitors? How has the magazine managed to survive and grow its brand as an independent in a tough industry?

Include some print media analysis (e.g. front cover) to help draw your own conclusions as well as your research findings.

Media conglomerates

As new technologies have emerged in a globalised world, so the number of media conglomerates has increased. We first encountered the term convergence to mean technological convergence – devices and platforms that now perform several functions in terms of communications and entertainments. The term convergence is also used to describe a number of companies that had different interests or originally produced products for different platforms, who have merged to form large media conglomerates. This form of merger, if the companies are at a similar stage in development, is known as horizontal integration. A globalised mass media, where the key elements involve the sale of goods and the technological advances used to distribute them, is often viewed negatively by media commentators. Many view them as doing very little to act in the interests of choice, and a buoyant, interesting and genuinely competitive market. This is also referred to as media concentration.

Vertical integration is another process that describes an alternative model for the merging of companies. In the case of vertical integration, we would usually see a company that owns one stage of media production acquiring others that offer different services within the production chain. This ensures smooth operation over the entire process, from product development through to distribution to audiences. Media companies that merge with one another benefit from the diverse experience they have, and can pool their knowledge to help target audiences in a more effective way. Today, much of this focusing process naturally concerns the improved targeting of advertising in order to increase its effectiveness and drive up revenue for the organisation as a whole.

Diversification is the term used when a media company adds to their core business and branches out into other areas. Diversification can be seen at work in most types of cross-platform marketing and production. It is also a common practice that results from any of the above behaviours in the formation of conglomerates. Profit is maximised and risk minimised by having a presence in more than one area of the market. It is a defining quality of modern, large media organisations.

Mass media convergence is a complex term that attempts to describe the huge changes that have taken place in the way in which the media industry now operates. Technological convergence has already been discussed, but there are other defining qualities. The social and cultural uses of media products and the appearance of innovative new products and ways of consuming them is also a feature of convergence. Convergence is only possible on the scale we see today because of communications technologies, and has shifted industry perspectives away from the notion of pure content and more towards services, sometimes across many platforms.

Alternative and independent media

Not all mass media production is owned by large corporations. Despite the challenges presented by the competition with such huge conglomerates, some independent media production companies continue to thrive. This is often because their unique position gives them an insight into the target market, which may be ignored by larger companies far more driven by a profit motive. This allows them to take risks that may not be taken by larger companies, which might view it as a waste of their time to cater for a niche audience. Some of these small media companies remain true to their independent values, whereas others are quickly bought out by larger media companies, and continue to exist in name only under the umbrella of the parent company.

Alternative and independent media are not the same thing, although the two terms are sometimes used together. Alternative suggests that the content of the media being offered provides some kind of ideological challenge to the mainstream, adopts a different aesthetic or has cult value. Independent media companies may have output that does this, but they may also simply be smaller companies freed from the constraints of conglomerate ownership and agendas.

Who owns a media production company, the influence they or their advertisers choose to exert on content, and the values held by the organisation can have an enormous impact on the media we consume. Many people are familiar with some of the political influences that come into play with the ownership of newspapers and their selection of news and angles on particular stories. It is not surprising that some smaller media producers seek to offer a product that might challenge mainstream ideologies, or offer content that appeals to a niche audience whose values fail to coincide with much of the mass media content available to them. Doing so can enable stories to be told or perspectives shared that would not have been considered commercially viable.

EXAMPLE: The journey of an independently made documentary from production to distribution

The Other Side of the Postcard (below right) is an independent documentary about human rights in Brazil. The following is an extract from an interview given for this book by the director, David Morris of Script2Screen Media.

> *The Favela Pacification Program was launched in 2008 to reduce crime and drug trafficking in Rio de Janeiro. In April 2015 … police shot and killed 10-year-old Eduardo in Complexo-do-Alemão. Communities began to realise that the program had become the very thing it was designed to destroy. Shot in the build up to the 2016 Olympic Games, this is the side to Rio you have never seen before.*
>
> *We had a budget of about £22,500. With this money we spent about £3,000 on equipment, £5,000 on flights and insurance, £7,000 on music licenses and legal fees, £1,500 on crew fees (only 3 people received payment, everyone else volunteered), £2,000 on artwork and printing costs and then a final (ongoing) £4,000 on festival submissions and marketing.*
>
> *With funding (which we were rejected for countless times) we could have done a cinema deal in Brazil with the Odeon. Due to music license fees, classification (where your film is given an age rating – which costs £9/min in the UK by the way) we couldn't take this path. In the end, we took an online distribution deal with TV4E in LA which included an Amazon [Prime] release. As well as this, more money would have meant more time on location and better kit. This may not have made the film any better, but it would have given us the chance to perhaps access the favela more and spend more time with our subjects.*
>
> *[The documentary was promoted] mostly through social media. Our festival run began in June 2016 and will run for two years. This will also help generate a lot of interest. In Brazil, we have done a lot of private screenings to politicians, professors and human rights organisations. In the UK, it's been a bit more mainstream, looking at radio and news interviews, as well as reviews, articles and print interviews for what feels like a million different publications. We did a live interview on a news channel in Brazil that went out to 12 million people.*
>
> *Being small, we slip under the radar, giving us greater access to things larger companies would shy away from. We also work in a close-knit group, with better camaraderie (our personality comes through a lot more this way), communication and ambition both within the company and with our clients. The challenge has always been resources and money. These things can be hard to come by, especially when we spend our profit on human rights causes – but this is just how we have decided to try and do some good with the little we have … and we love it. At the end of the day, if it were easy, it just wouldn't mean as much.*
>
> *We are developing another feature documentary in South Korea and I have just finished writing my second feature film 'Departures' which is a micro budget film shot in Dublin airport. We're also building a film school in the Jungle Refugee Camp in Calais, France, as well as another one in Complexo-do-Alemão in Rio de Janeiro.*

O Outro Lado do
Cartão-Postal
The Other Side of the Postcard

APPLY IT

Using the interview above with David Morris, can you sum up the advantages and disadvantages of being a small media producer operating in a global context?

If you have access to it, watch the documentary. Does it have mainstream appeal? Does it challenge dominant thinking about the situation in Rio? Did it educate you about some of the social issues faced by people in the favelas? Do you think that having a lower budget matters when producing this kind of media text?

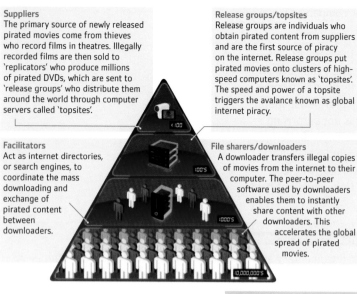

Suppliers
The primary source of newly released pirated movies come from thieves who record films in theatres. Illegally recorded films are then sold to 'replicators' who produce millions of pirated DVDs, which are sent to 'release groups' who distribute them around the world through computer servers called 'topsites'.

Release groups/topsites
Release groups are individuals who obtain pirated content from suppliers and are the first source of piracy on the internet. Release groups put pirated movies onto clusters of high-speed computers known as 'topsites'. The speed and power of a topsite triggers the avalance known as global internet piracy.

Facilitators
Act as internet directories, or search engines, to coordinate the mass downloading and exchange of pirated content between downloaders.

File sharers/downloaders
A downloader transfers illegal copies of movies from the internet to their computer. The peer-to-peer software used by downloaders enables them to instantly share content with other downloaders. This accelerates the global spread of pirated movies.

The pyramid of internet piracy

Piracy

Piracy is a huge challenge facing media producers today; in fact it has had a big impact on the way in which media content is distributed. The activity of watching streamed film or content on torrent sites has become so widespread that a poll of UK consumers in 2014 found that 30% of people consumed pirated TV shows and films. The effects of piracy include:

- Production companies having to reduce the timescales of staggered film and high-profile television releases around the world. Compressing the distribution process lessens the risk of people watching early because they don't want to wait for the official release in their country.

- The creation of digital locker systems that allow portability of content and viewing on different devices. This kind of service targets viewers who enjoy watching their films on a computer or tablet, and allows them to do so legally.

- In the music industry, piracy and illegal downloads have had a hugely negative impact, although the web has offered a showcase for bands struggling to get contracts. This led to the development of advertising-based streaming services.

- Loss of revenue for companies. Many consumers of pirated material don't think through the impact their viewing has on future production, which is very real.

- Piracy hits smaller companies harder, and in a climate where it is a struggle for small production companies to sell their products, this in the long term leads to homogenisation of content: less innovative and risky programming.

- Organised criminal gangs often benefit from media piracy.

EXAMPLE: Piracy, a programme-maker's perspective

In an interview in the *Guardian*, Gareth Neame, who was executive producer of the popular television period drama *Downton Abbey*, summarised the situation as follows:

> *Broadcasters will pay us money upfront, but it's not sufficient to cover the cost of the whole production, so we look at the long-term value of our product and, based on all the ways we can exploit this, we cashflow against anticipated revenues … Long term, movies and TV and other content simply won't be created in the first place. One may think an individual act of piracy doesn't matter, but if that becomes a way of life then the value of intellectual property becomes eroded, shows like Downton Abbey won't get made.* (Diana Lodderhose, 17 July 2014, 'Movie Piracy: Threat to the Future of Films Intensifies', *The Guardian*)

Highclere Castle, where *Downton Abbey* was filmed.

KEY TERMS

alternative	usually media products that offer some kind of alternative perspective to the mainstream
conglomerates	huge media organisations made up of several companies all with the same ownership
contested space	with reference to the internet, the ideological battleground between users and large media conglomerates

deregulation	reduction in governmental controls over media ownership
diversification	a feature of many media organisations as they try to increase their penetration of wider markets
horizontal integration	merger of media companies at a similar stage of development
independent	media companies not owned by larger organisations

mass media convergence	the coming together of many aspects of media businesses, including commercial, technological and cultural
piracy	the act of copyright infringement and theft
vertical integration	acquisition of one company in the production chain of another that offers a different service

6.4 How the commercial or not-for-profit nature of media organisations shapes the content they produce

Mass media production can be categorised in different ways. Primarily, the distinction can be drawn between commercial media organisations, which are the vast majority, and those that are not run for profit. The commercial nature of the majority of media organisations should not be forgotten when reading the content they produce, since this can make a significant difference to output.

How do we pay for the media we consume?

It's worth considering the number of examples of ways in which we might pay for the media we consume, and how this adds up in terms of the overall cost of media consumption per head. These are shown in the table below.

Commercial media product	Purchasing method
Magazines	• Single-issue purchase • Postal subscription • Digital subscription service
Newspapers	• Single-issue purchase • Regular order with newsagent • Postal subscription • Digital subscription service (mobile device or PC)
Satellite or cable television access to additional channel packages	• Subscription service per package • Pay-per-view, event purchase
Video-on-demand, such as Netflix, Now TV or Amazon Prime	• Yearly subscription • Monthly subscription
Computer games	• Monthly subscription • One-off physical purchase of game • Digital download of game or app • In-app or in-game purchases
Freeview television	• Licence fee required to watch or record BBC services on any device, and other channels on TV sets
Social media	• In-app purchases
Podcasts	• Cost per download • Subscription

The advertising contract

Many modern app developers for phones and tablet computers have recognised and used to their advantage the simple fact that many consumers will pay not to have to consume advertising. They exploit this by offering ad-free services at a premium to compensate the producer for the loss of revenue. Some companies offering subscription services were initially horrified at the thought of ad-skipping technologies, on television in particular. Over the years, a number of legal cases have been brought against the designers of software and hardware that permitted the consumer to skip ads.

For more on content see section '6.3 Issues of ownership and control'.

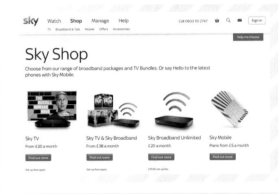

APPLY IT

Work out all the paid-for media consumption in your household, using the prompts in the table as a guide.

1 How much does your family spend on media entertainment in a year?

2 Which services do you think provide the best value for money?

3 Which other media entertainment do you think you or your family might use in the future?

4 If you are willing to do so, share your information with other members of your group. Bear in mind that family spending can be a sensitive topic, so be respectful.

APPLY IT

Keep an advertising diary for a day. List all the advertising you encounter across the whole range of media you consume, and in your local environment and during routines such as journeys. Use your findings to write a 350-word first blog entry reflecting on the exposure of teens to advertising.

For more on advertising space see section '6.1 The diverse nature of media organisations'.

The ways in which media industries target audiences through advertising are considered in more detail in section '5.1 How the media industry targets audiences'.

The arguments used have varied from copyright infringement in the rebroadcasting of material, to the suggestion that the consumer entered into a contractual agreement when purchasing the subscription – and part of the agreement was that the advertising was part of the package. It soon became clear, though, that an audience bombarded with advertising in almost every part of their consumption relishes the choice of ad-free services. This factor also benefits services such as Netflix and Amazon Prime, since the only realistic alternative to advertising revenue to sustain a company is subscription services, or a combination of subscription and paying to eliminate advertising content.

EXAMPLE: A legal test case on the advertising 'contract'

In 2012, a company named Dish, which sold a recording device that permitted as one of its functions advert skipping, was sued in the US by several TV networks. In 2013, following an intense legal battle, the Appeals Court ruled that such devices do not infringe copyright.

Some cultural commentators argue that the expansion of choice and proliferation of TV channels has led to a degradation in the quality of television programming, and that rather than engaging with the production of high-quality, original and exciting programme production, many channel owners opt instead to fill their schedules with cheaply produced, imported or repetitive content. Instead, channels may stick with safe content they know sells in order to attract advertisers to their services.

Print media audiences, particularly for magazines, are used to a large proportion of the item they paid for being taken up by advertising space. Content in magazines is often shaped around that month's advertisers, with linked topics receiving mentions in the editorial content itself, and articles known as advertorials making a regular appearance in newspaper supplements and magazines. These often promote goods through depiction of an aspirational lifestyle associated with fitness, luxury, beauty routines and so on.

Advertising rapidly becomes the norm on almost any new digital platform that begins advertisement-free. Some user-generated sites and web hosts use models where a percentage of revenue can be made by the individual whose contributions or sites gain the most traffic, and are therefore most valuable to advertisers. This encourages an acceptance among digital users who also generate content of advertising. Many social networking sites now personalise advertising, using data from our digital footprint – other sites we visit online as well as content we interact with on their platform – to generate strongly targeted adverts.

Synergy, a term from media marketing that can be used in a number of ways, is often used to describe co-promotional behaviours of companies that work together in economic relationships to maximise the impact of a particular campaign. The result benefits all parties involved. Like convergence, synergy has been enabled by communications and the digital revolution. The idea behind most campaigns that demonstrate synergy is that the message to the consumer is maximised due to increased exposure.

Public service broadcasting

Public service broadcasting (PSB) exists in some form in many parts of the world. It is difficult to define, with slightly different models of funding, purpose, broadcasting model and so on being used in different places, and even within regions in the UK. Usually, audiences can expect PSBs to exist for the benefit of audiences, not to excessively promote commercial interests, and to be impartial and fair in their content. In some parts of the world, PSB is seen as a poor relation of other channels, with second-rate content that struggles to compete in markets dominated by commercial television and its huge advertising revenues.

The BBC is held in high esteem worldwide for high-quality programming, but it is not the only PSB in the UK. In 1982, Channel 4 television first transmitted, having been authorised by the government to offer an alternative channel whose remit was specifically to cater for minorities and the arts. Many people, believing that PSBs do not carry adverts, are unaware of its contribution to the PSB sector. PSBs in the UK have a **remit**, which is a contract they must fulfil for their audience identified by the government and on which the conditions of its broadcasting licence are dependent. The overall mission statement for the BBC is familiar to many members of the public, and is derived from John Reith, the founder of the BBC's original vision:

> *To enrich people's lives with programmes and services that inform, educate and entertain.*

EXAMPLE: The BBC Charter

The **BBC Charter**, the set of conditions from the government under which it is permitted to broadcast, has six **public purposes**:

1   *Sustaining citizenship and civil society*

2   *Promoting education and learning*

3   *Stimulating creativity and cultural excellence*

4   *Representing the UK, its nations, regions and communities*

5   *Bringing the UK to the world and the world to the UK*

6   *In promoting its other purposes, helping to deliver to the public the benefit of emerging communications technologies and services and, in addition, taking a leading role in the switchover to digital television.* (www.bbc.co.uk/ bbctrust/governance/tools_we_use/public_purposes.html)

Separate remits are then provided for each channel, showing how each contributes to each of the purposes. The BBC is, at time of writing, held to account over fulfilment of its remits and public purposes by the BBC Trust, which represents the interests of the **licence payer**. This can include the investigation and sanctioning of channels if complaints are received about their content.

Even in the UK, the future of PSB is not secure. Recent changes, such as the switchover of BBC3 to online, only highlight the vulnerability of the service in a harsh and competitive economic climate.

EXAMPLE: BBC3

BBC3 was a channel previously available on Freeview, which offered 80% original content to a target audience of 16- to 34-year-olds. It ran on air until 2016, when the decision was taken to move the channel from a television service to an online-only version. This also resulted in a 50% cut in its budget.

There was a great deal of campaigning by viewers and high-profile people in the entertainment industry who united in a 'Save BBC3' campaign who were angered that it was programming for their age group, which was viewed as disposable by Director General Tony Hall. The BBC insisted it was right to go ahead with the cuts. The BBC also argued that the cuts occurred in an area that would lose fewer viewers, since many of the target audience already viewed the channel through iPlayer. The cut was part of a whole programme of redistribution of BBC funding among its departments.

 APPLY IT

Choose five contrasting programmes from across the BBC schedules that each seem to help fulfil at least three of the six purposes identified in the BBC Charter. Write around 100 words about each programme, explaining how it helps to fulfil the BBC's aims as a PSB. You don't necessarily have to view each one, as long as you are confident about its content.

For more on television regulation see section '6.5 How our media consumption is regulated in the UK'.

Source three news articles from different online news providers about the BBC, preferably covering different stories. Write a reflective paragraph to accompany each one, outlining the topic and content of the story, what it suggests to the reader about the BBC as an organisation, whether there is any evidence of a bias towards or against the organisation in the way the story has been presented or whether the story seems neutral. Use at least two quotations from each article to support your points.

The media landscape has changed so much since the simpler days of a handful of television channels, among which the defining qualities and purpose of the BBC stood out. It will be a continual struggle for the organisation to redefine its relevance in a climate where similar content can be found across the many commercial channels. Its very existence is becoming an ideological battleground for politicians struggling to agree on what the future of PSB should mean in the UK.

KEY TERMS

BBC Charter	the conditions upon which the BBC's licence depends		public purposes	the aims of the BBC as an organisation
licence payer	term for the viewing public who contribute to the funding of the BBC by payment of an annual licence fee		remit	the service provided by a PSB for its viewers
			synergy	mutually beneficial cross-promotional strategies used by media companies
PSB	public service broadcasting			

6.5 How our media consumption is regulated in the UK

How much of media regulation is enshrined in law, and how much consists of voluntary codes and an advisory role?

Not all media regulators have the legal power to enforce their codes, instead relying on consensus within the industry to serve the audience in a way that is in keeping with the spirit of regulation. After all, the codes created by most organisations are written with the best interests of the audience in mind, and in the majority of cases there is no vested interest on the part of an individual media producer in breaking the code. Codes are also designed to allow for an element of controversial and ground-breaking publication and broadcasting, and this is often carefully considered by media producers who produce such texts. Since broadcasting licenses in the UK for radio and television are issued by Ofcom, in extreme circumstances an organisation could lose its broadcasting privileges if it did not conform to Ofcom's broadcasting code, although imposition of a large fine is more usual.

Tabloid newspapers, however, have a history of publishing material that contravened the Press Complaints Commission (PCC) Code of Conduct. It was partly for this reason that, in the wake of the phone-hacking scandal that culminated in 2011 in the Leveson Enquiry, the PCC was re-formed into the Independent Press Standards Organisation (IPSO), which released a new Editors' Code of Conduct, shifting the emphasis to clearly making the editor of a publication legally responsible for the content published.

Consumer opinion about media regulation and censorship covers a wide spectrum, as with any public issue. More liberally minded consumers tend to argue that, in a media-saturated world and age of digital proliferation, it is up to the audience to educate themselves and to self-censor content they are likely to find offensive. The

Produce a visually appealing infographic designed to introduce the work of media regulators in the UK to an audience of 10- to 14-year-olds.

difficulty with this argument is that it relies upon everyone being able (or wanting) to decide what constitutes media content that is appropriate for them, able to see through misleading content and so on.

Some people would like media organisations to apply strict and often moral or political codes and frameworks to content regulation, to support the maintenance of a society that only exposes its consumers to content that is seen as wholesome. They advocate heavy censoring of the mass media, and this is deployed in many countries where media content is carefully managed in order not to promulgate material considered to be in some way:

- damaging to the interests of the state
- inconsistent with religious moral standards
- otherwise considered subversive.

Some global media franchises already concede to these countries, with heavily edited versions of their material being shown in some parts of the world to suit local laws and interpretations of taste and decency. Such state control takes a high level of investment to maintain, and involves not only controlling the point of distribution but also the point of access to mass media. Often, people who attempt to distribute or access forbidden material are dealt with harshly.

The main bodies responsible for media regulation in the UK and what they do

All regulatory bodies for the mass media in the UK are directly contactable by the public and publicise a procedure for doing so. That this process is easy to undertake is really important for issues of fairness and transparency. The following section gives a brief introduction to the main media regulators in the UK. It is highly recommended that you seek out copies of these codes in full and familiarise yourself with some of the content in more detail.

 APPLY IT

Source online and read the codes of practice set out by IPSO, the ASA and Ofcom. Create a revision grid that summarises the key points of each code.

Television, radio, Ofcom and the watershed

Ofcom, the main body responsible for the regulation of broadcast media content in the UK, is an umbrella organisation that regulates all broadcast material in the mass media. It was established in 2001. This was previously the job of a number of different regulators. In addition to issuing licences to channels based in the UK, it maintains a broadcast code, which all media channels licenced in the UK are expected to adhere to. It is a key stipulation of Ofcom's Broadcast Code that content broadcast between the hours of 5.30am and 9.00pm must be suitable for viewing by children. This is known as the watershed.

In the case of radio, content unsuitable for children cannot be broadcast at times they are most likely to be listening – this refers mainly to the mornings before school starts. The code includes all the areas that have historically been concerns of regulators, which would be familiar to most people – depictions of violence, substance abuse, sexual content and offensive language controls.

Regulation of advertising in the UK

The Advertising Standards Authority (ASA) has existed in the UK since 1962, and regulates both print and broadcast advertising across the media. It also offers guidance on pop-up and banner ads on British websites.

In the case of television and radio the ASA is supported by its co-regulator Ofcom, which is able to enforce judgements on advertising content should the company responsible for any contravention refuse to withdraw the content from publication or broadcast. In this case, Ofcom can impose a fine or, since individual licensed

TV channels are responsible for their advertising output, pursue this line. Print advertisers are likely to withdraw any adverts voluntarily that are investigated by the ASA, even if a formal ban is not imposed.

The ASA is also responsible for advertising content on British-hosted website pop-ups and banner advertisements. This is proving the hardest area in which to enforce regulation. Because of this, the ASA now includes on its website a list of 'non-compliant' web-based companies – those that have been asked repeatedly to change their advertising content but do not. In the ASA's report in 2016, web advertisements attracted the most individual complaints, although by volume television still had the highest number.

Regulation of print and news media

Print media publications in the UK are regulated by a body known as the Independent Press Standards Organisation (IPSO). IPSO was set up in 2014, and is responsible for ensuring that editorial standards outlined in its Editors' Code of Practice are adhered to and that journalism standards are maintained.

Any publication that is subject to an adverse adjudication must correct the facts prominently in a future publication. Complaints about the presentation of news stories in newspapers constitute the vast majority of the adjudications listed online for public inspection. The quality press, tabloids, local or regional newspapers in both rural and urban areas, and online versions of major national papers all feature in the list. The majority of upheld complaints concern accuracy, where something has been reported in a misleading way.

Contraventions of the code are less likely to occur for magazines. This could either be because their content tends to be less controversial in terms of what is covered by the code, or due to the nature of editorial practice in a publication that works to a monthly, weekly or even quarterly print cycle. Longer periods for legal checking and consideration of the code may result in fewer complaints.

Pressure groups

Pressure groups differ from regulatory bodies. They are often spontaneously formed from a group of individuals who share a particular concern or ideology regarding media output. These kinds of pressure groups may centre their activity on a particular issue, often regarding media content and representations – such as inclusion, visibility or suitability. There is an increased move towards people participating in single-issue pressure group activity rather than being involved in bringing about change through membership of a mainstream political party. This is particularly the case with younger people, who may feel distanced from traditional political processes. Sometimes these groups may represent other bodies, such as a religious group, charity, or other group of activists such as a gay rights organisation. Some are enduring, whereas others may spontaneously dissolve once an issue has been resolved.

🔗 See section '6.3 Issues of ownership and control'.

APPLY IT

Write a 250-word summary of three recent adverse judgements by the IPSO, and another 250-word piece on three recent subjects of rulings by the ASA that interest you. These can be readily accessed through the main websites of these organisations. You may use extracts from the actual wording on the websites, but make sure these are presented clearly as quotes connected by your own wording outlining each case.

Pressure groups therefore have a monitoring role that often prioritises a moral or representational concern shared by a minority of audience members. Pressure group activity might include writing letters to regulatory bodies and media producers themselves, persuading celebrities or MPs to support their cause and give it prominence in the public eye, the organisation of boycotts and small demonstrations, and the production of low-cost information points such as campaigning websites. Today, a common tactic is to try and create a groundswell of support through social media campaigns including petitions. All of this is facilitated by the features of Web 2.0, since voice and power – combined with the speed and immediacy of content made available – are defining qualities of Web 2.0.

EXAMPLE: Mediawatch-UK, an enduring pressure group

One of the most famous and enduring pressure groups in the UK is **Mediawatch-UK**. The group was founded in 1965 in response to increased liberalisation in society being reflected in television and radio content by Mary Whitehouse, a notorious campaigner, over issues of decency and Christian morals in television programming. Originally known as the National Viewers' and Listeners' Association (NVLA) it became Mediawatch-UK in 2001, partly in response to **mass media proliferation**.

Much of the emphasis in Mediawatch-UK's work today seems to focus on parental concerns about content. The 'latest news' section of its website, at the time of writing, links to stories from major news providers that appear to match its own campaign agenda – recent sex scenes on television, studies appearing to show harm caused by social media use, the negative influence of celebrity culture and the frequency of children's exposure to 'harmful' media images.

Mediawatch-UK promotes an effects-centric view of media consumption, meaning it believes there to be a cause and effect relationship between media consumption and a whole range of childhood issues. Campaigning for greater controls over content would theoretically enable children to grow up free from many of the pressures that media influence is thought to exert on them.

APPLY IT

Write a 500-word proposal for the creation of a new pressure group campaigning on a media issue. Include a clear statement of the reasons for the campaign, the methods you intend to use to get your message out there, and any target media organisations you feel need to hear your message. You don't really have to believe in your cause, but if you choose something that genuinely annoys you, the campaign ideas will flow more easily. Storyboard a one-minute promotional video for your campaign to be shared on social media, which raises awareness of the issue and contains a memorable campaign slogan.

KEY TERMS

Broadcast Code	Ofcom's regulatory framework for broadcast services
broadcasting licences	required for transmission of television or radio services
censorship	the blocking of certain media material from public consumption
co-regulator	the sharing of some aspects of regulation by more than one organisation
Editors' Code of Conduct	the IPSO's regulatory framework
IPSO	Independent Press Standards Organisation
mass media proliferation	the rapid expansion and growth of the mass media within a historically brief timeframe

MediaWatch-UK	well-established and influential pressure group
pressure group	group of individuals who campaign about a particular concern regarding media output
self-censor	action taken by the individual audience member to select media for consumption that does not offend or otherwise impact on them negatively
watershed	in the UK, the point (9.00pm) at which content of a more adult nature may be shown in a television schedule

6.6 New technologies and media regulation

Internet-based content is very difficult to regulate. Some householders may choose to install additional controls at the entry point for communications to supplement measures taken by some ISPs. A determined person with some quite limited technical knowledge can easily use a proxy server or virtual private network (VPN) to bypass many kinds of filter.

Since 2014, the majority of the main fixed line ISPs have responded to a government request to filter potentially harmful content at source, but smaller ISPs have either struggled to implement filtering at source, or seem reluctant to do so. Since legislation does not currently require it, this situation continues.

Ofcom also published a series of recommendations, as far back as 2004, requiring the blocking of unsuitable content to under-18s on phones, which are adhered to by most providers. These schemes are not without their critics; among them are some groups who complain of overblocking, where sites overly aggressively filter certain search terms and therefore restrict access to sources of information about issues with which people may be seeking help.

VoD services and subscription packages usually offer different password-protected user IDs and broad preference systems to help ensure that children are only able to select from appropriate material. It is increasingly common for mainstream news websites to preface their video content with warnings of graphic images that might be edited quite differently in a mainstream news report.

Social media sites are largely expected to regulate their content themselves, and given the huge volume of traffic that passes through the sites, it is unsurprising that unsuitable content is often only brought to the attention of moderators when it is reported by other site members. Since many younger users will lie about their age when joining such sites, the site owners have an easy defence – that they only offer content suitable for a certain age range because that is who they believe their membership to be.

Some recent arguments surrounding censorship of social media sites have centred on videos playing automatically. Many sites are constantly improving the algorithm to improve the user's ability to self-censor by requesting not to view similar content again. Adults may be capable of doing this, and have the confidence to tailor an experience of a network to one that suits their own sensibilities. Younger users subject to peer pressure or just natural curiosity may lack the skills or inclination to do this.

APPLY IT

Find out about and collect together the parental controls available on a range of TV player, VoD and popular subscription TV packages.

APPLY IT

Research the community guidelines and reporting procedures for a social media or user-driven site that you use. How effective in your personal experience are these guidelines? Do the majority of users abide by them? Write a 500-word case study introducing the site, how it aims to self-regulate, the role of moderation in the running of the site and any other interesting aspects of your findings.

EXAMPLE: YouTube's community guidelines

YouTube, in common with many sites that consist primarily of user-generated content, publishes **community guidelines**. These emphasise the collective responsibility that users of the site share with the site administrators. Guidelines cover nudity and sexual content, graphic violence, hate speech, misleading material, spam, threats, copyright and harmful or dangerous content.

The haphazard nature of relying on users to flag content as inappropriate, coupled with the sheer volume of uploads, means many breaches of the guidelines go undetected. The threat of removal from the site may be enough to deter some users but not all – particularly where multiple members of a subversive group or organisation are behind a coordinated and concerted effort to give that content a presence.

The Internet Service Providers' Association (ISPA) is a trade association, formed in 1995, that represents its members. As such, its methods and purpose differ from what we usually understand by media regulation. Its code, available from the website, does cover some of the standard practice we might expect to see in the body of other regulatory codes.

The ISPA has a sub-committee, which are responsible for internet safety, but this group does not deal directly with complaints from the public, instead supporting other groups. For example, it supported the founding of the Internet Watch Foundation (IWF), a charitable foundation that allows reporting of images of abuse, and liaises with the police over these.

We are left with a situation where ISPs agree in principal through their membership of the ISPA to attempt to regulate certain areas of internet content – and are encouraged to do so both by copyright holders attempting to protect their property and the government. In reality, they are not penalised for failing to do so. Most of their efforts necessarily surround engagement with controlling public access to more extreme content and preventing copyright infringement.

Computer games in the UK are certificated by the Video Standards Council (VSC). This is a non-profit-making company set up in 1989 at the request of the government to control video and DVD supply, and to make sure retailers and rental outlets understood their responsibilities in the supply of age-rated products. Under the name Games Rating Authority (GRA), this organisation applies the Pan-European Game Information (PEGI) age certification, which is an agreed standard across Europe. Importantly, the GRA does not have to agree with a rating awarded to games across Europe, but can veto a game's entry into the country under unusual circumstances, meaning it is not legal to distribute it.

Regulating computer games is not without its share of dilemmas. The PEGI system uses a methodology similar to that of film certification, where a game has certain instances of types of violence or behaviour and depictions. The actual certification definitions are necessarily broad, and certificates are issued that offer a fair interpretation.

EXAMPLE: The 'We Dare' PEGI controversy

In 2012, a party game release for the Nintendo Wii and Playstation, called We Dare, was given a PEGI 12 rating. The online advertising for the product, however, was highly suggestive and targeted the adult audience the game was, in fact, intended to reach. The *Sun* newspaper broke the story in the UK, causing its makers Ubisoft to withdraw the adverts due to negative publicity, and also taking the decision not to sell the game in the UK or US. PEGI defended the age rating given to the game, since it assessed only the game's content, not how it was advertised.

Some games that could be considered unsuitable for children by some adults would pass a PEGI 12 certificate. To assist parents in making suitability decisions, eight content labels are also included, which cover the categories of sex, violence, discrimination, online, drugs, fear, gambling and bad language.

As is the case with films, after the point of sale or access, it is largely up to parental supervision to ensure that age restrictions are adhered to. Another challenge is that no-one can reliably predict or measure the effect of highly immersive media on the individual, and the amount of time spent consuming the material. Another issue might be whether a person exclusively plays violent games, or whether they form part of a mixed diet of gaming and other media that would be viewed as diluting any potential 'effect'.

Research and write a 1,000-word opinion piece for an online technology and culture website on the problems presented by:

- self-regulation of digital culture
- the measures that already exist to try and protect users of new media against harmful content
- self-censorship strategies useful for users of all new media.

Use at least one source found using Google Scholar, and try to include a healthy balance of researched facts (which you should credit in the main body of the article) and a clear personal voice.

 For more on issues of how audiences respond to the media they consume see section '5.3 How audiences read the media'.

Collect and create a collage of PEGI ratings summaries of games played by the whole class. Using a word cluster generator such as www.wordclouds.com, create a word cloud for each of the PEGI age suitability ratings by inputting key words from at least five ratings summaries for different games. Print out, display and discuss the results.

KEY TERMS

community guidelines	means by which some websites ask their users to contribute to self-regulation
content labels	additional information provided by PEGI as part of its rating service
GRA	Games Rating Authority (a division of the VSC)

ISPA	Internet Service Providers' Association
IWF	Internet Watch Foundation
overblocking	internet filtering that is considered overly restrictive
PEGI	Pan-European Game Information
VSC	Video Standards Council

CHAPTER SUMMARY

- Huge changes have occurred in media industries in recent decades, driven by advances in digital and communications technologies. This has had varying levels of impact on different media sectors.

- Distribution and circulation patterns are measured in different ways in the UK. Most are monitored by organisations external to the main industry players, giving them impartiality.

- Patterns of circulation and distribution have changed and in some cases expanded due to globalisation of the media market.

- How the media is controlled and who owns it can impact on the content, as explored fully in the enabling ideas of Curran and Seaton in their book *Power Without Responsibility*.

- The mass media sector is constantly evolving. Media conglomerates are a key feature of the contemporary media landscape. Business strategies such as convergence and synergy abound.

- Some independent media companies survive and even thrive. Some of these produce products that are considered alternative, as they may cater for a niche audience or run counter to mainstream ideologies in either their product content or business practices.

- Piracy continues to be of grave concern to all media producers.

- Many media companies make a large proportion of their profit from advertising or subscriptions. Public service broadcasting is still an important feature of the contemporary media landscape in the UK, but has less significance worldwide.

- Media regulation in the UK is controlled by different bodies, each with their own powers. It is important to understand what each of these regulators can do, as well as their limitations. Self-regulation is also an important concept with the growth of the internet and mass global communications.

FURTHER READING

BARB, www.barb.co.uk.

James Curran and Jean Seaton (2009) *Power Without Responsibility*.

Jennifer Holt (2009) *Media Industries: History, Theory and Method*.

Jeffrey C. Ulin (2009) *The Business of Media Distribution*.

National Readership Survey, www.nrs.co.uk.

Ofcom, Ofcom.org.uk.
  Explore the Ofcom site for many interesting reports on aspects of media consumption and regulation in the UK.

RAJAR, www.rajar.co.uk.

The Media Studies specification identifies specific skills that you will need to demonstrate in your non-examined assessment (NEA) and your examination responses. This chapter will consider the underlying skills that you need to develop when studying the media and will make suggestions for the types of activities you can engage with to help you develop these skills further.

7.1 Introduction

Learning about the media can be daunting at first as there is so much to consider. You need to learn about what the media is, you have to engage with a huge range of media forms and products, and you also need to be able to consider media industries, audiences and products in light of the theoretical framework of ideas and concepts outlined in Chapters 1–6. Some of the media forms are so new that our understanding of them is only now starting to develop, while other forms and genres have been around for a long time and there is a huge and sometimes overwhelming range of theories, interpretations and concepts we can use to help us understand them. The media is constantly changing, so knowledge we have today may be inaccurate or out of date tomorrow.

Being an expert in each and every media institution, form or genre is an unrealistic goal. Learning ideas from the theoretical framework is important, but more important than just knowing something is knowing how to use that knowledge. Your knowledge needs to be applied to help you understand and discuss the way the media works, the way media products are constructed, and the way audiences and industries relate to one another. The ability to use your media knowledge is a skill that needs to be learned and practised. You should aim to be able to show that you can apply the knowledge to show your understanding of what you have learned. In the same way, the NEA may involve you making a product but your research, planning and production choices should be based on the application of your knowledge of the theoretical framework.

What you will learn in this chapter

- How to analyse and compare the way that media products construct and communicate meaning through the interaction of media language and audience response

- How to use key theories and subject-specialist terminology appropriately

- How to debate key questions relating to the social, cultural, political and economic role of the media

- How to communicate effectively using discursive writing

For more on the NEA see Chapters 10 and 11.

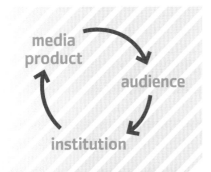

All analysis begins with media products as they are objects that can be examined in detail, so our understanding can increase. Analysis means asking lots of questions and considering media products in a number of ways including the interrelationships between product, audience and institution.

7.2 Analysis of media products and audience response

At the heart of Media Studies is the skill of analysis. Analysis is the act of seeking to understand how something works and why it works that way. In Media Studies, analysis demands a detailed examination of media products, audiences and industries.

We have already learned that media products are constructed using media language choices and that these choices are made carefully and deliberately by the media producers. Production decisions are made that attempt to appeal to, attract and please an audience. With this knowledge, analysis can begin by considering the effects that were intended by the media producer as well as the way the choices may have been interpreted by audiences. Before that though, it is worth taking a step back to consider what the media product is, and what, in broad terms, it is trying to achieve. You should aim to apply skills of analysis to close study products as well as your own choice of media products. You should analyse existing media products to help you make your own production decisions. When analysing media products your initial focus will be on the products themselves, as all the media language choices that have been made when creating the product will have been combined in an attempt to construct meaning.

Important in this communication process is the platform that is being used for **distribution**. The method of communication is always considered very carefully by media producers. It needs to be appropriate for the message itself as well as being the best way to reach the audience; the distribution of information may vary depending on the target audience. Modern celebrities who target teenage audiences will use social media to communicate because this is typically the best way to gain the attention of this demographic. Facebook was the social media of choice of teenagers for some time, but by 2012 only 43% of teens thought Facebook was the most important social media platform, with Instagram, Snapchat, Tumblr and Twitter all showing increases in popularity as Facebook declined. From 2008–2011/12, Facebook's take-up grew to a peak of over 800 million users. Users of Facebook are older than they were in 2008/9 as younger people moved to alternative social media platforms. It is important for media producers to have a good understanding of where the audiences are and how best to communicate with them.

Each form of media has its own **codes and conventions** in the way media language is used, and audiences will have **expectations** that vary across forms and genres. The audience's expectation of a news website will vary when accessing either a tabloid or broadsheet website. Audiences who watch adult drama such as *Happy Valley* will have a different expectation from those watching a sitcom like *Big Bang Theory*, and both television programmes try to meet the specific needs of their audience. Of course, some audience members could choose to read and view many different types of media product in different ways, depending on their mood and needs at the time. People can choose to move from news media forms that provide hard news to light entertainment, music, gaming or social interaction, as their personal requirements change.

Analysing products

The purpose of analysis is to engage with media products to see how they are constructed to make meaning. The theoretical framework can be used to structure your analysis, when you need to be able to:

- **identify media language** accurately so you can discuss the way a product has been constructed
- **discuss the representations and messages** conveyed within the product
- identify how the product attempts to **appeal to and engage its target audience**
- consider the impact of the **product's institutional context**.

These same ideas need to be applied when you are constructing your own production, when you need to be able to:

- use **media language accurately** so your product is recognisable
- **create representations** that are appropriate to the messages you wish to convey
- create a product that will **appeal to and engage its target audience**
- create a product that engages with the **appropriate institutional context**.

There are some key questions that you may find useful when it comes to using the theoretical framework to analyse existing media products. While you are developing and practising your analysis skills, you may want to follow the process outlined below. You will find that the more you practise analysis, the easier and more natural it becomes.

Following is an example of analysis focusing on the poster for the film *Suicide Squad* (2016, Ayer, D.).

Step 1

Before you start analysing, it is worth being very clear about what it is you are analysing and what its function is.

What is it?	A poster for the film *Suicide Squad*
What is it for?	This is an advertising and marketing product. The poster has been created to raise awareness of the film. The ultimate aim is to encourage people to go to watch the film at the cinema, in the first instance

If you ask, 'Why has the product been constructed this way?' your answer can be developed from the basic position that, as with every media language choice, it needs to raise awareness of the film and create a desire for the audience to watch it.

Step 2

Next you need to make some basic observations as to how the product has been constructed. At this stage you only need to observe but should try to look for details in the choices made.

What media language choices were made in the construction of the product?	• A pink and green background is used for the poster • The heads of the characters in the film are used in a montage • The montage is shaped like a mushroom cloud and contains a number of cartoon illustrations such as skull and crossbones, bulging eyes and eyeballs, explosions, etc. • The date of release is given prominence on the poster, as are the formats it is available in • The names of the main actors are given at the top of the poster

Step 3

The next step involves thinking carefully about the reasons behind these choices. Everything you have observed has been selected for a reason and often with a clear intended effect.

Why were these choices made? What connotations are created by the media language choices? What effect did the producer wish to achieve?	• The colours pink and green are not complementary, so they create a contrast that is jarring. In combination with the other images on the poster, the colours create connotations of chaos and while they create the idea of an explosion this is a chaotic comic book-style explosion of energy. These colours immediately set the tone of the film • The date of production, information about presentation formats and the names of actors are all important in the marketing of the product. Star names can help sell a film and some actors bring connotations because of their star or celebrity status. For example, Jared Leto is known for his film work and his role as lead singer for indie band 30 Seconds from Mars. Leto has tended to choose film projects that have allowed him to create quite exaggerated characters and he is often photographed on the red carpet in unconventional outfits and with non-traditional hairstyles. His star persona contains an edge of unpredictability that his role as a rock performer consolidates. His inclusion on the cast list brings an edge of unpredictability to the film. He and Will Smith bring different meanings to the cast and both actors may act to attract audiences • The use of characters' faces in the montage provides a literal illustration of what audiences can expect from the film. The characters are easily identified through their make-up. Fans of the comic book may be interested to see how famous characters such as the Joker are being interpreted • The use of cartoon illustrations provides information on the source material that has inspired the film • The mushroom cloud denotes a nuclear explosion. This creates connotations of the unleashing of unrestrained and destructive power. When combined with the tag line 'Worst. Heroes. Ever' this image suggests that the film will subvert the idea that superheroes create order from chaos. These 'heroes' look more likely to create mayhem and disorder

Step 4

The choices made are often connected to other ideas from within the media framework. Media language choices create representations, can communicate genre codes and can create narrative information. Some media language choices do all three things at the same time. Making these connections allows you to increase your understanding of the production process.

	Media language choices	Analysis
How does the product create representations of specific people, places, ideas or things?	Integration of character images within the animated style of the design of the illustration for the poster	The characters are shown clearly to belong to the comic book world. The make-up design is appropriate for the genre and the connection of the characters to the image of an explosion creates a representation that subverts the expectation of superheroes and shows that their characters are more likely to be villainous rather than heroic. This is reinforced by the Joker's (Jared Leto's) grimace and Harley Quinn's (Margot Robbie's) mischievous and coquettish body language
How does the product communicate narrative information?	*As above*	The representation of the characters shows their narrative roles (see above) and the fact that they are such unusual heroes implies that the group relationships could be quite fragile and may contain a lot of conflict. This conflict is likely to be violent. The idea about the type of narrative is reinforced by the image of a mushroom cloud

How does the product communicate its genre? Does it use genre conventions or subvert them?	As *above*	The representation of the characters subverts traditional genre conventions but the genre has become more knowing and its heroes less restricted, so, following successes such as *Super* (2010) and *Deadpool* (2016), this poster is clearly communicating the film's genre. The Joker is a recognisable character from several Batman films and the comic book drawings and tag line support a clear communication of the superhero genre – with some unconventional twists

Step 5

The final step involves thinking about things that may not be present within the poster but that can be inferred through the information presented. Again, using theoretical approaches helps here, as they provide useful questions to help you take your analysis further.

 APPLY IT Complete the table with some media language observations and ideas about how the poster has been constructed to attract and appeal to its audience, meet its institutional aims, and create brand identity, values or ideologies.

	Media language choices	Analysis
How does the product attempt to identify and attract its audience?		
How does the product set up audience expectations?		
What relationship does the product have with the producing institution?		
How does the product communicate a brand identity either for itself or the producing institution?		
What values or ideologies are created by the product?		
Is there a connection between the values communicated by the product and its target audience?		

All the steps taken in this analytical method provide ideas and information that help you answer the most important question:

- **How has the media product been constructed and how does its construction help it to achieve its aims?**

How does the construction of the film poster for *Suicide Squad* help it to raise awareness of the film and try to persuade audiences to go and watch the film?

The film poster for Suicide Squad aims to raise awareness of the release of the film and create anticipation in audiences that will lead to them wanting to go and watch the film. Box office takings are important for a feature film as not only do they create income for the film company, they also act as a marketing tool later when the film is released for purchase on DVD or as a digital download. In order to try and make it as easy as possible for audiences to access the film, the release date is positioned in the centre of the poster and information provided about the different formats the film will be screened in.

 TIP This type of analysis helps you to understand the thought process that has been followed during production. Thinking about media products in this way helps you understand how media producers use media language to help them communicate to their audiences and construct meaning. Identifying the techniques they use could help to inspire you as you start to plan your own production.

This method can be used to analyse a wide range of media products.

Find examples of the following media forms and use them to practise analysing the intended meaning of the products. Build up your analysis skills and broad media knowledge by ensuring you analyse several examples from all of the forms.

- **Moving image/audio**
  - television
  - music video
  - radio
- **Print**
  - newspapers
  - magazines
- **E-media**
  - online social and participatory media
  - gaming
- **Moving image/audio/print/e-media**
  - advertising and marketing

The genre of the film is clearly communicated. The tag line mentions 'heroes' and the illustrations refer to comic book styles in the use of images such as an explosion on the right-hand side and the repetition of 'action' words written in a font that holds connotations of the first television Batman series and graphic novels. Although the idea of this being a superhero film is clearly communicated, the representations of the characters and the film through the illustrations subvert the traditional codes and conventions of the genre. Traditionally, superheroes are either lone figures or members of a unified group who work to create order from the chaos created by comic-book villains. Here the heroes are a collection of comic book villains, easily identified by the image of the Joker. The characters appear as unconnected groups of individuals rather than a collective and they are pictured in the midst of an explosion. The audience is likely to interpret this representation as a subversion of the genre, and the fact that the poster maintains an enigma by not giving much narrative information, the intent is to encourage the audience to want to go to the cinema to see a new and surprising approach to the genre and discover how the characters will interact. The general look of the poster, the choice of colours, the use of a mushroom cloud, the disconnected images all reinforce the idea that this may be a more adult superhero film and audiences may expect more realistic violence and darker themes than usually seen in this genre. This could appeal to both superhero fans as well as audiences who may usually find the genre too simplistic or tame. This could broaden the audience of the film and so help add to its potential success.

Considering audience responses

It is always worth considering that, while media producers may wish to create a specific meaning when they create their media products, meaning is actually made by the audiences as much as by the producer. Audiences may accept the intended meaning of a media product and go along with the producer's intent in terms of the way the product is interpreted. *The X Factor* is constructed to provide light entertainment for a mass audience. A narrative is constructed through the show's competition element that helps audiences engage and become emotionally involved with the programme. The show provides safe and secure, mainstream entertainment with talented participants who create a spectacle with their performances. The earlier weeks also include a number of participants whose lack of skill can provide comedic relief or whose development of their skills provides inspirational narratives. Judges are represented as character-types whose responses can be predicted, and the brightness of the mise-en-scène and light musical choices all create an atmosphere of comfort and security for the audience. These are just some of the elements that make *The X Factor* a mainstream success year after year. Many millions of people accept this meaning and enjoy the programme as a simple but entertaining bit of fun.

The idea that people only access media that make them feel good may be a little simplistic. No doubt this is true most of the time but audiences do choose to access media despite the fact that they reject the intended meaning and may find

the product irritating or annoying. There is evidence that some audience members watch *The X Factor* 'ironically' – that is, they watch it while rejecting its values so they can mock and ridicule the programme and its contestants. Social media can bring these like-minded people together, who create a community by resisting the producer's intended meanings and sharing their own, alternative interpretations, as in the following reproduction of a Tweet:

nmccf 8 Oct 2016 21:40   1 ⬆

I can't sing a note but an considering entering next year. I'm going to shave my beard off, wear women's clothes and cover myself in glitter. I think I have a decent chance.

⤴ Share   Report

Dragonella → nmccf 8 Oct 2016 21:42   3 ⬆

What are you waiting for you sound perfect but leave the beard on. Be authentic??

⤴ Share   Report

nmccf → Dragonella 8 Oct 2016 21:46   2 ⬆

That is a fantastic idea. If it works out I'll let forward your commission.
:D

⤴ Share   Report

Of course, the producers don't really mind what motivates the audience to watch, as the fact that they are watching adds to the viewing figures. Even audiences that don't watch are part of the promotion of the product, as seen in the reproduction of a Tweet below:

HCollider1 7 Oct 2016 11:07   1 ⬆

I've never actually watched any episode of it ever but I am a attentive reader of the live blog because it's always very funny. It shows you don't have to watch a programme to find a write up of it amusing.

I feel if I watched the actual show it would ruin it. Plus the blog takes a few minutes to read the whole thing and you don't have to record it. It's far better than the show in all respects.

Weird outdated tv.

Good live blog.

Look forward to vomit laden Komodo dragons all through December.

None of these people seem very interesting but then surely this format ran out of steam about 10 years ago.

⤴ Share   Report

Some people take pleasure from resisting the intended meaning more directly. Debates and discussions online often provide evidence that various audience members will make quite different meanings from media products. For example, there are different and contradictory responses by audiences to the way the media portrays violence against women. Programmes such as *The Fall* (BBC) and *The Night Of* (HBO) have storylines that focus on the murder of women. Some see this representation as being misogynistic, focusing on women as objects and victims, while others see these programmes as being about the exploration of real-world events where women can be victims of violence. The producers' intents are not always clear in these types of programmes, so audience engagement with the issues and social media comments and discussions can help audience members engage with the debates and consider their own position on the issue. They may engage in a **negotiation** that considers the many levels of meaning that can be taken from a single media product.

Other, even more resistant audience members may enjoy provoking people by taking a deliberately oppositional position in online debates and discussions. They may be deliberately disrespectful towards a celebrity in order to provoke a response from their fans; they may criticise a TV programme or film with a large

The Fall (BBC2)

The Night Of (HBO)

and dedicated following; or they may offer oppositional political points of view on a news site that is known to have a specific political allegiance. Deliberately antagonistic comments, often identified as trolling, aim to create offence and/or make people angry. These comments seek to provoke arguments but they often act to strengthen the bond between like-minded audience members by helping them reinforce the more accepted interpretations within their community.

EXAMPLE: Pepsi advert (April 2017)

In 2017 Pepsi released an advert that was intended to contribute to the brand image of the soft drink manufacturer, create positive associations with the drink and, in doing so, encourage consumers to select Pepsi rather than its competitors' soft drinks. It chose a well-known celebrity who is admired by and influential to young people to front the advert (Kendall Jenner) and constructed an advert featuring imagery related to social protest, which, towards the end of the advert, turned into a real-world confrontation between protestors and the police.

Intended reading: Pepsi wanted the advert to create brand and product associations with:

- progressive ideas about individual power and challenging authority (in the context of the protests that marked the start of the Trump administration and Black Lives Matter campaigns)
- fashionable youth culture
- elite and beautiful social groups and individuals
- the promotions of peace
- solving conflict.

Many audience members may have made a **negotiated reading** when viewing the advert. Many people would have immediately made no logical connection between a sugary, soft drink and the lofty ideas in the advert but would still have had a positive response to the imagery and general message.

Kendall Jenner 'solves social tensions' with a can of Pepsi.

The dominant response from commentators on social media, though, was to resist the advert's aims and reject the intended meaning. **Oppositional** readings could be found on Facebook and Twitter as well as in the news reports that followed. Pepsi was accused of being culturally insensitive, reducing Black Lives Matter marches to fashion parades and offering simple solutions to complex social, economic and political issues. Confrontations between protestors and the police in the advert were peaceful and showed tolerance and mutual respect. This was argued to have belittled the situations, where confrontations with US police officers had led to violence and even death.

The pressure created by the oppositional readings led to Pepsi removing the advert from circulation, making a statement that they 'did not intend to make light of any serious issue'.

APPLY IT

Choose a popular media product or personality. Check social media responses to the product/personality and make notes of the different opinions and ideas that are being communicated.

Meaning is not simply within the text itself. There is an attempt to create meaning when media products are constructed but audiences construct meaning for themselves and can interpret them in ways that were not originally intended. The communication between audience members is part of this construction of meaning and some audience members may accept while others reject or negotiate the intended meaning of a product. It is worth keeping this in mind as you analyse media products.

> **NEA:** Your knowledge and understanding of how real media products are constructed and how audiences interpret and interact with media products should influence the way you create your practical production work.

Using key theories and subject-specialist terminology

As you learn about media theories it may be tempting to think of them as a body of knowledge that should be learned and then reproduced. Showing you understand the theories is more important than just showing you know them. You can show your understanding by applying the theories and ideas, and this goes beyond simple memory. Todorov stated that narratives follow a three-part structure:

- an **equilibrium** is first established and then **disrupted** before events **resolve** creating a **new equilibrium**.

Knowing this is only the starting point in Media Studies, as the knowledge needs to be applied in order to be of any value. In the exam you may be asked to define some Media Studies terms but you could also be asked to apply the ideas when analysing media products. Application of knowledge requires you to be able to use the knowledge to explain how a real media product creates meaning. When discussing media products you should always provide detailed examples to support the points you are making.

For example, in *The Night Of* (HBO) an equilibrium is created in the first episode. The lead character (Naz) is introduced and through media language choices that create narrative markers we learn that he is an ordinary, somewhat geeky college student – we first meet him in a maths lecture where he is taking notes. He appears to be an outsider to the dominant 'alpha-male' crowd who are basketball players presented as stereotypical frat-boys. Naz only interacts with them because he is offering maths tuition to one of the players. This equilibrium is **disrupted** when he is invited to a party with the basketball players and his desire to become part of their social group creates a situation that changes his life forever. The representations of Naz and his college acquaintances are constructed using media language choices and these representations are used to construct the narrative as outlined above.

There is no need to explain or describe Todorov's theory to show understanding of the ideas. Understanding is demonstrated in the way the ideas are used to explain the meaning being created by a media product. Key to being able to do this is the ability to use the terminology of a theory fluently and with confidence. The key terms provided in each chapter and the Glossary of key terms at the end of this book provide much of the subject-specialist terminology that you should start to use in your writing. Like analysis, using terminology is a skill that can be practised and the more you do it, the more confident you will become and the more natural it will feel. This is why your teacher sets essays and writing assignments – to help you improve your use of media terminology.

It is important not to forget that when you use a media term you need to provide a detailed product, audience or institutional example as evidence. It is not enough to say that *Strictly Come Dancing* aims to entertain its target audience (which it absolutely does). You need to be able to provide concrete examples as to how it does this.

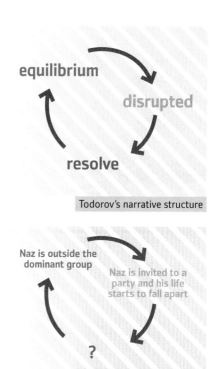

Todorov's narrative structure

Todorov's narrative structure applied to *The Night Of*

See the Glossary of key terms on pages 252–261.

Select some media terminology – you can use the following examples and then practise using other terms from the Glossary of key terms.

- **Moving image** establishing shot – codes and conventions – diegetic sound – character role – intended meaning – high-key lighting
- **Print** placement – compositional balance – headline – columns – anchorage – crop
- **Representation** mediation – stereotype – under-representation – self-representation – reinforcing of values – contextual meaning

- **Audience** demographics – target audience – audience appeal – consumption pattern – access – gratification
- **Institution** distribution – ownership – branding – marketing – regulation – income sources

Now, using media products/institutions you are familiar with, use the terminology to discuss how products make meaning, how audiences relate to media products and/or institutions, and how institutions attempt to engage with audiences and maximise their profits.

You may start by making simple observations in a bullet point list but you can develop your skills by building these points into a paragraph of more formal writing. Don't forget, though, that you need to provide examples to support each of the points you are making.

For example: Noel Fielding and Sandi Toksvig **appeal** to different **demographics** and create different **audience gratifications**. This will have been taken into account when casting for and **marketing** the Channel 4 version of *The Great British Bake Off* (left).

NEA: You will need to submit a Statement of Intent with your production work for the NEA. This Statement of Intent should demonstrate your knowledge of elements of the theoretical framework as it relates to the brief you have chosen. To demonstrate the extent of your understanding you should use appropriate terminology when explaining your production plans.

7.3 The social, cultural, political and economic role of the media

Media products are not just standalone artefacts. The media plays an important role in all our lives. It is part of the social, cultural and political context of our culture. The breadth and variety of the contemporary media mean that there are many ways to engage with the contextual role of the media. Following are just some examples.

Social

Sometimes a media product can be seen to have a social impact, even becoming part of our society.

For example, social media has become part of people's day-to-day lives in ways traditional media never could be. Social media can be used to access traditional media, providing links to news stories, videos, TV programmes, film trailers and podcasts being shared millions of times each day. Social media also provides audiences with games and are platforms that give access to and information about all manner of things including the media itself. Audiences share traditional media content with one another but they also get to create content themselves – whether this is a simple, 140-character Tweet or a video uploaded to YouTube. Social media has changed the way people communicate, the way they access the media, the way they share the things they create and their own ideas. These are all relatively recent social changes, so the long-term impact of this is still to be seen.

Cultural

The media is part of our culture. Media products are cultural artefacts and the experiences we share around the media influence the way we think about ourselves and one another.

For example, *The Great British Bake Off* (right) is a programme that grew in popularity over the seven years it was on BBC. The programme was initially broadcast on BBC2 and built from 2.7 million to over seven million viewers before moving to BBC1. Its audience grew again for three years peaking at 14.8 million. In September 2016 it was announced that the show was moving to Channel 4, who outbid the BBC for the rights to broadcast the show. Its cultural impact could be measured by the audience response to this news and the fact that the news media saw this as newsworthy. Audiences took to social media to express their disappointment and, at times, anger and outrage at the news that the show was moving channels, and broadsheet, tabloid, online and broadcast news providers all included this in their reporting over the course of the following week.

The show had a cultural impact as it moved the 'reality-competition' genre away from the back-stabbing (*The Apprentice*), the serious (*Masterchef*) and the mawkish back-story led (*Britain's Got Talent*) styles of programming to a gentler, more supportive and collaborative type of competition. Shows such as *The Great British Sewing Bee*, *The Great Pottery Throw Down* and *Hair* followed suit and used formats that were similar to *The Great British Bake Off* but, perhaps more importantly, kept the more positive, less combative tone of the original show. It was the friendly, positive and supportive nature of the show that audiences feared would be lost in its move to a commercial and more 'edgy' channel. The show had managed to create a mass market, mainstream hit that created reassurance for the audience and was based on positive values. This was a marked change in the culture of reality competition shows.

Political

The nature of most media is that it is political. The media reflects the political climate of the culture that produced it and in some cases can be seen to attempt to influence the political culture of the country.

For example, *Benefits Street* is a Channel 4 fly-on-the-wall reality show that hit a nerve in 2014. The show was filmed in a political context where 'austerity' was offered as a way out of the economic difficulties that were the fallout from the economic crisis in 2008/9. The political context of austerity created a culture where the way that public money was spent became a talking point. As there was less money being spent, the idea of who deserved it became a major issue, with 'welfare claimants' being identified by some politicians and some of the news media as being an undeserving, parasitic, lazy class of people – the 'shirkers' who took money from the hands of 'hardworking people'. *Benefits Street* itself didn't actually represent its subjects in such a simplistic and reductive way, but the response to the programme on social media and in the news was characterised by being divided. Some commentators and audience members criticised the participants within the show and judged their behaviours and lifestyles. Others criticised the makers of the show for exploiting poor people and creating what was called 'poverty-porn'. These two responses to the show broadly represent two political perspectives that can be described as right-wing (those in poverty are there because they have character flaws or have made bad choices in their lives) and left-wing (those in poverty are often there due to environmental and systemic issues that are often out of their control). The programme became a discussion point in the news and TV programmes were made to allow experts, commentators and the public a chance to discuss and debate the issues. *Benefits Street* can be seen as a touchstone for the politics of the era as it both reflected contemporary political issues and acted as a lightning-rod for political debate.

Some responses to *Benefits Street* on Twitter.

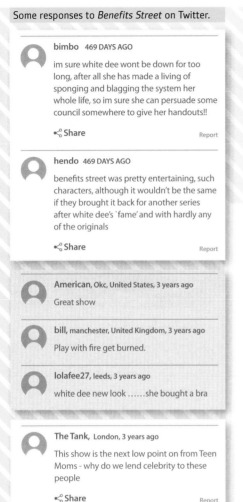

bimbo 469 DAYS AGO

im sure white dee wont be down for too long, after all she has made a living of sponging and blagging the system her whole life, so im sure she can persuade some council somewhere to give her handouts!!

⤳ Share   Report

hendo 469 DAYS AGO

benefits street was pretty entertaining, such characters, although it wouldn't be the same if they brought it back for another series after white dee's `fame' and with hardly any of the originals

⤳ Share   Report

American, Okc, United States, 3 years ago

Great show

bill, manchester, United Kingdom, 3 years ago

Play with fire get burned.

lolafee27, leeds, 3 years ago

white dee new look ......she bought a bra

The Tank, London, 3 years ago

This show is the next low point on from Teen Moms - why do we lend celebrity to these people

⤳ Share   Report

Anonymous 1326 days ago

hard people behind a computer u have no idea what your talking about why don't u go there and find out yourself what its like then just maube youll learn the truth as to what c4 really did do

Anonymous 1332 days ago

White Dee wants to get of her FAT A*** and get a job they are all born lazy And black Dee looks like she needs detox

these people should be drug and alcohol tested before they get any benefits

Anonymous 1333 days ago

would nt it be nice if our PM watched this!!! or then again this is out of his social bubble.

Anonymous 1333 days ago

This street shows what's wrong with Britain today .... we're over-run with scrounging, dishonest scum.

British newspapers are renowned for the fact they each have their own distinct political perspective. Most British newspapers are on the right politically, with notable exceptions being the *Daily Mirror* and the *Guardian*. Where broadcast news has a responsibility to try to stay impartial, British newspapers are free to promote whatever political perspective and whichever political party the newspaper management decides upon. The majority of the press have supported the Conservative party since 2010 and their reporting of the Labour party has been critical, regularly taking a mocking tone; even those 'on the left' tend to represent centrist views rather than those specifically from the left. Newspapers are free to report news stories that protect their own interests and promote their own values – making them an important part of the UK's political landscape.

Economic

Media industries aim to make profit and this leads the decisions made by them in the way they create products. They may make products that attempt to encourage people to pay in order to access or own the product, or they may make products that try to attract large audiences so advertisers can be persuaded to pay more for time or space.

For example, the music industry traditionally made most of its money through sales of music. Audiences would buy singles and albums on vinyl, cassette and, later, CDs. The sales of 'hard copies' of music have declined rapidly and music is now usually bought as a data file. However, access to music does not depend on buying the product. Music can be accessed free via streaming services. Free services such as Spotify are funded by advertising, although a monthly subscription often allows the audience to access music 'ad free'. Music can be accessed via YouTube and is often pirated – downloaded from file-sharing sites illegally. This economic context has changed the way in which musicians are paid and the music industry makes money. If music is to generate profit then income has to be generated in other ways rather than just music sales. For example, corporate sponsorship is often provided for tours, and product placement is common within music videos and in the social media of artists who have a large fan-base. Social media has become important in promoting an artist, and the number of followers on Twitter can influence the decisions of radio programmers when deciding which artists should go on a show's playlist. This leads to situations where small unknown artists may struggle to get radio air-play but a fictional 'group' satirising a musical subculture (DJ Beats and MC Grindah from BBC3's *People Just Do Nothing*) can host programmes and have their music played on national radio. These TV show characters have built a large social media following in a way that unknown artists cannot hope to do.

Product placement: screengrabs from music videos showing the inclusion of Beats headphones and speakers.

In order to be able to debate these issues, you will need to keep up to date with what is going on in our culture. This will mean engaging with the latest news stories that define our social, cultural, political and economic context. You will need to be informed on the general issues of the day but will also need to keep an eye on the developments in the media culture, learning about the latest institutional issues, and the debates that are happening around TV programmes, films, music and celebrities.

> **NEA:** Each NEA brief will ask you to produce a media product within a contemporary media context. When researching and planning for your production you might like to consider how the media product reflects or is influenced by social, cultural and/or political issues. You should also consider the economic context of your production. For example, a music video is an advert for a musician's brand and related media products, and a magazine front cover is constructed to try to persuade audiences to buy the product. Your knowledge of this economic context should be apparent in the production itself.

Do some research:

- Take some time to look through a few newspaper websites – both tabloid and broadsheet.
- Look through the 'media', 'culture', 'TV/radio', 'game' and 'film' sections of the *Guardian*.
- Have a look through the BBC news website.
- Watch a news bulletin on a non-BBC source.
- Watch some news on an online source.
- Access a review site such as 'Den of Geek'.
- Check what's trending on Twitter.
- Read some music news on the NME website.

Now try to identify some of the questions and concerns that are helping to define our contemporary culture. Some of these questions may be linked to the media and others may be broader social, cultural, political and/or economic issues.

7.4 Using discursive writing

Throughout your course you will no doubt complete a number of written pieces of work that aim to help you present your ideas formally. Some people find writing essays relatively easy, while others feel they struggle to communicate their ideas clearly. Everyone needs to work on developing a good writing style and it is practice that will help you improve this crucial skill.

Discursive writing is more than presenting a collection of facts or some information. Discursive means that your writing may need to present an argument or show the various sides in a debate. You may be asked to evaluate ideas or engage with theory and/or concepts. Crucially, though, discursive writing will give you an opportunity to show not only what you know, but also how much you understand the media.

When you construct a piece of discursive writing, you will usually be responding to a question. This means you have two important initial jobs to do:

1 Decide what the question wants you to do.

2 Decide what the question wants you to focus on.

1 What does the question want you to do?

Working this out should be fairly straightforward. All you need to do is look for the verb in the question. You should also look at how the question has been worded. This can give a clear indication of what is expected of you in your work.

The following table shows some of the words and phrasing you could be asked to respond to for a piece of discursive writing, with examples of possible ways to respond.

Key words/phrases	Expectation	For example
Compare	Show and explain similarities between ideas and/or products.	*Eastenders* and *Coronation Street* use the same narrative structure in the presentation of their stories.
Contrast	Show and explain differences between ideas and/or products.	BBC3 presents a range of programming for its target audience online. Despite being targeted towards the same group, programmes such as *Josh* and Stacy Dooley's documentaries offer very different gratifications.
Discuss	Present a logical and balanced argument with evidence for the ideas you are using.	In 2016, the fact that two black contestants were voted off *Strictly Come Dancing* first was used by some people on Twitter to accuse the audience (and the BBC) of racism. These accusations did not consider that many non-white contestants had won previous series of the show, with many more being ranked highly. This demonstrates that Twitter cannot be relied upon as a source of objective or even accurate information.
Evaluate	Present a logical engagement with the issue raised in the question. You will need to discuss the validity of ideas and show your analysis of strengths and weaknesses of ideas that relate to the issue raised in the question. You should be able to draw conclusions based on your knowledge of media products and theories.	The audience responses from Twitter support Stuart Hall's idea that some people resist the intended meaning of a media product.
Identify	You will demonstrate your knowledge and/or your observational skills. Much will depend on what the question asks you to identify. Some possibilities could include: • narrative techniques • genre codes and conventions • opportunities for interactivity • different editing styles. When you are asked to identify you should be as specific and precise as possible. You may find that a question asks you to identify and explain or analyse.	Katy Perry's video for her song *Roar* is a typical pop music video in many ways. For example: • The main visual focus throughout the video is on the singer. • Although other sounds are present at the start, the song is the primary communication in the video. • The song is upbeat and positive. • The colours are bright and the tone of the video is light-hearted. • The images reflect the general message of the song.
Analyse	To analyse is to engage with a detailed exploration of the elements and/or structure of a media product. Analysis begins with observation (usually based on media language choices) and then goes on to explain why each element was chosen and/or what effect these choices may have. It is often a good idea to use the theoretical framework to support the explanation provided.	See the example of a detailed analysis of a film poster on pages 137–139.

Key words/phrases	Expectation	For example
Explain	To explain is to offer a reason why. Explanations should be supported with examples from media products and reasons why should not just be an opinion or a personal perspective. Reasons why should be offered that show your knowledge of the theoretical framework or the context of production.	See the example of an explanation in the analysis of a film poster on pages 139–140.
Consider	Similar to evaluate. You should discuss ideas related to the question that show you have thought about them rather than simply repeated them. One way you can show you are considering the ideas is to apply the ideas you are considering to media examples/contextual issues. Considered ideas are not simply accepted as 'true' – they are applied, thought about and some may be rejected if they do not fit with the evidence from your analysis.	Although the representation of Stella Gibson in *The Fall* follows some conventions in the way women are usually shown, for example she is often presented as a beautiful and sexualised woman in a way that supports the idea of the male gaze (Mulvey), she also subverts these conventions. Stella is a powerful woman who is shown almost exclusively in a professional environment. She is shown being in control of her career and her romantic relationships. She defines herself and is not defined by her relationship to men.
What ...?	This question requires that you identify something ... ideas, media products, audience responses.	**Q:** What methods are used in the *Guardian* to engage the audience? **A:** The *Guardian* encourages **participation** to engage the audience.
How ...?	This question requires that you explain the way something is done. 'How' is usually answered using phrases similar to 'like this'.	**A:** Audience participation in the *Guardian* is used to engage the audience through the comment section at the end of some news stories.
Why ...?	This question requires that you explain the reasons that have led to your observations. 'Why' is usually answered using phrases similar to 'because'.	**A:** The comments sections under news stories in the *Guardian* help engage the audience, as they are able to engage in debates with others and they will recognise the fact that their participation makes them part of the wider cultural debate on a specific issue.
To what extent ...?	This phrasing is asking you to consider 'how much'.	**Q:** To what extent do mobile devices offer more freedom for audience? **A:** Plenty. For example ...

You should aim to use your perspective to present a reasoned and supported argument. The support for your argument is what will provide the evidence of the extent of your studies and your own understanding of the issue raised.

You will need to learn to present an argument but before you can do this you must have one to present. You will learn a range of arguments when you engage with the theoretical framework and hopefully you will hear more in class from your teacher and your fellow students.

What is important is not what other people think but what you think. In order to have an opinion on an argument you will need to engage with other people's ideas and then consider them in light of the media products you are studying.

So, if, for example, narrative theory tells us that narratives work on *conflicts driving a narrative forward until resolution is reached* you may want to consider:

- how soap operas and long-running serials need to manipulate this structure
- how some narratives don't offer conclusive resolutions
- how (and why) hard and soft news stories offer resolutions that are sometimes shown to be false.

To make the writing process easier, you must be sure where you are going in your essay before you start – you should know what your argument is.

This means that preparation is key. You will need to generate ideas when you:

- practise analysing media products
- practise applying media concepts
- practise using theoretical terminology.

The essay-writing process should start with a detailed, thorough and focused plan – get your ideas together before you begin.

Filming for *Benefits Street* on Kingston Road, Tilery, Stockton on Tees.

APPLY IT

Consider this 'why' question. (You can replace the media products for two other successful media products that have similar content if you prefer.)

Q: Explain why programmes such as *Benefits Street* and *Benefits and Proud* have been successful?

A: *Write down your first thoughts on how you would answer the question making sure that each response begins with the word 'because' and contains at least one reference to a media concept or theory.*

For example, because:

- *they attract **audiences** by offering a range of gratifications*
- ***audiences** often respond emotionally to these programmes*
- ***institutions** can target more than one audience group (**ideologically**)*
- *they encourage the use of **social media** benefiting the **institution** in **generating publicity***
- *they encourage the use of **social media**, providing **engagement** and the feeling of being involved for the **audience** members*
- *they fit in with the **current** political/media **narratives.***

Some of the ideas in the list above can be connected to or merged with other ideas from the list.

- *Once you have a list of ideas you are happy with put them in a rank order starting with your 'best' idea.*
- *Identify which ideas relate to the theoretical framework you could use to discuss your observation further (you could link to more than one theoretical idea).*
- *Identify what examples you could use to show how the idea works in the media products.*
- *Do this for all your ideas. You may find a table like the one on the following page can help you organise your ideas.*

Q: Why are programmes such as *Benefits Street* and *Benefits and Proud* successful?

Because ...? (add your own ideas)	Link to theoretical framework idea? (link your idea to an aspect of the theoretical framework)	Example from media product? (provide your own examples)
Because they encourage the use of social media, providing engagement and a feeling of being involved. This in turn helps the audience generate publicity for the institution.	Uses gratification theory; use of social stereotypes; construction of heroes/villains; viral marketing and marketing techniques; social media and herd mentality.	Examples of use of hashtags before ad breaks coinciding with controversial behaviour or comment from characters on the show. Selected Tweets from known opinion leaders and other Twitter users to show viral nature of social media.
Because		
Because ...		
Because ...		

From the above table an essay 'structure' can be formed. The reason for the programmes' success can be discussed and ideas can be supported by the **application of concepts** and **theory**, and **textual examples.**

To turn your ideas into an essay response you need to 'write up' three to five 'because' points giving detailed examples and explanations showing how your idea is related to the programme's success.

2 What does the question want you to focus on?

No question will ask you to discuss everything you know on a specific topic or issue. You will always be asked to focus on a specific, sometimes quite narrow, part of the issue raised.

Consider the following questions – all focusing on representation.

1 Identify and evaluate how race is represented in the media product.

2 Analyse and compare the way the two products represent race.

3 How might the representations of race in the product contribute to an idea of a collective identity (Gauntlett)?

All three of the questions are on 'representation' but each requires a very different response.

1 This question needs a focus on the specific representations of race in a given media product. The way media language has been used to construct the representations present. Semiotic analysis could be used to consider the way the media language choices create connotations that add to the possible interpretations that could be made by the audience. Specific examples will need to be given to show that techniques have been **identified** but a discussion on the meaning created by the media language choices and their potential impact would take an answer to this question into **evaluation**.

2 This is a question that is asking for similarities and differences between different products to be engaged with. Observations will be required but **analysis** needs to deal with why the representations are similar and/or different. This may lead to a discussion on genre codes, institutional values, narrative devices, audience expectations and/or the economic context of production, depending on whether you think the representations are the same/different.

3 This is a question that needs knowledge and understanding of a specific theoretical idea and how that idea works in media products.

It is crucial that, before starting to write, you have read the question carefully and you are clear on the focus you need to take. There are many ways you could be asked to demonstrate your knowledge and understanding of elements of the theoretical framework, but you will not be asked to simply write down everything you know about representation. You will always be asked to engage with a specific aspect of the element of the framework you are being assessed on and you will be rewarded for providing a focused response that selects theoretical ideas and media examples that are best suited to answering the question.

Writing style

When writing about the media you should aim to use media terminology, so practise discussing media text formally and integrating terminology into your writing.

There are some common errors that stop writing from being 'discursive'. Here are a few things that it is best to avoid when writing a discursive essay.

Avoid generalisations, assumptions and guesses

The idea that all women like soap operas or that older audiences don't understand social media is simply not true. These are just stereotypes based on the fact that some women may like soaps and not all older people understand social media, but these facts cannot be applied to all people in the group. To help you avoid generalisations, look for evidence to support what you want to say.

The producers of soap operas do assume that their audience will largely be female and the evidence of this can be found in the way they use stereotypes about women to construct their narratives. There is an assumption that domestic and emotional storylines will appeal to women. Evidence for this can be found in the narrative choices and the representations in the programmes and could be supported further by referring to research on audiences including the work of Morley, Ang and many others.

APPLY IT

Look at these statements about media products. Reword them using media terminology.

1 People really like this programme.

2 This newspaper provides more stories about celebrities than politics, economics and foreign affairs.

3 The drama was very exciting at the start.

4 The decoration in the room looked very posh.

5 The man in charge of investigation got the job done by being violent.

6 The artist was wearing beats headphones in the music video.

Avoid absolute statements (unless they can be supported by facts)

It is true that the BBC broadcasts *Eastenders* and that *The X Factor* is produced by Syco Entertainment, the production company owned by Simon Cowell. However, it is important to recognise the difference between a fact and an interpretation. To say that *Mrs Brown's Boys* is a comedy is a fact. This can be supported by looking at the way it uses the codes and conventions of the sitcom. It also uses a range of visual and lexical techniques that attempt to make the audience laugh. To say that the programme is funny, however, is an interpretation. Given its success, some people do find it funny and so audience numbers can show it is a successful sitcom and analysis of the techniques it uses can show it intends to amuse.

Simon Cowell

Avoid emotive language and value judgements

When analysing and discussing the media, it is best to avoid language that is based on emotion and judgements that are simply based on your own opinion. Saying that *Gotham* is 'brilliant' or that *Newsnight* is 'boring' shows that your comments are based on your own emotional response rather than analysis. Whether something is good or bad is subjective and there are no clear criteria to enable this kind of judgement. Many people attempt to write for Media Studies as if they are writing a review or a blog. Review writers and bloggers don't have to explain the reasons for their feelings about a media product (although good ones do) but Media Studies students won't be rewarded for personal responses unless they can support their responses by demonstrating a knowledge of the theoretical framework and an analytical approach to their interpretations.

Shooting an episode of the Fox series *Gotham*.

Avoid colloquialisms and informal language

Try to keep your writing as formal as you can. It helps you communicate clearly to your readers regardless of how old they are and where they come from. Try to avoid slang terms – TV shows shouldn't be described as 'cheesy'. If you feel they have been cheaply or poorly made then you could analyse the limitations of the mise-en-scène or the clichéd nature of the dialogue (for example) to discuss the way that they fail to draw the audience into the narrative. Your discursive writing should avoid using regional-specific vocabulary and fashionable turns of phrase that may be related to a specific age group or sub culture. Your job is to make your written work understandable.

Avoid cliché and metaphor

Try to avoid using phrases that have either lost their meaning or are metaphorical. TV shows can be described as being a success (evidence can be shown by highlighting viewing figures) but to say they are a 'big hit' is a cliché. For example, 'the protagonist of a drama had an "ace up his sleeve" that was the "final nail in the coffin" for the antagonist' uses two metaphorical clichés. You would be much better saying that the protagonist had a final plan/secret weapon/idea that helped put an end to the antagonist's actions.

Avoid too much description

You will need to provide some description as you have to give examples from media products to support your interpretations. Avoid retelling plot or providing extended descriptions of what you have seen. You should provide enough information on the product you are analysing to demonstrate the point you wish to make.

Avoid only stating what you think – explain or evaluate

Saying that Zoella's blog is a marketing product is a good observation. Identifying that Radio 4's *Today* uses an antagonistic technique when conducting interviews shows a real engagement with the radio show. Stating, however, is only the first

ANXIETY – THE UPDATE

11th October 2016 LIFE · THOUGHTS

part of analysis. You need to support your statement in the following ways:

1 Provide examples from the product to show that you haven't made your statement up.
2 Take care not to over-describe (see previous page).
3 Discuss the examples using ideas and terminology from the theoretical framework.
4 Offer an explanation as to why what you have observed is significant.
5 Evaluate the impact of your observation.

Some helpful (formal) words and phrases

Cause and effect	Comparison	Demonstration/exemplification	Position/relationship
As a result of	Alternatively	Exemplified by	Juxtaposed to
Because	Similarly	Incorporated (in)	In opposition (to)
Consequently	But	It is evident	In addition (to)
Hence	Considering	It is exhibited	Qualification
Necessarily	Correspondingly	It is noticeable	Could be described as
Nevertheless	Either ..., or ...	Presented with	In as much as
Therefore	Having first considered	This is manifest	It could be argued that
Thus	If ..., then...	This suggests	Can be seen to be
Yet	In contrast (to)		
Subsequently	Not only ... but also ...		
	Only so far as		

NEA: For the AS NEA you have only 400 words to show your knowledge and understanding so try to present your ideas as directly as possible and use media terminology to help your focus the points you are making.

CHAPTER SUMMARY

This chapter has dealt with the skills you will need to develop.

- You need to develop your **analytical skills** and your ability to discuss media products in detail to show how they create meaning.
- You need to use **media terminology** and ideas from the theoretical framework confidently and effectively.
- You need to be able to relate media products to the **social, cultural, political and economic contexts of production**.
- You need to be able to communicate your ideas clearly. You should aim to be able to produce formal, **discursive** pieces of writing.

Chapter 8 Close study products

Nine close study products will be selected by the exam board and you will need to study all of them for the exam. Three CSPs will be identified as products that need to be studied **in-depth**. 'In-depth study' means that you should aim to apply all areas of the theoretical framework to the named products. The remaining six CSPs are called **targeted CSPs**. This means that you will be told which areas of the theoretical framework you should focus on when you study these products. Three of the products will need to be studied focusing on media language and representations, and the final three need to be approached from an industry and audience perspective. It is important to use examples from most of the CSPs in the examination. It is possible that some changes may be made to the CSP list so you must make sure you refer to the most recent guidance material published by the exam board.

What you will learn in this chapter

- Alongside the theoretical framework you will also need to study some pre-selected media products known as **close study products or CSPs**.

For more information on the examination, see Chapter 9.

CSP focus	Media form
In-depth CSPs	Newspapers, radio, online and participatory media
Targeted CSPs – media language and representation	Video games, magazines and advertising and marketing
Targeted CSPs – media industries and audiences	Music video, television, film (industries only)

This chapter offers three **case studies** to demonstrate approaches to the close study products. The case studies provide examples of the analysis of three forms across the three platforms: print, broadcast and online. These case studies demonstrate the practical application of ideas from the **theoretical framework** and use media **terminology** to discuss the construction of media products and the way they create meaning for the audience. **Context** issues are also raised in each case study. The case studies should not, however, be seen as definitive ways to think about these products, as your own engagement with the theoretical framework will allow you to make interpretations of your own.

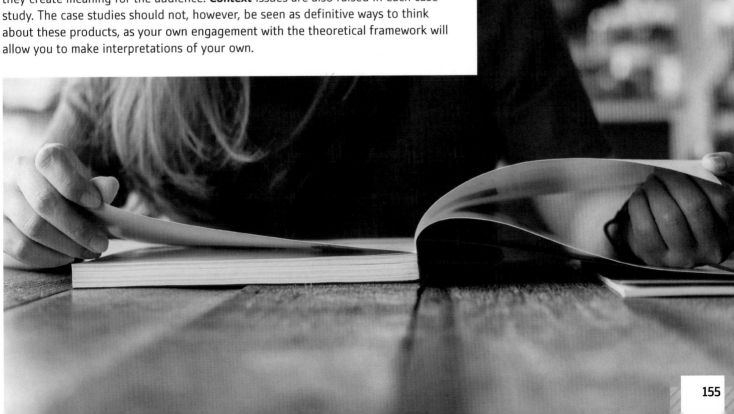

This chapter will also offer Apply It activities to help you practise the skills and use the ideas demonstrated to help you develop a fluent ability to apply theoretical ideas.

You can use this chapter to help construct your own case studies on these and other CSPs. When you complete the Apply It tasks you could use examples from the products here or from other CSPs to extend your understanding.

The CSP case studies use key terms from the theoretical framework discussed and defined in previous chapters.

The CSP case studies that follow provide examples of two targeted and one in-depth case study.

A level CSPs

Students taking the A level examination at the end of the second year will study specific close study products set by the exam board. The AS CSPs are also studied for the A level examination and the examples here are currently identified as **in-depth CSPs for the A level qualification**. As CSPs could change, do take care to check which CSPs are targeted and which are in-depth for your examination.

8.1 Introduction

Close study products should always be analysed and discussed using either the full theoretical framework or the targeted areas of the framework identified by the exam board. The CSP case studies that follow demonstrate how studying CSPs can be approached using the theoretical framework. The other products you study will raise different issues and allow you to explore the theoretical framework from different perspectives, so these case studies do not offer a simple template. The case studies should be used to familiarise yourself with the way media products can be analysed.

The following CSP case studies will demonstrate the study of **magazines**, **television** and **online, social and participatory media**. This chapter offers some examples of how to approach the application of theoretical ideas and demonstrates how the framework can help develop your understanding of the way media products create and communicate meaning.

The CSP case studies are as follows:

A **Targeted CSP** (media language and representation)
  - **Print case study: magazines: *Men's Health*:** a print case study with a close focus on the use of media language to create meaning and the way representations are constructed.

B **Targeted CSP** (audience and industry)
  - **Broadcast case study – television: *The Missing*:** A television case study with a focus on industry and audience issues.

C **In-depth CSP**
  - **Online, social and participatory media case study: *Teen Vogue*.** An online media case study looking at creating audience interest and appeal with ideas from all areas of the theoretical framework.

8.2 Case studies

A: Targeted close study product case study: *Men's Health*

- **Platform:** print
- **Form:** magazines
- **Product:** front cover, contents page and page 101 of the January/February 2017 issue
- **Targeted elements of the theoretical framework:** media language and representation
- **Assessment information:** your knowledge of *Men's Health* magazine may be assessed in Section A of the AS examination. You may be asked to compare the extracts from *Men's Health* magazine to an unseen media product.

Your knowledge and understanding of this media product will be assessed through your application of ideas and theories of **media language (including genre and narrative)** and **representations**. This analysis will refer to audience and industry issues to provide context.

Introduction: genre, audience and industrial context

Men's Health is a US-based magazine published by Rodale Inc. The magazine was founded in 1987 and is a men's health publication, as the name clearly indicates. Since 1987 it has grown into a global brand and currently publishes in 47 countries, with most of those countries publishing local editions.

The CSP is an extract from the UK edition of the magazine published in 2017.

The UK edition of *Men's Health* was first published in 1995 and has grown to become the best-selling UK men's magazine. At the time of its UK launch, *Men's Health* was entering a very competitive market. Men's magazines had become very successful in the 1990s and were largely grouped together under the **genre** term 'lads' mag'. This term defined an approach to content that focused on **stereotypical** men's leisure activities (e.g. sport, cars and socialising). Women were usually presented in a highly sexualised way in this genre. The archetypical example of this **genre** was *Loaded*, which was launched in 1994. Other magazines with a male target audience (such as *FHM, Maxim, GQ, Nuts* and *Zoo*) followed *Loaded*'s lead into providing **lifestyle magazines** that reflect aspects of 'lad culture'. Each one of these magazines attempted to find a **niche audience** within the target group to create its own **brand identity**. For example:

- *Loaded* targeted younger adult males and took a light-hearted and irreverent approach to its lifestyle content. Its tag line was 'for men who should know better'.

- *GQ* is less aggressively 'lad-ish' in approach as it targets slightly older, professional male readers. *GQ* is often associated with an idea of an urban, well-groomed masculinity, sometimes referred to as metrosexual. The magazine's tag line is 'look sharp – live smart'. *GQ* tends to feature men on its covers but, like *Loaded*, has also featured very sexualised representations of women both on its covers and in feature articles.

Men's Health offered a different type of content to the lads' mags of the 1990s, as it focused largely on health, nutrition and fitness. Over the years, *Men's Health* has developed and adapted to maintain **audience appeal** and, while it still features the content it was originally known for, it has moved away from the simple men's health **genre** and has become more of a **hybrid** magazine that also covers general male lifestyle topics, including fashion, celebrity interviews and travel.

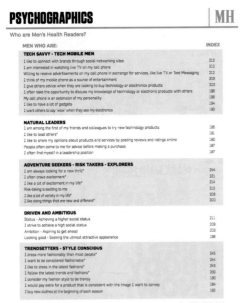

Despite some changes, *Men's Health*'s fundamental **brand identity** remains as it was in the 1980s and 1990s. It usually features muscular men on its front cover and most of its content focuses on having a fit and healthy lifestyle and a strong, toned body.

Men's Health identifies the median age of its readership as being 42½. Of its audience, 81.5% are male and over half of these are married men. Over 30% of the readership are college educated, 62% in full-time employment and 28% are defined as 'professionals'. This makes the magazine attractive to advertisers who have products that could appeal to these groups. It provides potential advertisers with detailed research on its readership and their interests.

Men's Health has managed to survive as a print magazine. Titles such as *Loaded*, *Maxim* and *FHM* have stopped publishing print magazines and now exist only online. *Men's Health* has **diversified** and offers a range of e-media products as well as the traditional print magazine.

BRAND REACH

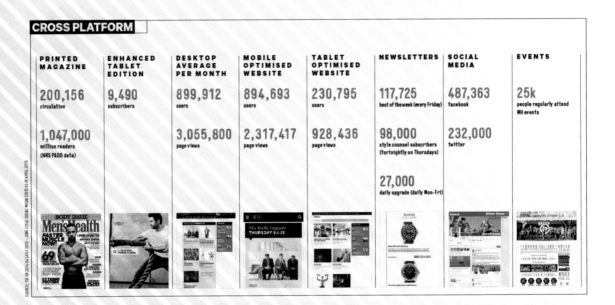

Media language and representation

The close study product focuses on three pages from one edition of the print magazine:

- the front cover
- the contents page
- one page from a feature article.

The magazine was published in January 2017.

The front cover

The **cover** features an image of Vin Diesel set in the centre of the page against a plain background. The cover contains several **cover lines** presented at the top and on the left and right edges of the page. The **title**, **dateline** and **cover price** are placed towards the top of the page. The front cover works on a 3 x 3 grid design. The vertical columns left to right offer cover lines on the left and right, and the image of Diesel is positioned in the centre column. Horizontally, the top third contains the title and Vin Diesel's chest and head. The cover lines become less dense towards the bottom of the page although the image becomes darker and less distinct.

The whole page uses a very limited **colour palette** of grey, blue and black. This is a typical magazine front cover but uses several media language choices that are specific to the **house style** of *Men's Health* such as the serif font used for the title, the mid-shot of a male figure dressed casually, and direct and exclamatory language in the cover lines.

It is a **genre convention** of lifestyle magazines to use recognisable stars or models on their front covers. Women's magazines and men's magazines such as *GQ* often use head and shoulder shots, whereas *Men's Health* often uses near full-body shots, and this has become part of the house style that makes the magazine distinct and recognisable. This focus on the whole body reflects the content of the magazine, as its main interest is in the male body. This longer shot ensures that the male torso and specific muscles become the dominant image. In the CSP, Diesel has been dressed in a simple grey t-shirt and what appears to be a pair of jeans or casual black trousers. His legs are visible but the **lighting** for the shot has been focused on the upper half of his body. He is posing with his arms tensed and the lighting (and possibly make-up and post-production editing) highlights muscle definition in his forearms and biceps. The use of **low-key lighting effects** creates highlights and shadow, which in turn creates a 'rugged' effect. His face in in partial shadow. He is looking directly into the camera and is frowning. Diesel is being offered to the audience to be gazed upon but he is actively returning this gaze. His body is fetishised and turned into an object for other men to desire but the use of shadow, the pose and facial expression, ensure that the gaze is not explicitly sexual. Diesel shows that he is in charge of his image rather than being presented simply for the pleasure of others.

The **cover lines** use a number of different fonts and sizes. Most of the cover lines are presented in capital letters but use lower case in supporting phrases. The fonts for the main cover lines are **sans serif**, which are easier to read when large sizes or capitals are used and when a lot of information is given in a small area. Serif fonts are used for some of the supporting phrases. Colour, size differences, underlining and emboldening are among the techniques used to ensure that all the information on the page is legible for the audience. Informal language and punctuation are used (e.g. 'Double your metabolism!') and the cover lines have been carefully chosen to create a powerful and active tone while giving an insight into the content of the magazine. The front cover acts to promote the magazine, so the cover lines create a level of **enigma** as they hint at the content that can be found in the magazine. The audience needs to buy the product to be able to read further and access the promised information.

The magazine's content reflects the **brand values** of the magazine. It promises a range of articles that are focused on health, nutrition and fitness, and this is what a regular reader would expect. Many of the cover lines are linked to the image of Vin Diesel, whether directly with 'Vin Diesel's Blueprint To Wage War On Flab' or indirectly in the line, 'Lose 8kgs Fast! Gut Gone in 60 Seconds'. The second example contains an **intertextual** reference as it refers to the film franchise *The Fast and The Furious* (featuring Vin Diesel) as well as the film *Gone in 60 Seconds*.

Similar but different. *GQ* and *Vogue* front covers compared to *Men's Health*.

Next to the image of Vin Diesel in a t-shirt is the cover line '103 Shortcuts To T-Shirt Arms'. The **anchorage** of the text and the image implies that the arms we see on the front cover can be achieved by following the 'shortcuts' in the magazine. Many of the cover-lines offer the readership ways to achieve an ideal body. From the front cover we learn than an ideal male body:

- will be fat free (with no 'gut')
- will be muscular (with a '6-pack')
- will have 't-shirt arms'.

Vin Diesel's image is used to exemplify this ideal.

The front cover also shows that the magazine values strength and healthy eating and, although it recognises that this physique requires some effort to achieve, it also offers several 'quick fixes': 'Burn 100KCals in 5 mins', '103 Shortcuts ...' and 'Lose 8kgs Fast!' seemingly making the ideal achievable for the magazine's audience.

The **lexis** chosen here such as **signifiers** like 'flab', 'gut' and 'junk food' create negative connotations that ensure the lifestyle that is **signified** by them appears unattractive and unappealing. Similarly, the active, 'masculine' signifiers such as 'blast', 'build', 'reboot' and 'demolish' create a more positive image of the lifestyle required to attain the ideal depicted here. In this way, *Men's Health* creates a clear set of lifestyle values and ideologies, and links these values to very specific ideas about masculine **identity**.

APPLY IT

The purpose of the front cover is to sell the magazine. To do this it needs to quickly communicate the genre of the magazine and its brand identity. It needs to appeal to its target audience and persuade them to spend £3.99 on this product.

What aspects of the media language choices made on the front cover do you think work to achieve these things?

Genre	
Brand identity	
Audience appeal	
Persuasion	

Vin Diesel is being represented on the front cover of *Men's Health*, and through him ideas about the target audience and the brand values of the magazine are communicated.

The choice of simple, casual clothing **represents** Diesel as being a 'chilled' and relaxed character. He is known to be successful but does not have to reinforce his power through expensive clothes or accessories. This is a convention of *Men's Health* and is part of its **house style**. Diesel's power and success are connoted by his physique – most specifically in this image in his muscular arms. Although relaxed, he has a serious facial expression and his physical size and strength connote a 'no nonsense' personality. His facial expression could be **interpreted** as being slightly aggressive but the frown could also **connote** a quiet thoughtfulness. This image represents the **stereotype** of the strong silent male. These **media language choices** create a specific idea of **masculine identity**.

In this case masculinity is defined by strength and having a lean, muscular body. In the **brand values** of this magazine, this physique is part of what creates masculine power. His 'cool', quiet demeanour is also part of his masculine strength and this is reinforced in the tag line just visible at the bottom of the page where Diesel is described as 'larger than life, smarter by half'. Size is important here but so too is intelligence.

The target audience may receive a **gratification** by **identifying** themselves directly with this idea of masculinity. They may see themselves reflected in this image, which could encourage them to read the magazine to have their own values reflected back to them, thus reinforcing their own identity. Other audience members may see this image and the attitudes communicated by the magazine as **aspirational**. This audience group may see the topics in the cover lines as being **solutions to problems** they perceive in their own lives. The magazine could be used as a product that may help them overcome what they see as their own shortcomings or, as Dyer would express it, **scarcities** within their lives. Being overweight, unfit or physically different from the idea presented to them in the magazine could be seen to be **problems** that need to be overcome. The audience may perceive themselves to be on a **quest** to achieve the ideal exemplified by Diesel, and the magazine becomes the **helper** to support them in achieving their goals. The front cover offers **causality**. It implies that by buying the magazine and following its advice the readership can achieve the masculine identity that it communicates.

The contents page

The **lifestyle values** and ideas about **masculine identity** are continued into the contents page, so can be assumed to be a **consistent message** throughout the magazine. The page is a continuation of pages providing information on the content of the articles that appear in the magazine. This information takes up approximately two-thirds of the page running horizontally. Reproductions of pages from the magazine are used to provide visual information on the magazine's content and a brief caption summarises each article's content. The articles maintain the consistent themes of health, nutrition and fitness. Information and advice are provided within the magazine to further define the lifestyle and help readers construct it for themselves. Articles on fitness classes, endurance challenges, skiing holidays and diet are within the magazine's own **conventions** and would meet **audience expectations**. Less traditional is the article on men's mental health. This article is presented as being a technology-based story but its inclusion in the magazine demonstrates the concerns that have been raised recently about the way society and individuals deal with male mental health issues. Articles such as this expand the scope of the magazine and enlarge the definition of men's health to not just physical health.

The two images used to illustrate both the mental health and nutrition stories are both **symbolic**. The illustration for 'Algorithms & Blues' is made up of items that hold **connotations** of things being broken and things that can mend (or heal). These images are **indexical** of mental health issues and treatments. Similarly, the 'Flour Power' article uses an **icon** of an arm but replaces the muscle with a pie. The pie is **symbolic** of the idea that certain foods are associated with unhealthy lifestyles. The images of the men in the final two articles reinforce the idea of masculine identity already created by the image of Vin Diesel on the front cover. The men are depicted with a quiet and calm yet powerful expression and they are defined by their physical achievements. The article on the sporting achievements of older men is an unusual representation of the older generation. Retired/elderly people are often **stereotyped** as being infirm and they are often shown as being dependent on others, in ill health or unable to care for themselves in some way. The representation of older men here is **positive** and **subverts** the **stereotypes**.

However, this unconventional approach to the **representation** of older men is included here because it **reinforces** the **ideology** of **masculine identity** communicated across the rest of the magazine. These men are valued for their physical fitness, strength and stamina.

Vin Diesel's image is used again at the bottom of the page. The image is from the same photoshoot as the cover picture. The focus of this smaller image is still on the upper part of his body although there is less **contrast** used in the **lighting**. The image selected for the contents page shows Diesel looking confident and a little aggressive. A caption with an arrow has been added and the magazine makes it explicit that Diesel is being offered to the audience as an **aspirational** figure.

The editorial comment to the right of the page **addresses the readers directly** and assumes them to be people who need a role model as well as requiring support and encouragement if they are going to be able to maintain the masculine ideal symbolised by Diesel and *Men's Health*. The editor's comment includes several **references** from popular culture, including: lyrics from John Lennon's *Happy Christmas (War is Over)*, 'So this is Christmas And what have you done?'; references to a historical figure (Nostradamus was a renaissance writer of prophecies); and Ancient Greek mythology (Sisyphus was a mythological character doomed to undertake a futile task over and over as a punishment). This may reflect the adult target audience for the magazine and an assumption on the part of the editor that they will understand these references. It could also indicate the way the audience is being **positioned** and **addressed**. The magazine represents itself as more knowledgeable than the reader and addressing them in this way positions the audience to feel that they need the magazine. *Men's Health* encourages the reader to trust and rely on the magazine, and this could lead to the development of **brand loyalty** as well as, importantly, repeat purchasing of the magazine. The editorial reinforces the narrative created on the front page, where the **heroes** (the readers) need help from the magazine to stay focused on their **quest**. The editorial identifies Christmas and the inevitability that people lose focus on their diet and fitness regimes as the **villains** in this **narrative** but they offer to step in to help get the reader back on track. To reinforce the authority of the editor, the magazine identifies that he was named as a 'BSME [British Society of Magazine Editors] Editor of the Year'.

In the layout of the contents page we can see the name of the magazine and the page number presented on the bottom right of the page, which is called a **footer**. This indicates that it is a right-hand page within the magazine. The magazine's web address is shown at the bottom left of the page.

Page 101: extract from a feature article

Page 101 is a continuation page of a feature article that began on page 96. This was identified in the contents page and it is clear that the article is still unfinished as an arrow has been placed in the bottom right-hand corner of the page as a **symbol** that the article continues overleaf. The title and the page number on the right of the bottom of the page indicate that this is a right-hand page.

The title for the feature is placed in the top-right corner, called the **running head**, and it can be assumed that this has been present on each page (or pair of pages) throughout the feature. This creates a coherent look for the feature article and indicates to the reader that the content on this page is connected to other pages in the article. The page uses a **five-column layout** with the image on the left taking up three **columns** and the text of the article placed in the final two columns. The main image is an 'action' shot showing the **subject** of the feature, Phillip Howells, running. Two **captions** have been overlaid on top of the image. The first is an inspirational quote taken from the interview. The second provides detailed information to identify the extent of his physical achievements.

A second smaller image, Howell's portrait, is placed in the fourth column as a header for the article. A box listing his accomplishments follows the portrait and this is followed by a Q & A interview. The heading for the interview identifies the subject by his accomplishments – 'The Marathon Man' (an **intertextual reference** to the film of the same name) – and this is followed by his name and age. The **selection** and **placement** of this information reinforces the purpose of the feature as identified on the contents page: to focus on senior citizens who continue to train and compete.

The interview is based on questions that focus on Howell's fitness, motivation, training and achievements. The questions and responses are short and to the point, making the article easy to read. The two-column layout presents the text in short lines, which increases readability, and the questions are presented in a bold font breaking up the appearance of text, again making it easier to read.

The subject of the article is older than the target audience, so acts as an **inspirational role model** for the readers. The questions in the interview help him reinforce some of the key **brand values** of the magazine – he sets himself challenges: 'I knew I had to do something'; he works hard to achieve his goal: 'In a week I'll run 30 miles, swim two miles and cycle 40.' Like the magazine itself, he reinforces the importance of nutrition and having a positive mental attitude. The image on the left-hand side of the page shows the subject 'in action' in a neutral studio setting. The pale background contrasts with the dark running clothes Howell wears. This creates a positive and active representation of a man who is nearly 70 years old and the exclusion of **props** and other **mise-en-scène elements** in the image encourages the audience to focus on him and his physical abilities. This representation subverts the idea that men will inevitably become weak in their retirement and shows that some older people can be fitter and stronger than younger men. The **masculine identity** of the subject of the article is linked to his strength and stamina. Although he does not have the muscular physicality of Vin Diesel, he **represents** similar **masculine ideals**.

In many ways, the **representations of masculinity** in *Men's Health* reflect traditional ideas and values. Men are defined by their strength and stamina, and this is reflected in their body size and sporting prowess. In the past, this idea of masculinity may have been thought of as a natural state inherent to men; however, *Men's Health* magazine puts forward the idea that this is something that needs to be worked at and can be achieved with effort and determination. This reflects a more modern way of thinking about **gender**, as the masculine identity shown in *Men's Health* is just one option that can be selected, worked on and created with exercise, a good diet and the right attitude. *Men's Health* shows idealised men to be stoic, focused and determined – again a traditional idea of masculinity – but they also acknowledge that men may suffer from mental health issues and could need support. These values and ideologies are communicated in the representations used by the magazine. These **representations** are created through the careful selection of **media language** choices , which also act to appeal to the **target audience**.

APPLY IT

According to the representations within the CSP, what words best define *Men's Health*'s idea of masculinity?

APPLY IT

Use this CSP (or another example of a print product) to answer the following questions:

1 How have the pages of the product been **constructed**?
   - Make detailed observations on
     - the layout and design of the pages
     - the construction of images, including the use of camera, costume, make-up, poses, mise-en-scène, lighting and post-production editing
     - the choices made in the written elements of the production.
2 What examples of **symbolic** communication can you find?
3 How is **anchorage** used to create meaning?
4 Does the product contribute to the construction of **cultural myths**?
5 How does the product use **narrative** techniques?
6 What can you say about the product's relationship to its form or **genre**?
7 What **representations** are created by the product? Does it use or subvert **stereotypes**?
8 Is there evidence of **misrepresentation** or **selective representation** within the product?
9 How does the product **position** its audience?
10 Does the product create ideas about **identity**?
11 How does the product attempt to control audience interpretation (**decoding**) of the **encoded** messages?
12 What **ideological** meanings are created?

B: Targeted close study product case study: *The Missing*

- **Platform**: Broadcast
- **Form**: Television
- **Product**: *The Missing*, with a specific focus on Series 1, Episode 1
- **Targeted elements of the theoretical framework**: Audience and industries
- **Assessment information**: Your knowledge of *The Missing* may be assessed in Section B of the AS examination.

Your knowledge and understanding of this media product will be assessed through your application of ideas and theories of **audience** and **industries**. This analysis will refer to media language (including genre and narrative) and representation issues as they relate to the audience and industrial contexts of the product.

Introduction: media language, narrative and genre

The Missing is a crime drama. Each series focuses on one investigation into a missing child. The initial episodes set up the **equilibrium** and the **narrative disruption**. Subsequent episodes chart the development of the investigation until the **resolution** is provided in the final episode, where a **new equilibrium** is established. The eight-episode **arc** maintains the central **enigma** (the location of the missing child). Further questions, problems and setbacks help drive the narrative forwards as the assumed **hero** is the character of the police officer who investigates the case. This character links the two series – each of which follows the investigation and consequences when a child goes missing.

Episode 1 of Series 1 of *The Missing* acts as an introduction to the characters, the plot and the location. The story is told across two timelines: 'the present day' and 'eight years ago'. **Media language** is used to ensure the audience can follow this **non-linear narrative**. Occasionally, a caption is added making it explicit which timeline we are in. Other devices are also used. For example, the characters have different haircuts in each timeline and, especially in this first episode, lighting and mise-en-scène are used to create a visual difference between the timelines. Once established, these media language choices become **temporal markers** for the audience. The first scenes of the episode are set in the present and the colours used are muted. The **colour palette** is based on greys and desaturated greens and blues. In contrast, the initial scenes representing 'eight years ago' are bright, sunny and full of primary colours. The characters' interactions reflect this sunny atmosphere, as the audience are introduced to a happy family holidaying in France. As the two stories develop, the muted colour remains in 'the present' but, as the disappearance of the child gets closer and finally occurs 'eight years ago', the sun has set and the family's world has been shattered. The lighting and colour that helped separate the two timelines becomes a **symbol** of the emotions of the characters.

The Missing: the muted colours of the present

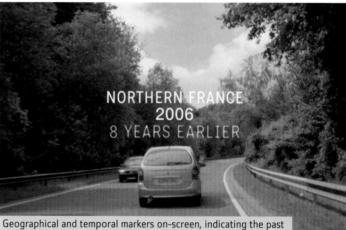
Geographical and temporal markers on-screen, indicating the past

The pastel colours and bright, spring-like mise-en-scène of the past.

The tragedy draws closer and the bright colour palette of the mise-en-scène moves towards the muted colours that symbolise the time after the child's disappearance.

Crime drama is one of the most popular **genres** of television programming. It has been popular for many decades and the genre has **adapted** over the years to reflect changes in society and to meet audiences' changing interests. This means that within this genre there are many different **sub-genres** – some feature individual detectives often with a helper, such as in *Sherlock*; others focus on investigative teams (such as in *Criminal Minds*). Some crime dramas are gruesome and have a dark tone (*The Fall*); others are much lighter (*Midsomer Murders*). Genres need to

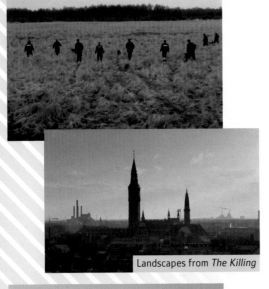

Landscapes from *The Killing*

Landscapes from *Broadchurch*

APPLY IT

Using the first episode of Season 1 of *The Missing* to provide examples:

- Identify the way the episode uses crime drama and/or Nordic-noir **codes and conventions**.

How does the episode offer new or **unconventional experiences** for the audience?

- Identify **narrative techniques** that are used to:
  - provide information about the plot
  - create temporal and geographical markers
  - give an insight into character roles' personalities
  - create a sense of drama, tension and suspense.

change and develop otherwise audiences will find them **predictable** and **clichéd**. The varieties of crime drama on offer allow the genre to remain popular with a range of audience groups who seek different experiences from it.

A relatively recent development of the genre was the rise in popularity of 'Nordic-noir' with English-speaking film and television audiences. This sub-genre of crime drama began in literature and was soon developed for film and television. TV programmes such as *Wallander* and films such as *Insomnia* and *The Girl with the Dragon Tattoo* began to find audiences for the sub-genre outside Scandinavia where it began. Nordic-noir uses **noir** genre conventions and relocates them from the traditional Hollywood film-noir US urban setting to Scandinavian locations – often with a focus on rural and/or industrial urban locations. *The Killing*, a Danish TV show, was broadcast on BBC4 in January 2011 – four years after the original Danish broadcast. The show became a **cult success** and attracted a regular audience, generating lots of discussion between fans online. Although its audience figures look small compared with other more mainstream television programmes, the fact that each week over half a million people were watching a **subtitled foreign drama** presented over 20 episodes on a **niche audience channel** made the importing of the show a ground-breaking moment. The success of *The Killing* has had a major impact. The show was remade for the US market and more European TV has been broadcast by the BBC. Channel 4 also now has a large collection of non-English-language programmes available, collected as 'Walter Presents'.

The Killing has also inspired the way new crime dramas are presented: Nordic-noir has a range of visual and thematic codes and conventions that have proved to be very popular. One of the most successful ITV dramas of recent years was heavily influenced by Nordic-noir: *Broadchurch* was broadcast in 2013 and its first season attracted eight to nine million viewers per episode, with over ten million viewers tuning in for the final season. *Broadchurch* used a number of conventions taken from Nordic-noir and so too does *The Missing*. Some of the conventions of the sub-genre include the following:

Some visual codes of Nordic-noir	Some thematic codes of Nordic-noir
Symbolic montage in the title sequence and/or use of melancholic music	The story will often be focused on crime and police investigations
Muted colours	Investigator is a 'lone wolf hero' who has personal problems to contend with and/or a dark past
Subdued and low-key lighting	Investigator 'hero' may struggle with personal relationships
Long slow pans and tracking shots over landscapes and landmarks	Other characters are shown to be complex and often flawed
Settings are often wintery	Authority figures cannot always be trusted
Rural landscapes are often presented as 'bleak'	Focus on the consequences of violent crime
Urban landscapes are often presented as industrial	Dramatic tension and suspense

Industrial context

The Missing is a television drama originally broadcast in the UK by the BBC on its main channel, BBC1. At the time of writing there have been two series of the programme. The first series of eight episodes was broadcast at 9pm on Sundays from October to December 2014. The second series was broadcast at the same timeslot in October and November of 2016. The series was successful in the UK, with the first series building its audience from just over six million for the first episode to 8.7 million for the series finale. The second series attracted over nine million viewers for the first episode but lost some viewers, with just over eight million people tuning in for the final episode.

Production and distribution

The Missing was financed by a collaboration between four production companies: Playground Entertainment, Company Pictures, New Pictures and Two Brothers Pictures, with investments from film and TV financers, including the Flemish Radio and Television Broadcasting Organisations and the Belgian national **public service broadcaster**. The BBC commissioned the show and were also involved in its production. The show was distributed by **all3media.**

Playground Entertainment is a global production company based in the UK and the US. The company was involved in other dramas such as *The White Queen* (BBC, 2013) and *Wolf Hall* (BBC, 2015).

Company Pictures is a UK-based production company that is a subsidiary of *The Missing*'s distribution company. Company Pictures was also involved in the production of *The White Queen*. Both *The White Queen* and *The Missing* were financed in collaboration with a Flemish production company.

all3media is identified as the UK's largest independent media **distributor**. Its function is to sell media products to broadcasters, cinemas and other **distribution** outlets. The **all3media** group owns several production companies, so is also involved in the **production** of media content as well as its **distribution**. It owns production companies around the world and has worked in collaboration with many other production companies. It is involved in many different genres of television, from dramas such as *The Missing*, *Skins* and *Midsomer Murders* to reality shows such as *The Only Way is Essex* and *10 Years Younger*, game shows such as *The Cube* and children's programming such as *Horrible Histories*.

all3media is owned by the US companies **Discovery Communications** and **Liberty Global**. Discovery own the Discovery Channels as well as having interests in other production and distribution companies. Liberty Global is a telecommunications company that runs phone, internet and cable network services around the world. Liberty Global has shares in Lionsgate and ITV plc. It owns Virgin Media and European mobile phone companies including Vodafone Netherlands.

In addition to the globalised nature of the funding of *The Missing*, its production was shaped by the fact that the production received tax incentives from the Belgian government to film there and employ local production staff. The show is set in France but was filmed in Belgium. The French setting, the casting of a French actor in the role of the police investigator and the use of British actors as the family at the centre of the **narrative conflict** will have helped to create a more global rather than narrow local appeal for the show.

Broadcasting and distribution

BBC1 is the flagship, mainstream BBC television channel. It broadcasts a variety of programmes for different audiences across the day and its 9pm Sunday slot is traditionally used for dramas that have adult appeal. As this is just after the **watershed**, the levels of violence, sexuality, swearing and tension can be higher than programmes broadcast before 9pm. When *The Missing* was first broadcast, the BBC Trust had an overview on the running of the BBC, including its programming. The Trust closed in 2017 and the BBC now has to follow Ofcom **regulations** regarding the material it broadcasts. The watershed is identified by Ofcom as being a process that acts to protect children from potentially 'harmful' or 'unsuitable material'. Unsuitable material is defined as including 'everything from sexual content to violence, graphic or distressing imagery and swearing'. The **scheduling** of *The Missing* identifies that the target audience for *The Missing* will be assumed to be 'adult' but the programme will not be overly graphic as the broadcast is still relatively early in the evening. *The Missing* was also available for audiences to watch on the BBC's streaming, catch-up service, **iPlayer**. Series 1 and 2 of *The Missing* are currently available to purchase on DVD – both separately and as a two-series box set. They can also be bought as digital downloads.

The Missing is currently available internationally to watch on Amazon's streaming service. Season 1 is free to watch for subscribers to the service. Season 2 can be bought or rented. *The Missing* has been broadcast internationally. It was broadcast on BBC First in Australia and on the US network Starz.

STARZ

Starz is a US **premium cable network**. It broadcasts film and television programmes to audiences who **subscribe** to its service. It buys programming from different producers but also funds its own original programmes. Within the Starz network there is a range of channels that target specific niche audiences. For example, **Starz Edge** targets 18- to 34-year-olds and **Starz in Black** targets black audiences. *The Missing* was broadcast on **Starz**, the network's main channel.

Amazon Prime is a film and television service that can be accessed via an annual subscription. Subscription allows access to a range of television and film titles either via streaming or as downloads that can be watched offline. **Amazon Prime** subscription also includes access to free next-day delivery when shopping on the Amazon website. Not all films and television programmes are free to watch within the subscription. Some titles are available for a small rental charge or can be purchased. Non-subscribers can also purchase film and TV products from Amazon.

Amazon has funded the **production** of original content but it also provides access to programming from many different producers around the world. Like Netflix, Amazon Prime provides a distribution model that removes the need for scheduling, and both companies have a global reach. Prime members now outnumber non-Prime customers. *Fortune* magazine reported that there were over 80 million Amazon Prime subscribers as of April 2017.

Advertising and marketing

The first season of *The Missing* was marketed in several ways in the UK. Ahead of its initial broadcast, information about the programme was communicated to other media outlets. The BBC provided **press releases** and a media pack containing information that could be reworked into articles and blog posts. Some press releases provided basic information while others provided much more detail. A detailed press release was released over six months prior to broadcast providing quotes from producers, a plot summary, biographical details on the stars and industrial information about production. This information is included so writers can choose the focus of their articles and provide the kind of information that will appeal to their readers. It is hoped that the early release of information will create audience awareness of the project, which in turn will encourage social media discussions. The press release shown on the right identifies James Nesbitt as the star of the show. He is a well-known actor and this information alone is likely to make the press release newsworthy for many entertainment journalists and could help encourage viral communication among fans and other audience members.

Press packs contain even more information. Images are provided that can be used to illustrate articles and posts. Detailed information on the cast and crew is presented as well as Q & A interviews with the stars, the writers and the director that can be published under the journalists' or bloggers' byline.

Extract from the BBC press pack

THE MISSING

BBC One (8x60mins)

28 October 2014, 9pm

The Missing is made by New Pictures and Company Pictures in association with Two Brothers Pictures and Playground. It is written by Harry and Jack Williams and directed by Tom Shankland.

The press pack includes character profiles and plot summaries – everything a writer would need to write a feature on the programme.

Trailers were also used to promote the programme. They were shown on television, featured on the BBC website and uploaded to YouTube. Trailers can be included within online articles and blog posts as well as being linked to on social media. As well as trailers, the BBC released interviews with the stars on YouTube. In addition to the promotion of the show, the BBC will also make an income from views on YouTube.

Company Pictures features its shows on its website and The Missing is used as an illustration on the site's homepage. The **BBC** created webpages for the show. It offers character and episode summaries, and clips from the programme. There is a feature on the writers and a behind the scenes blog written by the director. Additional content is also provided, with pages that focus on aspects of the **narrative** such as the significance of a drawing made by the missing child and background information on the father's past. This extra fictional information is presented realistically. The father's background is revealed through the content of a 'police file' and a suspect's 'medical file' can be read (as long as you can read French).

Filming starts on BBC1 James Nesbitt drama The Missing

News Jon Creamer   06 March 2014

Filming has started on 8 x 60 thriller series, The Missing, starring James Nesbitt and Frances O'Connor

The character driven drama, made by New Pictures and Company Pictures in association with Two Brothers Pictures and Playground, is written by Harry and Jack Williams and directed by Tom Shankland (Ripper Street).
It's due for TX on BBC1 and Starz in the US later this year.

Article from televisual.com

Company Pictures features its relationship with *The Missing* on its website.

The information on the website relates to the programme but the programme can be watched and understood without going online. For audience members who want to **immerse** themselves further into the mystery of the show, the website provides clues, information and discussion points. The BBC use Facebook and Twitter to promote their programmes. The hashtag #themissing has been used for both series of the programme. Pre-broadcast information is shared by producers, journalists and members of the public and it is possible to see how this creates an anticipation for the show.

Audience members share comments and theories about the show during its broadcast and also use the hashtag to share information related to the show or its stars. As the show trends on Twitter so more users, including other businesses and organisations, use the interest in the programme to raise their own profile.

The trends on Twitter are also picked up by more traditional news sources and so the programme and the audience response become news stories. Discussion in the press raises the programme's profile and this developing interest in the programme during its broadcast run can help explain its increasing audience during Series 1 and the fact that its audience numbers peaked at the start of Series 2.

APPLY IT

- Using examples from Episode 1, Series 1 of *The Missing*:
  - In what ways does the episode reflect the fact that its **funding** came from several international sources?
  - Whose **point of view** is the audience shown? How may this have helped with the marketing of the programme?
  - What **appeal** might the **setting** of the show create for UK audiences?
- How did **technology** help with the success of the show?
- Access the BBC website for *The Missing*, Series 1. www.bbc.co.uk/programmes/b04ph76g.
  - How would the website help **attract and maintain an audience** for the programme?
  - What **gratifications** does the website offer for the audience?
  - How could the website add to the **enjoyment** of the TV programme?
  - How does the website reflect **BBC1's brand image**?

Audience

The Missing is a successful show. It is popular with audiences and critics – it has a 90% rating on Rotten Tomatoes, a website where critical responses are analysed and aggregated. The advertising and marketing discussed above will have helped make people aware of the programme and, combined with social media discussions, this awareness spread during the broadcast of the first season. Catch-up services mean that people can join the audience later in the run.

Much of the programme's success will be down to the **gratifications** provided in the way the product is constructed, in its use of **genre codes and conventions**, in its ability to tell an engaging story and its use of interesting **representations**. Without this, advertising and marketing will not persuade people to return to a programme that they have not enjoyed. Audiences return to well-written and well-acted examples of this genre, as mysteries are intriguing and audiences engage with characters and their emotional journey.

The crime drama genre offers many **entertainment gratifications** from the **intellectual** engagement with twists and turns of the mystery and the ultimate reveal to the reassurance of the **myth** of 'good overcoming evil'. Traditionally, the crime drama would end with the capture or destruction of the criminal, so a danger is removed from society. More modern examples of the genre sometimes subvert this expectation, which could be seen as reflecting a more pessimistic view of humanity or, depending on your point of view, a more realistic one. Crime dramas allow audiences to explore dark emotions, behaviours and motivations in a safe environment. *The Missing* offers **vicarious** and **visceral** pleasures drawing the audience into the emotionally traumatised world of the distraught parents.

Crime dramas raise debates about the levels of violence they present and the impact that these may have on audiences. Crime dramas are sometimes accused of exploiting cultural fears, especially when the victims are children. The basic plot-line of *The Missing* reads as follows:

In 2006, a five-year-old from a middle-class family disappears whilst on holiday in Europe with their parents.

This mirrors the real-life events of the disappearance of Madeleine McCann in 2007. The McCann family tragedy became a major news story and over ten years later the search for Madeleine continues and theories as to what happened are still part of British culture.

The success of the genre can offer the audience an exploration of their fears and concerns but could also feed into what Gerbner calls '**mean world syndrome**'. The world of crime drama is filled with violence and appears to reinforce ideas that our modern world is a violent and dangerous one. The violence of crime drama is often random and the victims of violence are innocents. In *The Missing*, a family holiday turns into a tragedy, in *The Killing* a teenage girl is brutally murdered, and week after week in *Criminal Minds* innocent law-abiding citizens find themselves terrorised by psychopaths and serial killers. While there are incidents of horrific violence in the real world, they are rare and the exception rather than the rule.

Violent crimes will often be reported in the news, so the repetition of the idea that we live in a 'mean world', coming from both factual and fictional media, can lead to audiences believing the world is more violent than it really is. The risks of being a victim of violent crime are tiny and, according to Pinker, homicide rates are 'around half of what they were in 1990'. People tend to think that the risks are, however, greater than they are (Mueller).

Media producers know that tapping into audiences' fears and concerns is often a recipe for success. Dyer's **utopian solution theory** states that audiences like to consume media products that make up for a lack of, or help provide, temporary solutions to problems related to their real lives. The intensity of emotion and narrative twists and turns in a crime drama can enliven someone who feels their life is monotonous and predictable; the active nature of the investigation can invigorate someone who feels physically or emotionally exhausted. If the audience believes we live in a 'mean world', crime dramas reinforce their point of view. This may not provide reassurance but there is a pleasure that can be derived when the media confirms your existing beliefs.

The popularity of the crime drama genre means that media producers know there is a potential audience for more products within this genre. Fictional crime dramas attract audiences, as do documentaries about real-life crimes. One of the most popular Netflix shows in 2015 was a real-life documentary called *Making a Murderer*, and the podcast *Serial*, also a true-life crime drama, was a major success in 2014.

The Missing is a successful TV programme. Part of its success comes from creating a good marketing campaign but its popularity is largely due to the way the show is constructed.

- Audiences respond to compelling stories, appealing characters and intriguing mysteries.
- The programme generates social media engagement that benefits the media producers as it adds to the promotion of the show.
- Audiences also gain by being part of a group having conversations about the programme, where they are able to feel a sense of community.

APPLY IT

- What **gratifications** does the first episode of Series 1 of *The Missing* offer the viewer?

- How are these gratifications created?

- Are there any aspects of the programme that you think would encourage viewers to join in **social media discussions**?

C: In-depth close study product case study: *Teen Vogue*

- **Platform**: E-media
- **Form**: Online, social and participatory media
- **Product**: *Teen Vogue*
  - Website www.teenvogue.com/
  - Facebook page www.facebook.com/teenvogue/
  - Twitter feed https://twitter.com/TeenVogue
- **Assessment information**: Your knowledge of *Teen Vogue* will be assessed in Section C of the AS examination

Your knowledge and understanding of this media product will be assessed through your application of ideas and theories of media language, representation, audience and industries. As an example of online media, the actual content of the website, Facebook page and Twitter feed will have been updated when you study this CSP. Visit teenvogue.com and their accompanying social media pages as you read through this case study to relate their content to the analysis below. In your own work on *Teen Vogue* you should use recent examples to support your own application of the theoretical framework. This analysis of teenvogue.com is based on the content displayed on September 12th 2017. Some of the pages discussed here may still be available, others may have been amended or removed.

Industrial context

Teen Vogue is a magazine title owned and published by **Condé Nast**, an American media organisation that publishes over 20 magazines.

Condé Nast products started as print magazines but have **diversified** and become **cross-media products** produced online on websites, social media and video-hosting sites. Condé Nast products target different **audience groups** and offer different types of content. *Glamour* and *Vogue*, for example, target women while *GQ* targets men. *Wired* is a technology magazine and *The New Yorker* is literary publication offering reviews, commentaries, poetry and fiction.

Vogue was first published in 1892 and was purchased by Condé Nast in 1909. *Vogue* is presented as a high-quality publication focusing on fashion and, in its long life, has always had the brand image of being both the foremost authority on fashion as well as being an innovator in the way fashion is presented to its audience – as an art-form through its stylised photography. *Vogue* is a global brand and currently is published around the world, having specific editions in the UK, Italy, Paris, India, Saudi Arabia, and Mexico/Latin America. *Vogue* has two offshoots targeting specific demographics: *Men's Vogue* and *Teen Vogue*.

Teen Vogue was first launched in America in 2003. Its aim was to **target a youth audience** who may not have been attracted to the parent magazine. Attracting a teen audience and generating **brand loyalty** could actively help increase the sales of *Vogue* as the *Teen Vogue* audience grow older.

Teen Vogue was initially printed on smaller-sized paper than *Vogue* and was cheaper to buy than the parent magazine, making it more accessible for the target audience.

Like *Vogue*, *Teen Vogue* focuses on fashion, beauty and celebrities, but takes an approach to these topics that intends to meet the interests of teenagers. Again like *Vogue*, *Teen Vogue* published around the world and there was a British edition of the print magazine. Sales of print magazines have, however, been in serious decline as online media has become more accessible and popular, so *Teen Vogue* has **diversified** into online content and its website and social media are now the most successful parts of the brand. As a magazine, *Teen Vogue* recently announced that it is shutting the print version downtherefore it is an example of a media brand that has used **convergence** to maintain and expand its audience.

Teen Vogue: income sources

Teen Vogue offers the audience different ways to **access** its content and this means it has a number of different **income sources**. An income will be generated by the sale of **advertising space**. The money generated by the online and social media products is very important. teenvogue.com encourages their audience to register with the website for updates. Registration offers the audience access to exclusive content through the 'Insider' area of the website, and registration and subscription also provide the company with important **audience data** that can be used to sell online advertising and generate sponsorship deals.

Advertising space is a key source of income

Social media is also an important source of income

teenvogue.com features **advertising**, some of which is targeted specifically at the individual reader based on their browsing history. Other adverts are placed on the website to promote other Condé Nast titles and products, while others indicate the purchase of advertising space on the website.

In addition to the website, social media can also be a source of income. *Teen Vogue* has a **YouTube** channel and the company will receive an income based on the number of views each video receives. Twitter and Facebook provide alternative ways for audiences to access *Teen Vogue* content, and simultaneously act to promote the magazine and the website. **Twitter** and **Facebook** encourage audience members to share *Teen Vogue* content and so help extend the brand's reach. In addition, the brand is active on other social media including **Pinterest**, **Instagram** and **Snapchat**. *Teen Vogue*'s social media is largely used to promote articles published on teenvogue.com and encourage audiences to share the content and engage with other audience members in online discussions.

YouTube offers video content connected to the website content and also has topic-specific channels including 'Pop Feminist', 'Ask a Syrian Girl' and 'Guys Read', showing *Teen Vogue*'s commitment to both political content and broadening its audience base.

Fashion magazines exist to create a profit, but they are also part of the larger fashion industry. Their role is to communicate information to the audience about what products are available to buy and encourage the audience to desire these products. Advertising in the magazines and on the websites is explicitly part of this process but much of the **editorial content** of the magazines is also constructed for this purpose and **sponsored articles** are an important feature of the magazines and an important source of income.

Teen Vogue: genre and audience

Teen Vogue contains content covering topics that are traditionally seen as of interest to female audiences; however, fashion, style and beauty are increasingly seen as gender-neutral topics and the magazine has diversified into presenting political lifestyle and social content that would be of interest to teens regardless of gender. Although the magazine targets 'teens', its content has the potential to be of interest to people outside the **target demographic**. In its development, it has not only followed the codes and conventions of teen-targeted fashion and lifestyle magazines but has also expanded the **audience's expectations of the genre** to **broaden its appeal**.

The content of teenvogue.com is largely based in American culture but it has a **global appeal** as its content reflects the international nature of modern fashion and celebrity. Celebrities such as the Kardashians and models such as Cara Delevingne have international fame and teenvogue.com regularly features internet celebrities as well as music, TV and film stars. teenvogue.com reflects the interests of the audience by featuring people who are 'instafamous' and have become influential **opinion leaders** via social media.

As previously mentioned, teenvogue.com is expanding its brand image by diversifying content from just fashion, beauty and lifestyle into political and social commentary. A whole section of the website is devoted to news and politics and it has adopted a specific political and ideological position. teenvogue.com provides commentary on gender issues (pro-feminist and identities that are gender/sexually fluid), ecological issues (accepting the science of climate change) and has been highly critical of President Trump. teenvogue.com offers information on political and social issues that have a direct impact on the website's target audience. As such, the *Vogue* brand has been expanded and *Teen Vogue* not only seeks to sell clothes and make-up but also acts to inform and mobilise young people.

APPLY IT

Spend some time on the *Teen Vogue* website and identify the different topics covered by the magazine. Consider what this tells you about *Teen Vogue*'s assumptions about its **audience**.

How would you describe a *Teen Vogue* reader?

Media language, genre and narrative

The *Teen Vogue* website meets two of the most important criteria for a successful website: it is visually appealing and easy to navigate. Importantly for *Teen Vogue*'s **brand identity**, the site has a distinctive and consistent visual style that makes the brand recognisable.

The contents pages of the website are organised on a simple grid pattern. Information about the content of the website is included in two ways: links to the magazine sections are provided across the top of the page in a red banner and they can also be accessed via a menu on the left-hand side of the page. The contents at the top of the page change depending on where you are on the site, as they list the specific subsections of each area. The contents in the left-hand menu remain the same, giving visitors to the site easy access to other sections at any time. Every page features the *Teen Vogue* logo, which contains a **visual reference** to its parent magazine by using the same font as *Vogue* (a traditional, black, lightweight, upper-case serif font, with **connotations** of elegance, tradition and authority) combined with a modern presentation of the word 'teen', using a modern bold, lower-case, italic, sans serif font in red. The logo communicates the **brand identity** as being a mix of the old and the new, the traditional and the contemporary. *Teen Vogue* brings the authority of *Vogue* but updates it and gives it a modern, youthful twist.

The homepage provides access to a selection of stories from across the website.

The website menu is presented as a simple grid pattern.

At the very top of the page the main stories are grouped together to give quick and easy access to them. Articles are identified with a headline and an illustration. Both words and images act to appeal to the audience and encourage them to **click through** to the article itself. Advertising is often featured below the menu bar.

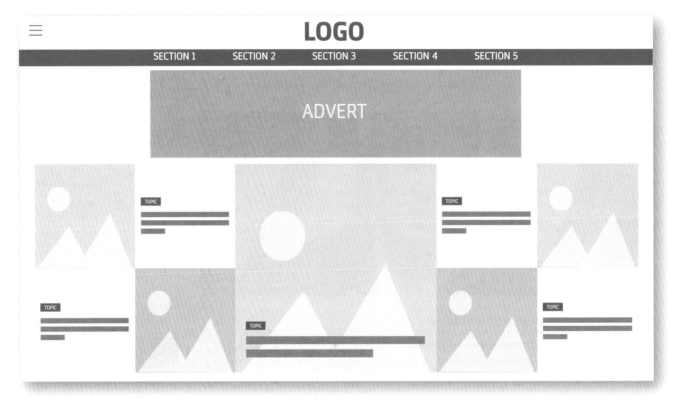

The '#TRENDING' feature is positioned just below the story montage. This section is updated regularly and features links to the most up-to-date stories based on recent events.

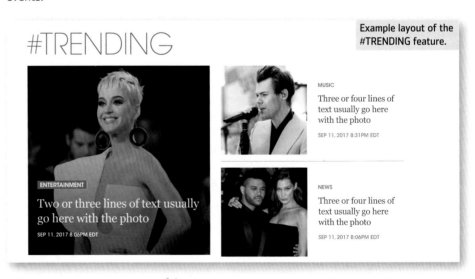

Example layout of the #TRENDING feature.

Further down the page the information is presented via an image and headline. The layout of the homepage depends on the format the audience is using to view it. In a large browser the information appears in the centre of the page with white space on either side. In this format, pop-up adverts appear on the right-hand side of the page. Sometimes they are third-party adverts and sometimes they are promoting Condé Nast products.

On mobile devices or in small browser windows, the information is on the left-hand side leaving room for the adverts on the right. On a mobile phone's smaller screen, there is no white space so adverts appear within the page itself.

teenvogue.com example layout on a tablet (left) and on a mobile phone (above right)

Examples of stories from the various sections of the website are featured on the front page, whether it is 'celebrity style' or 'news and politics'. The front page introduces the main stories within the website and provides an indication of the tone and content of the online magazine. The images used are a mix of red-carpet shots, casual Instagram-like images, promotional photos and exclusive photoshoots. Some stories are illustrated with stock images (see right).

Towards the bottom of the page teenvogue.com includes an advertising feature for the print version of the magazine, additional content such as videos and special features, and a section identified as 'sponsor content' containing links to **advertorials**.

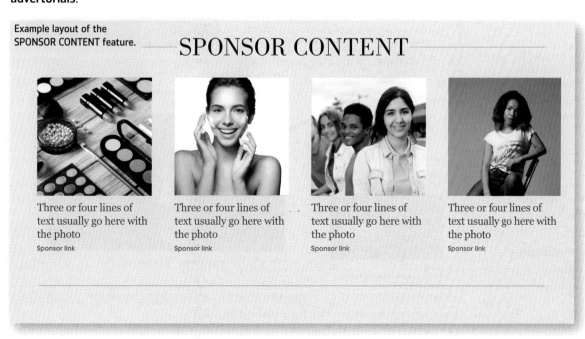

Example layout of the SPONSOR CONTENT feature.

SPONSOR CONTENT

Three or four lines of text usually go here with the photo
Sponsor link

Three or four lines of text usually go here with the photo
Sponsor link

Three or four lines of text usually go here with the photo
Sponsor link

Three or four lines of text usually go here with the photo
Sponsor link

The homepage of seventeen.com

The images on the homepage are simple and have been selected to appeal to the audience. Celebrities dominate the page but a dramatic image of the World Trade Center attack in 2001 (see screenshot on page 176) and the impact of Hurricane Irma are also used to capture the audience's attention and encourage them to read on. Capital letters are used to highlight certain words and add drama to the statements. **Anchorage** is created with the headlines. For example, the **intended meaning** of the story about Donald Trump is to be critical of the President. He is not identified by his formal title and the picture editor chose a shadowy image of Trump wearing a suit and standing at a microphone with his finger raised in a gesture that **connotes** a stern father figure. The fact that Trump has just nominated '42 U.S. Attorneys – and Only 1 Is a Woman' becomes a patriarchal act when combined with this image.

teenvogue.com provides the **familiarity** of a fashion/lifestyle online magazine but in its use of hard news stories and analysis of historical and political events it **subverts genre and audience expectations**. Of course, some readers may reject the less than traditional content but others, who may not have been drawn to a conventional fashion magazine, may find the variety of content appealing. This means that through a diverse mix of content and platform, teenvogue.com can attract a broader audience. teenvogue.com has also been influential in the genre, and other teen magazines online now feature a mix of fashion, celebrity and politics.

teenvogue.com is in itself following the lead of more politically focused blogs and online magazines that have become popular over the past few years. Online magazines such as *Jezebel* and *Rookie Mag* have targeted similar audiences but offer content covering political and social issues.

APPLY IT

Explore the websites for *Seventeen* and *Teen Vogue*. What **characteristics** do they both share?

APPLY IT

Explore rookiemag.com. How is it similar to or different from teenvogue.com?

Consider:

- the **design** of the two sites
- the way the sites use **images**/the types of **images** used
- the way the **audiences** are addressed
- the **content** of the websites.

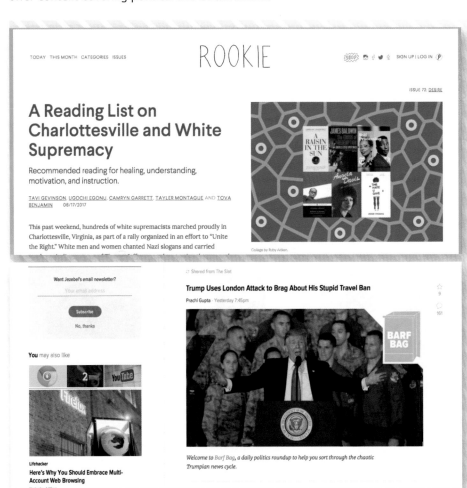

Extracts from rookiemag.com (top) and jezebel.com (bottom)

Following the traditional approach of fashion magazines, articles on teenvogue.com often promote products, brands and celebrities, and act as shoppers' guides. Articles are accompanied by images that feature the products and are constructed in a way to present the product as positively as possible. The headlines for the celebrity, fashion and lifestyle stories offer the audience some form of information, whether it's an insight into Kylie Jenner's psychology, personal information about Selena Gomez or what discussions are trending elsewhere online.

Media language and representation

Fashion

The feature on Skai Jackson's clothing line is clearly intended to raise awareness of the products, create an interest and desire and, hopefully, persuade some readers to purchase the products, or at the very least become actively engaged in the promotion of this article and the products, it is selling. The images used to illustrate the article follow the codes and conventions of a fashion shoot and are intended to make the products even more desirable. Skai Jackson's celebrity status is part of the appeal of the clothing line and she is also paid to represent *Teen Vogue* as a brand ambassador, so there is evidence of **synergy** here between the magazine, the clothing brand, the actress and the American department store Macy's, which receives positive promotion from this feature article. The article provides links to other areas of teenvogue.com and to external sites such as the Nowadays website, which then links to Macy's.

Skai Jackson is a teenvogue.com brand ambassador

The article reinforces the desirability of the products by declaring that the range offers 'everything you would ever need for fall [autumn]' and 'you're going to want literally everything…twice'. The use of the word 'adorable' positions the range as appropriate for a younger market and could be targeting the parent or guardian who would ultimately purchase the clothes. The images also create a relatively sophisticated image that would appeal to teenagers who wish to appear

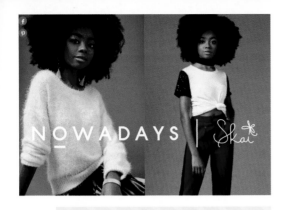

APPLY IT

Choose a fashion article from teenvogue.com. Identify the way the **media language** has been used to encourage the audience to desire and, possibly, buy the product or products featured in the article.

For more on Bandura's theory see page 180.

slightly more 'grown-up'. Skai's signature **positions** her as a young teen with the use of a flower for the dot over the 'i' but her styling creates a more mature image with the use of make-up and jewellery. The photographs are heavily stylised, with Skai posing in ways that reflect the way fashion models are often photographed. The images have been enhanced in post-production. Post-production in fashion photography is often used to smooth out models' skin, erasing any imperfections. It can enhance lighting effects and create flattering highlights. It is not uncommon for photographs of models' faces to be altered significantly before publication. Eyes can be brightened and widened, lips made fuller and cheekbones more pronounced. Models can be 'slimmed down' in post-production, as the images aim to present both the model and the clothes in as 'perfect' a way as possible.

Political, social and cultural contexts

Limited ideas of female beauty

This 'perfect' representation of models within fashion magazines has often been held up as a problem by people who worry about the impact of these images on the audience. With repeated viewing of 'beautiful' and extremely thin images, it is thought that some audience members would see this idea of the female body and appearance as a norm and even aspirational. **Bandura**'s social learning theory supports the idea that the observation of, in this case, images can influence the way people think and behave.

Attempts to link the representation of women to, for example, mental health issues and eating disorders have not been fully successful. A study of fitness magazines by **Thomsen** shows that there is no direct link to the reading of these magazines and the development of eating disorders. **Barthes** argued that the repeated presentation of an image as 'normal' can make it appear **normal** or **natural** to the reader. The **normalisation** of a limited definition of female beauty could create false expectations in the way females are 'supposed' to look and create pressures for women to conform to these ideals. Different audience members will react differently to the **representation** of these images. Some may respond in line with the magazine's intentions and seek to purchase products that will help them get closer to the ideal way to look. Some audience members will reject the definition of the ideal of beauty presented, while others may find the images impact on their self-esteem and they may be more susceptible to negative reactions to the representations presented in fashion magazines.

News and politics

The news and politics section of the website offers content that breaks with the conventions of fashion magazines. The question on the homepage, 'Are Americans Safer Since 9/11?', is intended to tap into contemporary fears of terrorist attacks and suggests that the article will provide answers to this question. This continues the form of address used in other areas of the website, where teenvogue.com positions itself as being knowledgeable and having authority. teenvogue.com maintains its position as a guide and advisor by reporting on hard-news stories with a serious tone, and it offers explanations of political issues and ideas. The website also uses some informal and colloquial language in its reporting; for example, 'many have taken to Twitter to call out Trump's nominating only one woman to the legal post'. This makes the stories accessible for the target audience. Social media and online sources are often referred to in these stories, as this reflects the media world that many of the readership find most familiar.

Across all sections of teenvogue.com the type of stories and images selected create a **narrative** about the world and reflect a **set of values** that are communicated across much of the content. teenvogue.com deals with the politics of gender and sexual identity, and reflects an attitude that accepts difference and seeks to help empower groups that may not have power in the wider society. An article on Lady Gaga's Superbowl performance of 'Born this Way' in 2017 is based on Twitter exchanges and argues that the performance carried a political message: 'performing a song that's so blatantly gay in front of an audience that includes Mike Pence, one of the most anti-LGBTQ politicians today, is absolutely political'. The positioning of the reports combines to create a political narrative that is largely progressive and often stands in opposition to the policies of the Trump administration. Social and political issues such as voting rights, immigration and child marriage are reported on alongside more general current affairs stories, and the online magazine offers its audience an opportunity to engage in active social protest, offering advice and guidance as well as a reading list and links to external agencies and organisations.

teenvogue.com supports ecological and feminist issues, and promotes racial inclusion both within the US and with a more global perspective. Much of its political reporting is currently focused on issues relating to the Trump presidency, and it is highly critical of the President and the politics his administration represents. teenvogue.com has become overtly political, even organising meetings across America between young activists.

teenvogue.com reports on issues related to the Trump presidency.

Teen Vogue's move into politics has raised the magazine's profile outside its audience base as it has been reported on in the more traditional news media. Some reports have been critical of the fashion magazine's diversification. In an interview for *Fox News*, *Teen Vogue* writer Lauren Duca was told to 'stick to the thigh high boots' rather than report on politics. She responded by saying that 'a woman can love Ariana Grande and her thigh-high boots and still discuss politics. Those things are not mutually exclusive.'

The *Guardian* reported that the teen magazine's move into political reporting has repositioned the magazine 'as a passionate and informed, if unexpected, voice

- How does teenvogue.com use **codes and conventions** of lifestyle websites?

- What **gratifications** does teenvogue.com offer its audience?

- How does **anchorage** work to create meaning in *Teen Vogue*?

- How is **narrative** used in:
  - the **construction** of a news or politics article?
  - the way choices are made about **which stories should be selected** for the news and politics section?
  - the **construction** of a fashion or beauty article?

- What does teenvogue.com offer **audiences** that printed lifestyle magazines don't?

- How does teenvogue.com encourage **audiences** to interact with its content and with one another on social media?

- Identify **income sources** for teenvogue.com.

- How does teenvogue.com **represent** teenage girls?

for the resistance', while the *Financial Times* observed that 'for this generation of teenagers, consumerism and idealism can go hand-in-hand'.

teenvogue.com presents a complex idea of female **identity**, where an interest in fashion and celebrity culture coexists with interests in news and current affairs. teenvogue.com promotes positive ideas about women and their potential, often featuring stories about powerful and successful women. The magazine offers a distinctive feminist perspective and counters the stereotype of females only being interested in 'trivial' issues or topics based in the domestic sphere. At the same time it still focuses on female appearance and places a high value on the way women look.

teenvogue.com has become a successful media product by adapting to changes in the way audiences wish to access their lifestyle and fashion content. It has learned from the success of other websites and the rise of 'amateur' fashion and beauty bloggers and vloggers, and has broadened its potential audience by diversifying and offering unconventional 'teen-mag' content.

It provides access to its content in a variety of ways that offer audiences choices and can appeal to different audience interests. teenvogue.com encourages audience interaction through its social media content and also mobilises audience members to share and promote the magazine. *Teen Vogue* reflects the changing nature of the media in a digital environment and also demonstrates a modern approach to creating content for teenagers, which engages with lighter topics such as style and beauty as well as more serious issues related to gender, sexuality and the current political context.

Chapter 9 The examination paper

9.1 Introduction to the examination

The AS level qualification requires you to complete two formal assessments:

1. **The non-examined assessment** (NEA) based on a practical production that is worth 30% of the AS level qualification
2. **One 2½ hour examination paper** that is worth 70% of your total mark.

The exam paper will consist of nine questions in three sections. Across the paper you will be assessed on your knowledge and understanding of:

- the theoretical framework
- the contexts of media and their influence on media products and processes.

You should aim to:

- apply your knowledge and understanding of the theoretical framework
- analyse media products in relation to their contexts
- make judgements and draw conclusions.

The content of the examination will be based on the detailed information given in the specification and the CSP guidance documents provided by the exam board.

The key areas for revision are:

- the **enabling ideas** for each aspect of the **theoretical framework**
- the **in-depth CSPs** and **targeted CSPs**.

There are three types of question that will be referred to here:

- **short-answer questions** (2–4 marks each)
- **longer-answer questions** (10–15 marks each)
- **extended-answer questions** (20 marks each).

What you will learn in this chapter

- This chapter will provide an overview of the AS level examination paper. By breaking down each section of the paper and the style of questions you can expect, this chapter will help you to prepare effectively.

- Sample questions will be provided and you will have the opportunity to practise responding to questions. Information on how to prepare for each of the examination's three sections will be provided. Non-CSP examples will be provided in this chapter.

For detailed information on the NEA see Chapters 10 and 11.

For more on the theoretical framework see Chapters 1 to 6.

For more on analysing media products see Chapter 8 and on making judgements and drawing conclusions see Chapter 7.

9.2 The exam paper

The examination is broad as it covers all areas of study – all four aspects of the theoretical framework will be assessed and you could be asked about any of the nine CSPs. In addition, the first section of the exam will include 'unseen' products – examples of media products that you will not necessarily have seen before. These products could be old or relatively new ones. They will, however, be examples of products from one of the forms assessed in section A (see the table below). You should aim to have a good knowledge and understanding of the theoretical framework and how it applies to the close study products set by the exam board. This means you should also be able to apply your knowledge to non-CSP media products. Each section of the examination will focus on specific media forms and identified aspects of the theoretical framework.

The precise allocation of marks in the exam can vary, with some questions being worth a few marks while others offer up to 20 marks. Each section of the examination will contain a combination of knowledge-based short-answer questions, longer-response questions and extended-response questions.

The AS Media Studies exam – quick summary

AS Media Studies exam	Theoretical framework areas assessed/CSP focus	Media forms assessed	Time allocation in the exam
Section A	**Media language and representation**: 2 x unseen products and targeted CSPs	Two of the following three: **advertising and marketing, magazines, video games**	45 minutes
Section B	**Audience and industries** using the targeted CSPs	Two of the following three: **television, music video, film (industries only)**	45 minutes
Section C	All four areas via the **in-depth close study products**	Two of the following three: **radio, newspapers, online social and participatory media**	1 hour

The following sections provide details on what to expect from each section in the examination. Please note that the types of question in each section will remain the same, although the questions may not always appear in the same order.

Section A

Theoretical framework	Media forms
Media language and representations	Targeted CSPs and two unseen media products from: • advertising and marketing • video games • magazines

In this first section of the examination you should aim to use your knowledge of **media language and representations** when you answer these questions.

Section A will be made up of four questions:

- **two short-answer questions** (10 marks in total)
- **one longer-answer question** (10 marks)
- **one extended-answer question** (20 marks).

These questions will be based on any two of these three media forms: **advertising and marketing**, **video games** and/or **magazines**.

Some of the questions will ask you to refer to targeted CSPs and others will ask you to consider the unseen products.

For more on CSPs see Chapter 8.

Unseen products

Section A will include two unseen media products. They will be included with your examination paper. You will probably not have seen these products before but they too will be products related to advertising and marketing, video games and/or magazines. The unseen products could be print products (e.g. advertising, pages from a magazine or a video game cover) or they could include printed examples of e-media (e.g. pages from a website or a printout of an online advert).

The unseen products could be for any target audience and come from any industrial context. You will need to be able to use the unseen products to answer questions on the way media language is used, and the way representations are constructed and make meaning.

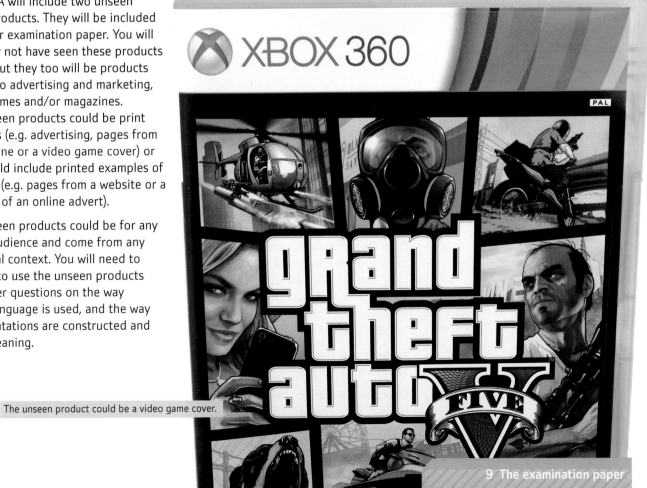

The unseen product could be a video game cover.

You will be asked to apply some aspect of your knowledge of media language or representation to one of the unseen products, and you will need to compare the second unseen with one of the targeted CSPs – again by considering how they use media language and how representations are constructed.

You may be given media products that you have never seen before or you may be given products you are very familiar with from your own media use. Don't worry about whether you are familiar with the unseen products. They are there to allow you to demonstrate that you are able to apply your knowledge of media language and representation to media products regardless of what they are and who they are for.

In section A you should be prepared to be assessed on the following:

Media language

- How different media forms use media language
- How media language choices make meaning
- How technology influences media language
- How genres develop in their use of media language
- How intertextuality creates meaning
- How audiences interpret media language:
  - semiotics (including Barthes)
  - narratology (including Todorov)
  - genre (Neale)

Representation

- How events, individuals and groups are represented
- The construction of versions of 'reality'
- The effect of social and cultural contexts
- Positive and negative stereotyping
- Under-representation and misrepresentation
- How representations convey values, attitudes and beliefs
- How audiences interpret media representations:
  - theories of representation (including Hall)
  - theories of identities (including Gauntlett)

Short-answer questions

There will be two short-answer questions in section A. Some of the short-answer questions could, however, have multiple parts.

Short-answer questions will focus on assessing your **knowledge** of media language and representations. These questions are likely to be based on your recall of terminology, your ability to show you understand what terms mean, or define ideas from the theoretical framework. The questions may be standalone or they may be directly related to one of the CSPs or unseen products relevant to this section. They may ask you a direct question that needs an explanation or one that asks you to observe and/or identify specific features. The short-answer questions could be multiple choice or require a brief explanation or definition. One of the short-answer questions will be based on one of the unseen products.

Example of a standalone question:
What is a stereotype?

Example of a question related to a specific media product (unseen or targeted CSP):
Identify some media language conventions used to make magazine front covers.

Example of a multiple-choice question:
An extreme close-up could be used to:

a establish the location of a scene

b create atmosphere

c focus the audience's attention on a specific detail of the mise-en-scène.

The longer-answer question

This will be a single question based on the second unseen product. You will be asked to demonstrate your ability to apply a specific idea from the theoretical framework for media language or representation.

This question will ask you to demonstrate your theoretical knowledge through the application of an idea you will have covered in class. The idea will be one of the main theoretical approaches for media language or representation, so questions could ask you about any one of the theories or enabling ideas from these areas of the framework. You could be asked to apply:

Media language

- Ideas from semiotics including Barthes' ideas about the construction of meaning
- Todorov's ideas about narrative
- Neale's ideas about genre

Representation

- Theories about representation, including stereotypes and countertypes, misrepresentation, hegemony, audience positioning, the construction of ideas
- Hall's ideas about encoding and decoding
- Gauntlett's ideas about identity

The question will ask you to analyse the given media product using a specific, named theoretical perspective. You will need to answer the question showing how the theory helps you to understand the way the media product creates meaning. You should demonstrate your understanding of the way media products are constructed by providing detailed examples from the product itself to demonstrate the theory in action.

For example:

How does this online advert demonstrate the way Todorov's ideas about narrative can be used to help promote a consumer product?

The advert's function is to sell Corsodyl mouthwash and it does this by creating a narrative disequilibrium (Todorov) by showing the image of the woman with one of her teeth missing. This disrupts the expectation of seeing a model in an advert with a perfect smile and so creates a problem that needs to be solved. The producers of the advert

APPLY IT

Answer the following questions.

1 What is a stereotype?

2 Identify three media language conventions of magazine front covers?

3 Which is correct: a), b) or c)?

An extreme close-up could be used to:

a establish the location of a scene

b create atmosphere

c focus the audience's attention on a specific detail of the mise-en-scène.

Would you be more careful if it was you that got pregnant?

Contraception is one of the facts of life.
Anyone married or single can get advice on contraception from the Family Planning Association.
Margaret Pyke House, 25-35 Mortimer Street, London W1 N 8BQ. Tel. 01-636 9135.

APPLY IT

Look at this example of a media product.

How does this advert* demonstrate the way Todorov's ideas about narrative can be used to help promote a consumer product or public service message?

* You can use this advert or the current advertising and marketing CSP to answer this question.

can safely assume that the people viewing it, regardless of age or gender, will want to actively avoid losing their teeth. The advert offers a solution to this problem – the mouthwash itself. The advert uses anchorage to encourage the reader to assume that the cause of the missing tooth is gum disease, a problem that Corsodyl offers to solve by taking the role of 'hero' in the advert's narrative …

The extended-answer question

One of the questions in section A will be worth 20 marks. This question will ask you to compare or contrast one of the unseen products with one of the targeted CSPs. You will be told which CSP you should refer to in your answer.

The question will be based on an idea from the theoretical framework and you will have to discuss both products in your answer. You might be asked to focus on differences or similarities between the two products or the question may ask you to make your own comparisons.

You should aim to analyse the unseen media product in light of the question. For the example question below, you should look at the way race is represented – looking for stereotypes and/or countertypes and identifying what media language choices were used in the construction of these representations and how they may create meaning for audiences. You should consider if the representations could be seen to be misrepresentations and/or if they contribute to or challenge hegemonic ideas about the racial group. You may consider if you think the representations could contribute to the construction of a racial identity or the way the representations attempt to create a preferred reading.

The question will indicate what you need to include in your answer as bullet points. You should aim to address each bullet point in your answer, although they don't all have to be covered equally.

> Compare the way two media products construct representations of race.

- How race is represented through the process of selection and combination.
  - *You can do this by ensuring you give specific details about how the two products use media language in the construction of the representations.*
  - *You should make sure that you use media language terminology to show how the representations in both products have been constructed.*
- The reasons for the choices made in the representation of race.
  - *You will need to explain why the representations are the way they are.*
  - *You should link your explanations to the theoretical framework.*
  - *Are the representations providing narrative information?*
  - *Are the representations part of the genre codes of the product?*
  - *Are the representations determined by industrial factors or related to the audience for the product?*
- The similarities and differences in the representations of race.
  - *How far are the two products the same/different?*
- How far these representations of race are influenced by historical, social and political contexts of media.

- *The specifics of your answer will depend on the products you are comparing.*
- *If one of them is from another era, can you see evidence that attitudes to race have changed over time?*
- *Do the representations contribute to a current political debate?*
- *Are the representations reflecting a specific social issue?*

When answering the extended-answer question, it is important that you provide evidence for your ideas. Your evidence could come from two sources:

1 Detailed examples from the media products (the unseen product **and** the named CSP as required by the exam question) to support your ideas.

2 Ideas and terms from the theoretical framework to support your ideas.

TIP You could use the bullet points in the question as a plan for your answer. The bullet points will provide a focus for each section of your answer.

Observation	Evidence from the posters	Application of theoretical framework
The advert above left treats people as individuals, the other (above right) puts people from similar racial groups in one anonymous group.	The OBV campaign uses a single figure who is named and shown looking into the camera. The UKIP poster uses an image of a large group of people. They are not named or identified in any way – many faces are out of focus.	The UKIP poster creates a **simplified representation** of a group based on the idea of mass migration. This is a **selective representation** as it does not reflect the reality of all members of the racial group. The OBV campaign attempts to empower a group who may share a racial **identity** by encouraging them to vote. The poster reinforces the **dominant idea** that democracy empowers people but the audience is addressed as individuals.

OBV = Operation Black Vote

While it is important to stay focused on the question, don't be afraid to show your knowledge of other areas of the theoretical framework as long as you are using the ideas to answer the question. For example:

- You could use **uses and gratification** theory to explain why representations are the way they are.
- You could use ideas about **marketing** to explain why the representations are the way they are.
- You could consider the influence of **globalisation** to explain why the representations are the way they are

You need to make sure you provide a logical and coherent argument that demonstrates your ability to analyse media products, use the theoretical framework (including terminology) and show your understanding of the influence of contexts on the products.

Section B

Theoretical framework	Media forms
Audience and industries	Targeted CSPs from: • television • music video • film (industries only)

Section B will assess your knowledge and understanding of **audience and industries**, and will ask you to provide examples from the targeted CSPs from **two** of these three media forms: **television, music videos and film (industries only)**. There will be no unseen products in section B and you should spend approximately 45 minutes on this section.

There are three questions in section B: one short-answer question and two longer-answer questions. These could be presented in the exam paper in any order.

In section B you should be prepared to be assessed on:

Industries

Processes of production, distribution and circulation:

- patterns of ownership and control
- the impact of economic factors
- how organisations attract and maintain audiences (national and global)
- media regulation
- the impact of digital technologies on media industries
- ideas about media power (including Curran and Seaton).

Audiences

- The grouping and categorising of audiences
- The targeting and creation of audience appeal
- Marketing, distribution and circulation to audiences
- Audience interpretation of the media
- Audience interaction with the media
- Media effects (including Bandura)
- Cultivation theory (including Gerbner)
- Reception theory (including Hall)

Short-answer questions

As in section A, the short-answer questions will assess your knowledge of one of the key ideas from the theoretical framework content on audience or industries. For example, you could be asked to define a term, select the correct term from a list or briefly explain a theoretical idea.

Longer-answer questions

Longer-answer question: understanding of audience or industries

In section B you will be asked to discuss a key idea related to audience and industry, using one of the targeted CSPs as examples to support the points you are raising. The audience/industry ideas raised in the question will be taken from the theoretical framework. You should aim to show you understand the theoretical idea raised in the question and your ability to apply it. It is important to demonstrate your ability to apply the ideas by using your CSP to show how the idea works in a real media context.

For example:

> Explain how media organisations attempt to create audience appeal when constructing media products.

Use the television CSP* you have studied to support your answer.

* The CSP you need to write on will be named in the exam paper.

In the exam, you will have approximately 20 minutes to provide specific examples from your CSP study to demonstrate how the product has been **constructed to attract and appeal** to its target audience and discuss the **importance of appealing to targeted audiences**.

- You should be able to demonstrate who the target audience is and provide support for your assertion from the product itself.
- You should be able to discuss the techniques and strategies used within the product to appeal to and maintain the audience.
- You should show an understanding of the importance of appealing to an audience from a media industry perspective.
- You should show how economic factors such as advertising, subscription or other economic models influence the way the product targets its audience – using examples from the economic context of the CSP.
- You should show how distribution, marketing and circulation are used to add audience appeal – using examples from the way the CSP is distributed, marketed and circulated.
- You should aim to select the most important points suggested by the CSP.
- You should offer specific details about the CSP in your answer and use media terminology to discuss the importance of audience appeal from a media organisation's perspective.

You should aim to select the most important points suggested by the CSP. You should offer specific details about the CSP in your answer and use media terminology to discuss the importance of audience appeal from a media organisation's perspective.

In order to prepare for this question, you should have analysed **all three CSPs** (television, music video and film (industries only)) by applying **all aspects of the audience and industry sections of the theoretical framework**.

TIP

Audience and/or industry?

One of the questions in section B will focus on audience or industry. As you will have discovered, though, audiences and industries are connected and to discuss either separately can be very difficult indeed. As long as you are focusing on the question and offering an answer that addresses the issues raised, you can use related ideas from other aspects of the theoretical framework.

APPLY IT

The stills on the right are from the Little Mix video for 'Shout Out to My Ex', which can be found on YouTube.

You can use this music video in answer to the following question:

> Explain how media organisations attempt to create audience appeal when constructing media products. Use a television or music video CSP to support your answer.

Longer-answer question: media contexts

Another type of longer-answer question will be based on a social or political context related to one or more of the CSPs. This type of question could come up in any part of the exam and the example here considers approaches to a media context question related to industries/audience ideas from the theoretical framework.

To study the context of a media product is to consider the issues from outside the media product that have influenced the way it has been produced and received by audiences.

Contexts can be discussed in light of the way they impact on the:

- actions of media organisations
- content and presentation of media products
- actions of audiences.

The contexts are identified as:

Social

- The impact of social factors such as contemporary attitudes, beliefs and behaviours

Economic

- The impact of economic factors in terms of both the media (e.g. funding, marketing, circulation) and cultural (e.g. capitalism, consumerism)

Political

- The impact of political factors such as dominant political ideologies, the influence of politicians and political strategies

Historical

- The impact of the era of production

Cultural

- The impact of cultural factors.

These contexts are all deeply interconnected.

Choose a television series you are familiar with (or the current television CSP).

Consider how the following contextual factors have impacted on the production and reception of the programme.

	Impact on production (media language, genre, narrative)	Impact on representations	Impact on ideas and values communicated by the product	Impact on the way audiences access and/or interpret the programme
The programme's industrial context				
Wider economic factors				
Contemporary audience behaviour				
The rise of digital technology				
Social attitudes and beliefs				
The context related to other media products				

For example:

The BBC comedy Peter Kay's Car Share was initially made available to audiences as a 'box set' on iPlayer. **❶** *The BBC later broadcast the show weekly on BBC1.* **❶** *This shows the influence of online streaming services such as Netflix,* **❶** *which regularly releases whole series to its platform to allow audiences who prefer the option to binge watch multiple episodes.* **❷** *As more people are watching television online they expect broadcasters to provide more flexible options for viewing* **❷** *and the BBC needs to compete with other television providers.* **❶** *The show itself reflects the rise in online viewing* **❷** *in the way it was produced.* **❸** *Many of the episodes focus on the driver and passenger in a car driving to or from work. The restricted location echoes the way vloggers often present their videos* **❸** *and the mundane setting* **❹** *reflects the popularity of the details of daily life in their work. Peter Kay's Car Share was released in 2015, a month after the first episode of Carpool Karaoke became a success. The timing of the two shows indicates that neither of these highly successful programmes influenced the other but both show the influence of vlogging style in their production choices.* **❸**

❶ Industrial factors influencing the distribution of the product
❷ The context of contemporary audience behaviour
❸ Media language choices
❹ The context of representations

For example:

> Explain how the social, political and cultural contexts of media influence how audiences may interpret the same media in different ways.

Use the television CSP to support your answer.

In the exam, you would have roughly 20 minutes to provide specific examples from your CSP study to demonstrate how the interpretation of the product has been influenced by the context of production and/or reception.

You will need to decide which context issues you wish to address in your answer. Don't try to cover everything but choose the context issues that you think are most relevant and that you can discuss confidently.

Some contexts that could be relevant in a discussion on the interpretation of a television product may include:

- **The context of production** – for example, special effects, star appeal, funding, models, advertising
- **The context of reception** – television broadcasts, streaming, mobile technologies
- **The social/political/historical contexts** – the reflection of specific cultural issues, the demonstration of current social issues, the relationship between the product and political values.

APPLY IT

How have the producers of *Peter Kay's Car Share* attempted to create audience appeal?

Peter Kay's Car Share

Carpool Karaoke

Zoella and Alfie Deyes

TIP Try to avoid:

- **Simply describing your CSPs** – use specific examples from your CSPs to show how the point you are making works. Provide analysis of the CSPs to connect them to the point you are making.
- **Using context to tell a story** – you should only refer to context to help explain why a media product is the way it is. You must demonstrate how the context has impacted on the product or its reception.

APPLY IT

Explain how the social, political and cultural contexts of media influence how audiences may interpret the same media in different ways.

Use the Little Mix video for 'Shout Out to My Ex'* to support your answer.

* Or a current CSP

Section C

Theoretical framework	Media forms
Media language Representations Audience Industry	In-depth CSPs from: • radio • newspapers • online, social and participatory media

Section C will ask you to demonstrate your knowledge of all four areas of the theoretical framework. There are two questions in this section and they are both extended questions worth 20 marks each. You will be asked to use **two of the three in-depth CSPs** in your answers – one CSP will be identified for each question.

As you have two extended-answer questions you are encouraged to spend one hour on this section – 30 minutes per question.

First extended-answer question (20 marks)

One of the extended answer questions in section C will ask you to show your knowledge and understanding of one theory from the theoretical framework. The theory will be named and you will be given a clear indication as to how to engage with the theory for the question.

Any of the theories could come up so it is important that you are familiar with the ideas that make up the theoretical framework.

You may find that the question includes a statement about a theory or a quote from a theorist. The question may offer an explanation of the ideas and terms it uses, as some theories and terms can be interpreted differently. Do read the question carefully to ensure you are clear which interpretation is being used for the purpose of the exam question.

You will be told which CSP to refer to, so you should focus on the preparation work you have done on this product. Even though the question will ask you to focus on a specific theory, you may find that other theories and/or aspects of the theoretical framework can be used to help you answer the question.

Specifically, you will be assessed on your 'ability to apply your knowledge and understanding of the theoretical framework of media to analyse media products through the use of academic theories'.

As this is an extended-answer question you are expected to provide a coherent discussion that uses media terminology and ideas from the theoretical framework accurately. You should be able to provide specific examples from the CSP to show how the ideas you are discussing can be demonstrated in action.

The theories that could come up in this section of the exam are named in the specification and on pages 186 and 190 of this chapter. They are discussed in more detail in Chapters 1–6 of this book.

You will show your knowledge of media language and representation in your analysis of the media product. You should show extended knowledge and understanding of the named theory in your answer, linking the theoretical idea to the CSP throughout. You must make sure that your answer is focused on the specifics of the question, and that any examples and application of theoretical ideas are always relevant to the question.

For example:

> Genre texts that simply follow conventions can become clichéd and repetitive but too much originality may be off-putting for the audience. Neale identifies that there is tension between the need for a media product to be both 'familiar' and 'innovative'.
>
> Discuss the way your in-depth CSP* uses genre conventions to offer familiar and/or unexpected experiences.

* A specific CSP will be named in the exam.

This question needs you to be able to engage specifically with the way the named CSP uses codes and conventions of the genre and why they are used in these ways. As part of the preparation for the exam you should have engaged with each CSP in terms of the way it uses media language in its construction and its relationship to genre. As you will have applied all aspects of the theoretical framework to the in-depth CSP, you will be aware that this question could be answered with reference to other aspects of the theoretical framework in this way.

Media language choices are used to replicate or subvert genre codes.	**Some representations** are part of the codes and conventions of a genre.	**Audiences** create expectations around their understanding of genre. This can be positive and may encourage loyalty to a specific product or genre.	**Industrial factors** may influence the choice of genres made. For example, soap operas aim to appeal to a large mainstream audience so are most often found on channels that audiences can access relatively freely.
Some genres have specific looks and/or sounds that help audiences identify them and help them construct a set of expectations.	Some genres use representations (and narrative) to present specific ideas and values to the audience. These values can be codes and conventions of the genre.	Fan behaviour is often linked to genres.	
Some genres use specific types or styles of narrative. Some genres use specific narrative characters that become part of its codes and conventions.		Audiences can feel part of a group and may identify with other audience members, based on a shared understanding of genre.	Cost may be part of the decision when an organisation considers which genres to invest in. Netflix is able to invest large amounts into production so can offer products more associated with film genres because of their cost – for example, the superhero genre.
		Different genres offer different gratifications for the audience.	
		Different genres have different target audiences.	

Most important, though, is your ability to engage with how the named CSP uses genre conventions.

- Is the product an easily recognisable, familiar and conventional genre product?
- Is there evidence of the influence of other genre products in its production?
- Does the product subvert or manipulate genre conventions in any way?
- Is it a hybrid product? Does it offer codes from more than one genre?
- Does it attempt to innovate, bringing new ideas to the genre?

Once you have decided on the way the CSPs use genre codes you should be prepared to go beyond simple description of the product.

Why is the product the way it is? You will be rewarded more highly if you are able to make judgements and draw conclusions in your answer.

APPLY IT

The Archers is a radio soap opera that is broadcast every day on Radio 4. It is the world's longest-running radio soap opera. It was first broadcast in 1950.

You can access past episodes of the show at: www.bbc.co.uk/programmes/b006qpgr.

Episodes can be downloaded or streamed from the website. To answer the following practice question you should listen to one 15-minute episode of the soap opera – or, of course, the current radio CSP.

Soap operas are ongoing narratives that deal with the day-to-day life of a group of people who are usually linked because they live in the same community. Television soap operas such as *Coronation Street* and *Eastenders* follow soap opera conventions in terms of the types of stories told (domestic dramas), the types of characters in the stories (heroes, villains, etc.), the extended nature of the story, with each episode ending on a cliff-hanger, and the way they prioritise family and community.

Genre texts that simply follow conventions can become clichéd and repetitive but too much originality may be off-putting for the audience. Neale identified that there is tension between the need for a media product to be both 'familiar' and 'innovative'.

Discuss the way *The Archers** uses genre conventions to offer familiar and/or innovative experiences for the audience.

* Or the named radio CSP

Second extended-answer question

The second of the extended-answer questions in section C is called the **synoptic** question. This just means that the question specifically seeks to assess your knowledge across the theoretical framework. Other questions on the exam **may** be answered using relevant knowledge from across the theoretical framework but you **must** reference a range of ideas from across the framework in your answer to the final question on the paper. You don't necessarily have to refer to all four areas of the framework but you need to show some breadth of theoretical knowledge in your answer. The question will ask you to focus on one of the three in-depth CSPs but this won't be the same one as the previous question. Specifically, you will be assessed on your ability to: 'apply knowledge and understanding of the theoretical framework of media to analyse media products including in relation to their contexts'.

You need to make sure you have prepared each of the in-depth CSPs thoroughly and have engaged with relevant issues and debates. You should carefully analyse the CSPs using as many of the theories and ideas from the theoretical framework as possible and be able to refer to specific aspects of the product to support your ideas.

For example:

Here is the front page of *Buzzfeed* on Monday 14 July 2017. The page (and the website itself) can be analysed using a range of ideas from the theoretical framework.

Media language

- How is the page/site encoded?
- How is the page/site presented?
- How is the page/site designed?
- How are images positioned?
- How are headlines used?
- How does the page/site use connotations to create meaning?
- Does the page/site feed into any cultural myths?
- Why is it presented this way?
- In what ways is it a typical or an atypical online news site?
- What genres of media influence its presentation style?
- How does the page/site use narrative in terms of its use of character roles or the disruption of equilibrium?

Representation

- How are people, identities, places and/or events represented?
- What meaning is created by these representations?
- Is there evidence of a 'version' of reality being presented?
- Does the page/site use stereotypes?

- What values and attitudes are being conveyed here?
- How might audiences decode the messages here?

Audiences
- Who is the target audience?
- How is the page/site attempting to create audience appeal?
- How might the page/site encourage audience interaction?
- Do you think the page/site could have positive or negative effects on the audience?
- What kind of world does *Buzzfeed* create for its reader?
- What type of behaviours are typical of online audiences when accessing pages/ sites such as this?

Industries
- How might the page/site encourage the broadening of its circulation?
- Who owns the site and how is it funded?
- How is the page/site attempting to ensure it generates an income?
- Might the page/site have global appeal?
- Is the page/site subject to the same rules as a traditional broadcast or print news organisation?

Context
- How is the site showing the audience's interest in soft news rather than hard news?
- How is the site reflecting the importance of celebrity culture?
- How is the site showing the impact of social media on the news?
- How does the site seem to be more 'modern' than more traditional news sources?

Of course, it will take time to come up with ideas and examples on all the theoretical framework questions here. The whole purpose of a CSP is that you have time to engage with the products over time and, in the case of the in-depth CSPs, you should explore the named radio, news and online products using most, if not all, of the ideas and theories from across the framework, as questions could be related to any of the issues raised above.

 APPLY IT **Using *Buzzfeed* or the online, social and participatory media CSP you are studying, make notes on the key ideas you would use to answer the following questions.**

> To what extent is the way the product is constructed influenced by economic factors?
>
> In your answer you should consider a range of economic factors such as competition from other media forms and products, advertising revenue and readership numbers.

This question has a clear focus on media industry issues (economic factors) but also needs you to provide details about media language use (product construction). You could show your knowledge of the product in the context of other media products (industry competition)

and the need for clicks (audience/readership numbers) to help raise advertising income (revenue). Your answer could, therefore, use theories about **audience** to discuss the economic issues and/or the choices made in the product's construction of **representations**.

> *Buzzfeed, like any other online news source, needs to attract viewers* ❶ *in order to generate an income.* ❷ *Much of the money made by Buzzfeed will come from advertisers* ❷ *who will pay Buzzfeed to feature their advertising content. This influences Buzzfeed to feature stories that have already proved themselves to be popular on other news and social media sites.* ❶ ❷ *For example, the hard news story about an attack on a woman on Putney Bridge in London went viral on social media.* ❸ *A video of the attack was made available on YouTube* ❸ *and within a week had attracted half a million views. The hunt for the attacker also became a trending topic on Twitter.* ❸ *This makes the story a potentially popular one for Buzzfeed audiences, which is why it is featured on its front page.* ❹ *The long headline* ❹ *makes it clear what information is offered within the story* ❹ ❺ *and positions it within the narrative of the ongoing story.* ❻ *A man had been arrested but has since been cleared. This means that the resolution* ❻ *to the narrative has been disrupted* ❻ *and so the enigma* ❻ *is reintroduced and the quest* ❻ *for the attacker continues.* ❻ *This maintains the audience's potential interest in the story* ❶. *Buzzfeed publishes these popular and ongoing stories in the hope that Twitter and other social media users would link to their version of the story and drive more readers to their site.* ❶ ❷ ❸ *This in turn would add value to the advertising space it needs to sell.* ❷ *It may also add to the appeal of its own site with audiences and, once they are on the Buzzfeed's front page, it would be hoped that the other examples of human interest and celebrity-based stories would encourage readers to stay and explore more of the site.* ❶

❶ Audience
❷ Industry
❸ Influence of social media
❹ Media language
❺ Representation
❻ Narrative

Using *Buzzfeed* or the current online CSP, make a list of other ways you could answer the question about the influence of economics on the construction and presentation of the page/site.

- Identify specific examples from the site that you could analyse and comment on.
- Identify specific ideas from the theoretical framework you could refer to.

> To what extent is the way the product is constructed influenced by economic factors?

In your answer you should consider a range of economic factors such as competition from other media forms and products, advertising revenue and readership numbers.

Use the same media product to answer the following question.

> How does the style of writing and the use of photographs create audience appeal?

In your answer you should consider specific media language choices and offer a range of reasons why they may be appealing.

SUMMARY

- At first, the examination paper may look daunting. Once you are clear on the way each section is structured, you should find preparation for the exam much more manageable. Remember:

Section A

- **Media language and representation**: two **unseen** products and two of the three **targeted CSPs**

Section B

- **Audience and industries**: two of the three **targeted CSPs**

Section C

- Two of the three **in-depth CSPs** and all areas of the **theoretical framework**
- You will need to study all nine CSPs in preparation but be clear which ones are 'targeted' and which ones are 'in -depth'.

Targeted CSPs

- Media language and representation
  - Advertising and marketing; magazines and video games
- Audience and industries
  - Television, music industry and film (industry only)

In-depth CSPs

- Media language, representation, audience and industries
  - Radio, newspapers and online, social and participatory media.
- You need to know and be able to apply the ideas from the theoretical framework.
- When studying your CSPs you will need to apply the relevant ideas from the theoretical framework and use detailed examples from the products to demonstrate the ideas in action.
- Every time you consider and apply ideas from the theoretical framework you are preparing for the exam. Every time you watch a TV programme, go on YouTube to watch a music video or trailer, read a webpage, listen to the radio, play a game, engage with an advert, read a newspaper or magazine you can be preparing for the exam. Try to get into the habit of thinking about your day-to-day media experience using the ideas from the theoretical framework and this will make it easier for you to apply the ideas to the CSPs and the unseen media products too.
- You should also practise writing up your ideas. With longer and extended answers in the exam need you to be clear and precise, and write relatively quickly. The best way to become clearer, more precise and more efficient in your writing is to practise.

For more advice on building the skills you will need to help you in the exam room see Chapter 7.

10.1 Introduction to the NEA

You need to complete a practical production for AS Media Studies. Three briefs will be provided and you will be able to select one of these. Each brief will outline the details of the production you are required to make and will contextualise the production in some way, usually providing you with a target audience and an institutional context.

You will be assessed on your ability to create a media product:

- **for an intended audience, by applying knowledge and understanding of the theoretical framework of media to communicate meaning.**

The three briefs will ask for different practical productions but they will always be related to eight of the nine media forms being studied for the examination. You will make a practical production related to one of the following eight forms:

1 Television (broadcast – moving image)
2 Radio (broadcast – audio)
3 Newspapers (print and/or e-media)
4 Magazines (print or e-media)
5 Advertising and marketing (broadcast: moving image/audio, print and/or e-media)
6 Online, social and participatory media (e-media, but could include audio/video content)
7 Video games (e-media)
8 Music video (moving image and/or advertising and marketing)

Film is not included here as a practical option, although you may be required to produce materials related to the film industry, for example marketing materials such as posters or websites.

What you will learn in this chapter

This chapter offers an introduction to the practical production work. If you are taking the **AS Media Studies** examination you will need to complete the non-examined assessment (the NEA) to be awarded the qualification. The NEA is worth 30% of the AS award.

A note about the A level NEAs:

If you are studying for the full A level award you do not have to complete an externally assessed NEA in your first year, but you will need to develop your practical production skills in preparation for the A level NEA that is completed in your second year.

The AS Media Studies briefs will be included within the A level briefs for the following academic year.

This chapter will consider some of the software and equipment requirements for different types of production and provide an overview of some of the different types of media that you may wish to create. It will consider the importance of both pre-production research and planning.

In addition, this chapter will look at the initial process of engaging with the AS NEA brief provided by the exam board. Through a sample brief, this chapter will offer guidance on the research required to prepare for production and you will learn how to use the theoretical framework in your research.

Further details on approaches to specific types of practical production can be found in Chapter 11.

For a sample Statement of Intent see page 219.

The first formal piece of work you do for the NEA will be a **Statement of Intent**. This is a 400-word written piece of work that sets out your ideas and intentions for the practical production. You will need to hand this Statement of Intent to your teacher before you complete the practical production task. The Statement of Intent is worth in the region of 17% of the NEA mark. It will be assessed on your ability to explain how you intend to use media language and representations to appeal to your target audience and meet the industrial requirements indicated in your brief. Specifically, you will need to show your knowledge of:

- media language codes and conventions appropriate to the form
- the expectations of your audience and methods that can be used to attract and appeal to them
- the way representations can be used to create meaning
- the industrial context of your production.

In order to create a good practical production, your work will go through the following stages:

1 Selecting one brief from the six available and engaging with the brief's instructions
2 Research
3 Production planning
4 Production

Your production must be an individual piece of work. You may, of course, need to work with others, for example if you require actors or models for your products, or to help with the practicalities of production by operating equipment. However, you must make all the practical and creative decisions for your production. Throughout the process of production, you should be using your knowledge of the theoretical framework to inform the decisions you make.

KEY TERMS

brief	information and instructions that set the remit and scope of the NEA
non-examined assessment (NEA)	a method of assessment where work you create over time is marked by a member of the teaching team in your school or college

Statement of Intent	a 400-word written document that is constructed after the completion of research and is part of the planning process. The Statement of Intent summarises what you will produce and why

10.2 Selecting your brief

Each brief identifies the form you need to produce and is based on a specific industrial context and target audience. The brief should be used as your starting point for production.

One of the first things you will need to do is select the brief you wish to work on for your practical production. Each of the three briefs will identify a specific media form that you will need to make. The form will be put into a media context and the brief may identify a target audience for the product and ask you to consider a specific idea or function for your product that should be addressed in your final submission.

Your choice of brief may be influenced by a number of factors, from your own levels of interest in a specific media form or area to the type of equipment and the software you have access to.

Here are some of the equipment/software needs for different types of production.

Media form	Equipment needs	Software needs
Moving image – including television, advertising and music video	**A moving image camera.** There are many specialist cameras for shooting moving image footage. You can use the camera on a mobile phone but make sure you have your phone in the correct aspect ratio (landscape mode) when you shoot your footage. You will need a tripod to stabilise your camera. This is especially important if you will be using a phone or a tablet to capture images as they can be very difficult to keep stable. Other equipment can be helpful when creating moving image work such as **lighting**, green-screen technology, etc. You may not have access to professional equipment but you can be creative. For example, not many people will have access to a dolly to create a tracking shot but could you come up with a low-tech way to achieve this effect? You could try moving the camera operator (carefully) on a wheeled chair perhaps or fixing your camera (firmly) on a skateboard that can be pulled along (carefully) by the camera operator. **Sound recording equipment.** You can capture sound in the camera but this can sometimes lead to problems with ambient noise and in-camera sound may not be as loud or clear as you would like. Using separate sound equipment to record sound gives you more control over your sound balance and allows you to add voice-overs, edit your sound recordings and create sound effects. Again, tablets and phones can be used to record sound. **A computer/tablet** that enables you to install post-production editing software.	**Editing software.** It may be possible to use a tablet to edit your work. Editing software (for still and moving images) can be accessed online and is often free (e.g. Filmora Video Editor) and there are many apps that can be downloaded for the most popular mobile phones and tablets (e.g. iMovie for video; Pixelmator for still images). You may have access to professional software such as Adobe Premier. These software packages are powerful but expensive, so before making any purchase of editing software check that the software/app can do what you want for your production. It is also worth checking that the software/app will allow you to save your moving image files in universally accessible formats such as MP4, avi, etc. If you are going to upload your work to YouTube you should check the list of accepted formats. If you are going to send your work on a disc or memory stick, you will need to make sure your work can be viewed on any PC or Mac.
Audio – including radio and podcasts	**Sound recording equipment.** You may have access to professional sound recording equipment but, if not, sound can be recorded on mobile phones and tablets. **A computer** that enables you to install post-production sound editing software or access the internet.	**Sound editing software:** as with video editing, a range of software is available from professional sound editing packages to be used on a computer to less complex programmes and apps for computers, tablets and phones. Free software can be accessed and used online too. You can also use moving image editing software to edit sound. Again, make sure the software you are using allows you to save your files to formats that are easily shared such as wav, MP3, etc.

Media form	Equipment needs	Software needs
Print – including newspapers, magazines and advertising	**A computer or tablet** that allows you to install desk-top publishing (DTP) and image manipulation software. **A camera, phone or tablet** for taking still images. 	A **DTP** package. Try to avoid using the templates provided by software packages – you should create your own designs. An **image manipulation** software package to help you edit, enhance and manipulate your still images.
e-media production	As most online, social and participatory media is a multi-media experience you would need access to equipment and software to allow you to **design the pages and the content** for these pages, **create and edit still images** to illustrate your work, and to create and **edit moving images and audio work**.	
a offline production	**A computer or tablet** that allows you to install **desk-top publishing** and **image manipulation software**. **A camera, phone or tablet** for taking still images and/or moving images. **Specialist equipment, a phone or tablet** for recording sound.	There are professional web design software packages. Research these before committing to a specific software as some are complex and may need you to learn coding – and this is not a requirement in Media Studies. DTP packages will allow you to, for example, design pages for a website. Alternatively, you could design your pages in an image manipulation software package and then import the image files into a DTP or web design package to add hyperlinks and multi-media features. If you use offline software to design your e-media production, you will need to consider how you will submit your work, the e-media productions will need to be viewable in a browser. This way your work can be viewed as a fully functional product. You may need access to post-production editing software to work on sound recordings, still images and/or moving image footage.
b online production	**A computer or tablet** that allows you access to the internet. **A camera, phone or tablet** for taking still images and/or moving images. **Specialist equipment, a phone or tablet** for recording sound.	There are lots of options for online production. Web design services such as wix.com allow you to create your website and host it online. These services have lots of features and can be used to create professional-looking websites. You might want to use a blog site such as WordPress or create social media pages on sites such as Facebook, Tumblr, Twitter, Vine and/or Instagram. If you use an online production tool, you will need to show your creative and technical skills in the content you produce for your e-media production. You may need access to post-production editing software to work on sound recordings, still images and/or moving image footage.

Media form	Equipment needs	Software needs
Video games	**A computer or tablet** that allows you access to the internet.	There are lots of online websites that provide users with the opportunity to create games online. Users can create games using game engines provided by resources such as Gamemaker, Unity, Unreal Engine and Source. There are lots of articles online and videos on YouTube that offer ideas and advice for novices with no technical skills who wish to make a game.

KEY TERMS

ambient noise	the background noise (such as wind, traffic, etc.) that is sometimes picked up when filming
aspect ratio	the correct width/height ratio
desk-top publishing software	software that enables users to create and design pages for offline or online publications. DTP allows users to control the layout and design of pages and the use of images and illustrations
dolly	a device that allows a camera to be pushed along a track to create a moving shot
editing software (video and audio)	software that allows video and/or audio files to be cut and spliced back together to allow footage to be used in a non-linear and more creative way. Additional audio tracks, intertitles and on-screen text, special effects and transition effects can be added during video and audio editing

footage	unedited video recordings
green-screen technology	filming characters in front of a green (or blue) screen allows backgrounds or other footage to be added in post-production
image manipulation software	software that enables users to crop, edit and add effects to photographic images
in-camera sound	sound that is recorded using the camera's internal microphone
tripod	a three-legged stand for a still or video camera

APPLY IT

- What production equipment do you have easy access to?
- What production software or apps do you have on your computer, tablet and/or phone?
- What production apps are available for your computer, tablet and/or phone?
- Research online production tools for image manipulation, DTP, web design and game design.

10.3 The NEA's eight forms: what could you be asked to make?

The three briefs will change each year, so the specifics of your production work are likely to be different from the examples given. Each set of briefs will include production tasks from three of the following eight forms:

1. Television
2. Radio
3. Newspapers
4. Magazines
5. Advertising and marketing
6. Online, social and participatory media
7. Video games
8. Music video

Within these forms, however, there are lots of different types of media product that you may be asked to create. All moving image products use the same basic media language elements.

Producers select camera and editing techniques, they dress and light the set, use music and sound effects, and some will use special visual or audio effects. The page design of print and e-media products is as carefully considered as the content of the pages. Print and e-media design has to consider the placement of images and the use of headings, columns, captions and fonts, as these are all important in the way a product generates visual appeal and communicates meaning. So, the form itself will define some of your approaches. However, a sitcom looks quite different from a news bulletin; a magazine uses different layout conventions from a newspaper. So, before you can start making media language choices for your production, you need to be clear not only on what form you are being asked to create but also on the specific nature of the media product you will be making in response to your chosen brief.

Following are some potential types of media that you could be asked to construct.

1 Television

Non-fiction programming could include news bulletins or reports, documentaries, quiz shows, sports programming, talk shows or magazine programming. Lifestyle programming such as cookery, travel and home improvement shows are factual and some reality TV would come under this heading too. If you are making factual programming you need to know who your target audience is and what type of information you wish to communicate. Having a clear idea about audience will not only help you to decide what the content of the programme should be but, importantly, will also help you decide how to present the information.

EXAMPLE: Television documentary styles

BBC3 offers a range of hard-hitting documentaries fronted by young presenters such as Stacey Dooley (left), Reggie Yates and Professor Green. These documentaries are informative and deal with issues such as homelessness, the lives of sex-workers, and violent homophobia and racism. BBC3 has a 'youth'-based target audience and, while the documentaries have a serious tone, the young presenters are able to communicate with the target audience in a way that creates identification and avoids the patronising approaches sometimes taken when adults attempt to discuss issues with young people. All of these presenters are on-screen and lead audience responses with their own, often emotional, responses to the situations they are reporting on. Information is given to the audience in a very direct way, with the presenter talking to the camera. Interviews are intercut with the presenters being shown immersing themselves in the situations they are reporting on. The effect is immediate, personal and emotional.

There are other styles of documentary, though. Some of the documentaries on BBC4, for example, and many of the films in the *Storyville* series use a cooler, more detached tone where the documentary maker is only ever heard from behind the camera or is often not heard or seen in the film at all. These documentaries attempt to present information with as little editorial input as possible. Audiences are free to interpret what they are shown for themselves. Of course, all documentaries shape the story they are telling and will influence the viewer's perspective but the BBC3 style of documentary making does this through the presenter, as well as in the way it presents its images and ideas.

Fictional programming is scripted and is all about telling stories to its audience. Again, different audiences may have different expectations as to how the story is told and knowing these expectations is important for all media producers. Fictional programming is created for all age groups whether it's the historical story-telling for children of *Hetty Feather* (BBC), adult dramas such as *Game of Thrones* (HBO) and *Happy Valley* (BBC), or situation comedies such as *The Big Bang Theory* (CBS) or the *Unbreakable Kimmy Schmidt* (Netflix). Some 'reality' TV is very close to being fiction. Programmes such as *Made in Chelsea* are sometimes called 'scripted reality', 'structured reality' or 'constructed reality' and, while the characters are not actors and they are being filmed living their own lives, they are often put into situations that have been constructed by the programme makers. The participants in these programmes respond to the situations in a way that is similar to the way actors improvise.

Of course, not all television-type programming is accessed on a television. Traditional television programmes are watched on computers, tablets and phones. Some traditional television is accessed on YouTube and Vimeo, and these video hosting services allow TV producers, both professional and amateur, to upload factual and fictional material. Non-mainstream news services such as *Vice* are available online and vloggers such as *Helmsley and Helmsley* and *Zoella* create television-type programming for their audiences – the former have also produced a more traditional television programme for Channel 4 called *Eating Well with Hemsley and Hemsley*. YouTube vlogs are developing their own visual language codes with some individuals creating their own visual style. These styles are based on conventional television media language codes but have been adapted to suit the more amateur approach that reflects the way many of these television-style programmes use webcams and hand-held cameras to create images in non-studio environments. Many of the bigger names in vlogging use high-tech equipment and a studio but carefully recreate the amateur look.

Eating Well with Helmsley and Helmsley

2 Radio (audio)

There is as much variety of programming in audio format as there is in television and moving image. Audio programming ranges from news and current affairs, documentaries and magazine programming to dramas, comedy, panel shows, interviews and debates, and, of course, music radio. **Local radio** programming – as the name implies – provides content with a local interest. Some local radio is provided by the BBC and some by commercial broadcasting companies. The latter make money by selling advertising space and the content of local radio is punctuated by audio advertising.

Podcasts are audio products that can be listened to online or downloaded to computers and/or mobile devices. Podcasts are made by professional media companies and can be online versions of radio programmes (such as *Mark Kermode's Radio 5 Film Reviews*) or they may be made specifically for online distribution. Just like radio, podcasts can cover a wide variety of topics and styles. Successful podcasts include *Distraction Pieces* (hip-hop and spoken-word poetry), *The Media Podcast* (superb for Media Studies students), *The Bugle/Page 94* (current affairs satire) and *The Infinite Monkey Cage* (light-hearted scientific discussions). Perhaps the most widely discussed podcast has been *Serial* – a documentary series using investigative journalism to challenge the outcome of a US murder case and its subsequent trial.

3 Newspapers (print and/or e-media)

Newspapers as print products are not accessed as much as they once were. Online news services have impacted on the circulation of print newspapers but many of the traditional print titles have an online version.

Newspapers can be divided into a number of different formats and genres.

- **Free-sheets** have no cover charge and some local editorial content, but these newspapers are dominated by adverts – the classifieds (text-based listings) and display ads (professionally produced adverts that contain some form of graphic design).

- **Local newspapers** cover a small geographical area such as a town or small city. They contain more editorial content than free-sheets but are mostly based on stories with a local interest. Local newspapers used to charge a cover fee but are now mostly given away.
- **Regional newspapers** cover a wider geographical area than local newspapers – a county or a larger city, for example. They report local news but will also cover national and international news and, where appropriate, will show how larger news stories may connect with local interests. Again, regional newspapers used to charge but they are mostly distributed free and, like local newspapers, they rely on advertising revenue to make a profit.
- **National newspapers** cover the stories that impact on national and international interests. They charge a cover fee in their print forms but content is usually available free online.

National newspapers can be further divided into two genres: tabloids and broadsheets. The terms come from the pre-digital era and refer to the size of paper each newspaper was produced on. The terms tabloid and broadsheet are now used to identify two different types of newspaper in terms of the papers' news values and reporting style.

	Broadsheets	Tabloids	
		Red-tops	**Compacts** (sometimes called **mid-market** or **black-top tabloids**)
Titles include ...	The *Daily Telegraph*, the *Guardian*, *The Times*	The *Daily Mirror*, the *Sun*, the *Daily Star*	The *Daily Mail*, the *Daily Express*
News values	Favour hard news over soft news; attempt to be factually accurate and provide information. Try to offer factual detail and provide an analytical overview. Tend to deal with the 'big picture' issues that stem from a news story. Look at wider implications of events and stories.	Favour soft news over hard news; attempt to appeal to the reader's emotions, focus on human interest stories, scandal, gossip, etc. Red-top tabloids tend to show how the news story has impacted on individuals or might impact on the reader him/herself.	Report hard news but soft news is a dominant feature; appeal to the reader's emotions, focus on human interest stories, scandal and gossip. All tabloids are likely to focus on individuals and personal aspects of a story. Black-top tabloids, like red-tops, often focus on how the news stories would impact on their readership – often in very personalised ways.
Reporting style	Attempt to be cool, detached and analytical. This does not, however, mean they avoid bias.	Red-tops go for a sensationalised style using lots of hyperbole and word-play to help create an emotional response. Images dominate in red-top tabloids.	Black-tops are less exaggerated in their reporting style than red-tops but they still employ emotive language and word-play that deliberately attempts to create an emotional response.
An example of front-page headlines: 14 August 2016 (the day after Theresa May began to construct her first parliamentary cabinet)	The *Daily Telegraph*: 'May Brings in the Brexiteers' The *Guardian*: 'May's Pledge to Brexit Britain'	The *Daily Mirror* (with a full-page picture of Boris Johnson on a zip-wire): 'Dear world ... Sorry' The *Star*: 'Psycho Seagull Girl's Horror Plunge'	The *Daily Mail*: 'Boris Bounces Back' The *Daily Express*: 'May's Team to Battle Brussels'

Online, these newspapers tend to follow the same reporting style and news values of their print versions. Online news is important to traditional newspaper companies, as free access to online news has made it almost impossible to generate a profit with print newspapers. To try and generate web views, broadsheets print lots of opinion editorials that create interest and discussion. They use social media to help generate interest in their stories, and having a story go viral is one way that online newspapers generate income. The *MailOnline* has become one of the most visited news websites in the world – largely because of its celebrity gossip reporting that attracts audiences from all over the world, not only the UK. The *Independent*, however, no longer has a print edition, as in 2016 it made a decision to focus its business on online publishing. Online doesn't just mean websites, as news producers also offer apps for mobile devices.

Online news is provided by other organisations as well as newspaper publishers. Broadcasters such as *BBC News*, *Sky News* and *Channel 4 News* have news websites, as do non-UK broadcasters such as *Russia Today* and *Al Jazeera*. The web allows audiences to access foreign news providers such as *Fox News* and *CNN* from the US, and there are many independent news organisations that publish online such as *The Young Turks*, *The Real News Network* and *The Canary*.

4 Magazines (print or e-media)

Like newspapers, the popularity of printed magazines has declined, as free content has become more accessible online. Magazines tend to fall into two basic categories:

- **Lifestyle magazines** have their roots in shopping catalogues and are guides to the products you may wish to buy to create and enhance your lifestyle. These products may include make-up, fashion, gadgets and holidays, and lifestyles may be defined through decorating, cookery, leisure activities, home improvements and gardening. Lifestyle magazines tend to cover a number of different topics that collectively help create a lifestyle (e.g. *Cosmopolitan*).

- **Special interest magazines** focus on a very specific topic area – one that may be a niche interest rather than a mainstream one. Special interest magazines offer buying advice but tend to be more focused on offering information (e.g. *Boating World*, *NME*).

Traditional publishers have expanded media brands online and so, for example, fashion magazines (such as *Vogue*), lifestyle magazines (such as *Red*, *FHM*) and music magazines (such as *NME*) exist in print form and online. Print and online versions of magazines share a number of visual codes that create consistency and make the brand recognisable. However, the design and content of the magazine in each platform will aim to meet the expectations of the specific audiences of print or e-media respectively.

Online versions of magazines are often used to try to encourage audiences to buy the print version and print magazines promote the online edition.

Mainstream magazines have always competed with one another for readers. Creating a clear brand in terms of content as well as attitudes and values allows audiences to create certain expectations that the magazine can meet. The institution hopes that this can create audience loyalty so readers will return again and again to a favourite and familiar magazine title.

A more recent form of competition for traditional magazines comes from new online magazines as well as both amateur and professional bloggers and vloggers. Online magazines are often based around a central writer/presenter, so they have an added advantage that their own personality and approach become their brand. Bloggers and vloggers often generate a loyal following who return regularly to websites and/or YouTube channels.

The style of presentation in both blogging and vlogging has influenced traditional

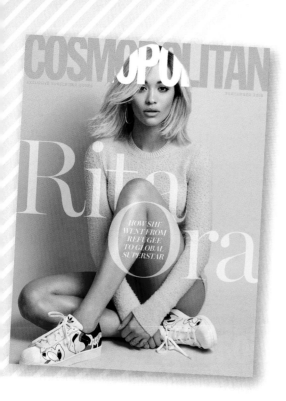

magazines to alter their approaches in print but most especially online. Magazine publishers now use bloggers as writers and they integrate moving image and audience interaction into their house style. Fashion and beauty bloggers have become increasingly influential, with titles such as *Vogue* and *Cosmopolitan* using conventions that come from blogging in their print and online editions.

5 Advertising and marketing (moving image, audio, print and/or e-media)

Advertising and marketing is not a specific media form. Both advertising and marketing have the same ultimate aims in that they use the media to create images and messages that aim to persuade the audience to act in some way. Advertising is easy to spot and identify. There are many forms of advertising including print adverts and billboards, moving image trailers and adverts, and, on e-media, advertising content appears on static text-based web pages, as well as on social media and streaming services. Commercial radio is funded by audio adverts and trailers are adverts for films. Marketing is often more subtle and is not always easy to identify. Music videos, for example, are media forms in their own right but they are created to promote the artist and market their music.

Advertising is content in the media that is paid for. Advertising space is sold in newspapers, magazines, in cinemas, by TV broadcasters and on the radio. Adverts can be created by media industries, for example trailers for BBC programmes. Many are created by a third party (an advertising agency) and the host media has no influence on the content of the adverts (other than to ensure they are meeting their own printing or broadcasting guidelines). Adverts on the internet are sometimes bought and paid for (e.g. the moving image adverts on All4), while others are generated by the data created when you access the internet.

Marketing creates awareness. There are countless methods of marketing and new strategies are continually being created. Marketing aims to build brand awareness, create a buzz around a product launch, insert the product into news and social media discussions, etc. The most successful marketing seeds some interest and then other parts of the media take the message out to the audience. Creating interesting materials that people will discuss and share is difficult, but when it is done well marketing spreads the message about the product across audience groups.

Marketing can occur through, for example, the creating of merchandising that is seen by audiences in shops. The media helps with the marketing of products by responding to marketing strategies. In 2016, with little traditional advertising, Pokémon Go became a huge success. The game created a buzz on social media and traditional news media, then picked up on its popularity and within a week of the game's release it had more active users than Twitter or Facebook. The game caught the interest of the mainstream news media, where the game's success and popularity made it newsworthy.

Some adverts hope to persuade the audience to buy a product they need (e.g. a shampoo). In this type of advertising, adverts attempt to persuade you to choose one specific product over all the other shampoos that are available. Some adverts try to create a desire for something the audience didn't know they wanted. When a brand-new product is launched, advertisers need to make it look attractive and turn it into an object of desire. Other adverts attempt to change viewers' behaviour – for example campaign-based advertising such as road safety adverts use images that shock and create fear to persuade people to change their behaviour on the roads.

There are many different types of advertising and marketing product, but all act to create a positive response to the product being advertised in some way.

6 Online, social and participatory media (e-media)

Much online media had developed from the older, traditional forms. A website can be created to advertise a product or provide news and information. Some websites provide the same service as a newspaper and others provide specialist information on a single topic. Some sites offer mixed content in a magazine style, and all types of website can offer moving image and/or audio content as well as the written word. Traditional media institutions provide some of the most visited websites such as *BBC News* and the *MailOnline*, and these sites have similar functions to their offline counterparts, although they will present the information in a different way to the traditional forms. An advertising website, just like a billboard or magazine advert, will try to create a positive response to the product being promoted in order to create desire and persuade the audience to purchase the product.

Some websites are created outside the usual institutional context of production, with smaller independent publishers and private individuals being able to publish online and having an opportunity to reach a large audience. Fashion bloggers have begun to challenge the power of fashion magazines and some individuals have become influential in their own right such as Susie Lau (*Style Bubble*) and Ella Catliff (*La Petite Anglaise*). The private individuals that do this are few and far between but bloggers such as *Deliciously Ella* (food), *Zoella* (fashion and lifestyle) and *Yogscast* (gaming) among others have managed to use blogs to launch media careers.

Participation

What also separates online media from traditional media is the fact that online media can be contributed to or created by 'the audience' as well as by media institutions. Participation encourages audiences to engage more with the material and provides a range of gratifications that cannot be offered by traditional media. Commenting on news websites can create connections between people who do not know one another and there can be a sense of community created that reinforces shared values when commentators agree with one another.

Giving people the opportunity to have a say in a public forum is something that traditional media cannot offer. Participation can take many forms, from comments and discussions to the ability to upload user-generated content and even participate in the development of a media product by, for example, contributing suggestions for character development in fiction or creating personal experiences within gaming – even creating their own missions (e.g. Infamous 2). News providers encourage audience members to send information, images and videos about developing news stories, as they do not always have journalists in situ when a story breaks and this citizen journalism has become important for newspapers and broadcasters that need to keep up to date with events as they unfold. Websites for musicians, bands and other celebrities try to ensure that fans feel part of a community. As well as providing news and information, celebrity or artist websites often offer some 'personal' communication to create the feeling that the fan is part of an elite group who can access 'insider information' and, importantly, have access to other members of this group – sometimes, access to the celebrity too.

The Bruno Mars website (www.brunomars.com) has a forum and an area where fans can upload their photos and artwork. The site operates a mailing list and encourages visitors to officially join the community by registering.

Muse (www.muse.mu) promote the interactive nature of their website on the front page, providing information about the size of the community and the extent they participate.

The Katy Perry website (www.katyperry.com) gives fans the opportunity to register for a newsletter but most of the real interaction for this fan group occurs via social media.

Social media

Different social media platforms provide different functions for their users. Facebook started as a platform for connecting with friends and sharing information through updates and the posting of images. Over the years Facebook has developed in order to attempt to offer different functions, as other social media platforms compete for users' time and attention.

Some social media is based around still photography (e.g. Pinterest, Instagram) others on moving images (e.g. Vine, Periscope), while yet others are based mainly on the written word (Twitter). Different social media platforms appeal to different audience groups and some have clearly identifiable demographics. Seventy-five percent of Periscope users are in the 16–34 age group (source: ccm.com) and 90% of Instagram users are under 35 (source: sciencedaily.com). Seventy-one percent of female internet users use social media but only 62% of males (source: pewinternet. org). Social media content producers consider the needs of their audience and try to construct ways to use the platform that help encourage the audience to share, communicate and interact with the content they provide.

7 Video games (e-media)

Video games cover a range of genres, are accessed using different platforms, use different types of gameplay and so attempt to appeal to different audiences. Some games are simple, to be played by individuals, while others create complex worlds where thousands of players can gather online to play together. Some games are produced by large companies that spend enormous amounts of money on their development and distribution, whereas other games are created by lone developers and end up being produced and sometimes distributed through independent companies.

Platform	Game	Genre	Gameplay	Institutional context
Mobile device, e.g. iOS/Android phones and tablets	Candy Crush	Puzzle	'Match-three' puzzle	Distribution by Activision/ Blizzard
Hand-held device, e.g. Nintendo 3DS	The Legend of Zelda: A Link between Worlds	Action adventure	Role-play game	Developed and published by Nintendo
Console, e.g. PS4	Uncharted 4: A Thief's End	Action adventure	Mixed gameplay including puzzle, platforming, third-person shooter	Developed by Naughty Dog and published by Sony Interactive Entertainment
PC	World of Warcraft	Fantasy	MMORPG (massively multiplayer online role-play game)	Distributed by Blizzard Entertainment
PC/console	Call of Duty	War	First-person shooter	Distributed by Activision
VR headset	Eve: Valkyrie	Action sci fi	Dog-fighting shooter	Developed by CCP Games and published by CCP Games and Oculus VR

8 Music video (moving image)

Music videos are another form of marketing. In the past, music videos were made to promote the sales of a specific music track that was released as a single. In turn, the single would promote the artist's album. Today, less money is made via the sales of music, so video acts to promote the artist's brand as much as the song itself.

A video is a visual way of reaching an existing audience and attempting to broaden an artist's reach. There are many different approaches to the creation of music videos: some videos offer a brief and relatively simple narrative that is directly related to the lyrics of the song; some offer a metaphorical visual connection to the lyrics; some are performance based; some use intertextual references to other cultural reference points such as specific historical periods, films or TV programmes; and some use apparently unrelated images for visual appeal.

Different genres of music use these techniques in very different ways. Musical genres have developed their own video codes and conventions, and sometimes these conventions are used so often that they are instantly recognisable but they become clichés. However, the music genre conventions often reflect the ideologies of the music genre itself as well as the brand image of the artist.

The main location of a rock performance video will often be a venue with a live audience. Rock often differentiates itself from pop by valuing the idea of authentic musical ability, including writing songs and playing musical instruments. This type of rock video reflects the way the genre favours live performance and demonstrates that the band is part of this tradition. Pop groups will often present a performance in their video, but the performance will be based on dancing in formation in a variety of locations. Pop groups tend to sing together and create harmonies, and pop is meant to be an upbeat, happy distraction that is largely marketed to young people. This youth audience prioritises socialising, and pop bands often reflect this in making their videos fun with lots of referencing to having a good time with friends. Pop music doesn't take itself too seriously, so it offers fun, frothy entertainment to its audiences. R&B music often focuses on ideas of wealth and power in the lyrics, as the genre itself reflects the ideologies of a culture where wealth equals status and demonstrates wealth as a sign of power. This is often reflected in videos where signifiers of wealth could be the choice of clothing and jewellery worn by the artist in the video or other symbols such as cars, houses, branded champagne and banknotes. These are indexes of success and power, and are used to demonstrate the wealth and power of the artist. Where the artist is male, women are often depicted as objects, indicating the artist's sexual power. Female R&B artists often try to re-appropriate the masculine power by creating images of female empowerment both sexually and within the culture.

Music videos developed with the rise of music television in the 1980s. At first only the biggest artists could afford to have videos made but today it is necessary for all artists to have a visual way to communicate. The most common way for music to be viewed today is via YouTube and the music video channel Vimeo. Artists and their recording companies receive money from YouTube views but there are many thousands of music videos available, so the biggest issue for artists is how to get audiences to watch their videos. Larger artists will have a PR team whose job it is to ensure as many people as possible know about the video, but creating a video with interesting or unusual visuals and/or content may encourage audiences to subscribe to share the video and/or subscribe to the artist's channel, so helping with the promotion of the artist. The more a video is watched, the more likely it is to be placed on YouTube's front page or 'most watched' playlists and so will generate more and more views, and more and more income for the music company.

The most important function of a music video, however, is to successfully reference genre conventions, to create representations that reflect the values of the genre

A rock performance video by Avenged Svenfold

Michael Jackson's *Billie Jean*

For further information on media language choices see Chapters 1–3.

that appeal to the existing audience and may be of interest to potential new audiences. All of this is achieved by the careful consideration of the media language choices made in the video's construction.

10.4 Sample brief

The following is an example of a brief.

> **The exam board will publish new briefs each year so make sure you are using the correct ones.**

Example brief	
Brief	**Minimum requirements**
Create print-based marketing materials for a new television game show targeting a mainstream, family audience. You will need to identify a genre of game show that would be appealing to a wide range of viewers. You should create two posters that present different aspects of the game to help it appeal to different segments of the audience. You should also create a two-page feature article for inclusion within a TV guide magazine. You may select your own approach to the feature article but it should be suitable for the genre of magazine. You will need to create your own images for each of the production pieces – a minimum of seven original images should be used. The posters should be significantly different.	**Posters** • Main image or images • Clear communication of key information (show title, presenters' names, broadcast information) • Clear identification of the genre and style of the game show • Clear identification of marketing strategy for specific audience segments **Feature article** • Headline, standfirst and subheadings • Original copy for the article (approximately 400 words) • Main image and at least three smaller images • Captions for images as appropriate • Pull quotes and/or sidebar • Considered use of house style, colour palette, fonts and columns • Identifiable marketing strategy for the game show

This example of a brief combines compulsory elements (the form and audience) and some options (the specific genre of game show to be marketed, the audience segments and the content of the feature article). In this case the brief instructs you to create two posters and a double-page feature article. The game show itself is targeting a mainstream family audience but each poster should focus on one segment of that audience. The feature article needs to be appropriate for a TV guide audience. The right-hand column provides details of the minimum requirement for each element of the production.

It is quite possible that the brief you choose will use terms and ideas you are not familiar with at the start of the process, but this is to be expected. You will need to undertake research before you begin, which will help you clarify precisely what the brief requires. Whichever brief you select, you will be assessed on the following:

1 Your understanding and use of media language choices that are appropriate and effective given the brief's requirements.

2 Your understanding and use of representations in a way that is appropriate to the audience, form and genre.

3 Your ability to engage your target audience and reflect the industrial context of your production – including the use of appropriate form, genre and industry codes.

APPLY IT

Read through this sample brief. Make a note of what you think are the key terms and ideas you may need to keep in mind as you plan and create your practical production.

10.5 Researching for the NEA

Whichever brief you choose and whichever form you are working in, you must be very clear before you start as to what the brief is instructing you to do and what choices you have to make:

- Is the form defined by the brief or can you choose?
- Is the genre defined by the brief or can you choose?
- Is the target audience defined by the brief or can you choose?
- Is the function of the product defined by the brief or can you choose?
- Is the content of the product defined by the brief or can you choose?
- Is the institutional context of the product defined by the brief or can you choose?

Once you have identified what you are being asked to do and the choices you need to make, you will need to start the first stage of the production process – research.

Practical tips for undertaking research

There are two main types of research you need to undertake:

- Practical research into existing media products similar to the one you are making
- Research into the theoretical framework and how it relates to the instructions in the brief and the product you are making.

Both types of research are closely related and need to be undertaken at the same time – hence, using the theoretical framework as a structure for your research may save you a lot of time. This research is crucial as you need to start to plan and then produce your product from a position of knowledge and understanding of media practices and of the theoretical ideas related to them.

	Existing media products	The theoretical framework
Media language	How is media language used in the production of this form? What are the codes and conventions of the form and the genres within it? How is media language use influenced by the products' target audiences? How is media language used to create narratives?	How can ideas from semiotics (connotation, denotation, myth, etc.) be seen in action in these media products? How are narrative codes constructed? Are genre conventions adhered to or subverted?
Representations	How are representations used to appeal to the target audience? What ideas are generated about specific locations, social groups, etc.	What stereotypes or countertypes are common in the media products? What evidence is there of selective representation? How might the representations contribute to hegemonic values? Do the representations contribute to ideas about identity?
Audience	How can the target audience be identified? How do the products attempt to reach and appeal to their audience? How do the products engage with the audience? Do they encourage interaction/action?	How do audiences use the product? What gratifications does the product offer? What would the conditions of consumption be? How might audiences interpret the meaning of the product?
Industry	How do the products contribute to their circulation and/or distribution? How has modern technology influenced the production of the products? What are the economic factors evident within the products?	How do the products fit in with the notion of a free market? Do the products raise issues regarding globalisation, surveillance, privacy, etc.

Using the theoretical framework in research

The purpose of your research is to gather the knowledge and develop the understanding that will enable you to create an appropriate and recognisable media product in your chosen form. You need to be able to:

- use **media language** accurately so your product is recognisable
- create **representations** that are appropriate to the messages you wish to convey
- create a product that will appeal to and engage its **target audience**
- create a product that engages with the appropriate **institutional** context.

To enable yourself to do this, you need to be familiar with the way real media products are constructed. The theoretical framework can be used to analyse existing media products and will help you engage with ideas that will enable you to create a more realistic and effective product.

While you are not expected to simply copy the styles and techniques you find, real media products should inspire you when you make your own production choices. You may decide that you wish to mix and match ideas from different media products or bring in ideas of your own so you take a more creative approach to production. You need to research codes and conventions of the form and genre you wish to create.

You cannot make an effective production if you do not have clear ideas about your target audience – who they are, what they expect and what might appeal to them. Your media language decisions will be shaped by your understanding of your audience. All media products will have a target audience in mind when they are created so you can learn a lot by looking at products similar to the one you wish to make or ones targeted towards the group you have chosen.

EXAMPLE: Game shows targeting different audiences

The game shows *The Chase* and *Copycats* clearly target different age groups. The gameplays of the two shows are quite different. *The Chase* is for adults and is based on a general knowledge quiz where contestants attempt to win large sums of money. This means it creates tension for the audience as there is real jeopardy for the contestants who are always in danger of losing their winnings. The show uses a 'chaser' whose job it is to try and stop the contestants. The mise-en-scène of the show follows the conventions of adult-oriented game shows by using a set that is decorated with neon lights, and by having a witty and charismatic host who puts contestants at ease. *The Chase* has contestants who represent the diversity of contemporary culture in terms of age, race and gender. It is a mainstream programme that attempts to appeal to a broad range of the population.

Copycats is a children's activity game show. The mise-en-scène is bright and garish, and the host is used to ramp up excitement and enthusiasm in the contestants, studio audience and viewers. The games and puzzles offer no real peril to the contestants. Contestants who lose are shown to be having lots of fun and they create amusement for the viewers.

Age and gender are two ways an audience can be defined but many products consider their audience less by how old they are and more by what type of person they are – what they like and what makes them happy. For example, if you were going to try to launch a new music magazine website you could define your audience as pre-teens, teenagers, young people under 30 or adults from 30 onwards. You could define your audience as males or females and both approaches would influence the creative decisions you make. You could also define the audience by their musical taste and their relationship with musical culture.

How would you approach creating a music website for the following audiences? Consider how the audience would influence various choices you would need to make when you create your media product.

	Casual pop fans	Serious fans of retro rock music	Avid dance music fans	Fans who are also musicians
The general tone of the website				
The style and design of the site				
The techniques you would use to try and encourage audience interaction				
The subject matter you will include – including musical artists and other features				

It is not just age that defines how someone will react. A fan of classic rock may be 60 or 16 and either male or female but regardless of age or gender they will want articles about rock musicians of the past – perhaps with a focus on guitar heroes – and will expect a magazine website aimed at their interests to take rock seriously and promote the idea that it has a value beyond simple entertainment.

Key to creating a successful product is knowing who the audience is and what it is likely to respond positively to. Media producers find out about their audience using a range of techniques from focus groups to analysing social media. You will need to research your target audience so you can shape your creative decisions to meet their needs. The best way to work out what your audience responds to is to engage with products it uses.

Classic rock fans want to read articles about rock musicians of the past.

Once you have a clear idea of your target audience you can focus on creating representations that communicate your message clearly and effectively to your chosen group. By accessing real media products you can see what type of representations are common in the area you are working in and what type of representations are used to communicate and appeal to your target audience. While analysing existing media products, don't forget to think about the industrial context:

- How would your product be distributed and circulated?
- Can you include any strategies that might make your product more successful and increase its circulation?
- What regulation issues would you need to be aware of when creating your product?
- What economic factors may impact on the way you construct your product.

When you have a good understanding of the form and its context of production you can start to plan your own practical work.

10.6 Planning for the NEA: practical tips for planning

The Statement of Intent should offer brief answers to the questions listed on the following page. It is a written document that summarises what you have learned while undertaking your research and showing how it has led you to make decisions about what you wish to make and what you want to achieve in your practical production. You should aim to make sure that your Statement of Intent is clear and that your production reflects your intentions.

See the sample Statement of Intent on page 219.

- **Media language**: What do you intend to create and how will you use media language to create genre codes, narrative, etc.?
- **Audience**: Who is this product for? How do you intend to appeal to them?
- **Audience/representations**: What is the intended function of the product? What does your product seek to achieve and how will you try to achieve this?
- **Industry**: What is the industrial context for your product and how will you consider this in your production?

The first formal piece of work you need to complete is the Statement of Intent.

Preparation and planning are vital to making a great product.

Production work always goes better when you have thought ahead and planned what you want to do — not only in terms of your ideas but also in the way you will construct your product. Creating print, moving image and e-media products is very time-consuming. Making adjustments to your production work when using software can take a lot of time and there is nothing more frustrating than editing with moving image footage that does not contain all the shots you need. Planning beforehand allows you to consider any restrictions that you may need to deal with and will ensure you have all the material you need when you come to working in desk-top publishing and editing.

Sample Statement of Intent

Media Studies AS level NEA Statement of Intent

Centre Name *Any School*   Centre Number *12345*

Candidate Name *Any Student*   Candidate Number *6789*

This form must be completed and given to your teacher before 1 April

How will you use media language and media representations in order to create a product that meets the requirements of the brief, would appeal to the target audience and also reflect the appropriate media industry? (Maximum 400 words)

Be specific about the ways in which you will use aspects of media language, media representations, target your audience and reflect the appropriate media industry for your chosen brief.

I will create marketing materials for a game show called 'Family Challenge'. It will be broadcast on BBC1 at 6pm on Saturdays and will be a hybrid game show where families compete for prizes, undertaking rounds that include quizzes, puzzles and physical challenges. The scheduling identifies the programme as being mainstream and its focus on families should appeal to a wide age-range of viewers. Although it is less common now than in the past, the time of broadcast could perhaps encourage families to view the show together. There will be four hosts – two in the studio (Mel and Sue) and two hosting the outside broadcasts (Joe Sugg and Casper Lee).

One poster will target adults and the other young people. Both posters will use a single image and minimal text. Both will include the broadcasting institution's logo and the time of broadcast, along with a hashtag and information about the programme's website and its availability on iPlayer. The celebrities will not be shown on the posters but their names will be included. The poster targeting adults will focus on the mise-en-scène of a traditional schoolroom to identify the quiz element of the game show. This will also tap into an element of tradition and nostalgia similar to the way the BBC's Great British Bake Off created appeal. This poster will identify Mel and Sue as hosts. The second poster will refer to the physical challenge aspect of the show. The physical challenges will be set in urban environments and include games based on parkour and skateboarding and identify Joe and Casper as the second pair of hosts. The two posters will offer different gratifications for the audience groups but both posters will address their audience with a challenge to attract them to the television show.

The feature article will be based on an interview with the hosts and will set up a fun 'conflict' between them based on the generation gap. The interview will be light-hearted including anecdotes from future shows to create audience appeal. The article will be illustrated with an image of the celebrities in an informal setting and smaller images showing families taking part in the show. The article will include broadcast information and the opportunity for readers to visit the programme's website and enter a competition. The feature article will use conventional layout and design codes from TV guides such as TV Quick and will have a clear and readable layout.

(400 words)

Print/e-media

Layout and design	You can create flatplans of your pages where you sketch out your basic layout and your page design.
	On these plans you can consider how you will arrange both text and images, considering the arrangements of columns and headings, and the placement and size of images.
	You can add details to your plan – ideas about your use of colour and, where necessary, your placement of standard design elements such as the institutional information on a film poster or page numbers in a magazine.
	You can create a flatplan of the basic style and design of any e-media products you choose to make. As with print, consider the relationship between text and image in your production, and use your plan to identify the size and proportions of the product you wish to make.
	If you are making a complex product, such as a website, you may want to plan the design of the site in terms of the way the pages will link together as well as the design of the individual pages. You can include e-media features in your plans to ensure you don't forget to add audience interaction and participation.
Photography 	You should plan your photoshoots carefully. Check out your locations. If you want to shoot outside, consider the weather and the quality of light you can expect at different times of the day. If you're shooting indoors, do you need to source additional lighting? Might there be any local issues you will have to deal with on the day?
	Before you shoot, consider whether you need to source make-up or clothes for your models. Do you want to include props in your images?
	Where you have practical limitations that make creating your images difficult, try to think of creative solutions to these limitations. You may want to create images with a view to using specific post-production techniques. If you need an image of one of your models on a Caribbean beach you could shoot your model in the pose you want against a plain background, then replace the background with a stock image creating the effect you want.
	When taking your photographs, don't just take one. Take a number of shots varying them slightly. Take some close-ups and long-shots. Ask your model to change poses. Take your shots from different angles and vary the position of the light. Many of these shots won't be used but you will have given yourself choices when you come to adding them to your production.

Video/audio

Script 	For any audio or video production you will need a script. This is the foundation of any production that includes dialogue and you need to work carefully on the script to ensure you are telling your story effectively and that you (where appropriate) have considered the creation of characters, relationships, conflicts and resolutions as necessary.
	You can use the script to start planning your video shoot or your audio effects. You can tell a story through images and sounds, sometimes more effectively than in words. You will also need a script for productions that do not contain dialogue where you are relying on visual or auditory storytelling.
Storyboard (video) 	The storyboard is a visualisation of the way the script will be shot and it should include information on the way the camera should be used and the transitions that are to be used in the editing process. This is an important document as it will save time when shooting because the types of shot required for each scene are clearly indicated. Scenes may need to be shot several times from different directions and angles. Footage might be needed to create intercuts, close-ups or long-shots. Having all the footage you need before you start editing will make the editing process quicker and far more efficient.
Location recce (reconnaissance)	Before you begin to shoot you should check the locations you wish to use. You may want to look at a couple of locations in order to find the one that works best for the effect you wish to create.
Sound effect plan	You may wish to create your own sound effects. Sound effects may be needed where in-camera sound recording for video work is not effective. Audio work also benefits from sound effects to break up the sound of voices and create atmosphere.

Using the sample brief, make some notes as to how you might approach the production task.

- Who is this product for? How do you intend to appeal to them?
- What is the context of this production? Do you intend to create user-generated content, self-representation or materials that emulate the production of a specific media industry or institution?
- What is the intended function of the product? What does your product seek to achieve?
- How do you intend to address the brief's theme and the focus question in your production?

KEY TERMS

flatplan	a page plan that shows how content, images and advertising will be laid out in the final production
in-camera sound	sound that is recorded using the camera's internal microphone
script	the text of a film or broadcast product

stock image	professional photographs that can be used without having to pay royalties
storyboard	sketches that represent the planned shots required for production. Storyboards often include examples of dialogue and other directorial choices such as sound, lighting and transitions

SUMMARY

This chapter has dealt with a range of different processes that need to be engaged with before you can start to create your practical production.

You need to:

1 Select the brief you wish to work on.

2 Engage with the instructions provided in the brief.

3 Undertake further research on the form, audience and industrial context as identified in the brief:

- research real media products looking at media language use and the use of codes and conventions
- research real media products looking at how they communicate to the audience
- research real media products looking at the construction of representations
- research real media products in their industrial context.

4 Create a Statement of Intent and plan your production, bringing together the knowledge and understanding you have gathered in your research.

Now you can start your production work.

Chapter 11 Making media

What you will learn in this chapter

- An introduction to the practicalities of production by offering some general information regarding the basic principles of producing work in print, e-media, audio, moving and still image.

- This information will support your practical production and should be supported by the research and planning discussed in Chapter 10.

- You will be offered ideas to help you create production work that is both effective and accurate. If you are confident in your understanding of codes and conventions and how technology can be used to help replicate them, you will have more time to create visually appealing and engaging products that succeed in communicating ideas to their audience and creating a product that meets the aims given in the statement of intent.

11.1 Print production

DTP software

When you are creating print production work you need to use software that gives you as much control over the different elements of a page as possible.

You need to be able to control:
- your font: its style, size and positioning
- your page size: different publications use different page sizes
- the presentation of your text: most print production has a lot of text and uses columns in the page design
- the presentation of your images and illustrations: you need to be able to position images accurately and resize them to fit with your page design.

Although you may take some time to work on your print production, something that should be considered as soon as you begin is printing. Most of your production decisions will be made while you are looking at your work on screen. What works on screen may not necessarily work on paper, so you should make test prints as often as you can to check how your work looks on paper. You will need to use a printer that allows you to print the correct size and weight of paper, and some productions need a printer that will print to the very edge of the page rather than leaving a margin.

Basic principles of page layout and design

Regardless of the format of your print production work, there are some basic principles of layout and design you will need to consider as you begin.

Page size and proportion

Before you start creating your layout and design, you will need to set up your paper size. Most desk-top publishing programs allow you to do this in centimetres, so this is a very easy job. You should base your page size on the conventions of the form you are making.

So, to ensure your finished work is accurate, you will need to find out what the correct size and page proportions are for your publication. You may be able to search for this information online but you can measure the media product that you are going to emulate so you know that your page size and proportion will be precise. Most printers use A4 paper and some A3, but not all print products match these sizes. Where your media product is too large to be printed at the correct size, you will need to set up your page for your product proportionally.

For example, a large billboard advertising poster measures 3,048mm high x 12,192mm wide. This means that a billboard poster needs to be (roughly) four times wider than it is high. You clearly can't create a life-sized billboard poster but you could use a template on a landscape A4 page that measures 10cm high x 30cm wide and your poster would have roughly the correct proportions.

Newspapers tend to come in two standard sizes:

- Tabloid 28cm x 43cm
- Broadsheet 60cm x 75cm

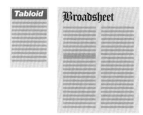

Magazines can vary in size. Smaller magazines called 'digest size', such as *Glamour*, have much smaller pages than a 'standard-sized magazine'. *Glamour*'s pages measure 7 7/8" x 10 7/8", whereas a standard-sized magazine measures 27.5cm x 21cm. Most magazines are taller than they are wide (*Elle* measures 28.5cm x 22cm) but others may be wider than they are tall.

If you are attempting to emulate a specific title for your production work you will need to measure the page size to be sure your finished work is accurate. If your pages are not the right size you are likely to get the proportions of the design elements incorrect and this will limit the effectiveness of your production. If you are creating your own newspaper or magazine title, you should check which page sizes are most often used in the form and genre you are working in.

Magazine and newspaper **adverts** are sized by the percentage of the page covered – so an advert's size is determined by the host publication's size. A half-page advert in the *Sun* would be larger than a half-page advert in *Glamour*. By identifying where your advert would be published you can demonstrate your understand that different publications are different sizes. You can also show you understand the relationship between your product and the target audience by placing your advert in a publication that shares your target audience.

You may be asked to create standalone advertising materials such as flyers or posters. The brief may be specific, detailing what type of advertising product or products you must create or it may allow you to make decisions on what advertising products are suitable for the given task. In either case, an understanding of your target audience should help you decide what forms of advertising product would be the most appropriate to get your message to the right people. As advertising products come in all shapes and sizes, you should decide on the placement of your advert and/or the distribution method so you can set up your DTP page accurately before production begins.

You should use existing media products to investigate the different approaches to print advertising used today. To get the full effect of your magazine or newspaper advertising, and to show your understanding of advertising and marketing, you might want to consider presenting your work within the page or pages of the publication it would be found. For standalone advertising, you could show it in its final location.

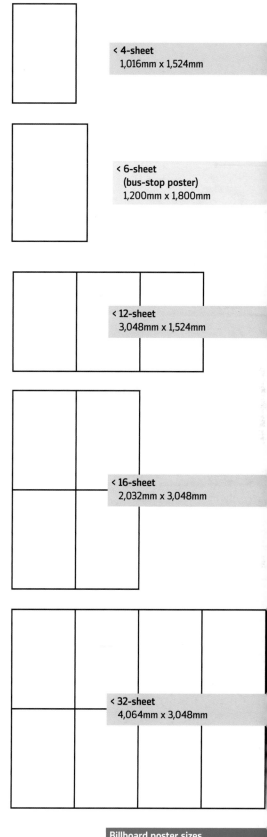

< 4-sheet
1,016mm x 1,524mm

< 6-sheet
(bus-stop poster)
1,200mm x 1,800mm

< 12-sheet
3,048mm x 1,524mm

< 16-sheet
2,032mm x 3,048mm

< 32-sheet
4,064mm x 3,048mm

Billboard poster sizes

However you approach your production, make sure that you set up your page correctly in your desk-top publishing software and, once your page size is set up, you should then start to consider your main design elements.

Proportion in design

You will have a number of design elements you will want to place on your print production page, including images and text and, depending on the form you are creating, you may have design conventions that you need to follow.

As we discovered earlier, a billboard poster is four times wider than it is high. If the billboard poster is to be used to sell a consumer product, for example a perfume, your poster would need to include:

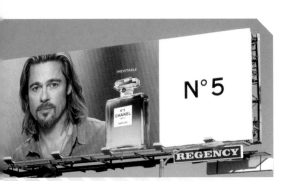

- the perfume's name/brand name
- an image of an aspirational model
- a background
- an image of the product itself
- a tag line (perhaps)
- a web address and/or hashtag (perhaps).

Before you start taking photographs or laying out your page you should create a flatplan to help you work out what you want your finished product to look like. When creating a flatplan you could consider how you would combine the poster elements on your page. You would need to consider where each element should be placed and also how large or small each element needs to be.

Looking at the real billboards on the left, it is clear that the names of the perfume, the perfume bottles and the images of Hollywood actors are the most dominant elements. If you look closely, each poster can be divided into three sections vertically and horizontally. The J'adore Dior and Chanel No 5 posters have one of the elements above in each section of the poster : the name/logo – then the bottle – then Charlize Theron; Brad Pitt – then the product – then the product name/logo. The Miss Dior poster uses the Hollywood star Natalie Portman across the whole length of the poster, so her face and the bottle are together in the right-hand section of the poster and this is balanced with the name of the perfume being placed in the top-left corner.

The conventional design elements of a poster are present in all these examples but the elements are used differently in each. The three posters all use images and text that are sized appropriately given the size of the poster. The information is clearly visible from a distance, faces are recognisable and the branding is clear. The posters work because all the elements are in proportion to the size and shape of a billboard poster. They look appealing because they are using the space in a way that feels balanced and logical.

 APPLY IT **List the design elements needed on one of the following print products:**
- a cover for a PC game
- the front page of a women's fashion magazine
- the back page of a tabloid newspaper
- a flyer promoting a club night.

Print layout and design

Whatever size or shape you choose for your page, you should try to apply the following design principles as you lay out your page.

Columns

As identified on the billboard posters, print pages are designed using a grid with each page being divided into vertical and horizontal sections. In text-based print publications, these vertical sections are used to divide text into **columns**. Magazines tend to use a three- or five-column layout depending on the size of the publication. Tabloid newspapers use a five-column layout and broadsheets often use six columns per page. Double-page spreads are often treated as a single page with column design, considering the look of both pages when seen side by side.

Page designers use columns to help them create pages that use pictures, text, adverts and headings in the most appealing way for the audience.

Columns make it easier for audiences to read text, thus making the content easier to follow. Long lines of text are hard to read and make it difficult to find the next line when returning to the left-hand side. Columns are used to ensure lines of text are neither too long nor too short for the reader.

Columns help designers create pages that are visually balanced and logical for the reader to access. When designing a page it is important that the reader knows which column follows on from the last.

Compositional balance

Compositional **balance** is created when the **weight** of the page is balanced top to bottom and left to right. The placement of your design elements will impact on the balance of the page. Large bold and black text is 'heavy', as are dense images. Small or thin fonts, black and white sketches and white space are 'light'. A balanced page has similar weight in the top-left and bottom-right sides of the page. This creates the feel of stability on the page and is pleasing to the eye. A well-balanced page guides the reader and makes it clear which images belong to which blocks of text.

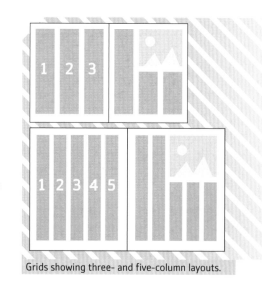

Grids showing three- and five-column layouts.

Heavy image

Light image

Heavy Text Light Text

Light pages

Heavy pages

Well-balanced pages

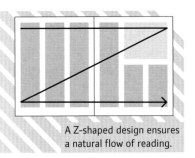

A Z-shaped design ensures a natural flow of reading.

Columns also help guide the way the eye travels across the page from left to right and ensures that images don't interrupt the natural flow of reading. Most readers don't take in the fine detail of the page at first. Readers tend to scan the page in a Z-shaped eye movement. This Z-shape eye movement is used across double-page spreads too.

Column design is one of the first steps in making sure pages look balanced, coherent, aesthetically pleasing and are legible.

As well as columns, page design considers the balance of the page on the horizontal. The page is usually divided into three and designers use these three spaces in addition to the columns to create **compositional balance** on the page.

Font style

Fonts are split into three basic types:

1 **Serif**: font styles that have small tails at the ends of the letters:
   * for example, Times New Roman or Georgia.
2 **Sans serif**: font styles that use simple forms for the letters:
   * for example, Arial and Gill Sans.
3 **Decorative** or **novelty** fonts: stylised fonts that can create a very specific look or feel
   * for example, Papyrus or *Snell roundhand* (the fonts that look similar to handwriting are sometimes called script fonts).

Serif and sans serif fonts are both very easy to read, whereas decorative ones can be more difficult for the reader and should never be used in large blocks of text.

When choosing font styles for your work, unless you have a specific reason for doing otherwise, consider choosing one font for your body text and a second for headings. It is possible to use the same font for both. Tabloid newspapers tend to use a sans serif font for headlines and a serif font for body text. Use decorative fonts sparingly and if you do use them ensure they are large enough so they can be read easily. A page that uses too many different fonts or that over-uses decorative fonts can look chaotic and unappealing to the reader.

Different styles of font have the potential to add meaning to your publication. Fonts create connotations, so make sure you choose fonts that create the tone and atmosphere that suits your publication, your message and your audience. Serif fonts are sometimes thought to look more formal and authoritative, whereas a sans serif font feels more friendly and accessible. Experiment with different fonts and see what kind of tone or feel they create. Consider the tone you wish to create and use fonts to help.

You may wish to create a publication that:

* is traditional (Bookman Old Style)
* is modern (Futura)
* is friendly (Comic Sans)
* is quirky (Bauhaus 93)
* looks typed (Courier)
* evokes the 'wild west' (Blackoak)
* is a little bit 1920s (Braggadocio)
* looks handwritten (Mistral)
* is formal (Times New Roman)
* is casual (Chalkduster).

Font size

Don't forget to use a font size that is appropriate to your publication. Posters tend to use small amounts of text and need to use large-sized fonts for visibility. Newspapers and magazines use large-sized fonts in headlines but smaller-sized fonts in the body text. Headlines can be as large as 72pt (pt = points – the numerical measurement of font size) in some newspapers, whereas the body type can be as small as 8 or 9pt. A typical font size for a magazine article is 9pt. Font size choices should also ensure that the content of the product is legible for the intended audience.

EXAMPLE: Different point sizes

1 This sentence may be difficult to read because the font is too small.

2 This sentence will look clumsy on the page because the font is too big.

3 This sentence should look just right as the size of the font has been considered very carefully in relationship to the size and general design of the pages in this book.

If you are creating your own original print publication rather than emulating an existing product, you can select your own page size and proportions as well as the general composition of your pages. You should use existing media products as guides, but have readability at the heart of all your design choices. If you are attempting to recreate an existing publication, these decisions have already been made. You should closely analyse the products to see how they use columns and fonts, so you can emulate their house style and the way they use design elements.

Approaches to different forms (magazine, newspaper)

In addition to general layout principles, for all print products different forms and genres use different codes and have their own conventions. You need to consider the theme and topics offered in the NEA brief but there is no constraint as to what type of product you make, so try to be creative as you make your production decisions. For example:

- You may choose to create a broadsheet- or tabloid-sized newspaper – you could show you understand the codes and conventions of the form and your chosen genre by replicating them, but you could subvert those codes in terms of the content you create.

- If you create your own magazine title you won't be tied to a specific page size. Once you've chosen the page size you wish to create, do some research to see how real magazines design content for their pages and then you can mix and match some of the best ideas you find.

- Advertising gives a lot of scope for creativity. You could create a range of flyers with similar design elements but content that targets a specific audience subgroup. You could come away from box-shaped designs and present your information in a much more appealing and interesting way. Perhaps you could be innovative in making booklets or flyers with unusual approaches to the presentation of the information?

Before you can be accurate and creative in your production work, you need to know what the conventions are.

Newspapers

Genre: tabloid

Each UK tabloid newspaper has developed its own house style based on page design choices in the fonts and page layout conventions used. While the house styles of the *Sun* and the *Daily Mirror* (red-top tabloids) or the *Daily Mail* and the *Daily Express* (middle-market newspapers) make each newspaper recognisable, they share presentation codes and conventions that mean they can all be identified as tabloid newspapers. Tabloid newspapers are not all the same size but they are significantly smaller than broadsheets. Tabloids tend to be printed on paper sized around 560mm x 430mm and this creates four pages of the newspaper (430mm x 380mm each).

Grid showing a typical double-page spread layout.

APPLY IT

Look at the front cover and two inside pages of a broadsheet newspaper. How does the layout and design of a broadsheet differ to that of a tabloid?

Write a detailed description of the page size, layout and composition of the front cover and two inside pages of a broadsheet newspaper.

The sheet of paper is printed front and back and then folded. The page has a print margin of approximately 1–2cm on all edges of the paper.

The horizontal top-third of the paper will contain the paper's masthead and a teaser for further content to be found inside the newspaper. The teaser will usually fill the full width of the page. The furthest top-right corner may advertise a special feature, a competition or perhaps a special offer. Promotions information will often be placed under the masthead. Traditionally, newspapers were displayed in newsagents folded so that only the top third of the page was visible. Sometimes they were kept in a large pile on or close to the ground. This makes the top third the most important part of the page when it comes to selling the newspaper. This section of the page is what was most likely to be seen by potential readers.

Front pages of tabloids tend to use a five-column vertical layout. The **headline** for the lead story often uses the first three columns from left to right and most of the lower two-thirds of the page. A standfirst often appears just beneath the headline, providing additional information or a very brief summary of the story. Standfirsts are usually presented in a contrasting font to the headline. The headline and/or an image will usually take up the majority of the space on the page leaving two or three short columns at the foot of the page for the first few paragraphs of the lead story. There may be subheadings within the article. The news story will continue inside the newspaper, as image and headline rather than text dominate the layout of a tabloid front page.

Unless the news story is particularly important there is usually a secondary story on the front page. This will often be a celebrity or human interest story and a photograph is likely to take up most of the remaining space on the page. A small headline covering the two-column width may be provided but, again, the detail on the story will be provided inside the picture itself.

Inside the newspaper, some pages are designed individually as single pages while some are double-page spreads. It is common for two pages to be split into five columns with one headline across both pages at the top. Where the copy for the article is quite long, the body text may be designed with pull quotes to help break up the text and two full columns may be followed by text only towards the bottom of the page with subheadings, images and captions filling the top two-thirds of the page. These illustrations may go onto the second page and the main article could end with a supplementary article containing additional or explanatory material in a sidebar, usually on the right-hand side of the page.

Not all feature articles take up the full double-page spread. Where this happens a different story will be positioned below, to the left or to the right of the feature, and will have its own headline, pull quotes and illustrations. The pages will be designed using different-coloured backgrounds, dividing lines and/or boxes to ensure the readers recognise that there are two different stories on the page.

Magazines

Genre: gossip

Gossip magazines are traditionally published weekly and are printed on relatively thin, coloured paper. The content of this type of magazine is primarily celebrity-based stories but they also contain beauty, travel, fashion and other lifestyle content for their predominantly female target audience.

Gossip magazines generally use close to standard magazine-sized paper. The front cover will feature the title of the magazine at the top of page and where the name is short enough (*heat*, *Now!*, *OK!*, etc.) it will be positioned on the left.

All gossip magazines will have their own brand and house style that differentiates them from one another, but there are conventions that are used across the genre. The gossip magazine cover tends to use a basic three horizontal x five vertical grid and there will be at least one celebrity on the front cover, normally in the middle section of the page positioned towards the right. The celebrity will usually be presented in mid- or medium-long-shot in this genre. Their eyes will be looking into the camera and they will generally be positioned towards the centre or centre top of the page. There will be small blocks of text in a large-sized font towards the left-hand side and the bottom of the page. The **coverlines** offer information to the audience on the content of the stories being published and they implicitly offer more detail inside the magazine itself.

Gossip magazines use bold, bright colours to get themselves noticed. Red, orange, bright pink and yellow are commonly used colours in this genre. The front cover will be **busy** with lots of text and maybe some smaller images that tease the reader by alluding to the stories that are expanded on inside the magazine.

There are many different types of layout used inside gossip magazines, as they contain lots of different types of feature, including beauty, fashion, cookery and celebrity lifestyles. Some pages are designed individually and, as with newspapers, some are treated as double-page layouts. It is not unusual to have a full-page image in a double-page layout with the story itself told in the bottom two-thirds of one page and the text being split between three or four columns. A large headline and sometimes a smaller subheading will fill the top third of the page and the two pages will feel **coherent**, as a limited colour palette will be used. Gossip magazines also often use geometric shapes and/or fancy fonts to add visual interest to a page. These shapes and fonts will often pick out a colour from the pages' palette.

3x5 grid

Create a written description of the layout of a front cover and selected inside pages of these other genres of magazine:

- men's lifestyle magazine
- home décor magazine
- cookery magazine
- TV listings magazine.

In your own print production, you should be accurate in your recreation of the codes and conventions used by the form and genre you are working in. Your work will be effective if it appeals to your target audience, so you should consider the content and imagery you choose so that they combine to create the message you wish to communicate in a way that meets your audience's expectations. You will need to use technology to reproduce the codes and conventions accurately but you can approach using these conventions creatively and with flair. Reproducing codes is not just about copying what has already been done but you should put your own spin on the way the conventions are used.

KEY TERMS

balance (page)	a balanced page has been designed to ensure that the heavy objects and lighter ones are positioned to create a harmonious feel
billboard	a large outdoor location for advertising. Traditionally a board for the placement of print adverts but electronic billboards can be found in some locations. Electronic billboards can present all types of video material but they are often used to broadcast adverts
busy	the effect of pages that are created with many design elements, font styles, etc. Busy pages are sometimes difficult for the reader to access and can be confusing and visually offputting

columns	a way to organise text and images on the page by dividing the page vertically
design elements	the individual parts that combine together to construct a page
DTP	a commonly used abbreviation for desk-top publishing that refers to software specifically designed to support the design and publication of print and, in some cases, e-media production
font	the design of the letters used within a specific typeface. Fonts have pre-defined proportions, weight and style. All letters and numbers within a font will be designed to harmonise
page proportions	the size of the page and the relationship between its height and length

subheading	a heading for a subsection of an article
teaser (newspapers/ magazines)	a brief indication of the content within the publication. Used to encourage the reader to purchase the publication to be able to read further
weight (visual)	a term used to refer to the effect of the depth, darkness and/or intensity of a design element. Large, dark, textured and warm-coloured elements tend to appear 'heavier' – they have more visual weight. Elements in the foreground or higher on the page tend to appear heavy on the page as do regular shapes and vertical (rather than horizontal) objects. Images of things that are actually heavy also have weight on the page

11.2 Producing and working with still images

Photography is an important part of media production. Photographs will be needed to illustrate print and e-media productions, and they can be used to demonstrate your knowledge of codes and conventions as well as creativity and technical skills.

The style and content of the photographs you need for your production will depend on what you are making, who your product is for and what your product needs to achieve. The best way to find inspiration for your photos is to look at the way photography is used in existing media products.

If you are making a newspaper product you will note that tabloids and broadsheets tend to use photographs that give information on the story being reported. Photographs are often simple illustrations of the 'who', 'what' and 'where' of the story being reported. News photographs are often sourced from **photojournalists** or **paparazzi** and can often look simple and denotative, as they are taken on the spot, giving the impression of immediacy.

News photos are selected to help reinforce the specific message a newspaper wishes to communicate and are carefully constructed and/or edited to create a specific effect.

Construction includes the positioning on the page, the size of the image, the way the image has been **cropped** and the anchorage that is added to the page. The presentation choices are made in an attempt to lead the reader towards a preferred reading of the events being reported. Newspapers also use maps, diagrams and graphs where these help communicate information to the reader. Broadsheet newspapers will sometimes use more metaphoric or symbolic images to illustrate a story, while tabloids prefer images that are directly connected to details within the story. Newspaper feature articles use posed portraits taken from photoshoots and they too are selected, cropped and possibly edited to reinforce the tone and values within the article itself.

You should take inspiration from products that are similar to the one you are making and/or that are trying to appeal to the same target audience when you start to think about how you will use images in your own production.

- Does your production need to communicate **genre** through images? How does this work in real media products?
- Will images be part of your creation of **audience** appeal? How does this work in real media products?
- Does your production need to use images to create **representations** that communicate values and **ideologies**? How does this work in real media products?
- Do you need to construct **narrative** information in your images? How is this done in real media products?

Once you have ideas about what you want to achieve with your photographs you should start to plan your photoshoot. In your planning, consider how you intend to use media language to construct the messages you wish to communicate.

Again, you should analyse the way the photographs in real media products are constructed. Breaking down the media language choices that are used helps you to create images that are effective and creative.

Your planning should include how you intend to create your mise-en-scène and should include ideas about:

- **Location** – what background to you want to use? Should your images be interior or exterior shots? Do you want to create a specific atmosphere or tone using the location or should your image be set in a certain place? You may wish to check out potential locations, even taking a few snapshots to see how the locations look on camera.
- **Make-up** – do your models need make-up and, if so, what effect are you aiming for? Are you intending to create character with make-up or use it to recreate a specific genre convention? You may wish to design the make-up you want in the planning stage. It's also a good idea to practise it before the photoshoot, again taking some snapshots to see how it looks.

Does your model need make-up and is special lighting required?

- **Wardrobe** – what should your models wear in your photographs? If you have any specific costume needs you may have to source items before your photoshoot.
- **Props** – what objects do you need in the shots? Should your models be holding items? Do you need a specific type of chair for your models to sit on? Are there items that you want to include in the mise-en-scène that you will have to source?
- **Lighting** – will you use natural light or do you want to have other light sources? Will you use the flash on your camera or an external flash? Do you want to try and control the colour, position or strength of the lighting? Perhaps you can use domestic lamps in interior shots? Can you access professional lights to help create tone and shadow in your photographs?

APPLY IT

What connotations about characters or situations might you make based on these mise-en-scène choices?

Style of décor	Connotation	Genre
Clean, modern décor with minimalist, modern art objects and functional furniture.		
A mix and match décor with a collection of retro objects in many different styles and colours.		
While clean and tidy the décor is shabby and in a state of disrepair.		

Mise-en-scène can be used to create a shorthand that communicates ideas and information quickly and efficiently. It can offer the audience clues to a character's background and personality, the historical or geographical setting, the economic status of characters and what they do.

For example, the following **props** give character information:

- a briefcase on the table can indicate that at least one of the characters is a professional
- ensuring that a character's wedding ring is in shot can indicate they are (or have been) married
- lots of pizza boxes lying around can indicate that a character is lazy.

Certain **settings** are common in specific genres:

- a cabin in the woods usually means something horrific will be on its way
- a British suburban kitchen will often be the location for family dramas or sitcom misunderstandings
- a steel and glass skyscraper will often be the setting for a corporate thriller.

Costumes can be used to indicate a character's personality, class position or profession and many genres have costume conventions.

You should also consider the **framing** and **composition** of your shots in your planning to ensure you have the content you want. You should consider how you need to position the people and objects in the frame. Do you want to create close-ups, mid-shots, and/or long-shots on your shoot?

Note: you can plan for framing and composition but it is always a good idea to take a variety of shots from different positions, angles and heights so you can select the ones that work best within your production.

Although this will be dealt with later, you should also consider what post-production effects you may want to create after the shoot. You should make sure you plan to take photographs that allow you to achieve what you need. For example, if you plan to insert one of your models into a stock background image you must take photographs of your model in front of a white or at least plain background. If you don't do this, you may find you cannot cleanly extract the image of the model from the original photograph when you are using photo-editing software.

There are no rules as to how you should approach planning your photoshoot but you may find using a **storyboard** template, similar to one you would use for moving images, helpful. You can sketch the images you want to create and make notes about specific effects you wish to create while taking your photos.

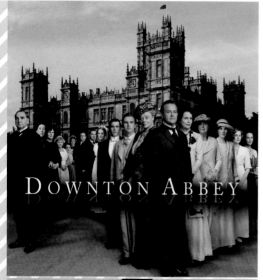

Downton Abbey and *People Just do Nothing*: costume, performance, props and setting communicating ideas of class, historical period and genre.

For more on post-production effects see pages 234–235.

Basic principles of photography

Photography has two stages: in-camera and **post-production**. Most digital photography offers a range of in-camera options, and lenses are usually automatically set up to take the best image possible given the conditions present at the time. This means that, today, many in-camera decisions are, in fact, made in post-production.

To save you time later in the process, you may try to ensure that the image taken is as close as possible to the one you need for your production. However, as you will see, many issues or problems can be sorted out later in image manipulation software.

Decisions about mise-en-scène and lighting should have been made before you take your pictures. During your photoshoot, but before setting up your shot, you should consider the following:

- **Focus** – relates to the sharpness of the image. What element of your photograph should be clearly in focus? Do you want any elements within your photograph to be out of focus? Mobile phones, tablets and most digital cameras will make focus decisions as the photograph is being taken. You can alter focus in post-production software but bear in mind it is easier to blur some aspects of the image than sharpen them. Try to make sure that the most important element in the shot is in focus when you take it.

- **Exposure** – relates to the amount of light that enters the camera when the shot is taken; an under-exposed image is too dark and an over-exposed image is too light. Digital cameras tend to use an automatic exposure calculated on the amount of light that is available at the time the picture is taken. Post-production software can create exposure effects.

- **Framing** – refers to the positioning of elements in the image. If you have a main subject for your image, do you want it to be the only image in the shot? Do you want it to be a small image to the edge of the frame? Do you want it to share the frame with other objects? When you look through the viewfinder you will create a frame for your image – your subject will be 'framed' by the edges of the lens – so you should make sure you have positioned your subject where you want it before you take your photograph.

- **Composition** – also refers to the positioning of elements in the image but in this case it is the way elements are positioned in relation to each other. A well composed shot has a clear **focal point**, considers the whole frame (often using the rule of thirds) and is well balanced.

Good photo

Bad photo

As you will be able to crop your image during post-production, you may think that you can create the framing and composition you need after the photoshoot. To an extent this could be true but some framing and composition errors are very difficult to correct. For example, it is difficult to correct an image where the subject does not stand out because the background in the composition creates a complex and muddled view. Similarly, if the head of your subject is outside the frame, this cannot be corrected in post-production.

Getting creative (on a shoestring budget)

Not all Media Studies students have access to professional cameras or equipment. The digital camera on your phone or tablet can create images that are perfectly suitable for a Media Studies production. You may have access to a digital stills camera. This will be fine too and may give you more control over exposure and focus.

You may be able to use the software provided with your camera, phone or tablet to create effects as you take your photographs. Internal software can alter the colour tone of the images you take and the aspect ratio of the image. You may prefer to take all your images using a standard setting and then make changes in post-

production. There may be limitations to the in-camera effects that can be created with these types of camera but there are ways to take creative photographs using a bit of imagination.

The easiest and cheapest way to create effects when taking photographs is to consider and vary camera distances and angles when creating your shots.

Try taking the same shot from a number of different **distances**:

- Put your subject in context with **long-shots** that include aspects of mise-en-scène that provide information to the viewer.
- Use **mid-shots** to show some aspects of the location but that allow your audience to focus more on your subject. This is a good position to use to communicate character through non-verbal communication codes. Head and shoulders shots can be used to exclude most elements of mise-en-scène.
- Use **close-ups** to show detail. Take care with focus – make sure that the focal point of the image is in sharp focus.
- Use extreme close-ups to exclude all information apart from one small detail.

An extreme close-up

Try taking the same shot from a number of **angles**:

- Use **low-angle shots** where you shoot your subject from below. This makes your subject loom large in the frame.
- Use **high-angle shots** where you shoot from above to minimise the subject or perhaps create the idea that they are being spied on.

  Unless you have the hardware, it can be difficult to get high-angle shots by hand. Take great care if you decide to climb up to create the shot. You may find it easier to use a selfie-stick to safely elevate your phone. Do test it first to make sure the selfie-stick will hold your phone securely.

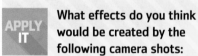
A low-angle shot

You could get even more creative by mixing your distances and angles or by experimenting with lighting effects during your photoshoots by:

- using torches or domestic lamps to create spotlights or low-key lighting effects
- creating reflectors made of card and tin-foil to create soft light fills or high-key lighting effects
- using objects to create shaped shadows in your image
- using natural light in a number of different ways, for example shoot with the light behind you, shoot with the light to the side or shoot with the light behind your subject. Each position will create a different effect.

During your photoshoot take lots of images using different types of shot and play with light effects, framing and composition as much as you can. Ask your models to try different poses, change the way you use props and alter make-up and costumes during the shoot. You can decide which images work best during post-production. It is always better to have too many photographs than too few.

APPLY IT
What effects do you think would be created by the following camera shots:

- low-angle mid-shots?
- high-angle long-shots?
- eye-level close-ups?
- low-angle close-ups?

Still-image editing and post-production

The work you undertake in post-production is where you get another opportunity to demonstrate your creative and technical skills. You can use standalone software to edit your photographs or you could use one of the many free editing packages available online, or an app for your phone or tablet.

Most post-production software offers similar functions. These are some of the post-production effects you may consider using to enhance your photos:

- **Cropping and slicing** – post-production software allows you to re-shape and re-size your photographs. You can remove parts of the image that you do not want to use by selecting an area of the photo to keep. Cropping usually allows you to keep a rectangular section of the image but some software allows other shapes to be selected. Cropping also allows you to improve the framing of your shot and, to a certain extent, its composition. Some software packages allow you to select and extract specific elements from the photograph, and add in elements from other photographs. Slicing allows you to select an area of the original image by dividing the image into sections and deleting the parts you don't need.

- **Colour/light editing** – post-production software allows you to alter the overall look of the photo by changing its colour. For example, colour images can be turned into black and white or can be 'aged' by colouring them in a sepia tone. The 'exposure' of the image can be changed as can the contrast between the dark and light tones. Shadows can be added and specific areas of the image can be brightened.

  The ability to edit the colour of photographs also allows them to be 'retouched'. Small areas of the photograph can be changed. This is a technique that is sometimes used to 'perfect' the look of models and celebrities. Skin blemishes can be removed and a common technique used to 'brighten' the face is to lift the corners of the mouth, the eyes and raise the arch of the eyebrows. Female models are often 'reduced' by erasing the edges of their body to produce a slimmer profile. This technique is often referred to by the name of one of the most well-known photo-editing software packages, Photoshop, and is known as 'photoshopping'. You don't need access to Photoshop to edit your images.

- **Effects filters** – post-production software offers a range of different finishes and textures that can be applied to photographs. Photos can be filtered to look like paintings and drawings; colour filters can create retro effects and leak or enhance the colours; some filters allow you to alter the depth of field while others can create grainy, glass or crackle effects.

KEY TERMS

colour tone	the properties of colour – its shade, hue, warmth, brightness, saturation, etc.	light fills	a light used to reduce the contrast between light and shadow within the frame
extreme close-up (ECU)	like the close-up, the camera is positioned close to the subject and a small detail fills the frame	low-key lighting	a style of lighting used to create shadow and areas of bright light within the frame
head and shoulders shot	a shot where the camera is positioned close to a human subject so that the frame excludes all of the body, apart from the head and shoulders	non-verbal communication	methods of communication that do not include words. Body language and modes of dress are both examples
high-key lighting	the use of light fills to create a low-contrast lighting effect	paparazzi	a professional photographer who seeks to capture informal images of celebrities or other people identified as being newsworthy
in-camera	decisions made to influence the look of images while shooting with the camera. This includes using camera settings as well as using external sources such as music, props and lighting to create specific effects	photojournalist	professional photographer who uses images to tell a story
		post-production	decisions made to influence the look of images after the footage or images have been captured. This is usually done using post-production software

APPLY IT

- Go online and search for 'image manipulation effects'.

- Scroll through some images to get an idea of the types of effect that are possible.

- Go online and search for 'free online image manipulation'.

- Access one of the websites and use one of your own photographs to explore the effects that you can create.

11.3 Moving image production

Creating a moving image production is an excellent way of demonstrating your knowledge of media concepts, your understanding of audience and institution, and your creativity and technical ability.

Whichever form you are creating you will need to think very carefully about the way you use technology and how you will present your work using **camera**, **sound**, **lighting** and **mise-en-scène**. You will **edit** the different shots you have taken and may also choose to enhance your work by adding special effects during **post-production**.

In order to ensure you get the footage you want and need, planning is key. Like photography, you may create the effects you want in-camera and/or in post-production, but you need to know what footage you will require so you can make sure you have everything needed when you come to edit. Before you begin to film you should research your locations, source your props and costumes, find your actors, and put together a storyboard and script. During your planning process you can consider whether you need to find light sources to help create the effects you want. One of the challenges in creating moving image productions is that you will inevitably need to work with others in some way – even if it's just with your actors – and this means you need to be able to plan carefully and be prepared to organise other people in order to get the footage you need.

There are many things you need to consider before you start shooting and it is easier to work out how to answer these questions while you are planning rather than during your shoot. Moving image productions need to be 'written' before they are filmed. A script is needed to give your actors dialogue, a shooting script adds images and direction to the words on the page, shot lists and storyboards help provide information on how to set up each shot and may also contain information about editing and other post-production elements. In addition to these production issues, there are decisions that need to be made that are dependent on the form and genre you have chosen to make, who your target audience is and what effect you are trying to create. These decisions should have been made during research so now you can think practically about how to achieve what you want in your production. For example:

- What are the conventions of the form you are creating? Which conventions will you follow? Which (if any) will you subvert?
- What are the genre conventions that you need to use? Do you wish to subvert the genre conventions and audience expectations? How will you do this?
- How will you approach telling the story? What visual devices will you use to create narrative information for your audience?
- What tone or atmosphere do you wish to create? How will you do this?
- What representations do you wish to create? How will you achieve this?
- How will you create audience appeal?

Basic principles of filming

Using the camera

You may have access to professional equipment or you may have to 'make do' with limited resources – either way there is still plenty of scope to make effective moving image production pieces. Mobile phone and tablet cameras can be used to capture your footage but do be aware of the difference between landscape and portrait modes and make sure you have selected the correct one for the form you are making. It is unlikely that you will want to use images recorded in portrait for many media productions unless you wish to replicate the type of user-generated content that is sometimes used in news reporting. News broadcasters, however, repackage this footage by adding visuals to the side of the original video to make it more appealing to viewers.

The size and portability of mobile phone cameras means that they can help create shots from perspectives and angles that may be difficult to achieve with larger cameras. If a tablet or mobile phone is used to create a media product that would usually be made by a professional camera, you may want to think about how you can make your work look as professional as possible. For example, using a tripod would help create steady shots and horizontal pans. Tripods are relatively cheap and they can make a big difference in the quality of your work. *Tangerine* (2015, Baker, S.) was filmed on an iPhone but the film still uses professional framing and filming techniques.

Whatever type of camera you are using, you need to familiarise yourself with it and what it can do. The best way to do this is to experiment and make some short videos using some of the settings and effects that are built in. You should test out the light-settings (if you have them) in different lighting conditions, both inside and outside. You should try some of the effects such as slow motion or time-lapse to see if they are effects you would like to use.

Setting up your shots – framing and composition

As with photography, you need to know how to frame your shots. You may wish to consider the composition of your shots by using a 3 x 3 grid to help you design the positioning of people and objects in it. Some cameras come with a grid visible in the viewfinder and this helps you to create balance in the frame. You should think about the **position** of your subject (or subjects) and the relationship between subjects and the background. How you compose your shots will depend on what you want to include in the frame and the effect you want to achieve. When composing the shot, you should consider the objects in the foreground and background and how they look together. You should also consider the balance between left and right areas of the frame as well as the top and bottom.

There are many things to think about when considering the position of the camera. Following are just some of the questions you should be addressing when you set your shot up.

- How high or low do you want your camera to be? What point-of-view do you wish to create?
  - Do you wish to create a high-angle or low-angle shot?
  - Do you want your camera to look straight ahead at your subject or look from the left or right?
- How far away should your subjects be?
  - Do you wish to create a long-shot, a mid-shot or a close-up?
  - Do you want to change the distance from your subject within the shot? Will you zoom in or out? Will you track in or out?
- Do you want subjects and/or objects to move within the frame? Will you move the camera during the shot?
  - Do you wish to tilt or pan during the shot?
  - Do you want to track the movement of subjects and/or objects in the shot? If so, how will you achieve a smooth camera movement?
  - Have you **blocked** the actors' movements so that the camera can follow them?

There are some basic rules that can be applied when setting up certain shots. Part of your research may be to look at media products and work out what conventions are often used.

Making a video filmed in portrait mode, suitable for broadcast

A video filmed in landscape mode

Tangerine

For example: filming a conversation

The conventional way to shoot a conversation between two people is to film the conversation three times from three different positions:

1 **The two-shot** – shooting the conversation with two people in the frame together (sometimes different two-shots will be from different positions or angles).

2 **Over the shoulder shots** – filming over the shoulder of one actor to capture the other actor's dialogue and their reactions to the first actor's lines.

3 A repeat of the **over the shoulder shot** from behind the second actor (the combination of these two shots is a **shot-reverse-shot** technique).

The conversation is then put together during editing, with shots being cut and edited together to show the conversation as one continuous event, but presented from a combination of positions and points of view.

1 **Find one of the following scenes (or similar) in a TV programme:**
- a family discussion around the dinner table
- a character walking down a city street
- a woman getting ready to go out
- a man meeting his friends at a sporting event.

2 **Select one minute from the scene and make a list of the shots used.**
- Consider camera angles, distance and movement.
- How many different shots are used in the extract?
- How are they edited together?

Lighting

You can use lighting to help with composition by highlighting certain parts of the frame. Lighting is often used to help create tone and atmosphere whether that is the high-key lighting that is used in hyper-real genres such as reality TV or sitcoms, or the low-key lighting that is a convention in horror. Sitcoms use off-screen lighting to create a brightness in the frame, whereas soap operas tend to attempt to create a more naturalistic effect with by using on-screen light sources such as lamps and candles, which can create contrast and shadow. The horror genre often uses low-key lighting to emphasise the contrast between light and dark and to create a mysterious tone. Shadows become as important as light in this genre, as what is hidden is often more frightening for the audience than what is seen.

A **three-point lighting** set up is often used on professional shoots and altering the position, strength and direction of the lighting can dramatically change the feel of the image being shot. The quality of the light (hard, bright or soft, diffuse light), the colour of the light (natural daylight, yellow-tone interior light, red light for effect) and the position of the light (from above, from the side, from below) all act to alter the feel of the image within the frame. The more you use and control light the more you can control the final look of your moving image footage and its impact.

When setting up your shots, consider whether the light you have is creating the effect you want. You may have to shoot outside at a specific time of day to get the shot you need for exterior shots. When shooting inside you may find using lamps, torches or other light sources helps you create the correct tone for your shot. When thinking about light, always bear in mind that shadows can be useful in a shot but can also be a nuisance. Try to avoid unwanted shadows by making sure you are aware of where the light source is in relation to the subject and the camera. Altering

your shooting angle or repositioning the frame can help you avoid unwanted shadows that may distract your audience. Don't forget, if your camera is between a bright light and your subject, you camera operator's shadow may appear in the shot.

Sound

Sound can be recorded in-camera at the same time as the images or can be recorded separately and then added in post-production. The latter technique is most often used where sound effects are needed to add to or replace the natural sound of the footage itself and is called foley. Voice-overs and soundtracks will be recorded separately and added to the footage in post-production but where there is dialogue within a scene, the most common approach is to record at the time of filming. Some cameras will have extremely sensitive microphones and others less so. You should create some test-footage with sound to see how well your microphone picks up conversations and the diegetic sounds you might want to include in your work. You should also see how much your microphone picks up the natural ambient sound within your location.

Unwanted ambient sound can be very irritating and you should try to shoot in a location where you can control noises as far as is possible. External sounds such as traffic, distant conversations, washing machines and telephones should usually be avoided. When shooting outside this can be very difficult and external noises such as the wind can drown out actors' dialogue if care is not taken. Of course, you may wish to use a certain amount of ambient sound in your scene to create a realistic environment. Before shooting, though, you should test the volume of the background noise and ensure that your actors can be heard. In order to control ambient noise some moving image producers record the ambient sound separately and then shoot dialogue in a quiet environment. When you see a club scene in a drama, the extras may be dancing in silence and miming their conversations in the background while the primary action is recorded. The sound of a club is then added in post-production, keeping the actors audible at the top of the sound mix. Not only does this ensure that the background noise does not become a distraction, it also means that the **continuity** issues that would come from cutting and editing a scene with music are avoided.

Controlling sound is often easier inside but it is worth checking the **acoustics** before capturing your footage. Some interiors can cause sound to echo or there may be **dead spots** in certain areas. Where there is dialogue, the most important thing is to ensure the audience can hear everything clearly. Creating test footage is the best way to check if there are likely to be sound issues when recording in-camera.

Getting creative (on a shoestring budget)

While using professional equipment can offer you lots of ways to show your technical skills when producing moving image productions, demonstrating how you have overcome technical and practical limitations to get the effects you want shows great creativity.

Camera

Don't be afraid to experiment and create new and unusual effects. Don't just stick to one type of shot in your moving image production, show creativity and use a carefully selected variety of shots. When conventions are overused they become clichés, so can you tell your story in a more interesting way by varying angles or shot distances? Without lots of equipment it can be very tempting to use a lot of static shots or create movement with hand-held shots. Often this can look unprofessional and a little dull so can you think of new ways to create movement in your camera work, maybe using home-made dollies as discussed in Chapter 10 or by using cheap equipment such as selfie-sticks in a creative and interesting way?

You may want to experiment with framing and composition. The directors of *Mr Robot* (an American drama) have broken lots of conventions in the way they place objects in the frame. This has amplified the unsettling nature of the programme and created an individual media language style. These images show how the programme positions characters and action towards the edge of the frame and the majority of the screen is often out of focus mise-en-scène.

Images from *Mr Robot*

Lighting

Lighting helps you control the tone and feel of your moving image production. You can use it to direct the audience to a specific part of your shot, create emphasis or hide elements of the frame. If you're feeling creative and have access to the equipment, you can use coloured lights or in-camera lighting effects such as strobing. You could use strong lamps to create shadows, halo effects, demonic faces or spotlights. Where professional lighting is not available you can use domestic lamps and torches to create specific lighting effects. Coloured lighting can be created using coloured transparent plastic, and soft lighting can be created with tissue paper placed carefully over a light source (but not touching the bulb itself, of course) or by using the reflection of light on the subject rather than the light source itself.

You could use light to create shadows for atmosphere but you could also create shadows to indicate an off-screen object or even a character. A small cardboard cut-out of a city skyline could be used to create a city-shaped shadow or a monster could appear only as a shadow or in silhouette using a back-light.

Sound/mise-en-scène

If your camera doesn't record sound well you could experiment with creating your production with no recorded dialogue, so all the sound, including voice-over, is sourced and recorded separately. You can then dub it in during post-production. When capturing your video footage you should be thinking about how you can tell your story using images rather than sound. Using a visual shorthand reduces the need for dialogue and may help you show how creative you can be with a camera. Early filmmakers told their stories through props, use of camera, setting and performance, and while some of these silent film techniques have become a little clichéd, visual storytelling can be very effective. The passing of time can be shown with a close-up of the hands of a clock moving (either fast or slowly depending on the idea being communicated) or the pages of a calendar peeling away. Narrative information can be provided using newspaper headlines or a montage of social media conversations – newspapers cut up and pinned to a wall can be used to communicate a lot of story information or it could show us the troubled workings of the mind of a serial killer.

Mise-en-scène

Mise-en-scène is a term that refers to everything that can be seen within the frame. It includes the location, set dressing, costumes, props and performance. Lighting is also considered part of the mise-en-scène. Your research should have given you a clear indication of what codes and conventions of mise-en-scène you need to try to emulate for your production. There will inevitably be practical limitations: if you live in a landlocked location, shooting a beach scene may be a little impractical, but you should choose your locations carefully to create the most appropriate backdrop possible for the message you wish to communicate.

A lot of information can be communicated through the mise-en-scène. The location you choose, and the objects you choose as set dressing and for the props can provide lots of narrative information in both denotation and connotation. For example, imagine you are to dress the set of a domestic living room for a broadcast fiction production. The style of décor and the objects in the room will communicate ideas about the characters and their situation to the audience. Perhaps some set dressing choices will also create connotations of a specific genre.

Unfriended (2014, Gabriadze, L.) used a range of images from social media platforms to help tell its story.

Editing and post-production

Post-production in moving image production usually means editing. It can also refer to the addition of visual and audio effects. What effects you are able to achieve will depend on the software you use, but you could consider changing the look of your footage by converting a colour image to black and white or heightening specific colours or textures. You can create titles and add on-screen text or animations to your moving image footage using editing software. Some software allows you to change your footage by adding backgrounds and other objects to your work. You may be able to create special effects such as explosions.

When editing you need to consider the speed and style that will best suit your production.

Speed

- **Fast editing** moves quickly from one shot to the next. An average shot length in a film is approximately eight seconds. In fast editing, each shot is shown briefly before moving to the next. Overly fast editing can be difficult for audiences to engage with, as they may struggle to make sense of the flashes of imagery that are shown. When done well, fast editing creates a dynamic and exciting scene. Fast editing is often used in music videos, action films and fight scenes. *Mad Max: Fury Road* (2015, Miller, G.) averaged 2.1 seconds as the average shot length and *Taken 3* (2015, Megaton, O.) 1.7 seconds.

- **A medium-speed edit** with average shot lengths of between three and six seconds allows the audience to take in more detail from the mise-en-scène and the dialogue. The edit still moves the images along fast enough to be visually engaging. This feels more 'natural'. A human blink averages 4–6 seconds, so moving image editing at this speed emulates the 'editing' of images we do ourselves as we look. Soap operas use a naturalistic style that includes medium-speed editing. They are shot on several cameras, so edits usually move from one angle to another with movements such as pans and zooms being created in-camera.

- **A slow edit** allows shots to remain on screen longer between cuts, so the action of a scene can feel slowed down. Long-shots often include camera movements such as tracking, and hand-held and crane/drone shots. Nordic-noir tends to use a lot of long edits to give a sense of place and atmosphere. *Children of Men* (2006, Cuarón, A.) presents three important action scenes in single shots, creating a sense of urgency in each. The use of hand-held cameras in the final battle scene (a single shot of over seven minutes) brings the audience into the action and the style has connotations of documentary footage or war reportage. This technique was used in *True Detective* (season 1, episode 4) when a drugs raid was filmed in a single, six-minute take. Slow editing can be used to create verisimilitude or can simply be used to slow the action down. Michel Gondry is known for his single shot or slow editing techniques in films and music videos.

Style

A **straight cut** is the most commonly used editing style. It mimics the human eye, creating a blink-like transition between shots. It feels like a natural way to move from one image to the next and often goes unnoticed by the viewer, hence it being part of the technique called invisible editing.

There are many ways to move from one shot to the next and different styles have different connotations.

- A **fade to black/fade up** transition seems to offer a firm end to the previous scene and allows the following scene to start a new part of the story, or change location or tone without it jarring the audience.

- A **dissolve** allows the first image to slowly dissipate and the new image to come in gradually. Dissolves can connote movement or the passing of time.
- When one image moves across the screen to make way for the next, this is called a **wipe**. Wipes can be simple – a 'barn door wipe' simply slides one image out of the frame and the second one in. Editing software offers a range of shapes for wipes from the simple iris wipe that uses a circle that grows (or shrinks) in the centre of the frame, to a clock wipe that sweeps across the frame like the hands of a clock, or matrix wipes that use patterned images to change from one shot to the next. Wipes can be obtrusive and tend not to be used very often. *Star Wars* films famously use lots of wipes.

Other uses of editing

Editing is often used to move between two different parts of the story. The edit may allow the audience to follow parallel narratives by swapping between the two storylines. These edits are called **cutaways**.

Edits should usually be subtle and unobtrusive. They should be smooth and show the viewer what they need to see, moving them gently between viewpoints or perspectives. It is best not to edit between long-shots and close-ups as this creates a jump for the viewer. Similarly, moving between shots of the same size (one close-up to a second) can also be jarring. Editing should maintain the continuity of the world being presented to the audience, so subjects should not be shown 'leaping' from one side of the screen to the other or changing in size or proportion. Continuity editing maintains the 'reality' of the world presented within the video production.

When capturing your footage you should plan for editing. When you are out filming you may want to consider filming a few seconds of 'run-in' and 'run-out' footage to give you space for your edit at the start and end of each shot. You should also shoot 'cover shots' – that is, long-shots of the scene you are filming as well as mid-shots and close-ups. Both these techniques give you more flexibility when you edit. You may also want to shoot images that give geographical or atmospheric information that can be added as intercuts.

Sound

You can add sound effects, musical soundtracks and voice-overs into your production work using editing software.

You could create your own foley (sound effects) by recording sounds using objects around you. For example, the sound of horses running is often created using coconut shells and helicopter propeller sounds can be made with plastic coathangers. You can also use post-production software to edit sound levels so that dialogue, music, sound effects and/or ambient sound are balanced correctly for the audience.

You can download copyright-free sound effects to use in your work, so you can create off-screen sounds or enhance and add to the sounds you recorded during filming.

Music is an important part of the creation of moving image productions. Again, you can download copyright-free music online and, if you select the music carefully and edit it into your work effectively, you can communicate your genre and help steer your audience's emotional responses.

Dialogue that has been recorded separately can be dropped in during post-production. This is a common practice in professional moving image production. The dialogue is first recorded in-camera and then the actors record another version in a controlled environment. They will use the moving image footage to ensure the second version is recorded at the same speed as the original and that **lip-sync** is possible. Sometimes sections of in-camera sound are replaced by studio recorded sound – this is not an easy technique as it can be tricky to get a match with the ambient sound and to get the sound to match lip movement. It is often used in professional media to add dialogue to the scene when the actor who is 'speaking' is not facing the camera.

KEY TERMS

acoustics	the sound qualities of a specific environment		lip-sync (synchronisation)	matching the lip movements of a moving image production to words recorded on a separate sound track – or recording the silent lip movements of an actor replicating pre-recorded dialogue or singing
back-light	a light positioned behind the subject			
blocking	the positioning of props and actors for a sequence that allows for specific camera moves and distances to be pre-planned			
			mise-en-scène (m-e-s)	everything that can be seen within the scene – set design, props, performance, lighting, costume and make-up, location and lighting
continuity/ continuity editing	the creation of logical and/ or visual coherence and consistency			
dead spot	an area created by local acoustics where sound is reduced in volume or flattened in tone		non-diegetic sound	sound that is heard but does not come from an on-screen source (e.g. a musical soundtrack)
dub	to add sound elements to recorded images		pan	a horizontal camera movement where the camera remains on a fixed point
edit (moving image/audio)	the arranging of images or sound to create a coherent visual or audio sequence		shooting script	the written text of a video/ film product including details of the use of camera in individual scenes
intercuts	to insert shots from other locations or narrative lines including flashbacks and flashforwards		shot list	a descriptive list of the shots required for a moving image production
invisible editing	an editing style that appears natural to the viewer, usually exemplified by straight cuts			

11.4 Audio production

Creating an audio production can be done quickly and easily using mobile phone and tablet technology. If you are lucky enough to have access to sound recording equipment you may have a microphone that provides a better sound quality in your recordings but the quality of mobile technology will usually be fine for your NEA production.

You may want to emulate music programming, create a podcast, a radio drama or a documentary. Your initial research into the form you want to make should help you break down the codes and conventions you want to recreate and inspire you to create interesting and engaging content for your audience.

Like moving image production there are some basic principles that should be considered when recording and editing sound, and there are techniques you may wish to experiment with when constructing your audio product.

Basic principles of recording

Be aware of your environment

Try to record all parts of your production in a similar environment (the same environment if possible) so that any recording done at different times has a similar audio quality. Make a note of the distance between the speaker and the microphone as this will help you set up the environment again should you need to. If you have access to a soundproof environment, that is ideal. If not, try to remove any exterior noise from your environment so that you are recording in as close to silence as possible.

If you are going to record on location, try to avoid loud, intrusive noises, and try to record all you need in one location at the same time so that the ambient noise sounds the same. You may even decide to record ambient noise separately and then add it to your 'studio recorded' voices in post-production.

Check your equipment

When you begin your recording, do some tests so you can check the sound levels and any ambient sounds that your microphone picks up. Here are some pre-production tips:

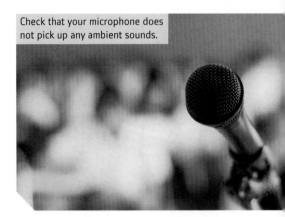

Check that your microphone does not pick up any ambient sounds.

- In a room or studio, record silence and listen to it on full volume. Have other sounds been picked up?
- On location, record the ambient sound and check how intrusive it is. Can you position your microphone closer to your subject to ensure the sounds you want are not being drowned out?
- Check to see if your microphone picks up the page turning of your notes or if your breathing is loud.
- Check the sound of your voice. Do you need to move your microphone a little to avoid it exaggerating your 'p' and 'b' sounds?
- If you are able to adjust your recording levels, experiment with them to see which work best for your environment.

You may have identified a number of elements that need recording or sourcing. This may involve going online to download music and/or sound effects, or you may record your own.

Depending on what you are creating, you may wish to create jingles and idents, intros, outros and even audio adverts. If you are creating audio drama you will need to record several voices and include sound effects to help tell the story. Audio documentaries often use incidental music to create tone or help steer the listener's emotional response. Audio products are rarely just one voice, so there is plenty of scope for you to show your creativity and technical ability in the recording stage of production. You will then need to use software to put all the various elements together for your finished production.

Editing and post-production

Sound editing, like moving image editing, is the bringing together of the different elements of sound that make up the audio production. Sound editing should move the listener from one sound element to another smoothly, so there should be no jarring movements, for example big changes in volume, as the audio production progresses. Sound can move simply from one sound to the next or transition effects such as fade-outs and fade-ins can be used. Transition sounds can be downloaded online and may include 'whooshes', 'swishes' or sound effects such as glass breaking or doors closing. Transitions like these should be used for specific sound effects – and then sparingly – or they can become irritating to the listener.

APPLY IT

Listen to the first couple of minutes of a podcast and write down everything you hear.

- What sounds could you source online?
- Make a list of all the recording you would need to do to recreate the start of the podcast.

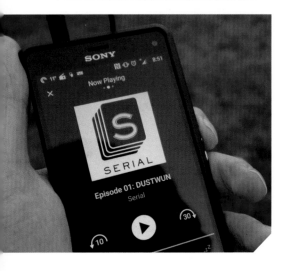

It is worth thinking about sound in layers as at any given time there may be several sounds playing at the same time. A presenter could be speaking over a music **sound-bed**. Post-production includes mixing the levels of sound so that some elements (e.g. music) sit below others (e.g. the presenter). In music programming, a DJ names the next track over the introduction and the music may be faded down towards the end as the DJ begins to speak again.

Serial season 2, episode 1 begins like this:

1 A 35-second, spoken word advert for 'Rocket Mortgage' is read out. They are the sponsors of the *Serial* podcast.

2 The presenter introduces the story and includes audio taken from the video source (audio from video is dropped below the voice and the presenter's voice dominates). The presenter describes the video and occasionally the audio from the video rises in the mix – sometimes it is the sound of voices and sometimes the sound of a helicopter. At the end of the description the audio abruptly cuts to silence.

3 The theme tune to *Serial* is played and the presenter announces the name of the podcast and she introduces herself. The sound of a military spokesperson, news reporters and politicians, including Donald Trump and his cheering followers calling for military deserters to be shot, can be heard as the music continues to play. The voices create a montage of sounds from various sources that provides a range of opinions on the podcast's subject matter and the opening ends with (what is assumed to be) the voice of the subject Private First Class (PFC) Bowe Bergdahl, a US soldier who had been captured by the Taliban after, according to some people, he had deserted his military post.

4 The presenter proceeds to outline the context of the story, as incidental music plays below the voice track and the voice of the subject of the podcast is heard.

To create this opening, the following sounds have been recorded or sourced from elsewhere:

Recorded	Sourced
The advert	Podcast theme tune
The script read by the presenter	Audio from a video
An interview with the subject	Incidental music

These six elements will have been edited together in post-production and great care will have been taken in the sound balance of the music and the audio from the video – the latter alters as the extract progresses.

KEY TERMS

idents	sounds used to identify the programme, radio station or brand. This could be a jingle or a theme tune
outro	the concluding piece of a recording

sound-bed	sounds, sound effects and/or music that plays below the main content of an audio production. Sound beds can communicate narrative information such as location or they can create a tone or atmosphere for the production

11.5 Approaches to e-media production

E-media production uses elements of all the production areas already outlined in this chapter, and it may:

- need to be designed in the same way as a print page. It will need to consider basic layout and design conventions but also the codes and conventions of the form being constructed
- need to use photographs as illustrations
- include moving image and audio productions as part of its presentation of content.

E-media is often a combination of different presentation forms that provide audiences with various ways to access and engage with the information being communicated. Of course, some e-media forms are simply replications of 'offline' formats. A podcast follows the conventions of radio programming and YouTube videos are very similar to television products that offer similar content. However, as user-generated content has developed, it has adopted some professional techniques while maintaining some of its amateur approaches.

Once you have decided what you are making, as with all the other production areas, you should undertake research of existing products to identify the approaches you could take in your own production. Although you need to show you can use software and equipment when making your productions, Media Studies does not require you to learn coding or other specific programming skills. You may have ideas that you would like to include in your production but lack the specialist technical skills to create them as fully functional elements. In this case you can indicate the feature that would be included in a real product even if it doesn't work fully. However, this is another great opportunity to show your understanding of contemporary media and your creativity using multi-media and audience participation. E-media products are more engaging when they contain movement and sound, so you could include moving image or audio recordings to your e-media work. Even a simple animation can give a visual interest to your e-media work that is not available in print.

E-media allows more audience participation and interactivity than other platforms and it allows audiences to communicate with producers and each other. E-media has changed the way audiences want to be entertained and a crucial part of any media production will be the way it is used to encourage and communicate audience participation. Interactivity can range from asking audiences to click on a simple poll to register their opinion, to providing opportunities for audiences to share ideas and opinions. Audiences could be persuaded to share media such as photos and videos or they could be encouraged to participate through competitions or getting involved in events and experiences in real life. It may be appropriate for your e-media product to include a comments section or be linked to social media. E-media products can offer choices that allow the audience to feel as if they are able to personalise their experience. For example, it is common practice for online adverts to offer the audience a choice of two or three different versions. Audiences can choose the version that looks most interesting or relevant to their needs and advertisers can use different marketing techniques for different parts of the target audience or offer further information, competitions and other ways for the audience to participate. Inspiration for the use of multi-media and encouraging audience participation can be found by researching existing media productions.

APPLY IT

Go online to the following websites and detail how the sites use multi-media to present information and how they try to get audiences involved.

Website	Multi-media?	Audience interaction?
www.theguardian.co.uk		
www.bbc.co.uk		
www.mailonline.co.uk		
www.loreal-paris.co.uk		
gillette.co.uk/en-gb		
www.zoella.co.uk		
www.manutd.com		
marvelcinematicuniverse.wikia.com		

Offline e-media production

You can create e-media productions using offline software such as specialised web design or desk-top publishing packages. You are not expected to be able to use computer code, so consider using software that allows you to design your e-media production and add in multi-media features. If you use offline e-media production software you will need to ensure that you are able to convert your work to an e-media format that will, in most cases, be accessible via a browser. Some offline software is complex to use and can limit the look and functionality of your finished production, so make sure you choose software that you can use effectively and that can achieve what you want to achieve.

Online production tools (to include websites, social media and video games)

It is very likely that you will want to use an online production tool to create an e-media production. You might use a blog site, a social media platform or an online game creation tool to create materials for your coursework. These tools allow you to use templates and pre-formed pages that make it very easy for you to present your work online. Some production tools require you to make design and layout decisions, and your choices will demonstrate your understanding of the platform, the form and your audience. As you won't be creating everything yourself you should spend time creating content for your online product. This means that you should be using still images, moving images and/or audio within your online production to create audience engagement and appeal and meet the function of your product.

Most of the online tools for e-media creation are intended to be simple to use and allow personalisation. Social media pages are often quite uniform in their layout and design but the choice of images and written content will set your pages apart from others. You will need to be sure about what you want your social media pages to achieve and how to best appeal to your target audience.

If you are creating gaming material using an online tool, you need to make a number of choices. You need to select the style of gameplay that is appropriate for the genre of game you wish to produce. You should also consider your target audience to ensure that you are making a game they will enjoy. You will select the style and design of the game as you choose the visual design of the locations, backgrounds and characters, and you will be able to choose the sounds and the music. You should try to ensure that your gameplay is both suitable and easy for the audience to engage with and that the codes and conventions you use accurately reflect the conventions of the genre and type of game you are replicating.

11.6 Reviewing and presenting production work

Practical tips for the presentation of production work

When you submit your work for assessment it should be presented in a way that is as close to the real thing as possible. You should check with the exam board's most up-to-date guidance for the submission of practical work.

Print

Print work should be printed in colour and on paper that is the correct size and as close to the appropriate weight and finish of paper as possible. Newspapers can be printed on lightweight porous paper, whereas many magazines use heavier paper with a satin finish. Using the correct type of paper helps create an accurate look to your production work. Transferring your production from the computer to paper is a technical skill in itself. You should make sure you do test prints throughout the process of production. Check to make sure your production fits correctly on the paper you are printing it on and that it looks the way you expect. Often, incorrect column layout or font size looks fine on a screen and problems are only identified when the work has been printed.

When you submit printed work you should also consider protecting your printouts by putting them in a plastic wallet or cardboard tube.

Audio/video

Probably the easiest way to submit audio and video work is online. You can upload videos to video streaming sites such as YouTube or Vimeo and audio files can be shared on platforms such as Soundcloud. You can create web or blog pages that can host your video or audio material.

If you are submitting audio or video work online, you must make sure that you publish the final version of your work in some way that will allow you to submit a web address (URL) for assessment. You can make an active link by copying the URL into a word-processing document and then sending the file on a pen-drive or disc. This is by far the best way to send work as you can check your link works before sending it and your work can be easily accessed.

Audio and video work can also be submitted as data files. Just make sure that you have saved them to universally accessible file formats such as MP3 (audio) or MP4 (video). You can save the files to a memory stick or a disc that can be used to submit the work.

Whichever method you use to submit your video/audio work, it is a good idea to check that it can be played or accessed on a number of different computers before submission.

E-media (including gaming)

With any e-production it is important that anyone can access the work. Most e-media is likely to be created online and so will be submitted as a working URL, as above.

If you create e-media work offline you should use the software to publish your production to a pen-drive or disc. Make sure you submit work that can be accessed using a web-browser rather than the original data files. As with online submissions, it is a good idea to open your e-media work on different computers and in a range of browsers such as Internet Explorer, Safari and Chrome. You should test all pages of your production where applicable and make sure all your images are visible and all multi-media features work correctly.

Final production checklist

What have I created and who is it for?	
What did I need to achieve in terms of the instructions in the brief?	
What is the institutional context of my production?	
How have I made my product appealing for the audience?	
How effectively does the product follow the conventions of the form?	
How successful have I been in replicating or subverting the conventions of the genre I am working in?	
What representations have I created and why?	
Is the content clear?	
Have I created meaning in a clear and understandable way?	
What ideas and values are being created by my production and why?	

Analysing your practical work in this way may give you some ideas as to how to improve your production work before it is submitted and marked.

SUMMARY

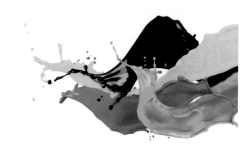

This chapter has dealt with a range of different things you need to consider when embarking on your practical production.

You need to:

- Choose one of the forms offered in the briefs.
- Identify or choose the genre to work on for your production.
- Consider the basics of the way the form is usually constructed by researching existing examples of the form.
- Consider the issues raised by the institutional context presented in the brief.
- Consider how to address the audience identified in the brief.
- Engage with the codes and conventions of the genre by researching existing media products.
- Consider what equipment and software you need to create your productions.
- Plan your productions carefully and taking your approach to the brief into account.
- Present your finished productions appropriately.

Glossary of key terms

24-hour-news culture	delivery of news around the clock on satellite and digital TV services since the 1990s, and its impact on the reporting and cultural perception of news
30-degree rule	one of the rules that constructs space in visual language – the camera must move more than 30 degrees in order to avoid an ugly cut
180-degree rule	one of the rules that constructs space in visual language – the camera must stay one side of an imaginary line when filming a scene, unless a cutaway or visible movement leads the audience to another perspective
accelerated motion	the speeding up of footage during editing
acoustics	the sound qualities of a specific environment
advertorial	an extended print advertisement that may resemble editorial in its use of codes, but will be clearly labelled 'advertisement' under UK media law
aerial shot	from in the air, often shot from an aircraft
AIDA	Awareness, Interest, Desire, Action
AIR	average issue readership
alternative	usually media products that offer some kind of alternative perspective to the mainstream
ambient noise	the background noise (such as wind, traffic, etc.) that is sometimes picked up when filming
analepsis	commonly known as a flashback
anchorage	does exactly what the name suggests – it fixes meaning. In print media texts, anchorage consists of lexical codes that firmly establish the connection between an image and the reason it has been used. They may appear as slogans, copy, headlines or captions accompanying an image. This can add value to the use of the image and maximise its impact
Andrew Crisell	author of *Understanding Radio* (1986), an important text and one of the few available that really explores radio from a Media Studies perspective
apparatus	term used for the equipment and methods used in media production
APS	average programme stream
arbitrary or symbolic sign	a sign that does not have an obvious connection with what it represents, but the meaning of which is agreed on by users of a particular code. Saussure referred to these types of sign as symbolic. Many road signs can be regarded as **symbolic** if you have to have read the *Highway Code* to understand what they mean
arbitrary relationship	a relationship between signifier and signified that is not obvious (e.g. the word 'cat' in the Roman alphabet and our mental image of the animal)
architecture	the structure and navigation of a website
aspect ratio	the correct width/height ratio
atmosphere/ soundscape	background sound, especially in fiction media texts, which is constructed to contribute to verisimilitude
attempt to repair	in Todorov's theory of narrative, attempts made by the protagonist or other characters to bring about a new equilibrium
auditory codes	sometimes also known as aural codes — sound and particularly its uses in radio and podcasting
aural code	term used to describe all the techniques relating to sound
backstories (in computer games)	contextual narrative information, often fed in through cut scenes
back-light	a light positioned behind the subject
balance (page)	a balanced page has been designed to ensure that the heavy objects and lighter ones are positioned to create a harmonious feel
banner	commonly used term for any block of information at the top of a website; can also refer to the site's 'masthead', its identity
BARB	British Audience Research Board
BBC Charter	the conditions upon which the BBC's licence depends
billboard	a large outdoor location for advertising. Traditionally a board for the placement of print adverts but electronic billboards can be found in some locations. Electronic billboards can present all types of video material but they are often used to broadcast adverts
binary oppositions	narrative theory proposed by Levi-Strauss that describes narratives as driven by pairs of opposing qualities that are in tension
binge-viewers	people who watch between two and six episodes of a given television show in one sitting
blocking	the positioning of props and actors for a sequence that allows for specific camera moves and distances to be pre-planned
bird's-eye shot	extreme high angle or directly from the sky downwards

blind medium	radio or podcasting – one that is wholly reliant on auditory codes
body text	the majority of article text, usually at the smallest size, appearing in a magazine or newspaper
boundary rituals	another term for framing devices in radio and podcasting
brand recognition	when an audience becomes familiar with a brand
brand value	the image a company intends to convey of its product or service
brief	information and instructions that set the remit and scope of the NEA
British Film Institute	(BFI) organisation that promotes the work of British cinema and studies cinema as a pastime among British people
Broadcast Code	Ofcom's regulatory framework for broadcast services
broadcasting licences	required for transmission of television or radio services
busy	the effect of pages that are created with many design elements, font styles, etc. Busy pages are sometimes difficult for the reader to access and can be confusing and visually offputting
byline	journalist's credit, usually at the start of an article
camera proxemics	sometimes known paraproxemics – the distance/relationship between subject and audience
captioning	the adding of subtitles to a video, sometimes used as another term for titling
canted angle	sometimes known as a 'Dutch' angle – a shot that leans over to the side
caption	written anchorage accompanying an image and fixing its meaning
card-based design	trend in web design that prioritises visual rectangular clickable links – 'cards' that often have a picture and captioning

celebrity endorsement	the process by which a celebrity is paid to become the face of a brand. This might include appearing in advertisements, using the brand in high-profile places, being a spokesperson for the brand
censorship	the blocking of certain media material from public consumption
centre of visual interest (CVI)	in newspapers in particular, the headline, photograph or graphic that intentionally dominates the page
chronology	the time order of narrative events
circulation	amount of copies of a print media publication sold (paid circulation) or distributed (free publications funded entirely by advertising)
citizen journalism	the passing of footage or photographs taken by witnesses as events to either mainstream or alternative news distributors
click-throughs	viewing of deeper website content
clicks	viewing of the homepage of a website
close-up	often just face and shoulders
co-presence	the audience's audio texts experience of almost being in the same room as the presenter and other listeners
co-regulator	the sharing of some aspects of regulation by more than one organisation
code	a system used to create meaning. Most forms of meaning production have specific codes: frameworks that are used to encode meaning. It is vital that codes are shared and their meanings agreed upon across a culture or they cannot be decoded. Where these are limited to a specific mode of expression in media productions or forms, they are referred to collectively as **technical codes**. The various kinds of code used in print media analysis are described in more detail in the technical codes and features used in print media texts

collective identity	aspects of our identity we share with others
colour tone	the properties of colour – its shade, hue, warmth, brightness, saturation, etc.
colourisation	the way in which the saturation or other elements of how we perceive colour may be altered post-production, either to harmonise footage from different shoots or locations, or to achieve a particular aesthetic
columns	a way to organise text and images on the page by dividing the page vertically
combining	using elements of more than one aspect of media language and form to achieve a desired representation
commercial revenue	profit generated by a media organisation
community guidelines	means by which some websites ask their users to contribute to self-regulation
compassion fatigue	the process by which the media audience lose empathy for victims of crime, disaster or war zones due to repeated exposure (especially to news)
composite image	presentation of images using a montage effect
compression of screen time	the way in which media texts, through editing, reduce the 'real time' in which events would unfold
conceptual map	our inner reference points dictated by the sum of our social and cultural experiences
conglomerates	huge media organisations made up of several companies all with the same ownership
connotation	the meaning evoked by a sign – what it makes us think. It can be thought of as the end result of reading a sign, the mental image we have of its meaning
constructionist approach	readers of a text or its producers can wholly fix meaning
content labels	additional information provided by PEGI as part of its rating service

contested space	with reference to the internet, the ideological battleground between users and large media conglomerates	cultural hegemony	described by Gramsci – the process of indoctrination through cultural products of the dominant ideologies in a society	democratisation of the mass media	increased ability of the audience to have their voices heard, and to interact with media producers and content
continuity editing	dominant mode of editing that does not draw attention to itself, allowing the audience to focus on the subject-matter	cultural identity	aspects of our identity that are derived from cultural influences such as region, religion or family	demographics	studying how populations may consume the media in different ways according to where they live
contrapuntal sound	sound that does not seem to match the action, often deliberately used to unnerve the audience or even create a blackly comic effect	cultural imperialism	transmission through the mass media of ideologies and/or cultural practices from a dominant media market to a smaller nation	denotation	may be understood as the literal meaning of a component of a code. You can also use the term as a verb, saying that an element of an image denotes – but be careful. The term is easily confused with **connotes**, which you would more commonly be using in meaningful semiotic analysis rather than description
copy	the term used for body text in a newspaper, print advertisement or magazine	cultural regime of verisimilitude	our connecting of a genre text with our wider cultural knowledge		
corpus	group of texts identified as belonging to the same genre	cultural shorthand	a way of understanding how stereotypes communicate ideas quickly to the audience		
counter-representation	a representation that offers an alternative to stereotypes			deregulation	reduction in governmental controls over media ownership
coverline	feature and secondary articles promoted on the front of a magazine	cultural tropes	plot elements, themes or figures of speech that are used repeatedly in literature or popular culture	desensitisation	the process by which media audiences can become used to seeing violent content and better able to tolerate it
crab	short tracking shot	cut scenes	non-interactive animated sections of games that contexualise an element of play	design elements	the individual parts that combine together to construct a page
crane shot	any footage taken using a crane – highly mobile and versatile in terms of movement	cutaway shot	footage that shows another subject before returning to the original	desk-top publishing (DTP) software	software that enables users to create and design pages for offline or online publications. DTP allows users to control the layout and design of pages and the use of images and illustrations
critical theory	an approach to the study of culture that considers how various forces are at work in its production	cutting rate	the way in which pace is controlled in editing – many shots of short duration lend a fast cutting rate; longer duration results in a slower rate		
cropping	the removal of sections of an image to emphasise its subject or remove clutter or unwanted signs			diegesis	the world of the media text, the 'story world' especially in fiction-based media
cross-cultural consumer categorisation	system developed by Young and Rubicam to categorise consumers outside of the usual factors. Also referred to as psychographics	cutting rhythm	the length of shots, particularly when edited to a soundtrack or score, when these appear to have rhythmic qualities	diegetic sound	refers to sound supposedly generated within the diegesis
cross-dissolve	the gradual fading of one shot into another	cybertext	a digital text that is constructed through effort by the reader in a non-linear and highly individual experience through the act of consumption	digital locker	system whereby a television show or film is purchased (sometimes as a physical copy) but also exists for that buyer to watch on other devices
crosshead	small amount of text enlarged as a hook for visual contrast with body text				
cultivation theory	branch of effects theory that looks at the effect of media saturation (particularly television) on the audience	DAB	digital audio broadcasting	digital revolution	sweeping changes brought about by the internet and advances in digital technology
		dead spot	an area created by local acoustics where sound is reduced in volume or flattened in tone		
		decelerated motion	the slowing down of footage during editing	digital subscription platforms	offering of traditional forms of publishing such as magazines and newspapers on tablets or other digital devices
cultural/ referential code	one of Barthes' five narrative codes; the frame of reference that is human knowledge	decoding	when audiences interpret a text, in order to make meaning		
		décor	selection of the appearance of interior locations		

direct/indirect address	the way in which a text addresses its audience; for example, where a subject is gazing into the lens of the camera, this could be said to be a direct mode of address
disruption	in Todorov's theory of narrative, an event that disturbs the equilibrium
distributed narrative	fragmented or fractured narrative distributed in different places and at different times
distribution	increased ability of the audience to have their voices heard, and to interact with media producers and content
diversification	a feature of many media organisations as they try to increase their penetration of wider markets
dolly	fixing for camera that allows it to be moved smoothly over a set floor or on a track
domestic markets	media content made by and for a particular country
drop cap	an enlarged first letter – an attention-grabbing aesthetic device
DTP	a commonly used abbreviation for desk-top publishing that refers to software specifically designed to support the design and publication of print and, in some cases, e-media production
dub	to add sound elements to recorded images
dynamic content	content that is regularly updated
edit (moving image/audio)	the arranging of images or sound to create a coherent visual or audio sequence
editing software (video and audio)	software that allows video and/or audio files to be cut and spliced back together to allow footage to be used in a non-linear and more creative way. Additional audio tracks, intertitles and on-screen text, special effects and transition effects can be added during video and audio editing
editorial content	original content written for magazines distinct from advertising
Editors' Code of Conduct	the IPSO's regulatory framework

effects theory	the collective term for media theories that explore the correlation between media consumption and audience behaviours or interpretations of the real world
elements of mise-en-scène	the individual components of mise-en-scène such as props or lighting
emasculate	to remove masculinity
enclosed narrative	a narrative that is complete
encoding	the process of creating particular intended meanings within a text
enculturation	the adjustment of people's values to mesh with the culture and society they inhabit
engagement	click-throughs or other interaction with a page or other digital content
entry point	a visually appealing and prominent spread in a magazine
equilibrium	in Todorov's theory of narrative, the stable situation or balance at the beginning of a narrative, and the new state achieved by the end
ergodic narrative	in ludology, a narrative that has different outcomes according to the interaction between the 'user' of the text and the 'rules' of the game
establishing shot	often exterior locations, but can be interiors – used to set a scene
ethnocentrism	seeing an issue from the perspective of your own cultural heritage – usually refers to a white European perspective
expectations and hypotheses	requirements to be fulfilled, and narrative and other predictions made by an audience based on their prior experience of a genre
extra-diegetic narration	voice-over provided by an unseen person from outside the diegesis
extreme close-up (ECU)	like the close-up, the camera is positioned close to the subject and a small detail fills the frame

eye-line match	usually means the pairing of a shot of a person with the object of their attention in the next frame
fade in/out	the gradual dissolution of a shot
fade through black	technique that allows the audience a moment to reflect, by placing a short breathing space over black between scenes
fish-eye shot	a shot, usually using a specific lens for the purpose, which brings in a range of angles of view
flag/masthead	the name of a newspaper or magazine
flatplan	a page plan that shows how content, images and advertising will be laid out in the final production
fly-on-the-wall documentary	style of documentary where the camera work is as unobtrusive as possible in order to capture events in a candid way. This technique can be created easily today by the miniaturisation of digital cameras that can be placed unobtrusively to capture many angles, as well as the habituation of subjects to the presence of cameras
focalisation	term used to describe our tendency to follow particular characters at individual points in a narrative, dependent on a range of encoded strategies and our own conceptual maps
focusing	building of a representation through techniques such as repetition or elimination of comparisons
folio	titling at the top of a section of a newspaper identifying the content in that section
following pan	movement where the camera remains in one position but is turned on its axis to follow an action
font	the design of the letters used within a specific typeface. Fonts have pre-defined proportions, weight and style. All letters and numbers within a font will be designed to harmonise
footage	unedited video recordings
framing	careful selection of what will appear in a final shot

framing (in radio)	contextualisation of sections or delineation between programmes in audio texts
generic regime of verisimilitude	the norms and laws of a genre; what is probable or likely in a genre text
Gérard Genette	French narrative theorist who proposed focalisation as an alternative to structuralist readings
gestural codes	the way in which we read expression through movement
global village	term coined by Marshall McLuhan in the 1960s to describe the impact of media technologies on global culture
globalisation	the increased interconnectivity of businesses and cultures worldwide
Google Analytics	market analysis of a website's performance
GRA	Games Rating Authority (a division of the VSC)
graphical elements	any graphics generated that do not consist of pure typography or photography
green-screen technology	filming characters in front of a green (or blue) screen allows backgrounds or other footage to be added in post-production
hand-held shot	footage taken using a camera operated by a person
hard news	news that focuses exclusively on serious issues relating to domestic or world events
hate radio	radio broadcast used to incite racial/ethnic hatred or persecution of minority groups
head and shoulders shot	a shot where the camera is positioned close to a human subject so that the frame excludes all of the body, apart from the head and shoulders
headline	large type promoting article content, especially on the front of a newspaper
hermeneutic code	one of Barthes' five narrative codes; enigmas or puzzles in a narrative
hero image	use of a large, dominating image that fills the majority of the viewable homepage before scrolling occurs

hetero-normative	using the perspective of heterosexuals (and therefore omitting alternative perspectives)
high angle	a shot positioned slightly higher than the subject that diminishes it
high-key lighting	the use of light fills to create a low-contrast lighting effect
historic specificity	belonging to a particular time period (e.g. a genre)
hook	any technique used to draw the audience into a narrative
horizontal integration	merger of media companies at a similar stage of development
house style	the way in which codes combine in print media to produce a familiar and recognisable brand
hybridisation	the mixing of one genre with another
hypertextuality	web 'intertextuality' – the linking from site to site of other content
hypodermic needle model	simple effects model that assumes the audience to be passive recipients of media content
iconic sign	looks like what it is representing. A portrait photograph is a good example of an iconic sign. Symbols such as the 'danger of death' sign you see on the side of an electrical substation are also iconic – they show someone being struck by a bolt of electricity, looking very much like the physical manifestation of electricity as lightning
iconography	repetition of certain visual images or symbols, usually associated in media with particular genres
idents	sounds used to identify the programme, radio station or brand. This could be a jingle or a theme tune
ideology	in the context of A level study, dominant ways of thinking in a society shared by many people within it
image manipulation software	software that enables users to crop, edit and add effects to photographic images

in-camera	decisions made to influence the look of images while shooting with the camera. This includes using camera settings as well as using external sources such as music, props and lighting to create specific effects
in-camera sound	sound that is recorded using the camera's internal microphone
in-groups	members of a dominant culture
independent	media companies not owned by larger organisations
indigenous media production	media products made by and for a particular culture or nation
individuality paradox	a known philosophical quandary in studying identity, that most people wish to simultaneously be seen as an individual while experiencing commonality and social belonging
indexical sign	has a relationship between the signifier and signified that could be described as causal or otherwise linked. The relationship between the two things is so widely recognised by users of the signification system that the indexical sign easily stands in for, or signifies, the concept it represents. Commonly used examples are smoke, which is an indexical sign of fire, a tear, which suggests sorrow, and footprints, which suggest someone was in a place
intercuts	to insert shots from other locations or narrative lines including flashbacks and flash forwards
intentional approach	approach that suggests meaning is imposed by the producer of the text
internet of things	connecting of appliances to online services using smart technologies
intertextuality	the process by which one media text consciously references another text or genre, therefore deriving further layers of meaning for a reader who has experienced both texts
intertitles	title cards used in silent cinema – a style of titling in modern video where the titles are placed in between other footage

intra-diegetic narration	voice-over provided by a person or character from within the diegesis
invisible editing	an editing style that appears natural to the viewer, usually exemplified by straight cuts
IPSO	Independent Press Standards Organisation
ISPA	Internet Service Providers' Association
IWF	Internet Watch Foundation
jib shot	any footage taken using a camera, remotely controlled, on a metal arm
jump cut	where the camera moves less than 30 degrees, creating an ugly and dissonant effect – sometimes used deliberately, but is not part of continuity editing style
laudatory stereotypes	stereotypes that contribute positively to views of social groups
lead article	in print media, this is usually clear from the front page or cover, where one article will be selected for promotion over others
left side third	area of a magazine cover where key content is usually positioned
lexical codes	words selected to generate specific effect
liberal pluralism	the belief that the mass media offers a range of ideologies that we can choose to accept or reject
licence payer	term for the viewing public who contribute to the funding of the BBC by payment of an annual licence fee
light fills	a light used to reduce the contrast between light and shadow within the frame
lighting temperature	the feel lent to a scene according to how it is lit – warm or cool, for example
linguistic analysis	detailed analysis of the ways in which language is used over a whole section of copy in the English language
linguistics	the study of structural aspects of language, with many sub-specialisms
lip-sync (synchronisation)	matching the lip movements of a moving image production to words recorded on a separate sound track – or recording the silent lip movements of an actor replicating prerecorded dialogue or singing
long-shot	full body at any distance
location	choice of place for an exterior shoot
logo	a design, sometimes consisting of typography and a symbol, that identifies a brand
low angle	a shot positioned slightly lower than the subject, which elevates it
low-key lighting	a style of lighting used to create shadow and areas of bright light within the frame
ludology	the study of games, especially video games
mainstreaming	in cultivation theory, the process of ideological alignment between media audiences and content
manufacture consent	the process, identified by Chomsky, that media institutions persuade audiences of the validity of national policies, particularly military
Maslow's hierarchy of needs	pyramid-based model offering a hierarchical visualisation of human needs
mass communication	a medium that has the power to communicate very quickly with large numbers of people
mass media convergence	the coming together of many aspects of media businesses, including commercial, technological and cultural
mass media proliferation	the rapid expansion and growth of the mass media within a historically brief timeframe
matched cut	pairs of shots that have a logical connection
mean world syndrome	in cultivation theory, the belief that the world is a more dangerous place than it actually is due to viewing of violent acts on television
media convergence	the coming together of many aspects of media businesses, including commercial, technological and cultural
MediaWatch UK	well-established and influential pressure group
medical model	approach to representing disability that perceives it as a flaw
medium-shot	mid-body shot
meme	an image, concept or behaviour that is rapidly disseminated online, mainly through social media
metalingual checks	in linguistics, elements of speech used to clarify understanding
MIDAS	measurement of internet-delivered audio services
mise-en-scène (m-e-s)	everything that can be seen within the scene – set design, props, performance, lighting, costume and make-up, location and lighting
mode of address	how the text 'speaks' to the audience – can be formal or informal – created by use of codes
montage editing	editing style where we are given a 'snapshot' of different clips
moral panics	term coined by Stanley Cohen to describe the press reaction to a negative event in the real world
multi-take	non-continuity technique, where a dramatic event may be filmed from several angles and the moment duplicated for effect
myth	this term is closely associated with Roland Barthes. A myth in critical theory is the way in which certain signs contribute to ideologies in our society. Myth is particularly helpful to print advertisers in promoting values that are consumerist and materialist in nature
narrative arc	the journey of an individual character
narrative closure	a narrative with a satisfactory ending

narrative enigma	puzzles or questions set up by the text to maintain audience engagement (see Barthes' five codes, Chapter 2)
narrative image	the expectations of a genre text based on its label, often passed by word of mouth
narrative resolution	the way in which a narrative concludes
narrative strands	different 'storylines' or subplots that usually contribute something to the main narrative subject
narratology	the structuralist study of narrative
news agenda	the priority given to particular news items by a news organisation
news values	the categorisation of news into types, some of which may be favoured more highly over others depending on the news agenda of an organisation. Refer to the work of Galtung and Ruge
niche publications	print media publications serving a special interest or with a small circulation
nodding shot	in documentary, used to show an interviewer is listening to the subject, but is often cut in later
noise (in radio)	the sum total of speech, sound effects and music in audio tracks
non-diegetic narration	voice-over created by an unseen person from outside the diegesis
non-diegetic sound	sound that is heard but does not come from an on-screen source (e.g. a musical soundtrack)
non-examined assessment (NEA)	a method of assessment where work you create over time is marked by a member of the teaching team in your school or college
non-verbal codes	in human subjects this is facial expression, posture, body language
non-verbal communication	methods of communication that do not include words. Body language and modes of dress are both examples
NRS	National Readership Survey
NRS PADD	National Readership Survey print and digital data
Ofcom	Office of Communications
omniscient narration	style of narration where the audience is privy to most contextual narrative information even where this is withheld from characters in the diegesis
on-demand viewing	viewing a channel or provider's content outside the traditional schedule
otherness	the state of being defined as 'different'– views of an outgroup held by an in-group
out-groups	minorities living within a dominant culture
outro	the concluding piece of a recording
over-the-shoulder shot	shot in which the back of someone's head and shoulder will be partially in view – often used to shoot dialogue – and makes the audience feel they are sharing in the exchange
overblocking	internet filtering that is considered overly restrictive
page proportions	the size of the page and the relationship between its height and length
pan	a horizontal camera movement where the camera remains on a fixed point
paparazzi	a professional photographer who seeks to capture informal images of celebrities or other people identified as being newsworthy
para-proxemics	sometimes known as camera proxemics – the distance/relationship between subject and audience
paralinguistic features	additional information we gain during a face-to-face conversation, which lends meaning to the words used – in audio-visual texts called non-verbal codes
parallel development	the apparently simultaneous presentation of another narrative strand in a text, which is actually achieved by alternating between the two spheres of action
parallel sound	a sound mix that meets the audience's expectations of a particular scene
participatory media	digital media that the audience interact with, help construct and distribute
passive audience theory	another term for effects theories, since they do not sufficiently explain the uses audiences may make of media consumption or how this varies from person to person
passive ideological state apparatus	according to Althusser, the function of the mass media in maintaining the status quo
patriarchy	a system where men predominate in power structures
PEGI	Pan-European Game Information
pejorative stereotypes	stereotypes who demean their subject
personal identity	identity made up of individual preferences and views
phatic remarks	talk that has a social function
photojournalist	professional photographer who uses images to tell a story
pick and mix theory	David Gauntlett's assertion, comparable with most liberal pluralist views, that audiences simply don't consume aspects of a media product or whole products that don't appeal to them or are not consistent with their sense of self
piracy	the act of copyright infringement and theft
plugins	additional features such as social media buttons or embedded YouTube players that encourage sharing and connectivity
podcasting	distribution of audio files using RSS (really simple syndication)
point-of-view shot	a shot that allows us to share someone's perspective
polysemic signs	possible multiple meanings of a sign
post-broadcast era	term sometimes used to define the shift away from scheduled media consumption
post-colonial theory	field that explores the legacy of colonialism by Western powers and how it contributes to race representation

post-modern theory	a school of thinking that questions the idea of 'reality' as anything other than a collection of constructs apparent in any culture – the mass media is seen as playing an important role since it helps shape and reflect our understanding of our culture. The movement resists solid definitions and answers in many disciplines within the arts, humanities and even sciences	puff	a call-out feature, often circular in shape, that draws attention to a price or promotion on a front cover	representation	the way in which people, places, abstract concepts and events are mediated in a particular way in media texts
		pull focus	shifting the focus in the frame in the same shot	resonance	in cultivation theory, the reinforcement of ideologies or experiences by mass media content
		pull quote	excerpt from interview, enlarged as a hook device and for visual contrast with body text	restricted narration	style of narration where information is withheld from the audience
post-production	decisions made to influence the look of images after the footage or images have been captured. This is usually done using post-production software	qualitative representation	using techniques such as semiotic analysis to draw conclusions about the nature of media representations	Sabido method	named after its creator, Miguel Sabido, who has acted as a writer and advisor on television serials in many parts of the world, and created a method for embedding educational messages successfully into the series
post-structuralism	later work on structuralism that both extends its ideas and critiques its approach	quantitative representation	using techniques such as content analysis to draw conclusions about representations in media texts		
press pack	information released by a company to promote its work, often to prospective investors or advertisers	quota	imposing a restriction on certain kinds of foreign media imports	schedule	traditional way of organising broadcasts in a chronological way to transmit at specific times of day
		radiogenic	a text that lends itself very easily to radio production	scheduling	in traditional television viewing, choosing the optimal time of broadcast to reach the highest potential target audience
pressure group	group of individuals who campaign about a particular concern regarding media output	RAJAR	Radio Joint Audience Research		
primary causal agents	the driving factors in a narrative, usually people	reach	the amount of people who see a link or site, for example in a newsfeed or search engine result	score	music composed specifically to accompany a media text – existing music redeployed in a text is usually referred to as soundtrack
primary image	the image that predominates visually where more than one has been used	reaction shot	demonstrates a response to an event or person		
proairetic code	one of Barthes' five narrative codes; units of resolved action through cause and effect	readership	the approximate number of consumers estimated to read a print media text	screen time	the amount of 'real' time a character is present on screen for, e.g. two minutes
		reception theory	considers that different audience members may interpret a single text in varying ways	script	the text of a film or broadcast product
profiling techniques	ways by which media producers discern their target audience			second order of signification	a layered and more subtle interpretation of a complex sign
prolepsis	commonly known as a flashforward	recognition	in Todorov's theory of narrative, the realisation that a disruption to the equilibrium has occurred	secondary image	an image that appears to be hierarchically less important when more than one is used
propaganda model of communication	the sustaining in media profile of a genuinely threatening event for political purposes	reflective approach	approach that suggests meaning is inherent in what is being represented	selection	choosing to represent one thing over another
proprietary fonts	fonts that are developed exclusively for a particular publication	remit	the service provided by a PSB for its viewers	selective focus	use of the lens where a particular section of the frame is in focus
props	items that are consciously added to a shoot because they contribute to meaning	repertoire of elements	identifiable aspects of texts belonging to the corpus in genre theory	self-censor	action taken by the individual audience member to select media for consumption that does not offend or otherwise impact on them negatively
proxemics	power relationships signified by relative positioning within the frame	repetition and sameness	the tendency of genre texts to repeat aspects of successful formulas – always in tension with variation and change		
PSB	public service broadcasting			self-contained narrative	a narrative that stands on its own
public purposes	the aims of the BBC as an organisation				

semantic code	one of Barthes' five narrative codes; connotations in a narrative	skyscraper	object positioned to run up the side of a website – sometimes a narrow advertisement	storyboard	sketches that represent the planned shots required for production. Storyboards often include examples of dialogue and other directorial choices such as sound, lighting and transitions
semiology	Saussure's term for the study of signs, which he regarded as a science	slug	a line in larger print introducing a feature that acts as a hook		
serial narrative	a narrative that may be extended over a number of episodes or editions	social learning theory	branch of effects theory that considers vicarious learning to be a highly significant factor in how people respond to media content	structuralism	a way of analysing culture that prioritises its form/ structure over function according to codified systems
shooting script	the written text of a video/ film product including details of the use of camera in individual scenes			studio shoot	a highly contrived photographic set-up, usually in an interior location
shot list	a descriptive list of the shots required for a moving image production	social model	approach to representing disability where society is to blame for failing to recognise what disabled people can do	sub-genres	the formulation of a new subgroup within a genre, which shares some of the qualities of the parent group but also has defining qualities of its own
sidebar	photographs or graphical elements in a newspaper to accompany an article and provide visual interest	social tensions	sources of displeasure in people's lives, compensated for by utopian solutions		
sign	the sum of the signifier plus signified. Most print media texts can be referred to as complex signs, since they often comprise many individual elements and codes that need to be decoded in order to understand fully what they represent	soft news	news that can be seen as focusing mainly on entertainment or celebrity-focused stories	subheading	a heading for a subsection of an article
		sound-bed	sounds, sound effects and/ or music that plays below the main content of an audio production. Sound beds can communicate narrative information such as location or they can create a tone or atmosphere for the production	supplements	extra inserts to newspapers that tend to have a specific focus; issued particularly at weekends or on a certain day of the week. May be themed by finance, business, arts or other categories
signified	works in tandem with the **signified**, and together these combine into a sign. We consider signifier and signified to work together, because the association happens so fast when reading a text			surveying pan	slow pan on the camera's axis, often to establish either exterior or interior environment
		split screen	simultaneous depiction of two events on screen by physical splitting of the frame	suspension of disbelief	allowing yourself to be immersed in a fictional world
signifying practices	techniques used to construct representations	standalone	prominent image without accompanying copy used to attract attention on the front page of a newspaper	sweet spot	position to the centre left of a single page of print media, where the eye naturally falls
signposting	in radio or podcasting, clearly signifying a change of some kind or designating structure and organisation of an audio text	standfirst	an introduction/introductory summary	symbolic code	one of Barthes' five narrative codes; deeper meanings and binary oppositions
		stereotypes	reduction of a social group to a limited set of characteristics		
silence	the deliberate absence of sound in a radio programme or podcast			synergy	mutually beneficial cross-promotional strategies used by media companies
		strapline	sometimes accompanies the masthead on a magazine – a promotional slogan		
skin	personalised look to software or apps – a style in web design where a background image such as a photograph is layered behind other content	Statement of Intent	a 400-word written document that is constructed after the completion of research and is part of the planning process. The Statement of Intent summarises what you will produce and why	systems of representation	identified by Hall – our conceptual map, and the language we use to navigate it
				teaser	(newspapers/magazines) a brief indication of the content within the publication. Used to encourage the reader to purchase the publication to be able to read further
skyline	strip often used to promote other content running along the top of a newspaper or magazine, sometimes referred to as a menu strip				
		stock image	professional photographs that can be used without having to pay royalties		

technological convergence	the gradual combining of separate technological devices into fewer devices or one device with multiple functions
technological determinism	the idea that technological advances dictate the path societies take
the other	the state of being defined as 'different' due to cultural differences
third order of signification	the relationship between the first and second orders of signification and myths and ideology
tilt down	movement where the camera is angled down on its axis
tilt up	movement where the camera is raised up on its axis
tilting	the use of lexical coding over black or over image – has become very common in digital media texts
tracking shot/ following shot	follows action by travelling alongside or behind it
traditional media	media forms that predominated before the digital age
transition	the way in which movement from shot to shot is managed in editing, most often a straight cut
transmedia narrative	product that exists over more than one media form, with different forms contributing different dimensions to the narrative
triadic model	common term used for Peirce's description of how we read signs
tripod	a three-legged stand for a still or video camera
TV player	service sometimes known as 'catch-up' television, where channels make content previously broadcast traditionally available to viewers on demand for a period of time following broadcast
two-shot	two people in the same shot, often implying a relationship between them
two-step flow	communications-based model that highlights the significance of opinion-leaders in the transmission of messages in the mass media
typographical codes	selection of font and graphical choices

universal themes	themes to which many people across cultures can relate
uses and gratifications theory	theory that suggested audiences make use of the media they consume for personal fulfilment
utopian solutions	gratifications-based model that suggests audiences use the media to make up for a lack of something in their lives
variation of change	the tendency of genre texts to reformulate with new qualities to prevent audiences from becoming tired of a formula
verisimilitude	appearing to be real or truthful
vertical integration	acquisition of one company in the production chain of another that offers a different service
virtual communities	groups of people who come together in cyberspace through a shared interest without geographical barriers
visibility	how high profile a particular issue, group or event is in media analysis
VoD	video on demand – any service where users can choose what they want to view and when
vox populi	soundbites and/or visual clips of different respondents discussing a topic or answering a question intended to reflect a range of opinions
VSC	Video Standards Council
watershed	in the UK, the point (9.00pm) at which content of a more adult nature may be shown in a television schedule
Web 2.0	phase of internet development summed up by increased human connectivity
Web 3.0/ semantic web	developments anticipated in internet use where user experience of the internet is much more highly personalised
web comics	comics that are published and designed to be read solely online

web series	a short form collection, usually fiction, of videos released online
webcasting	the streaming of live audio content online – 'internet radio'
webisode	individual 'episode' of a web series
weight (visual)	a term used to refer to the effect of the depth, darkness and/or intensity of a design element. Large, dark, textured and warm-coloured elements tend to appear 'heavier' – they have more visual weight. Elements in the foreground or higher on the page tend to appear heavy on the page as do regular shapes and vertical (rather than horizontal) objects. Images of things that are actually heavy also have weight on the page
whip pan	rapid following pan, widely used in action sequences
wide-angle shot	a shot, usually using a specific lens for the purpose, which shows a wide field of view
worm's-eye shot	extreme low angle or directly from the ground upwards
Young and Rubicam	one of the biggest advertising agencies in the world, established in New York in 1927
zoom	movement of the camera lens to bring a subject closer or to distance it

Glossary of key thinkers

Albert Bandura	(1925–) credited with developing social learning theory
David Gauntlett	(1971–) formulated ten influential criticisms of media effects theory
George Gerbner	(1919–2005) credited with developing cultivation theory
Jay Blumler and Elihu Katz	(1924– and 1926–) credited as two of the key developers of uses and gratifications theory
Stephen Neale	(1950–) Neale has written numerous books about film and genre, and is widely reputed as an expert in the field

Stuart Hall	(1932–2014) prominent cultural theorist. Born in Jamaica, Hall worked most of his life in the UK, and became a highly influential thinker respected for writing about cultural practices in many disciplines, including Sociology and Media Studies.
Tzvetan Todorov	(1939–2017) Bulgarian-French theorist who contributed to a range of academic disciplines in his time, including literary theory, anthropology, history and philosophy

Further reading

Aarseth, Espen (2008) *Cybertext: Perspectives on Ergodic Literature*.

Altman, Rick (1999) *Film/Genre*.

BARB, www.barb.co.uk.

Barthes, Roland (2014) *Mythologies*.

Berger, Arthur Asa (2011) *Media Analysis Techniques*.

Bjornstrom, E.E., Kaufman, R.L., Peterson, R.D. and Slater, M.D. (2010) 'Race and Ethnic Representations of Lawbreakers and Victims in Crim News: A National Study of Television Coverage', *Sociology Problems* 57(2).

Bryand, Jennings, and Zillman, Dolf (2002) *Media Effects: Advances in Theory and Research*.

Chander, Daniel (2007) *Semiotics: The Basics*.

Chignell, Hugh (2009) *Key Concepts in Radio Studies*.

Chomsky, Noam (1988) *Manufacturing Consent: The Political Economy of the Mass Media*.

Cobley, Paul, and Jansz, Litza (2010) *Introducing Semiotics: A Graphic Guide*.

Crisell, Andrew (1986) *Understanding Radio*.

Curran, James, and Seaton, Jean (2009) *Power Without Responsibility*.

Dyer, Richard (2002) *The Matter of Images*.

Dyer, Richard (2002) *Only Entertainment*.

Fowles, Jib (1976) *Mass Advertising as Social Forecast*.

Gauntlett, David (2008) *Media, Gender and Identity*.

Hall, Stuart (2013) *Representation: Cultural Representation and Signifying Practices*.

Handler Miller, Carolyn (2008) *Cybertext: Perspectives on Ergodic Literature*.

Hegarty, Stephanie (27 April 2012) 'How Soap Operas Changed the World', BBC World Service, www.bbc.co.uk/news/magazine-17820571.

Holt, Jennifer (2009) *Media Industries: History, Theory and Method*.

Jenkins, Henry (2008) *Convergence Culture: Where Old and New Media Collide*.

Kowart, Rachel, and Oldmeadow, Julian (2012) 'Geek or Chic? Emerging Stereotypes of Online Gamers', *Bulletin of Science Technology & Society* 32(6), https://www.researchgate.net/publication/258127460_Geek_or_Chic_Emerging_Stereotypes_of_Online_Gamers.

Mayra, Franz (2008) *An Introduction to Game Studies: Games and Cultures*.

Napoli, Philip M. (2012) *Audience: Evolution*.

National Readership Survey, www.nrs.co.uk.

Neale, Stephen (1980) *Genre*.

Neale, Stephen (1991) *Questions of Genre*.

Neale, Stephen (2000) *Genre and Hollywood*.

Ofcom, Ofcom.org.uk.

Ofcom Communications Market Reports, annually published at www.ofcom.org.uk/research-anddata/cmr/communications-market-reports.

Perkins, Tessa (1979) *Rethinking Stereotypes*.

RAJAR, www.rajar.co.uk.

Redfern, Nick (2015) 'Age, Gender and Television in the United Kingdom', *Journal of Popular Television*, www.researchgate.net/publication/274073135_Age_gender_and_television_in_the_United_Kingdom, https://nickredfern.wordpress.com/2013/04/11/agegender-and-television-in-the-uk/.

Thomas, Bronwen, (2015) *Narrative: The Basics*.

Ulin, Jeffrey C. (2009) *The Business of Media Distribution*.

Walker, Jill (2004) *Distributed Narrative: Telling Stories Across Networks*, http://jilltxt.net/txt/AoIRdistributednarrative.pdf.

Index

W

X

Y

Z

Photo acknowledgements

p1 Shutterstock / Dinga; p6 Kevin George; p7 (top) Jan Martin Will; p7 (bottom) Claudio Divizia; p8 (top) Public domain; p8 (bottom left) jara3000; p8 (bottom right) Kristo Robert; p9 (top) Sipa Press / REX / Shutterstock; p9 (bottom) Hector / Alamy Stock Photo; p10 (left) Vitezslav Valka; p10 (top right) Claudio Divizia; p10 (bottom right) Laura Pashkevich; p11 Africa Studio; p12 Zwiebackessser; p13 Brian A Jackson; p14 (left) © Telegraph Media Group Limited 2016; p14 (middle) The Guardian; p14 (right) Mirrorpix; p15 (top left) New Scientist; p15 (top right) Take A Break, Bauer Magazine Media p15 (middle right) Hearst Publications; p15 (middle left) Octonauts; p15 (bottom) Now; p16 (top) Entertainment Pictures / Alamy Stock Photo; p16 (bottom) Courtesy Mr President / Miele; p17 (top) Courtesy Mr President / Miele; p19 By Fronteiras do Pensamento [CC BY-SA 2.0 (http://creativecommons.org/licenses/by-sa/2.0)], via Wikimedia Commons; p20 Creative commons; p22 (top) The Print Collector / Alamy Stock Photo; p22 (bottom) Empire; p23 Thinglass / Shutterstock.com; p24 (all) True Crime Library; p25 (bottom left) Virgile S Bertrand / Wired © The Condé Nast Publications Ltd; p25 (top) AF archive / Alamy Stock Photo; p25 (bottom right) World History Archive / Alamy Stock Photo; p26 Claudio Divizia p27 IxMaster p29 Alexey Rotanov; p28 (top) s_bukley / Shutterstock.com; p28 (bottom) Kenzo World; p29 (top) photoJS; p29 (middle) urbazon p29 (bottom right); p29 bottom (left) Pavel L. Photo and Video; Top Photo Corporation; p29 (bottom left) DeymosHR; p30 (top) Piroviz; p30 (bottom) Angels, Chance; p32 Rocketclips Inc; p33 Take Me Out, ITV; p35 Syda Productions; p36 (top) Photofusion Picture Library / Alamy Stock Photo; p36 (bottom) Rawpixel.com; p37 (top) Nejron Photo; p37 (bottom) Syda Productions; p38 Creative commons; p39 Stranger Things, Episode 1, Netflix; p40 (top) Channel 4; p40 (bottom) bus109; p41 2015 John Lewis's Christmas advert 'Man on the Moon'; p42 (top) AF archive / Alamy Stock Photo; p42 (middle) Moviestore collection Ltd / Alamy Stock Photo; p42 (bottom) The Mighty Boosh; p43 Phillip Maguire; p44 (top) Courtesy Rick Altman; p44 (bottom) Swiss Army Man; p45 David J. Green / Alamy Stock Photo; p46 The Simpsons; p47 Courtesy Pirate FM; p48 IxMaster; p49 Peshkova; p50 (all) Humans; p51 La La Land; p52 (left) Glastonbury; p52 (right) Team GB; p53

Andrey_Popov; p54 (top) James Boardman / Alamy Stock Photo; p54 (bottom) LARPS; p55 (top) The Guardian; p55 (bottom) Corey Mason; p56 (top) lifewire.com; p56 (bottom) Maeril; p57 Iryna Tiumentseva; p58 (top) Courtesy Ben Prunty; Game Shots / Alamy Stock Photo; p59 (bottom) Elivind Senneset; p60 (top) Hitch the World; p60 (bottom) Things in Squares; p61 (left) Matrix; p61 (right) Creative commons; p62 Highrise; p65 (top) No Man's Sky; p65 (bottom) Game Shots / Alamy Stock Photo; p66 Peshkova; p67 Exodus: Our Journey to Europe; p68 Rawpixel.com; p69 Sorbis / Shutterstock.com; p70 (top) Patti McConville / Alamy Stock Photo; p70 (bottom) Javier Etzexarreta / Epa / REX / Shutterstock; p72 (both) Heat; p73 The Apprentice; p74 Pocholo Calapre; p75 When Louis Met Jimmay; p76 (top) WENN UK / Alamy Stock Photo; p76 (bottom) Jason Bourne; p77 (top) Joseph Gruber / Shutterstock.com; p77 (bottom) ArtOfPhotos; p78 Believe in Me, Barnardo's'; p79 Howard Davies / Alamy Stock Photo; p81 (left) Courtesy Emerald Life Home Insurance; p81 (middle) Holding the Man; p81 (right) iCandy; p82 Dean Drobot; p84 Exodus: Our Journey to Europe; p85 Hello!; p86 Phillip Maguire / Shutterstock.com; p87 Courtesy David Gauntlett; p89 Rawpixcel.com; p90 blvdone; p91 (top) Pearlstock / Alamy Stock Photo; p91 (bottom) Everett Collection Inc / Alamay Stock Photo; p92 The Oldie; p93 © I; p94 (top) FreemantleMedia Ltd / REX / Shutterstock; p94 (bottom) Condé Nast; p95 (top) attilio pregnolato; p95 (2nd top) Evgenlya Porechenskaya; p95 (3rd top) Rocketclips, Inc.; p95 (2nd up) Rawpixcel.com; p95 (bottom) Iakov Filimonov; p96 (top) Navistock; p96 (middle) Ysbrand Cosijn; p96 (bottom) Jeff Gilbert / Alamy Stock Photo; p99 (left) Guardian Online; p98 a-image; p99 (right) Telegraph Online; p100 Randy Miramontez / Shutterstock.com; p101 (top) Dedi Grigoroiu; p101 (bottom) Public domain; p102 (bottom) Granger Historical Picture Archive / Alamy Stock Photo; p104 Creative commons; p105 AF Archive / Alamy Stock Photo; p106 Creative commons; p107 Moviestore Collection Ltd / Alamy Stock Photo; p108 (bottom) Amazon Prime; p110 (top) BuzzFeed; p110 (bottom) Chuck; p108 (top) PCN Photography / Alamy Stock Photo; p108 (middle) Miguel Mataeo-Garcia / REX / Shutterstock; p109 blvdone; p102 (top) bergamont; p103 Creative commons; p111 blvdone; p112 Stuart Miles;

p113 (top) anistigesign; p113 (bottom) Niloo; p114 (top) ymgerman / Shutterstock.com; p114 (bottom) Everett Collection; p115 (top) chrisdorney; p115 (bottom); p116 Bloomicon / Shutterstock.com; p118 Georgejmclittle; p119 BARB; p120 pixnoo / Shutterstock.com; p121 (top) Mr Pics / Shutterstock.com; p121 (bottom) TC / Alamy Stock Photo; p122 (top) Leonard Zhukovsky / Shutterstock.inc; p122 (bottom) Okido Magazine; p123 Courtesy Script2Screen; p123 Sky; p124 (top); p124 (bottom) Margaret Smeaton; p125 Sky; p123 Sky; p128 Yavuz Sariyildiz; p130 Splash News / Alamy Stock Photo; p131 Mediawatch; p135 (bottom right) chrisdorney / Shutterstock.com; p133 Nintendo Wii; p134 Stuart Miles; p154 Naypong; p135 (left), p135 (middle right) Lenscap Photography / Shutterstock.com; p135 (top right) Thinglass / Shutterstock.com; p136 rvisoft / Shutterstock.com; p137 Suicide Squad; p140 Kathy Hutchins / Shutterstock.com; p141 (both left) The Guardian; p141 (top 2) The Fall; p141 (bottom 2) The Night Of; p142 (top) mozakim / Shutterstock.com; p142 (bottom) Pepsi; p144, p145 (top) Channel 4; p146 (top) Benefits Street on Twitter; p146 (bottom) Beats; p147 Dmytro Zinkevych; p150 ALANDAWSONPHOTOGRAPHY / Alamy Stock Photo; p153 (top) Featureflash Photo Agency / Shutterstock.com; p153 (middle) katz / Shutterstock.com; p153 (bottom) Zoella; p155 Farknot Architect; p157 (both) Men's Health, Hearst; p158 (both) Men's Health, Hearst; p159 (bottom right) Platon / GQ © The Condé Nast Publications Ltd; p159 (bottom left) Vogue, Condé Nast Publications Ltd; p161 Men's Health, Hearst; p162 Men's Health, Hearst; p163 Bopjan656; p165 (all) The Missing; p166 (top 2) The Killing; p166 (bottom 2) Broadchurch; p167 (top) Playground; p167 (middle) Company Pictures; p167 (bottom) all3media; p168 (top left) Starz; p168 (top right) Amazon Prime; p168 (bottom) The Missing; p169 (all) The Missing; p171 Marko Poplasen; p172 360b; p173 (top) Bloomicon; (bottom) Kolonko; p174 (top) tanuha2001; (middle) Allstar Picture Library / Alamy Stock Photo; (bottom) James McCauley / Alamy Stock Photo; p175 (top) JStone; p175 (bottom) Rob Kim / Getty Images; p176 (left) DFree; p176 (middle) JStone / Shutterstock.com; p176 (right) Ovidu Hrubaru / Shutterstock.com; p177 (left to right) 5 second Studio, popcorner, Daniel M Ernst, FabrikaSimf; p178 (top) Seventeen; p178 (middle) Rookie;